A Life Worth Living

Practical Strategies for Reducing Depression in Older Adults

Pearl M. Mosher-Ashley, Ph.D.
Worcester State College
Worcester, Massachusetts

and

Phyllis W. Barrett, Ph.D.
Holyoke Community College
Holyoke, Massachusetts

HEALTH
PROFESSIONS
PRESS

Baltimore • London • Toronto • Sydney

For my husband, George, who has made our life together adventurous and enjoyable

PMA

For my parents, Don and Doris Whiteside

PWB

Health Professions Press, Inc.
Post Office Box 10624
Baltimore, Maryland 21285-0624

Typeset by PRO-IMAGE Corporation, York, Pennsylvania.
Manufactured in the United States of America by
The Maple Press Company, York, Pennsylvania.

Library of Congress Cataloging-in-Publication Data
Mosher-Ashley, Pearl M.
       A life worth living : practical strategies for reducing depression in older adults / Pearl M. Mosher-Ashley
and Phyllis W. Barrett.
              p.   cm.
       Includes bibliographical references and index.
       ISBN 1-878812-03-3
       1. Depression in old age—Treatment.   I. Barrett, Phyllis W.
II. Title.
RC537.5.M67   1997
618.97'6852706—dc21   97-1679
                                                                                                                          CIP

British Library Cataloguing in Publication Data are available from the British Library.

Contents

Acknowledgments

The authors would like to express their gratitude to the many people who gave their time and expertise to the development of this book. Without their assistance, the variety of approaches could not have been addressed in as much detail. Appreciation is extended to the librarians and interlibrary loan assistants at Worcester State and Holyoke Community College: Mary Parker, Pam McKay, Linda Snodgrass, and Claire Wheeler. We are particularly indebted to the student assistants who, with great persistence and creativity, searched the literature and databases for relevant material: Jody Brooks, Karen O'Connor, and Sharon Gross.

Thanks also goes out to our friends and colleagues who provided assistance, ideas, encouragement, and emotional support during the lengthy period of writing: Dr. Mark Lange, Diane Lorenzo, Carol and Art Pogue, Valerie Vaughn, John Greene, and Phyllis's neighbors on Walnut Street and Cold Hill for their interest in and encouragement of this project. Special thanks to the wonderful staff of Health Professions Press for their encouragement, cheerful support, and recommendations during every phase of preparation: Anita McCabe, Barbara Karni, Melissa Behm, and Mary Magnus. They made the process of writing more manageable than we had expected.

Foreword

Depression is probably the most prevalent and well-studied serious mental illness among adults. In later life, depression has particularly serious consequences—it has been associated with substantial decrements in functioning and social relationships and increased rates of physical illness and mortality. Since 1987 alone well over 1000 articles have appeared in major research journals on the diagnosis, etiology, epidemiology, and treatment of depression in later life.

Making sense of the dizzying array of research findings is often an insurmountable challenge for the clinician working with depressed older adults. Many questions arise: What exactly is *depression in later life*? How is it different from depression in younger adults? What actually works in the treatment of depression? Must one change treatment regimens that are successful for younger people in order to make them effective for older adults? Answering such questions is difficult without excellent, clearly written, comprehensive, and up-to-date books such as *A Life Worth Living*.

As a graduate student in clinical geropsychology in the early 1980s, I came to rely on a particular book, Steven H. Zarit's *Aging and Mental Disorders*, to help me organize my thinking about depression in later life, develop appropriate treatments, and evaluate treatment efficacy. Its tattered appearance today is a testimony to the book's clarity and comprehensiveness as well as to my dependence on it. That was almost 20 years ago, and much has been learned about aging and depression in the intervening years. Obviously, it is time for a superb, clearly written book to provide a new "map" of the research literature on aging and depression to guide the practice of health care professionals who work with depressed older adults. *A Life Worth Living* is that map. Like any high-quality map, it provides accurate information and helps the user to plan and evaluate alternative routes.

The authors begin each chapter with a concise and useful review of the recent studies relevant to each topic (e.g., the nature and assessment of depression and life satisfaction, the effectiveness of different therapies). These reviews are outstanding—they provide in a few pages enough research detail to draw conclusions that are in keeping with more lengthy reviews such as those typically found in handbooks. Numerous appendixes supply references essential for clinicians who wish to do additional reading. But a careful review of the literature, however clear, concise, and comprehensive, is not enough. Clinicians need to be able to translate abstract and normative research findings into thoughtful practice. Unique to *A Life Worth Living* is the authors' narrative case examples, which merge themes derived from the research literature with descriptions of interventions and their impact on the lives of real clients. These narrative cases enable clinicians to conceive more clearly how research can be used to understand their clients' problems and develop appropriate treatments. By providing these narratives, the authors put information in the hands of practitioners in a uniquely effective way.

Finally, Mosher-Ashley and Barrett provide clear guidelines, based on the research literature, for implementing and evaluating a wide array of effective treatment modalities. The authors are careful not to provide a "cookbook" for different interventions, but they do describe those aspects of treatment that the research suggests can increase treatment effectiveness. Of particular significance is the emphasis throughout the book on keeping records and monitoring client progress. Mosher-Ashley and Barrett provide cogent methods for monitoring progress using standard, valid measures. In a climate of managed care and accountability, the monitoring of progress using standard methods is an excellent way to demonstrate the effectiveness of psychosocial interventions.

A Life Worth Living is an outstanding resource for the practitioner who seeks to assess, plan, execute, and evaluate psychosocial treatments for depression in older adults. I congratulate Professors Mosher-Ashley and Barrett and I look forward to *A Life Worth Living* becoming the authoritative and dependable reference for a cohort of clinicians, much as Zarit's *Aging and Mental Disorders* was in the early 1980s.

Andrew Futterman, Ph.D.
Associate Professor of Psychology
Director, Gerontological Studies Program
College of the Holy Cross, Worcester, Massachusetts

Introduction

The spectre of the stereotypical frail, lethargic, depressed older adult, slumped in a wheelchair in the common room of a long-term care facility, not even attending to a television droning on in the room, haunts many of us. Whether we have parents we fear for, projections imagined for our own futures, or a conscience that balks at such a compromised quality of life, we may not realize that this scenario is not, in fact, the natural conclusion to life. Nevertheless, it is more prevalent than it need be. Although there is some question as to the actual prevalence of depression among older adults, at least 15% of those living independently in the community and approximately 25% of those residing in long-term care facilities are thought to experience depressive symptoms. Most older people experience milder forms of depression at some time. Only 1%–3% of older adults have been found in epidemiological studies to display symptoms of major depression. Whether mild or more severe, however, depression has been viewed for far too long as an inevitable—and untreatable—part of old age.

Little attention has been directed to providing depressed older adults with suitable treatment, even though since the early 1980s professionals have advocated for more extensive psychiatric treatment for these underserved individuals. Even with more attention, barriers exist. Gaining access to transportation is challenging for some older adults, and few mental health centers provide outreach services. Economic conditions for physical and mental health suppliers have declined, making it unlikely that monies will be available to fund programs designed to improve or increase the number of traditional mental health services for older adults, who must compete with other groups for limited funds. In addition, older adults tend to be less informed about and less accepting of mental health services than younger people and, consequently, do not seek out such services.

Some authors, most notably Michael Smyer, have proposed the use of alternative approaches to the provision of mental health regimens. For example, peer counseling programs have been explored. A largely untapped resource is existing services. Health care and social services professionals are in an excellent position to provide treatment to mildly depressed older adults. Nearly every community makes available the services of the Visiting Nurse Association and home health care to older adults living independently. Every long-term care facility is required to employ a social worker, and many have a recreation therapist. Often, these professionals are the first to detect depressive symptoms in their clients and would be willing to intervene, given practical strategies for that purpose.

The 11 practical interventions described in *A Life Worth Living* are designed primarily for individuals experiencing mild depression, although some interventions may be appropriate for people with more severe depression who have refused traditional mental health services. The therapies may also serve a preventive function if offered to people whose circumstances (e.g., loss of spouse, loss of independent living situation, deterioration of health) may foment depression. Individual therapies can be matched to individual circumstances in an attempt to address the underlying reasons for depression. The interventions can be conducted without any psychotherapeutic training. However, they are not designed to replace psychotherapy as a treatment for depression. Instead, they are intended to expand the available resources for helping older adults cope with depression. Efforts to refer and treat older people using traditional psychotherapies must continue, but it is hoped that the interventions contained herein can substantially augment those services.

Developed specifically for health care and social services professionals who work closely with older adults, the book includes methods and forms for assessing depression and for tracking the older person's progress in overcoming it. In most cases the therapies are built around simple, easily recognized activities that offer many opportunities for interaction and enjoyment on the part of the older adult who has settled into passive and unrewarding patterns of existence. The procedures described in this book are drawn from clinical experience, published accounts of the experiences of others, and outcome research studies. In reviewing the literature for each of the chapters, several databases were consulted: PsycLit, CINAHL, MEDLINE, and ERIC. Although the literature review includes publications covering a 20-year span, emphasis has been placed on findings since the late 1980s.

The practical strategies of *A Life Worth Living* are presented in enough detail that the therapies can be carried out without need of additional source materials, although the numerous references and appendixes contained herein provide such information. Each chapter describes a complete intervention plan, including methods that are unique to home, community, and long-term care settings. In some cases procedures to use with frail, homebound individuals are included. In addition, information on how to obtain pre- and postmeasures for assessing the effectiveness of each intervention is included.

Case examples are drawn from the authors' personal experiences. Some cases are detailed descriptions of specific individuals who agreed to share their experiences. Efforts were made to protect the privacy of other individuals by changing some of the details such as gender or marital background. Some case examples represent a composite of several clients who had similar problems and participated in a similar treatment approach.

The interventions can be dovetailed with existing treatment programs, such as physical therapy or nursing services, in congregate or private living spaces. For example, visiting nurses and case managers can carry out many of these interventions in the homes of older adults or in elder housing complexes. Directors of adult day programs and senior centers can include some of the interventions among the activities they offer. Social workers or nurses can implement interventions for a single resident or a group in a long-term care facility, as can owners or directors of board and care facilities. The goal is to provide many opportunities for reducing depression and increasing life satisfaction for older adults, regardless of the setting.

*I know the bottom, she says. I know it with
my great tap root . . .*
Sylvia Plath, "Elm"

1

I Don't Want to
Get Up in the Morning

Depression

D epression is the most common psychological disorder among older people. Although there is some controversy as to the actual prevalence of depression among older adults, at least 15% of those living in the community (Blazer, Hughes, & George, 1987) and approximately 25% of those residing in long-term care facilities (Curlik, Frazier, & Katz, 1991) are believed to experience depressive symptoms. Of the older adults seeking outpatient services from community mental health centers, the majority are diagnosed with depressive symptoms (Mosher-Ashley, 1994; Speer, Williams, West, & Dupree, 1991).

Among older adults who experience depression, most have milder forms, such as adjustment disorders, rather than the more severe affective disorders. Epidemiological studies by Blazer et al. (1987) indicate that between only 1% and 2% of all older adults display symptoms of major depression. Although 23% of the older adults receiving outpatient therapy in a community mental health center presented with a condition characterized as purely depressive, less than one half of these individuals demonstrated symptoms sufficiently severe to qualify for a diagnosis of affective disorder (Mosher-Ashley, 1994). The majority of older adults with depressive symptoms in that study were assigned a diagnosis of *adjustment disorder with depressed mood*. Similar findings have been reported by others. Koenig and Blazer (1992) reported that among older adults adjustment disorders are more common than is major depression. Speer et al. (1991) also found the incidence of major depression to be much lower than that of milder forms of depressive disorders in older adults receiving therapy on an outpatient basis.

TYPES OF DEPRESSION

Disturbances in mental health are classified according to a system developed by the American Psychiatric Association and are listed in *Diagnostic and Statistical Manual of Mental Disorders, fourth edition* (DSM-IV; American Psychiatric Association, 1994). Depression is classified as one of three different mood disorders in DSM-IV. Two of the disorders, major depressive disorder and dysthymic disorder, are severe forms of depression and are considered to be affective disorders. *Affective disorders* are conditions that are characterized by serious impairments in mood. The third form of depression is a milder form and is classified as an *adjustment disorder*.

Affective Disorders

Two of the affective disorders recognized in DSM-IV are major depressive disorder and dysthymic disorder.

Major Depressive Disorder

A person with major depressive disorder experiences a severely depressed mood for most of the day each day for a period of several weeks (Busse, 1992). The specific criteria for a diagnosis of major depression, established by the American Psychiatric Association (1994), are listed as follows (these symptoms must be accompanied by considerable distress or impairment in social, occupational, or other important areas of functioning):

Primary Features[1]

- Depressed mood
- Markedly diminished interest or pleasure

Secondary Features[2]

- Significant weight loss or weight gain
- Insomnia or excessive sleeping
- Psychomotor agitation or retardation
- Fatigue or loss of energy
- Feelings of worthlessness or excessive or inappropriate guilt
- Diminished ability to think or to concentrate; indecisiveness
- Recurrent thoughts of death, suicidal ideation, a specific plan for suicide, or a suicide attempt

Major depression presents in two forms: *single episode* or *recurrent*. The recurrent form may be difficult to distinguish from the single episode form if the recurring symptoms wax and wane in intensity (American Psychiatric Association, 1994). The recurrent form is characterized by intervals of several months or years between episodes, during which the depressive symptoms abate. If periods of depression are interspersed with periods of elevated mood and manic behavior, the proper diagnosis is *bipolar disorder* rather than recurrent major depression.

A diagnosis of major depression should not be assigned to a person who has recently lost a loved one unless the bereaved person exhibits severe functional impairment, excessive preoccupation with feelings of worthlessness, or suicidal ideation. Depression may assume different forms among older adults than it does among younger adults. According to Knight (1992), in younger adults depression is often characterized by an unrealistic concern about bodily functions, which sometimes becomes a delusional belief that one is ill. Among older adults a similar process can lead to unrealistic concerns about memory, thought processes, and brain disease. In addition, depressed older people frequently withdraw from social activity, eat increasingly less, lose weight, and begin to appear frail (Knight, 1992). Complaints of memory impairment are common (e.g., older people may report difficulty remembering the plots of television programs or novels). Direct or indirect statements are made by depressed older people expressing feelings that life is not worth living or that they would be "better off dead." Depressed older adults may be mistakenly perceived as developing cognitive impairments because of the aging process or a dementing illness.

Dysthymic Disorder

If a person is severely depressed without abatement for more than 2 years, the condition is called *dysthymic disorder*. The criteria for a diagnosis of dysthymic disorder are presented in the following (American Psychiatric Association, 1994):[3]

---

[1]Either of these two symptoms must be exhibited daily for a 2-week period.
[2]Any four of these secondary symptoms should be observed or reported.
[3]Any two of these symptoms should also be observed or reported.

Primary Feature
- Depressed mood (must be exhibited for a period of not less than 2 years)

Secondary Features
- Poor appetite or overeating
- Insomnia or excessive sleeping
- Low energy or fatigue
- Low self-esteem
- Poor concentration or difficulty making decisions
- Feelings of hopelessness

Individuals with dysthymic disorder will exhibit or report having little interest in life and will be very self-critical, often considering themselves uninteresting or less capable than other people. Because the symptoms become such a part of individuals' everyday experience, the symptoms of dysthymia are not often reported unless directly inquired for by someone familiar with the disorder (American Psychiatric Association, 1994). This form of chronic depression is more common than is major depression in older adults (Blazer, 1990b). For example, Speer et al. (1991) found that 29% of the older adults receiving outpatient services in a community mental health center were diagnosed with a dysthymic disorder, although only 3% were classified as experiencing a major depression. Although this condition is usually less severe, dysthymia can coexist with a major depression. The pattern of coexistence is one whereby dysthymic disorder develops into a major depression, resulting in a situation Blazer (1990b) terms "double depression" (p. 67). Dysthymic disorder is more likely than is major depression to have been caused by psychological and psychosocial factors.

Adjustment Disorders

An adjustment disorder is a condition in which individuals experience distress or considerable impairment in social or occupational functioning that is attributable to a psychosocial stressor (American Psychiatric Association, 1994). DSM-IV identifies several different types of adjustment disorders, which develop 3 months after the onset of the stressor and usually are resolved within 6 months. The primary symptoms associated with the six subtypes of adjustment disorders are listed in Table 1.1. All adjustment disorders are classified into one of two categories, acute or chronic, based on the duration of the symptoms. The acute form is characterized by symptoms that do not persist beyond a 6-month period. The chronic form lasts longer than 6 months and is a response to a chronic stressor or a stressor that has enduring consequences.

Adjustment Disorder with Depressed Mood

An adjustment disorder with depressed mood is observed frequently in older adults (Mosher-Ashley, 1994; Speer et al., 1991). The stressor that most commonly leads to this type of adjustment disorder is physical illness (Blazer, 1990b). Additional stressors may include retirement; financial difficulties; difficulties adjusting to a

Table 1.1.   Six subtypes of adjustment disorders and their symptoms

Subtypes	Primary symptoms
With depressed mood	Depressed mood, tearfulness, or feelings of hopelessness
With anxiety	Nervousness, worry, or jitters
With mixed anxiety and depressed mood	Combination of anxiety and depression
With disturbance of conduct	Behavior that violates the rights of others or social norms and rules
With mixed disturbance of emotions and conduct	Combination of depression or anxiety with disturbance of conduct
Unspecified	Maladaptive reactions, from physical complaints or social withdrawal to psychosocial stressors, not covered by the previous subtypes

Adapted from: American Psychiatric Association (1994).

new social role; marital problems; and a change of residence, particularly to a nursing facility. Bereavement is not classified as an adjustment disorder. Despite the similarity in symptoms, bereavement is considered to be a normal response to a serious loss and part of the universal human experience (Blazer, 1990b). The symptoms associated with the loss of a loved one, particularly a spouse or child, can persist for up to 2 years (Sanders, 1989).

Difficulty in Diagnosis

Identifying depression in older adults is complicated by the overlap of the symptoms of depression and the physical illnesses that are common in later life (Steiner & Marcopulos, 1991). For example, decreased energy, loss of appetite, sleep disturbances, and decreased sexual appetite and interest are common in nondepressed older adults and are related to the physiological changes that accompany aging (Osgood & Thielman, 1990). Even healthy older adults can experience decreased ability to sleep, more frequent nocturnal awakenings, and decreased deep sleep (Webb, 1982). Decreased concentration and memory problems have been reported in both nondepressed and depressed older adults (Kaszniak, Sadeh, & Stern, 1985).

Suicide

Although depression does not often result in suicide, suicide is preceded by depression. Suicide ranks as the 10th leading cause of death in people over age 65 (Busse, 1992). The suicide rate of older adults is 50% higher than that of younger adults (Osgood & Thielman, 1990). Individuals at greatest risk tend to be Caucasian men age 75 and older. The rate of suicide in women increases until middle age (mid-40s to mid-50s) and declines thereafter. Suicide is more common in people who live alone, particularly in those who have undergone a change in living arrangement (e.g., death of a spouse). Older adults who have lived with others but, for whatever reason, are now living alone are at special risk (Osgood & Thielman, 1990). Other risk factors for suicide include poor health, a history of previous suicide attempts, low socioeconomic level, recent bereavement, and lack of social support.

Older adults who are at risk for suicide should be referred for mental health services. Frequently, health care and social services professionals are reluctant to bring up the subject of suicide in the mistaken belief that doing so could provide their client with the idea to try it. If an older adult has mentioned or attempted suicide, it is obvious that he or she has been thinking about it, and broaching the subject will not cause the individual to be more willing to try it. When evaluating the risk of suicide in an older person, the health care professional should carefully question the older person as to whether he or she has made any prior attempts and whether a means of carrying out the act has been contemplated. A key indicator would be an affirmative response with details. A useful scale to assess suicidal ideation (contemplation of suicide) can be obtained from the address at the bottom of the chapter appendix.

Older adults who express their suicidal thoughts should be taken seriously. In general, older adults are less likely than younger adults to express suicidal thoughts, but they are more likely to succeed when they attempt suicide (Osgood & Thielman, 1990).

Health Status and Suicide

Concern about health is one, if not the most common, reason for suicide (Copeland, 1987). Diseases with chronic, debilitating courses are frequent triggers to suicidal behavior (Blumenthal, 1990). The disorders most often associated with suicide are cancer, Huntington's chorea, musculoskeletal disorders, and AIDS. Blumenthal (1990) points out that for some individuals the choice to die by suicide may be a rational act to avoid suffering and loss of dignity. She cautions that research indicates that suicide by physically ill people rarely occurs without an accompanying psychiatric disorder. The accompanying psychiatric disorder may be severe depression or an organic mental disorder such as delirium, which can result in perceptual, cognitive, and mood changes leading to impaired judgment. Suicide is also thought to be an impulsive act rather than one that has been planned over time (Busse, 1992).

Older Adults in Long-Term Care and Suicide

In general, older adults who reside in long-term care settings are not perceived to be at risk for suicide. As a consequence, suicide attempts may not be recognized, and sometimes the person involved is not referred for therapy. For example, it was only after three unsuccessful suicide attempts that one of the authors' clients, who was a resident in a nursing facility, was referred for mental health services. The resident was in an early stage of Alzheimer's disease. He would wander away from the facility, as might be expected of a person with dementia, but he always walked in the same direction—toward a busy highway—and, in each case was caught stepping in front of an oncoming car.

Although little research has been done on this topic, it is known that young-old (age 60–74) men in residential care are more likely than are women or old-old (age 75 and over) men to attempt suicide. Suicidal old-old people, both men and women, tend to engage in indirect life-threatening behavior, such as refusing to eat or drink (Osgood & Thielman, 1990).

Overlap Between Depression and Dementia

In some older adults severe depression may be mistaken for a dementing illness. This overlap has been referred to as *pseudodementia* and has received much attention since the mid-1970s. It was thoughtfully reevaluated in the 1990s (Teri & Wagner, 1992). In a few cases psychomotor retardation and apathy resulting from depression can cause older persons to appear to have cognitive impairments; once the depression is treated, the cognitive impairments disappear. Several patterns that were thought to be indicative of pseudodementia have been identified as a reversible condition called *delirium*, which is caused by some depressive symptoms, such as loss of appetite, but not by depression itself. In other cases depression accompanies the early stage of a dementing illness. It is regrettable that the criteria that are often employed to distinguish between pseudodementia and dementia (e.g., preoccupation with memory loss, poor effort responses, apparent recent onset) do not effectively discriminate between people who are depressed and demented and people who are simply depressed (Osgood & Thielman, 1990).

FACTORS INFLUENCING THE DEVELOPMENT OF DEPRESSION

Before the late 1980s people generally accepted that depression was common in later life because they experience many losses as they age. The findings of a 1989 study indicate that older adults actually exhibit lower rates of depression than do younger adults (Newman, 1989). Older adults are believed to possess better coping skills than do younger cohorts and, thus, have lower rates of depression. Depressive symptoms are the most frequent mental health problem encountered in later life, and, given their common occurrence, there is a need for proper attention and treatment (Blazer, Hughes, & George, 1987).

In both men and women depressive symptoms have been associated with chronic diseases, poor general health, impairment in performing activities of daily living, cognitive impairment, and recent stressful life events (Busse, 1992). Most researchers believe that depression is caused by an interplay of biological, psychological, and social factors. To some extent, the primary contributing factor will depend on the type of depressive disorder being experienced (e.g., an adjustment disorder with depressed mood is caused by psychosocial factors) (Blazer, 1990b).

Physiology

Frequently, depression coexists with other illnesses, most notably Alzheimer's disease, AIDS, brain tumors, multiple sclerosis, Huntington's chorea, and Parkinson's disease. Cardiovascular illnesses, such as congestive heart failure and myocardial infarction, are known to cause depressive symptoms. Lupus and rheumatoid arthritis are also implicated. Because of the amount of medications many older adults take, they are at particular risk for drug-induced depression. Kinzie, Lewinsohn, Maricle, and Teri (1986) found that of the major depressions found in a community sample, more than one third were associated with medication use. Several agents used in the treatment of cardiovascular conditions (e.g., propranolol, methyldopa, digitalis, clonidine, prazosin) have been found to cause depression. Medications used to treat anxiety, psychosis, sleep disorders, hypertension, and nerve disorders such as Parkinson's disease have been shown to cause depression as well. Hormones such as estrogen, progesterone, and prednisone may cause physical changes that can induce depression (Reynolds, 1995).

Researchers have proposed that some adults are at greater risk for depression because of disregulation of neural receptor sites for specific neurotransmitter substances in their brains. Other researchers believe that chronic stress can trigger a disregulation of the endocrine system, specifically the concentrations of cortisol. Although the evidence for a physiological basis for depression is inconclusive, the findings are promising (Blazer, 1990b).

Health Status

Physical illness is a primary contributor to depression in older adults (Koenig, Meador, Cohen, & Blazer, 1988). As previously mentioned, physical illness is the most common stressor leading to an adjustment disorder with depressed mood (Blazer, 1990b). The relationship between depression and physical illness appears to hold for severe conditions such as a major depression, as well as for milder forms (Hall, Gardner, Stickney, LeCann, & Popkin, 1980; Kinzie, Lewinsohn, Maricle, & Teri, 1986). This relationship is complex; all three spheres of influence (e.g., physiological, psychological, social) have an impact on an individual's mood. Either the illness or the medications taken to treat it could trigger depression. An individual could experience a psychological change as he or she loses the resources needed to maintain self-esteem (Allen & Blazer, 1991). Social factors leading to depression could include loss of friends, loss of opportunities to socialize, and feelings of guilt associated with the burden of care thought to be placed on family members.

Gender

Women demonstrate a higher prevalence of depressive symptoms than men at all ages (Krause, 1986; Myers et al., 1984; O'Hara, Kohout, & Wallace, 1985). In part, this prevalence has been attributed to an underreporting of such symptoms by men (Vaux, 1985). However, many researchers believe that gender is not a true risk factor. When studies have controlled for disability level or living with a spouse, gender differences have disappeared (Feinson, 1987).

Status of Intimate Relationships

People who are unmarried (i.e., never married, divorced, widowed) and alone are at greater risk for depression than are those who are married or who have a partner (Phifer & Murrell, 1986). Having a "significant other" has been associated with social support, which can mediate stress. However, being married or having a permanent relationship should not automatically be taken as an indicator that social support needs are being met; not all spouses or life partners are supportive. The level and quality of social support received from a spouse or life partner should be established when evaluating a person for depression (Kurlowicz, 1993).

Minority Status

Relatively little information is available concerning depression in culturally diverse minority groups. Several studies have reported that prevalence levels in minority groups appear to be comparable to those of Caucasians (Blazer & Williams, 1980; Linn, Hunter, & Harris, 1980; Waxman, McGreary, Weinrit, & Carner, 1985). However, Smallegan (1989) found the number of depressive symptoms to be lower in African Americans than it is in Caucasians. Upper-income African Americans, in particular, have lower levels of depression. These lower levels are attributed to family and community support.

As is the pattern among older Caucasian adults, older Hispanic and African American women report more depressive symptoms than do older men from the same cultures (Mui, 1993). Common predictors of depression in older Hispanics and African Americans are greater numbers of physical illnesses, poorer perceived health, more perceived unmet needs, and perceived lack of control over their lives.

Socioeconomic Status

Older persons with low socioeconomic status are more likely than older people with better socioeconomic status to have high rates of depression (Blazer, Hughes, & George, 1987; Goldberg, Van Natta, & Comstock, 1985). This finding has been attributed to increased stress that results from a lack of financial resources and higher rates of physical illness among economically disadvantaged people. Without adequate financial resources, individuals are not likely to obtain regular medical checkups, which can forestall or prevent some chronic conditions. Financial limitations may even prevent some older people from obtaining treatment for existing medical conditions. Many of them must decide between purchasing medication and paying for other needs.

Social Support

Support from family and friends can also reduce the risk of depression (George, 1991). Social support provides a sense of security, a sharing of concerns, a feeling of worthiness and belonging through kinship ties, a chance to give and receive nurturing, and a way of receiving guidance and assistance with the tasks of daily life (Goldberg, Van Natta, & Comstock, 1985). Social support is believed to mediate the effects of stressful events (Kurlowicz, 1993). It is not the size of the support network available but the perceived adequacy of the support that is critical (George, Blazer, Hughes, & Fowler, 1989). Having one intimate confidant has been associated with high morale and improved mental health (Lowenthal, 1965).

Problems with interpersonal relationships, specifically arguments with family and friends, were found by Linn, Hunter, and Harris (1980) to be among the stressful life events associated with depression in older community-dwelling adults. Similar findings were obtained by Smallegan (1989), who examined life stresses and depression in culturally diverse older adults. The psychological distress experienced by older adults who are having interpersonal problems with family members is supported by Mosher-Ashley (1993), who found that conflict with family members was the most frequent reason older adults referred themselves for outpatient therapy at a community mental health clinic.

Loss of Control

Later life is frequently a period in which major losses take place, and depression may be a reaction to them. In older adults depression may be perceived as a form of learned helplessness (Knight, 1992). In many cases older adults are unable to exert personal control over their losses, which can include the illness or death of friends and loved ones. The concept of personal control also extends to belief systems through which people interpret events. Events that are perceived as unpredictable and uncontrollable instill feelings of helplessness, which result in depression. In addition, a person who is depressed believes that he or she is responsible for the situation, that things are unlikely to get better, and that life is a hopeless mess. These beliefs are manifested in negative thoughts that become automatic and repetitive and serve to sustain the symptoms of depression (Thase & Beck, 1993).

Death of a loved one, according to Yost, Beutler, Corbishley, and Allender (1986), is one of the major precursors for depressive symptoms in older adults. Prolonged bereavement can have all of the characteristics of a major depression. A common reaction in the initial phase of bereavement is disbelief, which can manifest itself in confusion and a sense of being "off-balance." The individual has difficulty thinking clearly and has a shortened attention span. Confusion is accompanied by restlessness, which interferes with sleep. This restlessness extends well into the second phase of a five-phase process (denial and isolation, anger, bargaining, depression, and acceptance) that can last up to 2 years. In addition, the grieving individual experiences loss of appetite and severe emotional distress (Sanders, 1989).

Dementing Illnesses

Many older adults who are in the early stages of a dementing illness such as Alzheimer's disease experience depression. Between 15% and 57% of people with Alzheimer's disease have coexisting depression (Busse, 1992). During the initial stages of Alzheimer's disease and other dementing illnesses, the affected individual is frequently and painfully aware of the changes in intellectual functioning (Cohen, 1988). This recognition leads some individuals to withdraw and even deny what is happening in an effort to cope with ongoing losses. Others, with help from their families, seek answers from physicians and specialists in neurology. Once the diagnosis of Alzheimer's disease is made, the individual frequently moves into a depressed state.

The rate of depression among people who are in the early stages of a dementia will probably rise by the year 2000, as knowledge about the disorder, specifically its course of progressive deterioration and subsequent disabilities, becomes more widespread. As previously noted, Huntington's chorea, which has a degenerative course and outcome similar to that of Alzheimer's disease, is one of the illnesses that most commonly causes older adults to consider or commit suicide.

Although people with Alzheimer's disease experience considerable distress about their condition (Flowers & Mosher-Ashley, 1996), few receive treatment from mental health professionals (Thompson, Wagner, Zeiss, & Gallagher, 1989). Because of their failing cognitive abilities people with Alzheimer's disease are not viewed as appropriate candidates for therapy by most clinicians (Eisdorfer, Cohen, & Preston, 1981; LaBarge, Rosenman, Leavitt, & Cristiani, 1988). However, researchers indicate that individuals with Alzheimer's disease can benefit from therapeutic interventions, even psychotherapy (Eisdorfer, Cohen, & Preston, 1981; LaBarge et al., 1988; Teri & Gallagher, 1991; Yale, 1995). Although psychotherapy and other interventions cannot make an impact on the underlying progression of changes taking place in the brain, gaining insight into the dementing disorder and "venting" feelings can lead to some degree of acceptance and a reduction in the symptoms of depression (Hinkle, 1990; Solomon & Szwabo, 1992). Reducing depressive symptoms can also lead to some improvement in cognitive functioning. Depression alone can cause temporary impairments in thinking. An overlay of depression with a dementing illness tends to produce even greater declines in cognition.

The treatment of depression in people with a dementing illness is similar to the management of depression in nondemented older adults. However, some slight modification of the therapeutic approaches may be needed to compensate for the individual's declining level of cognitive functioning (Ellis & Donnelly, 1993; Taft, Delaney, Semen, & Stansell, 1993). Teri and Gallagher (1991) report that people with mild dementia respond well to cognitive therapy, whereas individuals with advanced dementia benefit more from a behavioral approach. People with dementia have responded well to therapeutic interventions that use gentle but persistent stimulation to improve conversational abilities and to increase activity level (Brody, 1981). The chapters on cognitive-behavioral therapy (Chapter 3) and support groups (Chapter 11) describe interventions that have been carried out successfully with depressed people with Alzheimer's disease.

Coping Skills

Although many of the stressors examined have been associated with depression, the relationship between stressors and depression is not a direct one. An increase in a given stressor or even the presence of multiple stressors does not automatically result in depression. An individual's lifelong pattern of coping is probably a more influential factor than are stressors. Individuals with effective coping skills can tolerate high levels of stress without experiencing depressive symptoms. Other persons who have less effective coping skills may experience depressive symptoms after being exposed to relatively low levels of stress (Blazer, 1990b).

OLDER ADULTS LIVING INDEPENDENTLY AND DEPRESSION

Lillian was a 78-year-old woman residing alone in a multigenerational apartment building. Her closest friend and only living relative was a sister, Sarah, who resided across town. The sisters spent a great deal of their time together. Both women had married early in life but were divorced at a relatively young age. Neither sister had children. Lillian had married into a wealthy family and received a generous settlement upon her divorce. She had elected not to work, and she invested her money and lived modestly. Unfortunately, the combination of inflation and some poor investment decisions left her with a limited income in later life. Sarah, who had worked, retired early, and received a modest pension, preferred to spend her financial resources on travel. Both women prized their independence, but agreed to share some resources. Lillian owned a car, and she frequently escorted Sarah to appointments. Sarah had a telephone that Lillian used whenever necessary. The sisters, who were delightfully eccentric, also had a common circle of friends.

At age 78 Lillian experienced a series of strokes that severely affected her visuospatial abilities and, subsequently, her vision. The strokes also affected her ability to drive her car, a major source of independence. Lillian hired a companion who came in to help her a few hours a day so that she could continue living independently. As Lillian became more visually impaired, many of her friends drew away. What had been enjoyed by others as eccentric behavior was now perceived as irritating in an old, physically disabled woman. Sarah was very much involved with Lillian's care, but felt unable to provide the extensive physical assistance Lillian needed. Over time, Lillian sank into a deep depression. She experienced difficulty sleeping, spending her time awake brooding about the changes in her life. She also spent much of her time weeping and lamenting her losses to anyone who stopped by to see her. These behaviors further alienated friends and, eventually, even Sarah.

Finally, a few close friends convinced Lillian to speak with her physician about her depressive symptoms. Lillian was placed on an antidepressant medication, which greatly improved her mood. With the improvement in her mood, her revitalized vivacious manner and witty comments drew some of her old friends back, which made her feel confident to manage living alone.

Although depressive symptoms are common in later life, older adults who live independently in the community have been underrepresented in the caseloads of mental health centers, averaging only 6% of the clients served (Swan, Fox, & Estes, 1986). Negative attitudes toward mental health services have been implicated (Waxman, Carner, & Klein, 1984), as have therapist prejudice (Casey & Grant, 1993) and lack of accessibility to services (Hagebak & Hagebak, 1980). Knight (1985–1986) demonstrated that the assumptions of therapist prejudice and lack of accessibility were not based on empirical evidence and are false. Lack of education concerning psychotherapy and its uses has been proposed to be the primary reason for the low levels of participation by older adults (Knight, 1992; Lasoski & Thelen, 1987; Lundervold, Lewin, & Bourland, 1990). Support for this interpretation can be seen in work conducted by Mosher-Ashley (1993), who found that, in general, older people do not refer themselves for outpatient therapy. Older adults who do refer themselves also tend to be younger. It is interesting that adults over age 75, who are more likely to hold negative attitudes toward therapy, are as likely as younger older adults (age 60–74) to accept and take part in counseling (Mosher-Ashley, 1995).

Older adults who exhibit symptoms of depression should be referred to and treated by mental health specialists. However, this is not always an option. Some older adults may not be willing to consider treatment at a mental health center, the type of mental health services needed may not be available (e.g., group interventions), or transportation may not be available. In such cases professionals in other disciplines who work closely with older adults may be in a position to provide treatment.

OLDER ADULTS LIVING IN LONG-TERM CARE FACILITIES AND DEPRESSION

Dora passed away at age 94 in a nursing facility. She had lived there for $8\frac{1}{2}$ years. Her only surviving relative, a nephew, visited twice a year, at Easter and Christmas. He was her only visitor. Dora's physical condition had deteriorated over the years, and for the last 4 years of her life she was unable to walk unassisted. She also needed assistance in moving from her bed into her wheelchair or into the easy chair in her room. Dora rarely propelled the wheelchair on her own, relying on the staff to take her from place to place. In the several years before her death Dora showed little interest in her surroundings. On most days a nursing assistant would help her with her morning care and bring her to a large sitting area on the ward. Although a television set located there was turned on, Dora paid little attention to it. Staff members would pass by periodically and speak to her, but she rarely acknowledged them.

Yolanda, a nursing assistant, developed a particular fondness for Dora. During morning care, she was able to encourage Dora to chat a bit. Yolanda was surprised to discover that Dora's thinking processes were intact. Dora could remember what she had eaten for dinner the night before and could even describe how some of the other residents' visitors were dressed. When Dora was questioned about her feelings, she said that she was waiting to die. She reported that there were few pleasures and little purpose in her life. Yolanda tried to interest Dora in some of the activities held in the facility. She would wheel Dora to Monday morning coffee hour, arts and crafts classes, entertainment programs, and bingo games. Dora sat in her chair patiently, but rarely participated or even looked interested.

Older adults who reside in long-term care facilities have been found to exhibit high rates of psychiatric disorders (Borson, Liptzin, Nininger, & Rabins, 1987; Curlik, Frazier, & Katz, 1991). Although many residents have dementing illnesses, a large proportion have emotional problems (Mosher-Ashley, 1994). As many as 20% (Busse, 1992) or 25% of residents (Reynolds, 1995) are believed to exhibit depressive symptoms.

Numerous factors contribute to depression in older adults living in long-term care facilities. According to Masand (1995) these factors include the following:

- Loss of independence resulting from structured mealtimes, bedtimes, and recreational activities
- Loss of loved ones

- Chronic physical illness
- Difficulty adjusting to the facility and coping with the many social changes that living in long-term care facilities brings

Living in long-term care facilities also isolates older individuals from family and friends and limits residents' acquaintance to other infirm and dying people. In an effort to provide medical care and physical assistance, these facilities frequently sacrifice quality of life, making living in them even less appealing to some residents than death (Yost et al., 1986). The challenge is to help residents regain a sense of hope and provide some degree of meaning to their lives.

Although older adults in residential settings experience a high incidence of mental health problems, they are unlikely to receive treatment (Burns et al., 1993; Rovner, 1993; Sakauye & Camp, 1992). Many factors contribute to this situation, including insufficient finances, lack of appropriate training programs for staff members, lack of referrals, and a general lack of knowledge of methods to feasibly implement treatment programs in long-term care settings (Bienenfeld & Wheeler, 1989; Gatz, Popkins, Pino, & VandenBos, 1990). Since the early 1990s some gains have been made in providing mental health services to residents of long-term care facilities (Brooks & Mosher-Ashley, 1996). The impetus for these gains can be attributed, in part, to the Omnibus Budget Reconciliation Act (OBRA; Omnibus Budget Reconciliation Act, 1989). OBRA regulations mandate that residents of nursing facilities who have a primary or secondary diagnosis of a major mental disorder must receive treatment for their psychiatric symptoms (*Federal Register*, 1989). Also, this treatment must not be limited to psychotropic medications. Alternative strategies (e.g., behavior therapy) must have been attempted prior to the use of chemical restraints. Periodic dose reductions and "drug holidays" are required as well. A number of private vendors have sprung up in several states to help meet this need. The vendors usually offer an array of services and are willing to treat residents with adjustment disorder as well as those with more serious psychiatric disorders. Funding for these mental health services comes primarily from Medicare, commercial insurance companies, HMOs, and private billing (Brooks & Mosher-Ashley, 1996).

It is important to treat depression in older adult residents of long-term care facilities because depressed residents have a 59% greater likelihood of death (Rovner, 1993). This increased mortality has been attributed to two factors: 1) reduced nutritional intake, leading to malnutrition and electrolyte imbalances, which can predispose residents to infections, loss of skin integrity, and poor control of chronic diseases; and 2) changes in cardiac function and immune response. Psychotherapeutic interventions are easy to carry out in residential settings. An outreach therapist can see several individuals during one visit to a facility. Interventions provided in a group format are particularly well-suited to long-term care facilities because they house large numbers of older adults with similar problems. Once initiated, strategies that employ environmental change to treat depression must be continued, particularly in long-term care settings. Initiating change and then withdrawing it may be worse than not initiating the change at all (Schultz & Hanusa, 1978). Giving residents hope that things can improve and then dashing their hope is demoralizing.

ASSESSMENT OF DEPRESSION

In order to treat depression in older adults, the type and level of depression must be assessed.

Presence of Symptoms

Great care should be taken when assessing older adults for the presence of depressive symptoms. Many of the symptoms of depression are similar to characteristics that are associated with increasing age (e.g., increased forgetfulness, decreased physical stamina, increased "aches and pains"; see also the exhibit on p. 16). A vital initial step in assessment is a thorough physical examination because many illnesses and medications can induce or mimic the symptoms of depression (Reynolds, 1995). Once physiological factors are ruled out as the primary cause of the depression, older adults who exhibit clear signs of a major depression or who score high levels of depression on a standardized assessment scale should be referred for professional mental health services. Most community mental health centers offer specialized services for older adults. At the very least, older people may be seen as eligible for the services that are available to adults in general.

Assessment devices that stress somatic (body) functioning are particularly susceptible to indicating depression when it may not be present. In addition, some of the questions listed on scales that were developed for younger age groups may not be suitable for older adults. For example, questions about sexuality may put many older people on the defensive (Kivela, 1992). Questions about whether life is worth living or whether one is hopeful about the future may have different meanings for older adults than they do for younger adults.

Assessment of depression in older adults can take many forms. The most common assessment approaches developed include self-rating scales and interviewer-rater scales. Considerable work has been carried out in establishing the effectiveness of self-report measures with older adults; far less effort has been expended on assessing the suitability of the interviewer-rater scales. Self-report measures are susceptible to two common problems in clinical assessment: social desirability responses and an overreporting of symptoms. Gallagher (1986) reports having observed both in older adults. Some older adults tend to underreport depressive symptoms in an effort to appear healthy or because they are not well-informed about the nature of psychopathology and how it might relate to their own experience (Thompson, Gong, Haskins, & Gallagher, 1987). Other older adults overreport depressive symptoms because of their generally negative self-perceptions. Gallagher (1986) has observed that underreporting of symptoms is more common in men. In contrast, women with histrionic and/or dependent personality characteristics tend to overreport depressive symptoms. Because of

Recognizing the *Signs* and *Symptoms* of Depression

This list can be used to determine whether a formal assessment should be conducted. If one or more of these signs or symptoms persists for longer than 2 weeks, professional help should be sought.

Extreme sadness

Excessive crying

Anxiety

Low or lack of energy; apathy

Too little or too much sleep

Restlessness (clinicians call this *psychomotor agitation*)

Hopelessness

Worthlessness/low self-esteem

Inability to concentrate

Inability to enjoy life

Preoccupation with negative thoughts about self and events

Weight gain

Little or no appetite

Weight loss

Overwhelming guilt

Poor personal appearance

Fear that nothing will change or get better

Recurrent thoughts of death and/or wish that death would come more quickly

Suicidal thoughts

Suicide threats or attempts

A Life Worth Living: Practical Strategies for Reducing Depression in Older Adults, by Pearl Mosher-Ashley and Phyllis Barrett. ©1997 Health Professions Press, Inc., Baltimore.

these barriers to properly assessing an older individual for depression, many clinicians advocate a comprehensive approach, in which both a self-rating measure and an interviewer-rater scale are administered to determine the nature and severity of the disorder.

Self-Rating Scales

Two excellent, reliable, and valid self-report inventories can be administered by professionals who are not necessarily mental health specialists to assess depression in a wide range of older adults: the Geriatric Depression Scale (GDS) and the Beck Depression Inventory (BDI). Both the GDS and the BDI can be administered and scored by social workers or health care professionals to determine the presence of mild depression. Two additional scales, the Zung Self-Rating Depression Scale (ZSDS) and the Center for Epidemiological Studies Depression Scale (CES-D), are described because they are used commonly with older adults and may provide useful alternatives for professionals. All four scales have been assessed for validity, internal consistency, and test-retest reliability, although the Zung scale has not been standardized to community-dwelling older persons. Information on ways to obtain the scales is listed in the appendix to this chapter.

Geriatric Depression Scale

Developed by Yesavage et al. (1983), the GDS was designed specifically for older adults. The GDS is made up of 30 items that are answered independently in a yes/no format. Administration is simple and brief, requiring an average of only 5–7 minutes. The scale can be self-administered or used to interview and question an older person. None of the items are related to somatic symptoms, which makes the scale suitable for use with physically ill people, including people with stroke (Agrell & Dehlin, 1989). The scale can be used with both independent-living older adults (Olin, Schneider, Eaton, Zemansky, & Pollock, 1992) and older, frail residents of nursing facilities (Abraham, 1991). The GDS appears to be useful with older adults who have mild cognitive impairment as well as with healthy older adults (Parmelee, Katz, & Lawton, 1989). Olin et al. (1992) report that the GDS may be simpler than the BDI for older adults to complete. The four-point scale used in the BDI to measure the intensity of a symptom was found to result in multiple responses from some older adults, particularly those who were depressed. Older adults had less difficulty responding to the yes/no format of the GDS.

The GDS can discriminate among nondepressed, mildly depressed, and severely depressed older participants more effectively than can the ZSDS (Yesavage et al., 1983). It is also sensitive enough to measure changes taking place during drug trials (Kivela, 1992).

Beck Depression Inventory

Developed by Beck, Ward, Mendelson, Mock, and Erbaugh (1961), the BDI was designed for all adults, but has been found to be a useful screening instrument for identifying clinically depressed individuals over 60 years of age (Brink, 1986;

Teri, 1991). It contains 21 items rated on a 4-point scale and measures the frequency and severity of symptoms experienced. Often, the BDI is completed by the individual who is being evaluated. The person usually completes the scale independently and is asked to choose the response that best describes the way he or she has felt over the past week. Like the GDS, administration of the BDI is simple and brief. The BDI also can be quite useful in evaluating bereaved older adults for signs of a more serious depressive state. Gallagher, Breckenridge, Thompson, Dessonville, and Amaral (1982) found that both depressed and bereaved older people reported being tearful, sad, and dissatisfied with themselves. Depressed older people were more pessimistic, felt more like failures, showed greater self-dissatisfaction, were more irritable, cried more, felt less personally attractive, and had greater fatigue and health concerns than did bereaved older people. Gallagher (1986) reports that the BDI can be a useful indicator of change and need for medication in treatment interventions. Administering the BDI session by session permits a therapist to focus on the symptoms being experienced by depressed older clients.

Because concentration and some memory skills are needed to complete the BDI, it may not be suitable for older adults with cognitive impairment. An eighth-grade reading level is required to understand the items and the gradations in the response choices fully (Gallagher, 1986). The scale may not be suitable for older adults with minimal education or for those who are not sufficiently fluent in the English language. This scale also should be interpreted with caution when assessing physically ill older people because some of the items deal with somatic symptoms (Gallagher, 1986).

The BDI was upgraded (BDI-II) in 1996 to correspond to the diagnostic criteria of DSM-IV. In the revision the items concerning weight loss, changes in body image, and somatic preoccupation have been replaced with work difficulty, agitation, concentration difficulty, worthlessness, and loss of energy (Beck & Steer, 1996). The change in items may make the BDI-II more applicable for use with older adults, particularly those with physical impairments.

Zung Self-Rating Depression Scale

Developed by Zung (1965), the ZSDS is one of the most popular of the self-report scales. It contains 20 items designed to assess common symptoms of depression along a 4-point scale that ranges from "none of the time" to "all of the time." Questions linger regarding its appropriateness for people over age 70 (Thompson et al., 1987). Some of the items are related to somatic symptoms, and it is difficult to differentiate between depressive features and the signs of normal aging. As a result, the ZSDS has been found to indicate elevated levels of depressive symptoms in healthy older people (Kivela, 1992).

Center for Epidemiological Studies Depression Scale

The CES-D, developed by Radloff (1977), is also widely used to assess depressive symptoms. Like the ZSDS, the CES-D contains 20 items that assess common aspects of depression on a 4-point scale. A number of the items deal with somatic symptoms. As a consequence, this scale should be used cautiously with individuals who are physically ill. The CES-D is believed to have lower sensitivity and lower predictive power than the ZSDS or GDS (Agrell & Dehlin, 1989). In addition, not all of the older adults who score high on the CES-D are depressed (Kivela, 1992). The author of the scale indicates that people with a high average score may be seen to be "at risk" for depression and in need of treatment (Kivela, 1992). However, this finding has not been substantiated in older adults.

Interviewer-Rater Scales

Several different interviewer-rater scales are used commonly to assess depression in adults. None of these scales are recommended for use by health care and social services professionals with older people. The scales used most frequently are presented here in an effort to enlighten the reader concerning the difficulties inherent in each. Given the wide use and revision in 1994 of the Hamilton Rating Scale for Depression, information on how to obtain this scale has been included in the appendix to this chapter. An older adult who is believed to be depressed should be referred for assessment of depression by a person trained in the use of one of the following scales.

Schedule for Affective Disorders and Schizophrenia

The Schedule for Affective Disorders and Schizophrenia (SADS), developed by Spitzer and Endicott (1978), is the most respected of the interviewer-rater scales. The SADS should be administered by a trained clinician (Thompson et al., 1987); consequently, it is not suitable for use by health care and social services professionals unless they have received the lengthy training and clinical experience required.

Diagnostic Interview Schedule

The Diagnostic Interview Schedule (DIS), developed by Regier et al. (1984), can be administered and scored by individuals with minimal formal training in psychology or psychiatry. However, the DIS contains many items pertaining to drug abuse and acting-out disorders that are believed to be inappropriate for use with older adults. Thompson et al. (1987) report that the type of questions and the manner in which they are presented may curtail an older adult's inclination to disclose information. Also, the DIS contains 254 questions and takes about 1 hour to administer. Its length may prove taxing for some old-old people.

Hamilton Rating Scale for Depression

The Hamilton Rating Scale for Depression (HRSD), developed by Hamilton (1967), is the most commonly used of the interviewer-rater scales. Some training and experience is needed to administer the scale properly. The HRSD was revised in 1994 and is available in two forms: the Clinician Rating Form and the Self-Report Problem Inventory. Both forms assess the same symptoms and provide the same score. They differ only in who completes the form, the clinician or the client. The scale comprises 76 items and takes approximately 10 minutes to complete. The self-report inventory can be used by people with only a fourth-grade reading ability. No information has appeared in the literature concerning the applicability of the revised HRSD to older adults. The previous version of the scale was criticized for its reliance on somatic information, which could result in elevated scores indicative of depression in medically ill older adults (Teri, 1991). The revised scale still includes a number of items that rely on somatic symptoms. Consequently, scores on the revised HRSD could be influenced by physical ailments in some older adults and should be used with caution.

Episodes of Crying

Although crying is perceived frequently as a symptom of depression, the relationship between crying and depression is actually weak (Hastrup, Baker, Kraemer, & Bornstein, 1986). In some individuals crying episodes appear to function as a release of tension and can be an adaptive coping strategy in response to stress. Thus, the genesis of crying should be evaluated with caution. Busse (1992) proposes that in older adults crying may be more an expression of normal grief than it is an indication of depression.

Additional Considerations

In addition to the physical examination and self-report and interviewer-rater scales, the older person's health status and medication usage should be assessed. These issues should be addressed with the older person's physician. Older adults living independently should be encouraged to speak with their physicians about whether the prescribed and/or over-the-counter medications they are taking can cause depressive symptoms. The physician may be approached directly if the older person resides in a long-term care setting. Regardless of the living arrangement, having a close collaborative relationship with the physician during assessment and treatment is beneficial. It is important, however, not to disempower the older person in the process. Whenever possible, older people should take an active role in the remediation of their depressive symptoms. Interpretations of the assessments should be discussed with them and interventions planned together.

TREATMENT OF DEPRESSION IN OLDER ADULTS

The treatment of depression can include a variety of alternatives, depending upon the cause and severity of the disorder. Pharmacotherapy (drug therapy) can often be quite effective. Treatments once considered inappropriate for older people, including electroconvulsive therapy and psychotherapy, should be given consideration under certain circumstances. In addition, there are numerous psychosocial alternatives worthy of exploration.

Pharmacotherapy and Electroconvulsive Therapy

Pharmacotherapy and electroconvulsive therapy are usually advocated in the treatment of a major depressive disorder (Steiner & Marcopulos, 1991). The use of these treatments is based on the assumption that underlying physiological factors are wholly or partially responsible for the affective disorder. According to Blazer (1990a), early studies suggested that the levels of neurotransmitters, specifically serotonin and norepinephrine, in certain areas of the central nervous system were responsible for depressive symptoms. This chemical imbalance perspective has given way to a more sophisticated view that a disregulation of the receptor sites that receive the neurochemical messengers is at fault. An explanation of the neurophysiological causes of depression in later life is beyond the scope of this book. The reader who wishes to pursue such information is advised to consult Blazer (1990a) for an in-depth description of the neurological dysfunction, medical disorders, and medications found to give rise to depression in older adults.

Pharmacotherapy

Medication can be useful, particularly when the cause of depression is believed to have a neurological basis or when the factors influencing the depression cannot be changed. In cases in which the individual is experiencing severe losses such as cognitive decline, bereavement or other losses, and serious adjustment problems, antidepressants combined with a psychotherapeutic intervention can be an effective approach. Also, antidepressant medication can have the advantage that it results frequently in an improvement in mood and a reduction in depressive symptoms, such as difficulty in sleeping, providing older people with renewed hope that things can change for the better and with the motivation to work toward additional change.

The most serious drawback to pharmacotherapy is that as people age, they are less able to process medications physiologically. The side effects of antidepressant medication can include anticholinergic and cardiovascular changes as well as sedation (Casey & Grant, 1993). Confusion, urinary retention, dry mouth, blurred vision, and tachycardia are common symptoms. In some cases impaired gait, which can increase the risk of falls, has also been observed. Another problem with pharmacotherapy is that older adults are likely to be prescribed many different medications because of a variety of medical problems (i.e., polypharmacy) (Eisdorfer, Cohen, & Veith, 1980; Salzman, 1992). Many drugs used to treat depression can interact with medications used for other conditions, producing additional side effects that may impair an older person's functional capacities.

Electroconvulsive Therapy

Electroconvulsive therapy is believed to reset the receptor sites that receive neurochemical substances responsible for mood (Blazer, 1990a). This treatment has been found to be a safe and effective alternative to medication even in old–old persons. At Duke University Medical Center, 228 persons were treated with electroconvulsive therapy over a 3-year period. Nearly 50% were over the age of 60 and 28% were over 70 (Blazer, 1990a). Fogel and Kroessler (1987) found that 92% of depressed medically ill patients over the age of 80 responded well to electroconvulsive therapy. However, this form of treatment is usually reserved as a last resort for severe depression that has not responded to pharmacotherapy. Older adults who are prospective candidates must be fully informed of the treatment and its potential side effects. Although electroconvulsive therapy is being used safely and effectively with older adults, the effects on their memory have been poorly studied (Blazer, 1990a). Blazer (1990a) points out that some evidence indicates that electroconvulsive therapy induces impairments in concentration, short-term memory, and learning, but that there is better recall of remote (i.e., long-term) memories. The impairments observed following electroconvulsive therapy treatments usually dissipate by 6-month follow-ups.

Psychotherapy

Psychotherapy and social interventions have several advantages. They lack the potentially dangerous side effects of pharmacotherapy, and some therapeutic interventions can teach individuals coping skills that they can use to mediate stressors after the therapeutic intervention ends (Steiner & Marcopulos, 1991). Some questions have been raised in the 1990s regarding the effectiveness of psychotherapeutic interventions for older persons. Scogin and McElreath (1994) conducted a meta-analysis of 17 studies describing psychosocial treatments for depression among older adults. Their results indicated that the treatments provided were reliably more effective than no treatment on self-rated and clinician-rated measures of depression. Scogin and McElreath propose that greater emphasis be placed on providing psychosocial interventions. Given the paucity of research on psychotherapeutic interventions, they were unable to identify the mechanisms underlying the efficacy of the procedures reviewed.

The psychotherapeutic intervention that has received the most systematic study in older adults is cognitive-behavioral therapy. This therapeutic approach is particularly well suited to older adults who exhibit intractable beliefs as part of their depressive symptoms. These beliefs are called *cognitive distortions* and usually take several forms, as follows:

- Unrealistic expectations of the self or others
- Belief that a current situation will have an impact on all aspects of one's life
- Belief that experiencing one bad incident means that all future incidents of a similar nature will end badly
- Belief that a problem or upcoming event will be horrendous and unbearable

Cognitive-behavioral therapy emphasizes the role of thinking and behavior in the development and maintenance of depression. Thought content and thought processes are viewed as mediators between life experiences and emotional responses.

Thompson, Gallagher, Nies, and Epstein (1983) found that nonprofessionals were as effective as were mental health professionals in implementing a cognitive-behavioral program to reduce depression in older adults. The major factor influencing effectiveness was an adherence to the structural format of the therapeutic approach. The nonprofessionals involved in the study were described as individuals who worked in senior centers, adult day programs, and retirement hotels. Their level of education ranged from high school to postgraduate training in fields not associated with the mental health profession. Given this finding, cognitive-behavioral therapy is an appropriate treatment for use by professionals in the medical and social services fields.

Psychosocial Alternatives

Depressive symptoms may be caused by a variety of factors. Knight (1992) suggests that one source of depression involves the tendency of many older people to give up previously enjoyed activities because of the onset of a debilitating illness or a drifting away from the activities. (The authors' experience is that the latter is likely to occur following the death of a spouse.) Knight also points out that many older adults believe that old age is not expected to be enjoyable. This belief becomes a self-fulfilling prophecy as these older adults begin to "act old," engaging in sedentary, less enjoyable activities. Knight's proposal is based on Lewinsohn's view (1974) that depressed individuals engage in fewer self-reinforcing activities or enjoyable events than do nondepressed individuals. Older adults are thought to have less access to social reinforcers of all types and to experience more unpleasant events than do younger adults. The challenge in developing a psychosocial intervention for a mildly depressed older person is to match the individual's history of pleasurable events to the intervention approaches described in subsequent chapters.

When an assessment indicates a mild level of depression or when a severely depressed older adult refuses traditional mental health services, the alternative forms of treatment described in this book may be helpful. Alternative approaches that have an impact on the underlying reasons for the depression are increasing in number and are particularly effective. For example, research has shown that a substantial number of older adults report problems coping with loneliness (Mosher-Ashley, 1994). Having an animal companion or participating in a group based on one of the described treatment approaches can help to relieve some of these feelings. Other older adults have reported problems coping with losses associated with diminished or lost work-role. In such cases role replacement strategies may help them to overcome these losses. Feelings of sadness, one of the issues most commonly reported by older adults in therapy (Mosher-Ashley, 1994), may be ameliorated through music therapy, art therapy, or bibliotherapy (reading books). Older people who are experiencing difficulty coping with the eventuality of death or with the sense that they have not spent their lives productively may profit from reminiscence therapy. One of the benefits of this form of treatment is that it provides the individual with an understanding of the continuity of life and diminishes the importance of the individual in the sequence of time and events. Engaging in reminiscence or horticulture therapy as well as any of the other therapeutic approaches may also increase the frequency of pleasurable events, experiences that can decrease the symptoms of depression.

Role of Health Care and Social Services Professionals

Health care professionals are in an excellent position to assess and treat mild depressive symptoms in older adults. The majority of older people experiencing their first psychiatric crisis will seek medical rather than psychiatric treatment

(Blumenthal, 1990). In addition, visiting nurses, physical therapists, and occupational therapists who come into regular contact with older adults are more likely than are nonprofessionals (e.g., friends, family) to be the recipients of confidences concerning emotional difficulties and to recognize the symptoms of depression.

Social services professionals such as case managers and senior center directors are also in an advantageous position to recognize and treat mild forms of depression. Like health care professionals, they come into frequent and regular contact with older adults. They are also apt to be used as confidants. Even more than that of health care professionals, the training social services professionals receive usually stresses the use of psychosocial interventions to increase life satisfaction in older adults. This training, along with the review of findings concerning the implementation of the psychosocial interventions in subsequent chapters, can empower social services professionals to develop systematic programs to treat depression or circumvent the risk of it in older adults.

Support for encouraging health care and social services professionals to take on the treatment of mild symptoms of depression in older adults may be drawn from Gallagher's work (Foster & Gallagher, 1986; Gallagher et al., 1982) in comparing professionals and nonprofessionals in undertaking group interventions. Thompson et al. (1983) found group facilitator competence to be more a function of the willingness and ability to apply the treatment approach accurately than a function of professional status. Admittedly, mental health specialists are superior in effecting treatment, but, in their absence, much can be accomplished by health care and social services professionals. A notable example is Irene Burnside, who, as a nurse, pioneered group interventions with older people. Others have also begun to recognize the importance of compelling professionals in other fields to implement therapeutic interventions with older adults (Kozlak & Thobaben, 1992; Myers & Salmon, 1984; Quinlan & Ohlund, 1995). Even paraprofessionals and peers can provide some supplementary care (Smyer, Zarit, & Qualls, 1990). That health care professionals who are not mental health specialists, paraprofessionals, or peers can implement psychotherapeutic interventions is also advantageous in that some older adults harbor negative feelings about being treated by professionals in the mental health system.

Outreach social workers who implement a highly structured program of intervention on a frequent basis in the setting in which the client lives can have a considerable impact. Bush, Langford, Rosen, and Gott (1990) found that when case managers provided intensive outreach to adults with psychiatric disabilities, the result was significantly fewer days of inpatient care and better adherence to medication regimens and agreed-upon service plans during the project.

Introduction of Treatment

Health care and social services personnel should not expect their depressed patients and clients to welcome the intervention approaches described in this book. Foster and Gallagher (1986) found that, in general, depressed older adults did not perceive the coping strategies commonly used to reduce stress and feelings of depression to be helpful. This perception was attributed to their depressive symptomology, which negatively biased their view of the situation. When possible, it is best to develop a close, trusting relationship with the older person and to follow up with an approach in which both individuals work together to resolve the feelings of despondency. Having a clear plan in mind is necessary to ensure a cohesive approach. However, the plan should be modifiable based on the desires and individual needs of the client. Although a strict adherence to procedure is needed for a cognitive-behavioral intervention, the other interventions described in this book can be implemented in many different ways. With sufficient background, imagination, and compassion, it is possible to offer older people many stimulating, life-enhancing alternatives to stagnation and despair.

REFERENCES

Abraham, I.L. (1991). The geriatric depression scale and hopelessness index: Longitudinal psychometric data on frail nursing home residents. *Perceptual and Motor Skills, 72,* 875–880.

Agrell, B., & Dehlin, O. (1989). Comparison of six depression rating scales in geriatric stroke patients. *Stroke, 20,* 1190–1194.

Allen, A., & Blazer, D.G. (1991). Mood disorders. In J. Sadavoy, L.W. Lazarus, & L.F. Jarvik (Eds.), *Comprehensive review of geriatric psychiatry* (pp. 337–351). Washington, DC: American Psychiatric Press.

American Psychiatric Association. (1994). *Diagnostic and statistical manual of mental disorders (4th ed.).* Washington, DC: American Psychiatric Press.

Beck, A.T., & Steer, R.A. (1996, Spring). Beck depression inventory-II. *Behavioral Measurements Letter, 3*(2), 3–4.

Beck, A.T., Ward, C.H., Mendelson, M., Mock, J., & Erbaugh, J. (1961). An inventory for measuring depression. *Archives of General Psychiatry, 4,* 561–571.

Bienenfeld, D., & Wheeler, B. (1989). Psychiatric services to nursing homes: A liaison model. *Hospital and Community Psychiatry, 40,* 793–794.

Blazer, D. (1990a). Depression in late life: An update. In M.P. Lawton (Ed.), *Annual review of gerontology and geriatrics* (Vol. 9, pp. 197–215). New York: Springer Publishing.

Blazer, D. (1990b). *Emotional problems in later life: Intervention strategies for professional caregivers.* New York: Springer Publishing.

Blazer, D., Hughes, D.C., & George, L.K. (1987). The epidemiology of depression in an elderly community population. *Gerontologist, 27,* 281–287.

Blazer, D., & Williams, C.D. (1980). Epidemiology of dysphoria and depression in an elderly population. *American Journal of Psychiatry, 137,* 439–444.

Blumenthal, S.J. (1990). An overview and synopsis of risk factors, assessment, and treatment of suicidal patients over the life cycle. In S.J. Blumenthal & D.J. Kupfer (Eds.), *Suicide over the life cycle: Risk factors, assessment, and treatment of suicidal patients* (pp. 685–733). Washington, DC: American Psychiatric Press.

Borson, S., Liptzin, B., Nininger, J., & Rabins, P. (1987). Psychiatry and the nursing home. *American Journal of Psychiatry, 144,* 1412–1418.

Brink, T.L. (1986). *Clinical gerontology: A guide to assessment and intervention.* New York: Haworth Press.

Brody, E.M. (1981). The formal support network: Congregate treatment settings for residents with senescent brain dysfunction. In N.E. Miller & G.D. Cohen (Eds.), *Clinical aspects of Alzheimer's disease and senile dementia* (pp. 301–330). Ann Arbor, MI: Books on Demand.

Brooks, J.A., & Mosher-Ashley, P.M. (1996, January). Resources for on-site mental health services: How private vendors are serving nursing homes in Massachusetts. *Nursing Homes, 45,* 26–28.

Burns, B., Wagner, H., Taube, J., Magaziner, J., Permutt, T., & Landerman, L.R. (1993). Mental health service use of the elderly in nursing homes. *American Journal of Public Health, 83,* 331–336.

Bush, C.T., Langford, M.W., Rosen, P., & Gott, W. (1990). Operation outreach: Intensive case management for severely psychiatrically disabled adults. *Hospital and Community Psychiatry, 41,* 647–649.

Busse, E.W. (1992). Quality of life: Affect and mood in late life. In M. Bergener, K. Hasegawa, S.I. Finkel, & T. Nishimura (Eds.), *Aging and mental disorders: International perspectives* (pp. 38–55). New York: Springer Publishing.

Casey, D.A., & Grant, R.W. (1993). Cognitive therapy with depressed elderly inpatients. In J.H. Wright, M.E. Thase, A.T. Beck, & J.W. Ludgate (Eds.), *Cognitive therapy with inpatients: Developing a cognitive milieu* (pp. 295–314). New York: Guilford Press.

Cohen, G.D. (1988). One psychiatrist's view. In L. Jarvik & C. Winograd (Eds.), *Treatment for the Alzheimer patient: The long haul* (pp. 96–104). New York: Springer Publishing.

Copeland, A.R. (1987). Suicide among the elderly: The Metro-Dade County experience 1981–83. *Medical Science Law, 27,* 32–36.

Curlik, S.M., Frazier, D., & Katz, I.R. (1991). Psychiatric aspects of long-term care. In J. Sadavoy, L.W. Lazarus, & L.F. Jarvik (Eds.), *Comprehensive review of geriatric psychiatry* (pp. 547–564). Washington, DC: American Psychiatric Press.

Eisdorfer, C., Cohen, D., & Preston, C. (1981). Behavioral and psychological therapies for the older patient with cognitive impairment. In N.E. Miller & G.D. Cohen (Eds.), *Clinical aspects of Alzheimer's disease and senile dementia* (pp. 209–226). New York: Raven Press.

Eisdorfer, C., Cohen, D., & Veith, R. (1980). *The psychopathology of aging.* Kalamazoo, MI: Upjohn Pharmaceuticals.

Ellis, M., & Donnelly, P. (1993). Defeat depression: Depression in dementia must be treated. *Geriatric Medicine, 2,* 50–59.

Feinson, M.C. (1987). Mental health and aging: Are there gender differences? *Gerontologist, 27,* 703–711.

Flowers, E.M., & Mosher-Ashley, P.M. (1996, March). *Caregiver attitudes toward counseling for persons with Alzheimer's disease.* Idea exchange presented at the American Society on Aging conference, Anaheim, CA.

Fogel, B.S., & Kroessler, D. (1987). Treating late life depression on a medical-psychiatric unit. *Hospital and Community Psychiatry, 38,* 829–831.

Foster, J.M., & Gallagher, D. (1986). An exploratory study comparing depressed and non-depressed elders' coping strategies. *Journal of Gerontology, 41,* 91–93.

Gallagher, D. (1981). Behavioral group therapy with elderly depressives: An experimental study. In D. Upper & S. Ross (Eds.), *Behavioral group therapy* (pp. 187–224). Champaign, IL: Research Press.

Gallagher, D. (1986). The Beck Depression Inventory and older adults: Review of its development and utility. *Clinical Gerontologist, 5,* 149–163.

Gallagher, D., Breckenridge, J.N., Thompson, L.W., Dessonville, C., & Amaral, P. (1982). Similarities and differences between normal grief and depression in the elderly. *Essence, 5,* 127–140.

Gatz, M., Popkins, S., Pino, C., & VandenBos, G. (1990). Psychiatric interventions. In J.E. Birren & K.W. Schaie (Eds.), *Handbook of the psychology of aging* (pp. 755–785). San Diego, CA: Academic Press.

George, L.K. (1991, November 4–6). *Social factors and depression in late life.* National Consensus Development Conference Diagnosis and Treatment of Depression in Late Life. National Institutes of Health, Bethesda, MD.

George, L.K., Blazer, D.G., Hughes, D.C., & Fowler, N. (1989). Social support and the outcome of major depression. *British Journal of Psychiatry, 154,* 478–485.

Goldberg, E.L., Van Natta, P., & Comstock, G.W. (1985). Depressive symptoms, social networks, and social support of elderly women. *American Journal of Epidemiology, 121,* 448–455.

Hagebak, J.E., & Hagebak, B.R. (1980). Serving the mental health needs of the elderly: The case for removing barriers and improving service integration. *Community Mental Health Journal, 16,* 263–275.

Hall, R.C.W., Gardner, E.R., Stickney, S.K., LeCann, A.F., & Popkin, M.K. (1980). Physical illness manifesting as psychiatric disease. II: Analysis of a state hospital inpatient population. *Archives of General Psychiatry, 37,* 989–995.

Hamilton, M. (1967). Development of a rating scale for primary depressive illness. *British Journal of Social and Clinical Psychology, 6,* 278–296.

Hastrup, J.L., Baker, J.G., Kraemer, D.L., & Bornstein, R.F. (1986). Crying and depression among older adults. *Gerontologist, 26,* 91–96.

Hinkle, J.S. (1990). An overview of dementia in older persons: Identification, diagnosis, assessment, and treatment. *Journal of Mental Health Counseling, 12,* 368–383.

Kaszniak, A.W., Sadeh, M., & Stern, L.Z. (1985). Differentiating depression from organic brain syndromes in older age. In G.M. Chaisson-Stewart (Ed.), *Depression in the elderly: An interdisciplinary approach* (pp. 161–192). New York: John Wiley & Sons.

Kinzie, J.D., Lewinsohn, P., Maricle, R., & Teri, L. (1986). The relationship of depression to medical illness in an older community population. *Comprehensive Psychiatry, 27,* 241–246.

Kivela, S.L. (1992). Psychological assessment and rating scales: Depression and other age-related affective disorders. In M. Bergener, K. Hasegawa, S.I. Finkel, & T. Nishimura (Eds.), *Aging and mental disorders: International perspectives* (pp. 102–123). New York: Springer Publishing.

Knight, B. (1985–1986). Therapists' attitudes as explanation of underservice of elderly in mental health: Testing an old hypothesis. *International Journal of Aging and Human Development, 22,* 261–269.

Knight, B. (1992). *Older adults in psychotherapy.* Beverly Hills, CA: Sage Publications.

Koenig, H.G., & Blazer, D.G. (1992). Mood disorders and suicide. In J.E. Birren, R.G. Sloane, & G.D. Cohen (Eds.), *Handbook of mental health and aging* (pp. 380–407). San Diego, CA: Academic Press.

Koenig, H.G., Meador, K.G., Cohen, H., & Blazer, D. (1988). Depression in elderly patients with medical illness. *Archives of Internal Medicine, 148,* 1929–1936.

Kozlak, J., & Thobaben, M. (1992). Treating the elderly mentally ill at home. *Perspectives in Psychiatric Care, 28*(2), 31–35.

Krause, N. (1986). Stress and sex differences in depressive symptoms among older adults. *Journal of Gerontology, 41,* 727–731.

Kurlowicz, L.H. (1993). Social factors and depression in late life. *Archives of Psychiatric Nursing, 7*(1), 30–36.

LaBarge, E., Rosenman, L., Leavitt, K., & Cristiani, T. (1988). Counseling clients with mild senile dementia of the Alzheimer's type: A pilot study. *Journal of Neurological Rehabilitation, 2,* 167–173.

Lasoski, M.C., & Thelen, M.H. (1987). Attitudes of older and middle-aged persons toward mental health intervention. *Gerontologist, 27,* 288–292.

Lewinsohn, P.M. (1974). A behavioral approach to depression. In R. Friedman & M. Katz (Eds.), *The psychology of depression: Contemporary theory and research* (pp. 157–185). New York: John Wiley & Sons.

Linn, M.W., Hunter, K.I., & Harris, R. (1980). Symptoms of depression and recent life events in the community elderly. *Journal of Clinical Psychology, 36,* 675–682.

Lowenthal, M.F. (1965). Antecedents of isolation and mental illness in old age. *Archives of General Psychiatry, 12,* 245–254.

Lundervold, D., Lewin, L.M., & Bourland, G. (1990). Older adults' acceptability of treatments for behavioral problems. *Clinical Gerontologist, 10,* 17–28.

Masand, P.S. (1995). Depression in long-term care facilities. *Geriatrics, 50,* S16–S23.

Mosher-Ashley, P.M. (1993). Referral patterns of elderly clients to a community mental health center. *Journal of Gerontological Social Work, 20,* 5–23.

Mosher-Ashley, P.M. (1994). Diagnoses assigned and issues brought up in therapy by older adults receiving outpatient treatment. *Clinical Gerontologist, 15,* 37–65.

Mosher-Ashley, P.M. (1995). Attendance patterns of elders who accepted counseling following referral to a mental health center. *Clinical Gerontologist, 16*(2), 3–19.

Mui, A.C. (1993). Self-reported depressive symptoms among black and hispanic frail elders: A sociocultural perspective. *Journal of Applied Gerontology, 12,* 170–187.

Myers, J.E., & Salmon, H.E. (1984). Counseling programs for older persons: Status, shortcomings, and potentialities. *Counseling Psychologist, 12,* 39–54.

Myers, J.K., Weisman, M.M., Tischler, G.L., Holzer, C.E., Leaf, P.J., Orvaschel, H., Anthony, J.C., Boyd, J.H., Burke, J.D., Kramer, M., & Stoltzman, R. (1984). Six-month prevalence of psychiatric disorders in three communities. *Archives of General Psychiatry, 41,* 959–967.

Newman, J.P. (1989). Aging and depression. *Psychology and Aging, 4,* 150–165.

O'Hara, M.W., Kohout, F.F., & Wallace, R.B. (1985). Depression among the rural elderly: A study of prevalence and correlates. *Journal of Nervous and Mental Disorders, 173,* 582–589.

Olin, J.T., Schneider, L.S., Eaton, E.M., Zemansky, M.F., & Pollock, V.E. (1992). The Geriatric Depression Scale and the Beck Depression Inventory as screening instruments in an older adult outpatient population. *Psychological Assessment, 4,* 190–192.

Omnibus Budget Reconciliation Act, 54 Fed. Reg. (1989), 42 C.F.R., Part 405.

Osgood, N.J., & Thielman, S. (1990). Geriatric suicidal behavior: Assessment and treatment. In S.J. Blumenthal & D.J. Kupfer (Eds.), *Suicide over the life cycle: Risk factors, assessment, and treatment of suicidal patients* (pp. 685–733). Washington, DC: American Psychiatric Press.

Parmelee, P.A., Katz, I.R., & Lawton, M.P. (1989). Depression among institutionalized aged: Assessment and prevalence estimation. *Journal of Gerontology, 44,* 22–29.

Phifer, J.F., & Murrell, S.A. (1986). Etiologic factors in the onset of depressive symptoms in older adults. *Journal of Abnormal Psychology, 95,* 282–291.

Quinlan, J., & Ohlund, G. (1995). Psychiatric home care. *Home Healthcare Nurse, 13*(4), 20–24.

Radloff, L.S. (1977). The CES-D scale: A self-report depression scale for research in the general population. *Applied Psychological Measurement, 1,* 385–401.

Regier, D.A., Myers, J.K., Kramer, M., Robins, L.N., Blazer, D.G., Hough, R.L., Eston, W.W., & Locke, B.Z. (1984). The NIMH epidemiologic catchment area program: Historical context, major objectives and study population characteristics. *Archives of General Psychiatry, 41,* 934–941.

Reynolds, C.F. (1995). Recognition and differentiation of elderly depression in the clinical setting. *Geriatrics, 50,* S6–S15.

Rovner, B.W. (1993). Depression and increased risk of mortality in the nursing home patient. *American Journal of Medicine, 94*(5A), 195–225.

Sakauye, K., & Camp, C. (1992). Introducing psychiatric care into nursing homes. *Gerontologist, 32,* 33–49.

Salzman, C. (1992). *Clinical geriatric psychopharmacology* (2nd ed.). Baltimore: Williams & Wilkins.

Sanders, C.A. (1989). *Grief: The mourning after.* New York: John Wiley & Sons.

Schultz, R., & Hanusa, B.H. (1978). Long-term effects of control and predictability enhancing interventions: Findings and ethical issues. *Journal of Personality and Social Psychology, 11,* 1194–1201.

Scogin, F., & McElreath, L. (1994). Efficacy of psychosocial treatments for geriatric depression: A quantitative review. *Journal of Consulting and Clinical Psychology, 62,* 69–74.

Smallegan, M. (1989). Level of depressive symptoms and life stresses for culturally diverse older adults. *Gerontologist, 29,* 45–50.

Smyer, M.A., Zarit, S.H., & Qualls, S.H. (1990). Psychological intervention with the aged individual. In J.E. Birren & K.W. Schaie (Eds.), *Handbook of the psychology of aging* (pp. 375–404). New York: Academic Press.

Solomon, K., & Szwabo, P. (1992). Psychotherapy for patients with dementia. In J. Morley, R. Coe, R. Strong, & G. Grossberg (Eds.), *Memory function and aging-related disorders* (pp. 295–319). New York: Springer Publishing.

Speer, D.D., Williams, J., West, H., & Dupree, L. (1991). Older adult users of outpatient mental health services. *Community Mental Health Journal, 27,* 69–76.

Spitzer, R.L., & Endicott, J. (1978). *Schedule for affective disorders and schizophrenia (SADS).* New York: New York State Psychiatric Institute, Biometrics Research Division.

Steiner, D., & Marcopulos, B. (1991). Depression in the elderly: Characteristics and clinical management. *Nursing Clinics of North America, 26,* 585–600.

Swan, J.H., Fox, P.J., & Estes, C.L. (1986). Community mental health services and the elderly: Retrenchment or expansion. *Community Mental Health Journal, 22,* 275–285.

Taft, L.B., Delaney, K., Semen, D., & Stansell, J. (1993). Dementia care: Creating a therapeutic milieu. *Journal of Gerontological Nursing, 19,* 30–39.

Teri, L. (1991). Assessment and treatment of depression. In P.A. Wisocki (Ed.), *Handbook of clinical behavior therapy with the elderly client* (pp. 225–243). New York: Plenum.

Teri, L., & Gallagher, D. (1991). Cognitive-behavioral interventions for treatment of depression in Alzheimer's patients. *Gerontologist, 31,* 413–416.

Teri, L., & Wagner, A. (1992). Alzheimer's disease and depression. *Journal of Consulting and Clinical Psychology, 60,* 379–391.

Thase, M.E., & Beck, A.T. (1993). Overview of cognitive therapy. In J.H. Wright, M.E. Thase, A.T. Beck, & J.W. Ludgate (Eds.), *Cognitive therapy with inpatients: Developing a cognitive milieu* (pp. 3–34). New York: Guilford Press.

Thompson, L.W., Gallagher, D., Nies, G., & Epstein, D. (1983). Evaluation of the effectiveness of professionals and non-professionals as instructors of coping with depression: Classes for elders. *Gerontologist, 23,* 390–396.

Thompson, L.W., Gong, V., Haskins, E., & Gallagher, D. (1987). Assessment of depression and dementia during the late years. In K.W. Schaie (Ed.), *Annual review of gerontology and geriatrics* (Vol. 7, pp. 295–324). New York: Springer Publishing.

Thompson, L.W., Wagner, B., Zeiss, A., & Gallagher, D. (1989). Cognitive/behavioral therapy with early stage Alzheimer's patients: An exploratory view of the utility of this approach. In Light, E. & Lebowitz, B.D. (Eds.), *Alzheimer's disease treatment and family stress: Directions for research* (pp. 383–397). Rockville, MD: National Institute of Mental Health.

Vaux, A. (1985). Variations in social support associated with gender, ethnicity, and age. *Journal of Social Issues, 41*, 89–110.

Waxman, H.M., Carner, E.A., & Klein, M. (1984). Underutilization of mental health professionals by community elderly. *Gerontologist, 24*, 23–30.

Waxman, H.M., McGreary, G., Weinrit, R.M., & Carner, E.A. (1985). A comparison of somatic complaints among depressed and non-depressed older persons. *Gerontologist, 25*, 501–507.

Webb, W.B. (1982). Sleep in older persons: Sleep structures of 50- to 60-year-old men and women. *Journal of Gerontology, 37*, 581–586.

Yale, R. (1995). *Developing support groups for individuals with early-stage Alzheimer's disease.* Baltimore: Health Professions Press.

Yesavage, J., Brink, T., Rose, T., Lum, O., Huang, O., Adey, V., & Leirer, V. (1983). Development and validation of a geriatric depression screening scale: A preliminary report. *Journal of Psychiatric Research, 17*, 215–228.

Yost, E.B., Beutler, L.E., Corbishley, M.A., & Allender, J.R. (1986). *Group cognitive therapy: A treatment approach for depressed older adults.* New York: Pergamon Press.

Zung, W.W.K. (1965). A self-rating depression scale. *Archives of General Psychiatry, 12*, 371–379.

Appendix
Assessment Scales for Use with Older Adults

Obtaining the Scales

Some of the assessment scales may be obtained by locating the original publication listed. This may be accomplished by contacting a local hospital library or university library that may own the journal in which the scale was initially published. Some libraries require that you come in and make a copy of a desired article; others will mail a copy for a transaction fee. If the journal is not available locally it may be obtained through the library's interlibrary loan system. One need only submit a formal request and a librarian will contact another library that owns the journal and have a copy of the article forwarded. Again, a transaction fee may be involved.

Self-Rating Scales for Depression

Geriatric Depression Scale (GDS)
A copy of this scale can be obtained free of charge from T.L. Brink, 1103 North Church Street, Redlands, California 92374.

Beck Depression Inventory
BDI-I—See Beck, Ward, Mendelson, Mock, & Erbaugh (1961) in chapter reference list.
BDI-II—Available for a cost (cost unavailable) from The Psychological Corporation, 555 Academic Court, San Antonio, Texas 78204-2498.

Center for Epidemiological Studies Depression Scale (CES-D)
See Radloff (1977) in chapter reference list.

Zung Self-Rating Depression Scale (ZSDS)
See Zung (1965) in chapter reference list.

Interviewer-Rater Scales for Depression

Hamilton Rating Scale for Depression-Revised (HRSD-R)
This scale is available for $70.00 from the Western Psychological Services, 12031 Wilshire Boulevard, Los Angeles, California 90025-1251.

Suicidal Ideation

Scale for Suicide Ideation
A copy of this scale (cost unavailable) is available from the Center for Cognitive Therapy, Room 602, 133 South 36th Street, Philadelphia, Pennsylvania 19104.

An aged man is but a paltry thing,
A tattered coat upon a stick, unless
Soul clap its hands and sing, and louder sing
For every tatter in its mortal dress . . .

William Butler Yeats, "Sailing to Byzantium"

2

Turning the Tide

Achieving Life Satisfaction

The achievement of life satisfaction in older adults has been of great interest to social scientists since the 1960s (Larson, 1978; Willits & Crider, 1988). *Life satisfaction* is defined as an outcome of an evaluative process that involves a comparison between current circumstances in one's life and personal standards or ideals (Rapkin & Fischer, 1992a). Different individuals can use considerably different frames of reference to evaluate their lives. Rapkin and Fischer (1992b) found that older adults vary substantially in what they want out of life, with some rejecting or ignoring what others find essential. Although different people want different things out of life, research has indicated that perceived health is consistently related to life satisfaction. A variety of additional factors has been found to play a role, but their association with overall life satisfaction has been somewhat weaker. This weaker association probably reflects the types of goals different individuals set for themselves (Rapkin & Fischer, 1992a, b).

Inherent in the concept of life satisfaction is the assumption that a state of well-being reflects an effective adaptation to the stresses and losses experienced, particularly as people age. Rapkin and Fischer (1992a) propose that when older adults experience a change in their functional capacities, they must realign their goals to maximize satisfaction. In some cases the goals are modified to accommodate the losses and obstacles; for example, someone who has traditionally served the food at large church suppers can instead contact volunteers by phone to ask what they can make for the meal. In other situations the environment is modified so that a desired goal is more easily attained; for example, independent living in an elder housing complex can be an acceptable substitute for remaining in a large family home.

PREDICTORS OF LIFE SATISFACTION

Numerous factors have been cited by older adults as critical to achieving life satisfaction; the ones cited most often are included here.

Physical Health

The most salient predictor of life satisfaction in older adults is health. The association between health and subjective well-being has been recognized for some time (Larson, 1978) and has been reliably replicated by numerous researchers, even when other, confounded variables were controlled (George & Landerman, 1984; Okun, Stock, Haring, & Witter, 1984; Willits & Crider, 1988; Zautra & Hempel, 1984). The association between health and life satisfaction appears to apply to adults of all ages (Herzog, Rodgers, & Woodworth, 1982) but increases in strength as people age (George, Okun, & Landerman, 1985; Willits & Crider, 1988). Health has been found to be equally important to the well-being of men and women (Willits & Crider, 1988).

Older adults who are sick or physically disabled are less likely to report being content with their lives (Larson, 1978). However, the subjective assessment of health is more critical than the actual extent of the physical condition. For example, studies that relied on physician or nurse ratings of health have not shown the same strong relationship between health and life satisfaction as have self-ratings (Okun et al., 1984). Expectations and desires can mediate how people view their objective physical status (Willits & Crider, 1988). Older adults who are over age 80 may assume that discomfort from chronic conditions such as arthritis is to be expected, and they may be less affected by their physical condition. Although the type of medical condition does not appear to be a factor, increases in functional disability have been associated with lower levels of life satisfaction. Visual impairments appear to be a particularly influential disability. Self-reported vision loss was found by Garfein and Herzog (1995) to be one of the few variables that distinguished people who age successfully from their less-well-functioning counterparts. They also found that visual impairments can limit independent functioning. Older adults who are blind or have poor eyesight are at great risk of losing the ability to dress, use transportation, shop, and carry out other activities of daily living.

Physicians tend to underestimate the quality of life of people who are chronically ill (Pearlman & Uhlmann, 1988). It is likely that others in the medical field and those in the social services field also perceive older adults who are ill or disabled to have lower levels of life satisfaction. Along with the assumption that individuals who have poor health must have a lower quality of life goes the underlying belief that poor health is a good reason for being unhappy and that little can be done about the situation.

Pearlman and Uhlmann (1988) note that quality of life is a complex, multidimensional construct that extends beyond the simple associations with health and functional disability. Even when perceived health is poor, there are factors that can buffer or reduce the detrimental effects. Krause (1990) found that older adults who received assistance with personal care and help with household chores and meal preparation from formal sources such as community agencies reported higher levels of well-being than did older adults who received assistance from informal sources such as friends and family. This difference was attributed to the strong feeling of older adults that they do not want assistance unless they can reciprocate or recompense it in some way. Failure to reciprocate may lead to diminished feelings of well-being. Consequently, helping older adults to locate affordable assistance from community agencies and local tradespeople may help increase psychological well-being. Regrettably, most older adults who encounter health problems usually turn to informal sources of assistance that, over time, can lead to lower levels of life satisfaction (Krause, 1990).

Social support for individuals who are experiencing physical problems may also mediate psychological well-being. Self-help groups for people who share common medical problems (e.g., coronary heart disease) have been found to have positive consequences for well-being (Hildingh, Segesten, Bengtsson, & Fridlund, 1994). Support groups conducted by therapists and other professionals can help individuals with serious medical problems, such as dementing illnesses (Yale, 1995), strokes (Puppolo, 1980), and visual impairments (Evans & Jaureguy, 1981), to come to terms with their conditions and to develop coping skills.

Although perceived health plays an important role in the psychological well-being of older adults, individuals who are content with their lives and situation may also rate their health more positively (Willits & Crider, 1988). Strengthening aspects that contribute to psychological well-being may result in a more positive outlook on life even in older adults with poor health. One approach that has been particularly effective in helping older adults is described by Rybarczyk et al. (1992), who used cognitive-behavioral therapy to reduce depression and anxiety in chronically ill older adults (see Chapter 3).

Several additional factors have been associated with overall life satisfaction, although they tend to be secondary to perceived health. These factors include relationships with family and friends, adequate income level, perceived control over one's life, personality traits, pursuit of leisure activities, and meaning in life.

INTERPERSONAL RELATIONSHIPS

Interpersonal relationships are found consistently to be associated with psychological well-being. Even older adults in poor health report that interpersonal relationships are a factor in their psychological well-being (Pearlman & Uhlmann, 1988). Social contacts and supports help people cope effectively with stress (House, Landis, & Umberson, 1988).

Family

Older adults residing with a spouse report fewer psychological problems and higher morale than do those who reside alone (Mindel & Wright, 1982, 1985). Having a spouse can serve two major purposes in the emotional well-being of the partner (Dykstra, 1995). The first purpose served involves increased opportunity for social interaction. Many activities are oriented to couples, making it easier for a couple to be involved than it is for a single person. The second purpose served is that the spouse frequently provides protection. "Protection" consists of positive exchanges in responding to adverse events and in preventing some of them from occurring. For example, discussions in which a spouse's role in a conflict is minimized can relieve the person of guilt. In addition, a discussion in which the perspective of the other person involved in the conflict is reframed in a more positive light could reduce the potential of an even greater breech in the relationship. Living with a spouse is also related to greater independent functioning (Roos & Havens, 1991). As noted in Chapter 1, although individuals who are involved in a partner relationship generally have access to support, not all relationships are supportive.

When a relationship with a spouse ends in later life, usually because of death, frequently, the surviving partner experiences loneliness and declines in psychological well-being. For some older adults, the loneliness can be diminished through reliance on a network of friends (Dykstra, 1995). This pattern is common among women. Men tend to rely less on friendships and tend to maintain a focus on an exclusive relationship with a partner. Men also have a greater tendency toward remarriage. In general, a relationship with a partner appears to be of greater importance to the well-being of men than of women (Dykstra, 1995). However, for both men and women, if being with a partner is more desirable but is perceived to be unattainable, the individuals are likely to feel lonely. Also, if these individuals lack a strong network of friends, they are likely to feel even more alienated and lonely. Low self-esteem has been associated with a perception that obtaining a partner or friends is not feasible. People with low self-esteem tend to feel unattractive to others and have little faith in their ability to improve their relationships.

Some people who do not have a life partner do not feel a need for one. This is particularly true of people who have never married or who have become accustomed to being on their own, such as individuals long widowed or divorced (Dykstra, 1995). Alternatively, many older adults who have lost a spouse and who do not have supportive friends may be in need of intervention. One approach is to work on increasing the individual's support network. Involvement in group activities, particularly support groups, can be helpful.

Reminiscence as an activity or therapeutic modality also has shown some promise. Engaging in reminiscence appears to be related to life satisfaction for older adults who live alone but not for older adults who reside with a spouse (DeGenova, 1993). This finding was attributed to the ability to sort through memories and to learn to understand and find meaning in the past. It is also possible following the death of a spouse—the most common reason for living alone in the study conducted by DeGenova—that the surviving spouse will come to rely on reminiscing as a pleasurable activity and mediator of stress, whereas conversations with the spouse may have fulfilled this role previously. The finding that reminiscence is associated with life satisfaction in older adults residing alone means that it has potential as an intervention. The relationship between reminiscence and well-being has been reported by other investigators. Fallot (1979) and Atkins (1980) observed that engaging in reminiscence-type activities was associated with lower levels of depression. The therapeutic uses of reminiscence on psychological well-being have also been recognized since the 1970s (see Chapter 4).

Research on relationships with children as a source of well-being for older adults is inconclusive. Long, Anderson, and Williams (1990) found the rearing of children to be the most frequently reported accomplishment and related this finding to personal well-being. However, Kehn (1995) did not find the number of children and grandchildren to be good predictors of happiness. Hess and Soldo (1985) propose that parent–child relationships are weakly correlated with happiness because these relationships are not based on choice. A more critical feature in the prediction of well-being may be the nature of the relationship rather than the presence of children. Support for this position can be found in the study by O'Connor (1995), who found that the quality of the relationship was more closely related to life satisfaction than was the frequency of contact. Stevens (1992) found reciprocity (i.e., specifically the giving of instrumental support on the part of older adults, in the form of assistance with household tasks, baby-sitting, transportation, or money) to be related to life satisfaction. Giving instrumental support was more important than giving social support in the form of affection.

The research findings have important implications. The children of older adults need to be aware of the need their parents have to provide them with assistance. It is common for middle-age adults to become concerned about the welfare of their parents, resulting in a tendency to make decisions for their parents and dictate what needs to be done. In addition, younger adults frequently have a desire to do something for their parents without expecting anything in return. Older adults who feel worthless may need to explore how they can help family members. Assistance can come in many forms and should reflect practical approaches in which the older adults are willing to engage. However, Stevens (1992) notes that older adults should not take or be taken advantage of. Older adults who are doing most of the giving should be encouraged to explore what types of assistance they would like to receive in return.

Friends

The number of friends a person has was found by Willits and Crider (1988) to be the second most important factor, after health, related to achieving life satisfaction. Dykstra (1995) proposes that the quality of the personal relationships is the critical factor. High-quality relationships with friends have a greater impact on psychological well-being than do positive relationships with one's children (O'Connor, 1995). Several reasons have been proposed for this unusual finding. It is possible that older adults who have positive relationships with friends are simply better-adjusted people. Another possibility is that older adults may report that their relationships with children are more favorable than they are. O'Connor (1995) proposes that older adults may perceive the quality of family relationships from a "wanting-to-feel-close" perspective. Also, relationships with children tend to be emotionally charged. O'Connor found criticism and intrusion from family members to be negatively associated with the motivation to interact with the family member, the mood of the interaction, and the quality of the relationship. Criticism is often perceived as indicative of incompetence, and intrusion can threaten self-determination, both of which are detrimental to psychological well-being. Older adults may be sensitive to criticism and to their lives being intruded on because the aging process tends to reduce competence and increase dependence on others. It is interesting to note that in O'Connor's study older adults reported receiving more criticism and perceiving acts of intrusion from their friends than from their children, yet they continued to perceive their relationships with friends as positive. The older adults were more likely to report that the quality of their relationships was less positive when they received criticism and acts of intrusion from their children. Family relationships may be based on feelings of obligation, a factor that is believed to reduce warmth and closeness (Ishii-Kuntz, 1990).

Friends can fulfill a wide range of needs (Dykstra, 1995). These needs include love, understanding, respect, positive regard, and trust. Friends also validate a person's beliefs, judgments, and behaviors. In addition, they can be a source of information, advice, and aid in times of difficulty, satisfying social and material needs. As mentioned previously, they can help to compensate for the loss of a partner. Friendships are understood to have ups and downs, but on average they are perceived to be voluntary and positive (O'Connor, 1995).

Ill health can place stress on friendships. It can limit opportunities to engage in social activities. In addition, it can lead to expectations or provisions of care that are uncomfortable. The discomfort usually results from an imbalance of exchanges, which is common in caregiving relationships (Allan, 1986). The imbalance can lead to uncomfortable feelings of obligation on the part of the receiver or resentment on the part of the caregiver and can disrupt the friendship. This scenario may be one of the reasons that older adults in poor health prefer to receive assistance from formal sources. An exception to the pattern can be seen in Jerrome's work (1990), which revealed that long-term friends will provide people who are terminally ill with the type of care usually provided by family members. To reject the assistance would imply a rejection of the friendship.

It is important to remember that there are people who do not have supportive relationships and do not feel their absence. These people tend to cherish their privacy or prefer solitude and need few friends. However, older adults who do have strong relational needs can be assisted in meeting these needs.

Adequate Income Level

Adequate income level was found by Willits and Crider (1988) to be the third most important factor, after health and friends, related to achieving life satisfaction. Numerous researchers also have noted the consistent finding that adequate income level is associated with life satisfaction (George, 1981; Rapkin & Fisher, 1992a). Pearlman and Uhlmann (1988) even found finances to be a factor in the well-being of older adults with chronic illness. Although having sufficient financial resources to live comfortably certainly adds to life satisfaction, income level can also have an impact on other factors that have been associated with psychological well-being. High socioeconomic status can ensure better medical care and prevention of some chronic conditions, thereby influencing health status. Older adults who are comfortable financially are also better able to provide instrumental support to their children than are older adults who are not financially secure, a source of psychological well-being (Stevens, 1992).

On average, older adults tend to be satisfied with their financial status as long as they feel they can manage basic necessities and are able to live comfortably (Gray, Ventis, & Hayslip, 1992). The level of satisfaction appears to be influenced by a comparison of one's economic situation with that of others. When older adults perceive themselves as comparable to or better off than others, life satisfaction is high (Usui, Keil, & Durig, 1985). If they perceive themselves as having less than others, their level of life satisfaction may be viewed as lower.

Stressful Events

Empirical evidence indicates that older adults assess feelings of satisfaction within specific areas of life and then synthesize these domain-specific views into an overall sense of satisfaction with life as a whole (Krause, 1991). These areas of life are affected strongly by stressors such as illness, disability, or financial losses or limitations. Experiencing fewer significant life events in the few years before the assessment has been found to contribute to successful aging (Garfein & Herzog, 1995).

Traditionally, retirement has been viewed as being a stressful transition in the lives of older adults (Martin Matthews & Brown, 1987). The loss of the work-role and subsequent feelings of rootlessness can cause discontent, anxiety, or depression (Richardson & Kilty, 1991). However, evidence indicates that most people do not experience negative effects such as loneliness or lowered self-worth following retirement and that retirement may not be as stressful as believed previously (Kasl, 1992). Research concerning the effect of retirement on life satisfaction indicates that several factors are involved. People who wish to retire tend to have less difficulty adjusting to the change (Martin Matthews & Brown, 1987). Many older adults fill the time work once occupied with new activities and interests (Pearlin & Mullan, 1992). (Although if the new activities are un-rewarding, a sense of loss can be experienced.) Also, forced retirement due to poor health or job loss can lead to a decline in psychological well-being (Atchley, 1982; Beck, 1982; Cavanaugh, 1997). However, planned retirement with suffi-cient financial resources and fulfilling activities can lead to increases in life satis-faction (Atchley, 1989; Cavanaugh, 1997; Walker, Kimmell, & Price, 1980–1981). Several studies indicate that as a group, retired adults report lower levels of stress than do adults who are still employed (Bosse, Aldwin, Levenson, & Workman-Daniels, 1991; Midanik, Soghikian, Ransom, & Tekawa, 1995). Re-tirement is perceived as lacking in stress and does not lead to declines in well-being in those who are able to continue the patterns in status, income, health, and social relations that they had formed prior to retirement (Richardson & Kilty, 1991).

Few differences have been observed between men and women in postre-tirement satisfaction (Richardson & Kilty, 1991). However, women who were retired from low-status jobs experienced greater declines in well-being than did women who were formerly employed in professional positions. This finding was attributed to the greater accessibility of professional women in retaining profes-sional contacts, involvement in professional groups, and part-time professional employment. Women of low occupational status also reported the greatest dis-satisfaction with social contacts following retirement. As Richardson and Kilty (1991) point out, it is possible that these women were affected more by the loss of contact with co-workers.

Martin Matthews and Brown (1987) suggest that some older adults who experience critical life events, including retirement, that result in considerable stress have not developed adequate coping mechanisms to manage their stress. In a longitudinal study involving groups of four different generations, Fiske (1980) found a sizable number of individuals whose lives were filled with stress but who appeared to be challenged by it. These individuals seemed to be unaffected by the stress and paid little attention to it. They were able to maintain close interpersonal relationships and were open to new experiences. Alternatively, many individuals in all age groups were found to be overwhelmed by the stress in their lives. These individuals dwelled at great length on the stressors they experienced and were preoccupied with stressful events that occurred in the past and those that might occur. Few of these individuals had close interpersonal relationships. Fiske posits that experience in coping with stress early in life helps older adults cope with the stresses and losses in later life. Without early exposure to stress, many older adults do not gain the experience needed to ward off thoughts and beliefs that stress cannot be handled.

Perceived Control

The continued opportunity to make choices, exercise responsibility, and nurture others is believed to contribute to well-being (Reker, Peacock, & Wong, 1987). A sense of control has been linked to hardiness, a disposition that refers to the ability to remain healthy under high stress (Kobasa, 1979). Control as a factor tends to emerge when the individual feels threatened by its potential loss or when control over one's life has been assumed by some external force. For older adults "threats of potential loss" may be seen in the concerns older adults have about their middle-age children's intrusions on their lives. "Assumption of control" may be seen in older adults who are required to reside in long-term care facilities because of physical disability. Rapkin and Fischer's (1992a) point about differential goals in older adults must be kept in mind: Not all older adults will want considerable control over their situation. Bowsher and Gerlach (1990) report that the level of control some people want changes with their perception of their ability. Older adults who express or demonstrate a high expectation of control should be helped to maintain as much as is realistic.

Locus of control, which is more of a personality trait or coping style, also has been found to be associated with life satisfaction. Having an internal locus of control, believing that one is ultimately in charge of oneself and one's situation, has been associated with a higher level of life satisfaction. Having an external locus of control, the sense that other people have ultimate control over one's life, is associated with lower levels of well-being (Hickson, Housley, & Boyle, 1988).

Personality Traits

Personality traits have been found to affect life satisfaction in later life. Mussen, Honzik, and Eichorn (1982) found that certain traits observed at age 30 correlated with life satisfaction at age 70. Women who at 30 were mentally alert, cheerful, satisfied with their current situation, self-assured, and not worried or fatigued were likely to display high levels of satisfaction in later life. Men who at 30 were relaxed, emotionally stable, and in good physical condition had high levels of life satisfaction at age 70.

Research conducted by Costa and McCrae (Costa & McCrae, 1980; McCrae & Costa, 1983) indicates that certain personality traits are associated with life satisfaction. Of the five dimensions of personality they have proposed, four (extroversion, openness, agreeableness, and conscientiousness) are believed to enhance life satisfaction and one (neuroticism) diminishes it. If individuals score highly in neuroticism, which is characterized by anxiety, hostility, depression, vulnerability, impulsiveness, and self-consciousness, they will tend to view the problems encountered in later life as crises and will be at risk for negative emotions and maladaptive behavior that can carry over into many situations (Costa & Mc-Crae, 1980). If individuals score highly in extroversion, which is characterized by the subtraits of warmth, gregariousness, excitement-seeking, and assertiveness, they tend to have an increased ability to make friends, resulting in reports of greater happiness. In addition, extroverted individuals have reported greater satisfaction with postretirement life. Individuals who score highly in openness are intellectually curious, have an awareness of inner feelings, and have a need for variety in activity. Costa and McCrae propose that one's desire to explore new ideas and find new sources for enjoyment other than work would be more satisfied. Those who score highly in conscientiousness and agreeableness are also believed to enjoy enhanced life satisfaction.

Sociocognitive skills (the ability to think about the self, other people, and social relationships) also have been related to achieving life satisfaction (Gray, Ventis, & Hayslip, 1992). Understanding others (i.e., the ability to recognize certain characteristics about others such as their interests and beliefs) and the ability to seek out support when needed are believed to be helpful in facilitating a successful adjustment to critical life events. Other aspects of sociocognitive functioning related to life satisfaction include assertiveness, independence, and decisiveness.

Pursuit of Leisure Activities

Researchers have found an association between leisure activity and life satisfaction (DeGenova, 1993; Ekerdt, Bosse, & Levkoff, 1985; Kelly & Ross, 1989; Lomranz, Bergman, Eyal, & Shmotkin, 1988). Involvement in leisure activity has been linked to better health (Lawton, Moss, & Fulcomer, 1982; McAvoy, 1979) and the absence of depression (Lomranz et al., 1988). Leisure activities are believed to be even more important in later life (Hersch, 1990). Younger adults resolve many of their intellectual and social needs through work. For older adults, these needs are met through their leisure activities. Leisure activities also provide older adults with a source of identity following retirement (Atchley, 1976) and help them find meaning in their lives (Neulinger & Breit, 1971). Leisure can encompass a variety of activities, including study and contemplation; play or recreation; and volunteer, nonpaid service (Havighurst, 1969). Bevil, O'Connor, and Mattoon (1993) found that people who were satisfied with their lives reported engaging in the greatest number of activities per week and gave numerous reasons for participating in the activities. Engaging in activities had an impact on several areas of life (i.e., Krause's concept of domain-specific areas of functioning) that are important in providing older adults with psychological well-being.

Leisure activities tend to be regarded by most people as recreational and nonproductive. Traditionally, services that do not generate income have tended to be devalued and not be recognized (Glass, Seeman, Herzog, Kahn, & Berkman,

1995). In reality, many older adults, even old-old people, continue to engage in nonpaid productive leisure activities, such as volunteer work and the provision of help to friends, family, and neighbors (Herzog, Kahn, Morgan, Jackson, & Antonucci, 1989). Kahn (1986) found that 90% of older adults do some productive activity, and this productive activity has been linked to life satisfaction (Stevens, 1993). Most of the decline in productive activities takes place because of physical disability and impairments. People who remain active tend not to diminish the intensity with which they pursue productive activities. Productive activity in old age has an impact on many aspects of life. Older people who are active and engaged in some meaningful, productive activity tend not to be perceived as "old" either by themselves or by their families (Kaufman, 1986; Stevens, 1993). Moreover, activity, whether it is productive or not, has been shown to delay the onset of chronic disability and death (Mor et al., 1989).

According to Hersch (1990), numerous aspects of leisure have been found to be linked to satisfaction with life. The most notable of these aspects are challenge seeking, concern with recognition and reward, family focus, social competence, and amount of volition and interest. Presumably, people who are not depressed will engage in a particular activity in order to enjoy one or more particular aspects of the leisure activity they seek. For example, an older person may volunteer in a political campaign in order to receive some sort of recognition in the community and to increase his or her level of social competence.

Rapkin and Fischer (1992b) found that depressed older adults and those with lower levels of life satisfaction most frequently reported the goals of reducing activities and stabilizing life circumstances. Although initially, loved ones may endeavor to support older adults' wishes to simplify their lives, it is important to remember that one of the major symptoms of depression is apathy. As these older adults sink further into depression, they increasingly constrict their social world and decrease their involvement in activities. In doing so, they cut themselves off from social support and the activities that give their lives structure and meaning. In time the lack of support and activities fuels the depression. Intervention will necessitate some increase in activities. (Before undertaking such a step, the reader is advised to consult Chapter 3.)

Meaning in Life

Having meaning in one's life is a strong and consistent predictor of psychological well-being (Zika & Chamberlain, 1987). It is also related to positive mental health. When a person's search for meaning is blocked or lost, it causes frustration. Finding positive meaning in life has been related to strong religious beliefs, self-transcendent values, membership in groups, dedication to a cause, purposeful activity, and clear life goals (Zika & Chamberlain, 1992). These sources of meaning tend to change over a person's life (Yalom, 1980), although the strength of the relationship between what provides meaning and psychological well-being remains consistent (Zika & Chamberlain, 1992). The importance of purpose in life also has been found to increase as people age (Reker, Peacock, & Wong, 1987).

Often, personal meaning is accompanied by feelings of satisfaction and fulfillment (Zika & Chamberlain, 1992). These feelings are linked to belief systems and serve to motivate the individual. It is unclear whether the effect of personal meaning on positive well-being is direct or whether personal meaning functions as a moderator of stress. For example, people who are chronically ill undergo role losses as they become disabled and often adopt a mantle of sickness, which robs them of a sense of meaning in life (Rybarczyk et al., 1992). Their belief that they can no longer be productive causes them to question their worth, contributing to a descent into depression. The loss of role also reduces opportunities for these individuals to engage in pleasant activities and to receive the respect and periodic appreciation usually accorded to people who are involved in helping others and doing for themselves.

Loss of meaning in life can be precipitated in part by an aspect of Western culture, which does not adequately prepare adults for personally meaningful lives in retirement (Maultsby, 1991). Also, issues regarding the productivity, purposefulness, and meaningfulness of older persons residing in long-term care facilities have rarely been discussed (Saul, 1993).

When meaningful activity is incorporated into therapeutic interventions, it can augment personal effectiveness. Yost, Beutler, Corbishley, and Allender (1986) note that in group therapy, older adults gain as much from helping others as they do from the opportunity to socialize.

LIFE SATISFACTION IN OLDER ADULTS LIVING INDEPENDENTLY

Art, age 67, lives with his wife, Carol, in a former henequen hacienda in a rural part of Mexico's Yucatan Peninsula. In his mid-50s he found himself caught in the transition from large, mainframe computers to small, primarily single-user machines. His skills in setting up systems and programming were not easily transferred to the new personal computer business, which relied heavily on marketing skills. After a few years of contract work in computers and part-time teaching, Art opted for early retirement. By this time, he was in a depressed state and questioned his abilities and sense of worth. Carol, a resourceful, action-oriented person, encouraged Art to act on a dream they shared to leave the United States and start a new life in Mexico. Art and Carol sold the family home in Florida, packed a car with some basic necessities, and drove to the Yucatan.

Although they had vacationed there several times, they had no firm plans for where they would live or how they would spend their time. In the process of looking for a home they found a century-old hacienda in great disrepair. Art was captivated by the challenge of restoring it. Carol groaned, but agreed to the purchase. Living conditions were primitive. For example, the bathroom consisted of a metal sheet suspended between two trees and a bucket in the field behind the main house. Art and Carol spent the first year repairing roofs and walls where trees had established extensive root systems. After 6 years of intense work, the restoration of the main house with its 5000 square feet of living space was completed. The 13 acres of grounds were immaculately groomed and royal palms lined the long driveway into the complex of eight buildings, a chapel, and a combination pool/irrigation holding tank. The dramatic transformation of the hacienda was a frequent source of praise for the couple, who had undertaken the task out of enjoyment and not for altruistic purposes. The positive feedback they received encouraged them in their efforts until it was no longer feasible financially to keep making changes.

Art's son told him about the neem tree (*Azadirachta indica*), which is indigenous to India but has been successfully planted in South America and some parts of Mexico.

The tree provides good lumber and is a source of firewood. Twigs can be used as a natural toothbrush, and the seeds form a natural insecticide when ground in oil. Art began to propagate seeds and grow these trees. His goal is to try to encourage the neem tree as an alternative crop to be produced in the Yucatan. Cultivating it would require little capital investment and would fit in well with the agricultural skills of the Yucatecos. Art dreams of establishing a processing plant in the back acreage of the hacienda and forming a nonprofit cooperative with local Mexicans. He is realistic and does not know if his efforts will succeed, but the venture itself brings him much satisfaction. Art is growing 100 trees and hopes to germinate several hundred seeds in 1997. His short-term goal is to develop a "road show" to take to surrounding villages, where he will hand out free seedlings.

Many retired older adults have combined leisure activity or hobbies with productive goals, such as Art's goal. These goals and activities provide a sense of integrity at a time when people tend to perceive older adults as unproductive and a drain on the Social Security system. These activities also contribute to overall life satisfaction.

Most of the research on life satisfaction has been carried out with older adults who reside in the community; most adults lived alone or with a spouse. (The findings were summarized in previous sections.) One area that has not been addressed fully is the impact of living arrangements on older people. Older adults prefer to live independently and only resort to living with others, most often their children, when health declines to the point that living alone is no longer feasible (Magaziner, Cadigan, Hebel, & Parry, 1988). Older adults living alone report fewer mental health problems and higher morale than do older adults who reside with others. Older adults who reside with their adult children tend to report the lowest levels of happiness (Kehn, 1995). Issues of reciprocity and feelings of being a burden may play a role in these findings. In addition, difficulties over territoriality, privacy, and differences in theories of child rearing can lead to feelings of discomfort. Living with a spouse has been found consistently to be associated with higher morale and life satisfaction among older adults in the United States as well as older adults living in other countries (e.g., Israel; Shmotkin, 1991).

LIFE SATISFACTION IN OLDER ADULTS LIVING IN LONG-TERM CARE FACILITIES

Agnes is a 69-year-old woman who had to enter a nursing facility because of a massive cerebrovascular accident (stroke). She and her husband, who had passed away 3 years earlier, had run a small farm where they grew organic vegetables for the city markets. They had no children, but a succession of nieces and nephews lived with them during school vacations. Following her husband's death, Agnes sold the farm and moved to a cottage nearby, where she was able to work a small vegetable and flower garden. She sold vegetables and plants by the side of the road and talked with those who stopped by.

The stroke took place during the night. Agnes was not discovered until noon the following day. Despite 6 months of physical therapy, the damage to the brain left her paralyzed on the left side and in a wheelchair, and she required much assistance in carrying out basic self-care tasks. Agnes was left-handed, and the loss of the use of that hand particularly impeded her functioning. She spent much of her time in the nursing facility sitting by a window and looking out. She showed little interest in the recreational activities offered. Agnes's social worker explored various options, all to no avail.

An administrator from a local school approached the social worker about establishing a pen pal program between students in a fourth-grade class and some of the residents of the nursing facility. The goal was to expand the writing skills of the students through some purposeful activity. When Agnes was approached about the project, she was not particularly enthused, but she agreed to participate. In pairing the residents with an appropriate student, the social worker recommended that a child with an interest in plants or gardening be assigned to Agnes. Using an old typewriter and laboriously picking out the keys with her right hand, Agnes was able to write a suitable letter. After five letters, a meeting took place between the pen pals. Agnes met her pen pal, Robby, and spent a lively half hour discussing organic gardening with him. The two continued to correspond until the end of the school year. The following year, Robby was involved in a gardening club at his school, and Agnes became a "consultant" to the club, providing assistance in dealing with common problems such as finding nonchemical pesticides. The emerging concern over environmental issues made Agnes a valuable resource to the club. She communicated with the club primarily through Robby, who would write letters describing the club's activities and forward questions presented by members. On occasion, he would telephone her. Agnes's involvement with the club led to the preparation of a lengthy list of the most effective gardening techniques that she and her husband had used over the years. She was assured that this information would be added to the club's collection of materials.

Old-old adults (age 80 and over) who reside in nursing facilities tend not to report a favorable view of later life (Becker, Blumenfield, & Gordon, 1984). It has been assumed that older adults prefer to live independently and, when ill with a chronic disorder, wish to receive health care in their own home (DeCrosta, 1984). Several studies have questioned whether life satisfaction is indeed higher in older adults living on their own as compared with those of similar physical condition residing in long-term care facilities. Salamon (1987) found that residents of nursing facilities have higher life satisfaction ratings than those receiving home health care. He attributed his finding to the limitations imposed by the environment on older adults with physical disabilities living independently. Salamon proposed that these older adults were not as able to socialize or engage in a variety of activities and that they may not have received the full amount of medical care needed at home. He also pointed out that older adults living independently are more likely to experience low self-esteem as a result of their poor health. Older adults residing in long-term care facilities have greater opportunities to be exposed to others with similar or worse health problems, making them feel less unusual. These older adults can spend their time socializing with family members rather than engaging in physical care.

Perceived Control in Residential Settings

It is likely that long-term care settings differ in the types of environment provided to residents and that these differences can have an impact on life satisfaction. An example of this impact can be seen in the findings of Vallerand, O'Connor, & Blais (1989). These authors found that residents who lived in nursing facilities

that provided them with more control or self-determination had greater life satisfaction than did residents who lived in more restrictive settings. Similar findings
were obtained by Shary and Iso-Ahola (1989), who reported that confidence and
self-esteem increased in residents of nursing facilities when they were provided
with staff communications worded in a manner that promoted self-determination.
These studies support earlier studies that found a positive interaction between
perceived control and well-being (Langer & Rodin, 1976; Rodin & Langer, 1977,
1980).

Bocksnick and Hall (1994) propose that the manner in which activities are
conducted in long-term care facilities and presented to residents can influence
perceived control strongly. In an investigative study they found that little or no
communication existed between therapists and residents as to the objectives of
recreational activities. Also, although both administrative personnel and therapists
strongly believed that older adult residents should have control over how they
decide to spend their time, both condoned and legitimized persuasive techniques
such as coaxing and physical guidance, in which the therapist or staff member
took the resident's hand and directed him or her to the activity. Bocksnick and
Hall uncovered several factors that they believe maintained this pattern of interaction. Administrators based their perception of program effectiveness on the
number of participating residents, putting increased pressure on recreational therapists to plan large group activities and encourage as many residents as they could
to attend. Administrators condoned assertive behavior on the part of therapists in
recruiting participants. Frequently, therapists had to assume tasks that were not
directly related to their jobs, such as fund-raising campaigns to purchase needed
supplies. Although this activity may be justified in that it will benefit the residents,
the amount of time and energy expended takes away from other initiatives to be
pursued.

Another factor that promoted the negative interaction pattern involved program design: Residents were given little opportunity to provide input. Residents
who wished to provide input were expected to do so by individually approaching
the therapist or addressing their wishes through bureaucratic channels, such as the
residents' council. In both situations the initiative for providing input rested with
the resident. In fact, most of the control residents had over recreational activities
was limited to the decision to participate or not, and even then they could be
coaxed or guided to the activity by staff members. Some residents reported feeling
guilty if they did not participate because the therapist had invested so much time
in planning the activity. Despite these findings, the administrators and recreational
therapists believed sincerely that their residents had free choice.

Interventions that foster control, along with changes in administrative policies and the manner in which activities are planned and carried out, can help to
encourage self-determination. An excellent example of such an intervention was
developed by Christenson (1985). In a group format participants learned to set
short-term goals and work toward achieving them. Assertiveness training and
planning leisure time were also incorporated.

Activities in Residential Settings

Other factors have been found to contribute to quality of life in long-term care settings: flexibility in care practices (Clark & Bowling, 1990); individualized recreational activities such as music, reading, and personal hobbies, as well as group activities such as exercise sessions and current events readings (Clark & Bowling, 1990); and human relationships and social contact with others (Kayser-Jones, 1990; Ross, 1990). Aller and Van Ess Coeling (1995) conducted in-depth open-ended interviews with 8 residents of a 150-bed nursing facility. The residents reported three common themes that contributed to life satisfaction. The first and strongest, as reflected by the number of times the theme was repeated, involved the ability to do things for others. The second was the ability to care for themselves, and the third theme was the opportunity to engage in social interaction with other residents and staff members. Recreational activities and the hobbies engaged in were perceived primarily as a way to pass time and relieve boredom. This perception on the part of the residents was also reported by Bocksnick and Hall (1994). Although the number of participants in the study conducted by Aller and Van Ess Coeling (1995) is limited, the study does reveal some important findings concerning the needs of residents in long-term care settings. However, as Rapkin and Fisher (1992b) have pointed out, residents may have different goals, and it is essential to assess residents as to their specific desires.

Several purposeful activities have been recommended by Saul (1993) for residents of long-term care facilities. These activities include the development of a resident newspaper, an oral history program, art classes with the results displayed throughout the facility, and a drama group for the entertainment of other residents (see Chapters 4, 10, and 13).

ASSESSMENT OF LIFE SATISFACTION

One can find numerous reasons for assessing the perceived life satisfaction of older adults. Doing so enables health care and social services professionals to obtain information about clients in a relatively quick manner. Professionals with large caseloads can use a standardized scale that can be completed by the client independently. A formal assessment also facilitates obtaining information from reticent clients who may be experiencing problems in well-being but who are reluctant to burden others. Many older adults find life satisfaction scales to be less threatening to complete than the traditional depression or anxiety scales (Salamon, 1985). Individuals with low levels of well-being can be referred for social services, counseling, or other forms of intervention depending on the nature of the source of dissatisfaction. Measures of life satisfaction can be used to monitor treatment effects as well (Conte & Salamon, 1982).

Although the life satisfaction measures may be less threatening to older adults, some may still find it difficult to report what they perceive to be highly personal information. Asking a person who has a good rapport with the older adult to administer the measure is recommended (Salamon, 1988). Also, it is important to keep in mind that an older adult may be particularly unhappy with one domain in his life but satisfied with the remainder (Veenhoven, 1984). If this domain is not represented in the scale being used, the individual may appear to feel more life satisfaction than that which truly exists. In addition, the individual may be satisfied with most domains in life but the impact of one area of dissatisfaction can reduce the overall sense of well-being considerably. Pavot, Diener, Colvin, and Sandvik (1991) recommend using a global measure for the initial screening of life satisfaction.

Several life satisfaction scales are available. The preferred scales are self-report measures, because a subjective judgment is being sought. Three scales have been widely used and have undergone considerable analysis as to their psychometric properties. They can be used reliably with older adults. A fourth scale is included as a quick screening measure, which can be added to an intake process with minimal expenditure of time. The latter scale will provide little information other than a global sense of life satisfaction and should not be used as part of an in-depth determination of an individual's psychological well-being.

Life Satisfaction Index A

The Life Satisfaction Index A (LSIA) was developed by Neugarten, Havighurst, and Tobin (1961) and is the most commonly used scale. The scale consists of 20 items representing the following five components:

1. Zest for life against apathy
2. Resolution and fortitude against merely accepting that which life has given
3. Congruence between desired and achieved goals
4. Respondent's social, psychological, and physical self-concepts
5. Mood tone (optimistic versus pessimistic attitude)

Scoring of the items involves three options: agree, disagree, or undecided. Some question has arisen as to whether these five factors truly represent independent domains in functioning. Adams (1969) demonstrated empirically that only four factors were truly representative. Factorial studies have reduced the number of components in the LSIA to three: zest, mood tone, and congruence (Shmotkin, 1991). Rao and Rao (1981–1982) experienced difficulty separating the various dimensions in terms of the items as they are stated. They reported that it is difficult to find a set of distinctive factors that effectively discriminates between the components, which they reduced to four. This type of situation is not a problem if one perceives life satisfaction as a comprehensive judgment of well-being. However, if one ascribes to the idea that life satisfaction indicates a cumulative judgment representing assessments of well-being across several domains of functioning, the LSIA may be of limited use.

The LSIA has been tested for reliability and validation across several groups of older adults [e.g., middle-class, urban (Neugarten, Havighurst & Tobin, 1961); rural (Wood, Wylie & Sheafor, 1969); African American (Rao & Rao, 1981–1982); British (Bigot, 1974), and Israeli (Shmotkin, 1991)]. A shortened version of the LSIA was developed by Wood, Wylie, and Sheafor (1969). They reduced the original 20 items to 13 and made some minor changes in the scoring system. This scale is called the Life Satisfaction Index Z (LSIZ). Neugarten, Havighurst, and Tobin (1961) also developed a shorter scale, consisting of 12 items, called the Life Satisfaction Index B (LSIB).

A copy of the LSIA is available by obtaining the original publication (Neugarten, Havighurst, & Tobin, 1961) and following the steps described for obtaining depression scales in the appendix to Chapter 1.

Philadelphia Geriatric Center Morale Scale

The Philadelphia Geriatric Center Morale Scale (PGCMS) was developed by Lawton in 1972 and was revised in 1975. The revised scale contains 17 items and consists of 3 categories:

1. Agitation—This category includes items that reflect negative emotions and cognitions such as anxiety, anger, sadness, becoming upset, and belief that life is hard.
2. Attitude toward own aging—This category compares current life experiences with those from an earlier period in one's life.
3. Lonely dissatisfaction—This category examines feelings associated with social relationships and discontent.

The scoring of the PGCMS yields an overall indication of life satisfaction, although individual subscores are available for the three categories. The PGCMS has been used successfully with older Japanese adults (Liang, Bennett, Akiyana, & Maeda, 1992), but Stock, Okun, and Benito (1994) reported that the scale produced lower reliability estimates than did the LSIA when it was used with Spanish older adults. The PGCMS can be administered by assistants who have no background in health care after some training (Edwards, Feightner, & Goldsmith, 1995).

A copy of the revised PGCMS is available by obtaining the original publication (Lawton, 1975) and following the steps described for obtaining depression scales in the appendix to Chapter 1.

Life Satisfaction in the Elderly Scale

The Life Satisfaction in the Elderly Scale (LSES) was developed by Salamon and Conte (1984) as a multifactor scale for measuring life satisfaction. Eight categories of functioning are addressed:

1. Pleasure in daily activities—This category measures the individual's degree of satisfaction with numerous, unspecified daily activities
2. Meaningfulness of life—This category reflects the individual's positive attitude toward life as a result of a sense of usefulness and purpose in his or her life
3. Goodness of fit between desired and achieved goals—This category matches the individual's degree of satisfaction with his or her present stage of life as compared with previous stages

4. Mood tone—This category is a measure of general positive affect, happiness, or optimism, nonspecific with regard to one's environment or social situation

5. Self-concept—This category is the degree of personal self-regard and favorable self-appraisal

6. Perceived health—This category is a self-assessment of overall physical well-being

7. Financial security—This category reflects one's satisfaction with his or her present and recent financial situation

8. Social contact—This category is the perceived level of satisfaction with the number and quality of social contacts that are characteristic of the respondent's usual routine

The first five of the eight LSES categories overlap with those of the LSIA. The three additional factors were included to take into account research findings on psychological well-being. The 40 items comprising the LSES are scored using a summative Likert 5-point range (Conte & Salamon, 1982). Because there are 5 questions for each of the 8 factors, the scores can range from 5 to 20 for individual factors, or 40 to 200 for the complete LSES. The items are written in the first person, which may make it easier for older adults who are not accustomed to filling out measurement devices to complete them. The LSES has been used with both older adults living independently and residents of long-term care facilities (Salamon, 1988).

It should be noted that the LSIA and PGCMS were not designed to be used in clinical assessments (Stock, Okun, & Benito, 1994); in contrast, the LSES was designed for this purpose. Because of the comprehensive nature of the LSES, the authors recommend its use by health care and social services professionals. Although administration of the 40 items may be time consuming, a clearer picture of the clients and their needs will emerge with the use of this scale.

A copy of the LSES may be obtained from Michael J. Salamon, Ph.D., Adult Developmental Center, Inc., 1728 Broadway, Suite 1, Hewlett, New York 11557. Phone (516) 596-0073, Fax (516) 599-5698. The test manual is $8.00 and 50 test booklets and 50 scoring sheets are $35.00. Given the cost of most assessment tools, these amounts are quite modest.

Satisfaction With Life Scale

The Satisfaction With Life Scale (SWLS) was developed by Diener, Emmons, Larsen, and Griffin (1985) and consists of five items that are designed to assess a global sense of life satisfaction based on respondents' overall judgment of their lives. The scale has demonstrated both validity and reliability, using external criteria such as peer reports and the traditional pen-and-paper measures of well-being (Pavot et al., 1991). The scale has been used effectively with adults of all ages in the Netherlands as well as in the United States (Arrindell, Meeuwesen, & Huyse, 1991). The advantage of the SWLS is that it can be incorporated easily into the intake or admission process as a quick assessment of older adults' well-being. It can also be used to monitor life satisfaction in a large number of clients or patients.

A copy of the SWLS is available by obtaining the original publication (Diener, Emmons, Larsen, & Griffin, 1985) and following the steps described for obtaining depression scales in the appendix to Chapter 1.

AN INTERVENTION PLAN

Following assessment of life satisfaction, older adults experiencing dissatisfaction can be helped by being referred for services either to an appropriate agency or to a professional in the community. Depending on the source of the dissatisfaction, one of the interventions described in this book may be helpful. It is important to note that helping behaviors will be effective only if they satisfy the specific needs or demands of the individual involved. In most cases the best person to make this decision is the older adult. Optimally, older persons should be active participants in the selection, planning, and implementation of interventions to remediate dissatisfaction with life or their current situation. Focusing helping behaviors initially on an assessment of older adults' goals in promoting life satisfaction should take into account their priorities (Rapkin & Fischer, 1992a).

REFERENCES

Adams, D.L. (1969). Analysis of a life satisfaction index. *Journal of Gerontology, 24*, 470–474.

Allan, G. (1986). Friendship and care for elderly people. *Ageing and Society, 6*, 1–12.

Aller, L.J., & Van Ess Coeling, H. (1995). Quality of life: Its meaning to the long-term care resident. *Journal of Gerontological Nursing, 21*(2), 20–25.

Arrindell, W.A., Meeuwesen, L., & Huyse, F.J. (1991). The satisfaction with life scale (SWLS): Psychometric properties in a non-psychiatric medical outpatients sample. *Personality and Individual Differences, 12*, 117–123.

Atchley, R.C. (1976). *The sociology of retirement.* New York: Halstead Press.

Atchley, R.C. (1982). Retirement: Leaving the world of work. *Annals of the American Academy of Political and Social Science, 464*, 120–131.

Atchley, R.C. (1989). A continuity theory of aging. *Gerontologist, 29*, 183–190.

Atkins, A. (1980). Research finds distortions in the elderly. *Psychiatric News, 15*(7), 32.

Beck, S.H. (1982). Adjustment to and satisfaction with retirement. *Journal of Gerontology, 37*, 616–624.

Becker, D.G., Blumenfield, S., & Gordon, N. (1984). Voices from the eighties and beyond: Reminiscences of nursing home residents. *Journal of Gerontological Social Work, 8*(1–2), 83–100.

Bevil, C.A., O'Connor, P.C., & Mattoon, P.M. (1993). Leisure activity, life satisfaction, and perceived health status in older adults. *Gerontology & Geriatrics Education, 14*, 3–19.

Bigot, A. (1974). The relevance of American life satisfaction indices for research on British subjects before and after retirement. *Age and Ageing, 5*, 113–121.

Bocksnick, J.G., & Hall, B. (1994). Recreation activity programming for the institutionalized older adult. *Activities, Adaptation & Aging, 19*(1), 1–25.

Bosse, R., Aldwin, C.M., Levenson, M.R., & Workman-Daniels, K. (1991). How stressful is retirement? Findings from the normative aging study. *Journal of Gerontology: Psychological Sciences, 46,* P9–P14.

Bowsher, J.E., & Gerlach, M.J. (1990). Personal control and other determinants of psychological well-being in nursing home elders. *Scholarly Inquiry for Nursing Practice, 4,* 91–101.

Cavanaugh, J.C. (1997). *Adult development and aging* (3rd ed.). Pacific Grove, CA: Brooks/Cole.

Christenson, I. (1985). Self-help groups for depressed elderly in the nursing home. *Physical & Occupational Therapy in Geriatrics, 3*(4), 39–47.

Clark, P., & Bowling, A. (1990). Quality of everyday life in long stay institutions for the elderly: An observational study of long stay hospital and nursing home care. *Social Science and Medicine, 30,* 1201–1210.

Conte, V.A., & Salamon, M.J. (1982). An objective approach to the measurement and use of life satisfaction with older persons. *Measurement and Evaluation in Guidance, 15,* 194–200.

Costa, P.T., Jr., & McCrae, R.R. (1980). Still stable after all these years: Personality as a key to some issues in adulthood and old age. In P.B. Baltes & O.G. Brim, Jr. (Eds.), *Life-span development and behavior* (Vol. 3, pp. 65–102). New York: Academic Press.

DeCrosta, T. (1984). Home health care: It's red hot and right now. *Nursing Life, 4,* 53–60.

DeGenova, M.K. (1993). Reflections of the past: New variables affecting life satisfaction in later life. *Educational Gerontology, 19,* 191–201.

Diener, E., Emmons, R.A., Larsen, R.J., & Griffin, S. (1985). The satisfaction with life scale. *Journal of Personality Assessment, 49,* 71–75.

Dykstra, P.A. (1995). Loneliness among the never and formerly married: The importance of supportive friendships and a desire for independence. *Journal of Gerontology: Social Sciences, 50B,* S321–S329.

Edwards, M., Feightner, J., & Goldsmith, C.H. (1995). Inter-rater reliability of assessments administered by individuals with and without a background in health care. *Occupational Therapy Journal of Research, 15,* 103–110.

Ekerdt, D.J., Bosse, R., & Levkoff, S. (1985). An empirical test for phases of retirement: Findings from the normative aging study. *Journal of Gerontology, 40,* 95–101.

Evans, R.L., & Jaureguy, B.M. (1981). Group therapy by phone: A cognitive behavioral program for visually impaired elderly. *Social Work in Health Care, 72,* 79–90.

Fallot, R.D. (1979). The impact on mood of verbal reminiscing in later adulthood. *International Journal of Aging and Human Development, 19,* 191–201.

Fiske, M. (1980). Tasks and crises of the second half of life: The interrelationship of commitment, coping, and adaptation. In J.E. Birren & R.B. Sloane (Eds.), *Handbook of mental health and aging* (pp. 337–373). Englewood Cliffs, NJ: Prentice Hall.

Garfein, A.J., & Herzog, R. (1995). Robust aging among the young-old, old-old, and oldest-old. *Journal of Gerontology: Social Sciences, 50B,* S77–S87.

George, L.K. (1981). Subjective well-being: Conceptual and methodological issues. In C. Eisdorfer (Ed.), *Annual review of gerontology and geriatrics* (pp. 345–382). New York: Springer Publishing.

George, L.K., & Landerman, R. (1984). Health and subjective well-being: A replicated secondary data analysis. *International Journal of Aging and Human Development, 19,* 133–156.

George, L.K., Okun, M.A., & Landerman, R. (1985). Age as a moderator of the determinants of life satisfaction. *Research on Aging, 7,* 209–233.

Glass, T.A., Seeman, T.E., Herzog, A.R., Kahn, R., & Berkman, L.F. (1995). Change in productive activity in late adulthood: MacArthur studies of successful aging. *Journal of Gerontology: Social Sciences, 50B,* S65–S76.

Gray, G.R., Ventis, D.G., & Hayslip, B. (1992). Sociocognitive skills as a determinant of life satisfaction in aged persons. *International Journal of Aging and Human Development, 35,* 205–218.

Havighurst, R.J. (1969). Research and development goals in social gerontology, Gerontological Society Committee on Research. *Gerontologist, 9*(4), 17–33.

Hersch, G. (1990). Leisure and aging. *Physical & Occupational Therapy in Geriatrics, 9,* 55–78.

Herzog, A.R., Kahn, R.L., Morgan, J.N., Jackson, J.S., & Antonucci, T.C. (1989). Age differences in productive activities. *Journal of Gerontology: Social Sciences, 44,* S129–S138.

Herzog, A.R., Rodgers, W.L., & Woodworth, J. (1982). *Subjective well being among different age groups.* Ann Arbor, MI: Institute for Social Research.

Hess, B.B., & Soldo, B.J. (1985). Husband and wife networks. In W.J. Sauer & R.T. Coward (Eds.), *Social support networks and the care of the elderly* (pp. 67–92). New York: Springer Publishing.

Hickson, J., Housley, W.F., & Boyle, C. (1988). The relationship of locus of control, age, and sex to life satisfaction and death anxiety in older persons. *International Journal of Aging and Human Development, 26,* 191–197.

Hildingh, C., Segesten, K., Bengtsson, C., & Fridlund, B. (1994). Experiences of social support among participants in self-help groups related to coronary heart disease. *Journal of Clinical Nursing, 3,* 219–226.

House, J.S., Landis, K.R., & Umberson, D. (1988). Social relationships and health. *Science, 241,* 540–545.

Ishii-Kuntz, M. (1990). Social interaction and psychological well-being: Comparison across stages of adulthood. *International Journal of Aging and Human Development, 30,* 15–36.

Jerrome, D. (1990). Frailty and friendship. *Journal of Cross-Cultural Gerontology, 5,* 51–64.

Kahn, R.L. (1986, November). *Productive activities and well-being.* Paper presented at the 39th Annual Meeting of the Gerontological Society of America, Chicago.

Kasl, S.V. (1992). Stress and health among the elderly: Overview of issues. In M.L. Wykle, E. Kahana, & J. Kowal (Eds.), *Stress and health among the elderly* (pp. 5–34). New York: Springer Publishing.

Kaufman, S.R. (1986). *The ageless self: Sources of meaning in late life.* Madison: University of Wisconsin Press.

Kayser-Jones, J. (1990). The environment and quality of life in long-term care institutions. *Nursing and Health Care, 10,* 121–130.

Kehn, D.J. (1995). Predictors of elderly happiness. *Activities, Adaptation & Aging, 19,* 11–30.

Kelly, J.R., & Ross, J. (1989). Later-life leisure: Beginning a new agenda. *Leisure Sciences, 11,* 47–59.

Kobasa, S.C. (1979). Stressful life events, personality, and health: An inquiry into hardiness. *Journal of Personality and Social Psychology, 37,* 1–11.

Krause, N. (1990). Perceived health problems, formal/informal support, and life satisfaction among older adults. *Journal of Gerontology, 45,* S193–S205.

Krause, N. (1991). Stressful events and life satisfaction among elderly men and women. *Journal of Gerontology: Social Sciences, 46,* S84–S92.

Langer, E.J., & Rodin, J. (1976). The effects of choice and enhanced personal responsibility for the aged: A field experiment in an institutional setting. *Journal of Personality and Social Psychology, 34,* 191–198.

Larson, R. (1978). Thirty years of research on the subjective well-being of older Americans. *Journal of Gerontology, 33*, 109–125.

Lawton, M.P. (1975). The Philadelphia Geriatric Center Morale Scale: A revision. *Journal of Gerontology, 30*, 85–89.

Lawton, M.P., Moss, M., & Fulcomer, M. (1982). *Determinants of the leisure activities of older people.* Philadelphia: Philadelphia Geriatric Center.

Liang, J., Bennett, J., Akiyana, H., & Maeda, D. (1992). The structure of PGC morale scale in American and Japanese aged: A further note. *Journal of Cross-Cultural Gerontology, 7*, 45–68.

Lomranz, J., Bergman, S., Eyal, N., & Shmotkin, D. (1988). Indoor and outdoor activities of aged women and men as related to depression and well-being. *International Journal of Aging and Human Development, 26*, 303–313.

Long, J.D., Anderson, J., & Williams, R.L. (1990). Life reflections by older kinsmen about critical life issues. *Educational Gerontology, 16*, 61–71.

Magaziner, J., Cadigan, D.A., Hebel, J.R., & Parry, R.E. (1988). Health and living arrangements among older women: Does living alone increase the risk of illness? *Journal of Gerontology: Medical Sciences, 43*, M127–M133.

Martin Matthews, A., & Brown, K.H. (1987). Retirement as a critical life event: The differential experiences of women and men. *Research on Aging, 9*, 548–571.

Maultsby, M.C. (1991). Prescribed therapeutic self-help for the elderly: The rational behavioral approach. In P.K.H. Kim (Ed.), *Serving the elderly: Skills for practice* (pp. 137–165). Hawthorne, NY: Aldine de Gruyter.

McAvoy, L.H. (1979). The leisure preferences, problems, and needs of the elderly. *Journal of Leisure Research, 11*, 40–47.

McCrae, R., & Costa, P. (1983). Psychological maturity and subjective well-being: Toward a new synthesis. *Developmental Psychology, 19*, 243–248.

Midanik, L.T., Soghikian, K., Ransom, L.J., & Tekawa, I.S. (1995). The effect of retirement on mental health and health behaviors: The Kaiser Permanente retirement study. *Journal of Gerontology, 50B*, S59–S61.

Mindel, C.H., & Wright, R. (1982). Differential living arrangements among the elderly and their subjective well-being. *Activities, Adaptation & Aging, 3*, 25–34.

Mindel, C.H., & Wright, R. (1985). Characteristics of the elderly in three types of living arrangements. *Activities, Adaptation & Aging, 6*, 39–51.

Mor, V., Murphy, J., Masterson-Allen, S., Willey, C., Razmpour, S., Jackson, M.E., Greer, D., & Katz, S. (1989). Risk of functional decline among well elders. *Journal of Clinical Epidemiology, 42*, 895–904.

Mussen, P., Honzik, M.P., & Eichorn, D.H. (1982). Early adult antecedents of life satisfaction at age 70. *Journal of Gerontology, 37*, 316–322.

Neugarten, B.L., Havighurst, R.J., & Tobin, S.S. (1961). The measurement of life satisfaction. *Journal of Gerontology, 16*, 134–143.

Neulinger, J., & Breit, M. (1971). Attitude dimensions of leisure: A replication study. *Journal of Leisure Research, 3*, 108–115.

O'Connor, B.P. (1995). Family and friend relationships among older and younger adults: Interaction motivation, mood, and quality. *International Journal of Aging and Human Development, 40*, 9–29.

Okun, M.A., Stock, W.A., Haring, M.J., & Witter, R. (1984). Health and subjective well-being: A meta-analysis. *International Journal of Aging and Human Development, 19*, 111–132.

Pavot, W., Diener, E., Colvin, C.R., & Sandvik, E. (1991). Further validation of the satisfaction with life scale: Evidence for the cross-method convergence of well-being measures. *Journal of Personality Assessment, 57*, 149–161.

Pearlin, L.I., & Mullan, J.T. (1992). Loss and stress in aging. In M.L. Wykle, E. Kahana, & J. Kowal (Eds.), *Stress and health among the elderly* (pp. 117–132). New York: Springer Publishing.

Pearlman, R.A., & Uhlmann, R.F. (1988). Quality of life in chronic diseases: Perceptions of elderly patients. *Journal of Gerontology: Medical Sciences, 43*, M25–M30.

Puppolo, D.H. (1980). Co-leadership with a group of stroke patients. In I.M. Burnside (Ed.), *Psychosocial nursing care of the aged* (pp. 253–270). New York: McGraw-Hill.

Rao, V.N., & Rao, V.V.P. (1981–1982). Life satisfaction in the black elderly: An exploratory study. *International Journal of Aging and Human Development, 14*, 55–65.

Rapkin, B.D., & Fischer, K. (1992a). Framing the construct of life satisfaction in terms of older adults' personal goals. *Psychology and Aging, 7*, 138–149.

Rapkin, B.D., & Fischer, K. (1992b). Personal goals of older adults: Issues in assessment and prediction. *Psychology and Aging, 7*, 127–137.

Reker, G.T., Peacock, E.J., & Wong, P.T.P. (1987). Meaning and purpose in life and well-being: A life span perspective. *Journal of Gerontology, 42*, 44–49.

Richardson, V., & Kilty, K.M. (1991). Adjustment to retirement: Continuity vs. discontinuity. *International Journal of Aging and Human Development, 33*,151–169.

Rodin, J., & Langer, E. (1977). Long-term effects of a control-relevant intervention with the institutionalized aged. *Journal of Personality and Social Psychology, 35*, 897–902.

Rodin, J., & Langer, E. (1980). Aging labels: The decline of control and the fall of self-esteem. *Journal of Social Issues, 36*, 12–29.

Roos, N.P., & Havens, B.H. (1991). Predictors of successful aging: A twelve-year study of Manitoba elderly. *American Journal of Public Health, 81*, 63–68.

Ross, M. (1990). Time-use in later life. *Journal of Advanced Nursing, 7*, 167–176.

Rybarczyk, B., Gallagher-Thompson, D., Rodman, J., Zeiss, A., Gantz, F.E., & Yesavage, J. (1992). Applying cognitive-behavioral psychotherapy to the chronically ill elderly: Treatment issues and case illustrations. *International Psychogeriatrics, 4*, 127–139.

Salamon, M.J. (1985). A clinical application for life satisfaction. *Clinical Gerontologist, 3*(4), 60–61.

Salamon, M.J. (1987). Health care environment and life satisfaction in the elderly. *Journal of Aging Studies, 1*, 287–297.

Salamon, M.J. (1988). Clinical use of the life satisfaction in the elderly scale. *Clinical Gerontologist, 8*, 45–55.

Salamon, M.J., & Conte, V.A. (1984). *The Salamon-Conte life satisfaction in the elderly scale.* Odessa, FL: Psychological Assessment Resources.

Saul, S. (1993). Meaningful life activities for elderly residents of residential health care facilities. *Loss, Grief and Care, 6*(4), 79–86.

Shary, J.M., & Iso-Ahola, S.E. (1989). Effects of a control-relevant intervention on nursing home residents's perceived competence and self-esteem. *Therapeutic Recreation Journal, 23*, 7–16.

Shmotkin, D. (1991). The structure of the life satisfaction index A in elderly Israeli adults. *International Journal of Aging and Human Development, 33*, 131–150.

Stevens, E.S. (1992). Reciprocity in social support: An advantage for the aging family. *Families in Society, 73*, 533–541.

Stevens, E.S. (1993). Making sense of usefulness: An avenue toward satisfaction in later life. *International Journal of Aging and Human Development, 37*, 313–325.

Stock, W.A., Okun, M.A., & Benito, J.G. (1994). Subjective well-being measures: Reliability and validity among Spanish elders. *International Journal of Aging and Human Development, 38,* 221–235.

Usui, W.M., Keil, T.J., & Durig, K.R. (1985). Socioeconomic comparisons and life satisfaction of elderly adults. *Journal of Gerontology, 40,* 110–114.

Vallerand, R.J., O'Connor, B.P., & Blais, M.R. (1989). Life satisfaction of elderly individuals in regular community housing, in low-cost community housing, and high and low self-determination nursing homes. *International Journal of Aging and Human Development, 28,* 277–283.

Veenhoven, R. (1984). *Conditions of happiness.* Hingham, MA: Kluwer Academic Publishers.

Walker, J., Kimmell, D., & Price, K. (1980–1981). Retirement style and retirement satisfaction: Retirees aren't all alike. *International Journal of Aging and Human Development, 12,* 267–281.

Willits, F.K., & Crider, D.M. (1988). Health rating and life satisfaction in the later middle years. *Journal of Gerontology: Social Sciences, 43,* S172–S176.

Wood, V., Wylie, M., & Sheafor, B. (1969). An analysis of a short self-report measure of life satisfaction: Correlation with rater judgment. *Journal of Gerontology, 24,* 465–469.

Yale, R. (1995). *Developing support groups for individuals with early-stage Alzheimer's disease: Planning, implementation and evaluation.* Baltimore: Health Professions Press.

Yalom, I.D. (1980). *Existential psychotherapy.* New York: Basic Books.

Yost, E.B., Beutler, L.E., Corbishley, M.A., & Allender, J.R. (1986). *Group cognitive therapy: A treatment approach for depressed older adults.* New York: Pergamon Press.

Zautra, A., & Hempel, A. (1984). Subjective well-being and physical health: A narrative literature review with suggestions for future research. *International Journal of Aging and Human Development, 19,* 95–110.

Zika, S., & Chamberlain, K. (1987). Relation of hassles and personality to subjective well-being. *Journal of Personality and Social Psychology, 53,* 155–162.

Zika, S., & Chamberlain, K. (1992). On the relation between meaning in life and psychological well-being. *British Journal of Psychology, 83,* 133–145.

I have been one acquainted with the night.
I have walked out in rain—and back in rain.
I have outwalked the furthest city light.
I have looked down the saddest city lane.
I have passed by the watchman on his beat
And dropped my eyes, unwilling to explain.

Robert Frost, "Acquainted with the Night"

A Leopard *Can* Change Its Spots

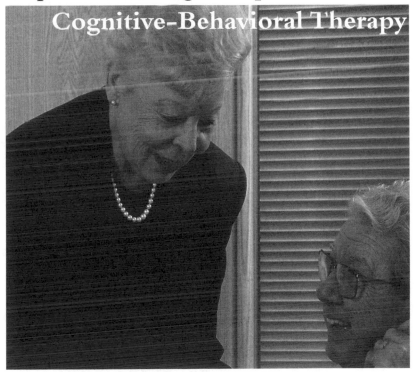

No therapy can fully address the effects of aging and the inevitability of death. However, like everyone else, older people can be helped to improve the quality of their daily lives and to experience less depression, hopelessness, and despair. Cognitive-behavioral therapy is one important strategy for altering the assumptions and changing the behaviors that can lead to isolation, inertia, and a deterioration in body and spirit. Although older people may be reluctant initially to act as full partners in their therapeutic process, the very act of doing so will help to reinstate them in the human community.

When people are depressed, their thoughts usually center on negative perceptions of the self, their situation, and their future. These negative thoughts lead to hopelessness, helplessness, pessimism, and self-blame. Illogical, rigid, and automatic thought processes keep these depressive perceptions alive and prevent constructive problem solving (Kemp, Corgiat, & Gill, 1991–1992). The goal of cognitive-behavioral therapy is to help people learn more effective methods of coping with troubling thoughts, feelings, and behaviors. Cognitive-behavioral therapy addresses the situational difficulties that may foment depressive symptoms and the underlying cognitive reasoning that gives rise to the depressive disorder (Thase & Beck, 1993).

Cognitive-behavioral therapy is an extension of cognitive therapy and behavior therapy. Three schools of thought drive cognitive therapy: Albert Ellis's rational-emotive therapy (RET), Aaron Beck's cognitive therapy (CT), and David Meichenbaum's self-instructional training (SIT). All three approaches assume that negative thoughts and distorted perceptions reinforce negative self-concepts and can lead to depression. The goal in all three models is to transform negative, irrational thoughts into adaptive interpretations of reality.

RET uses an A–B–C construct to describe the processes that result in psychological distress and self-limiting behaviors. *A* represents activating events (i.e., events perceived to be distressful and that often lead the individual to seek treatment), which are mediated by *B*, which represents the beliefs the individual holds, that in turn give rise to *C*, which represents the emotional, behavioral, and cognitive consequences. RET involves training the depressed person to identify, challenge, and modify his or her irrational beliefs. Various strategies are used, including self-monitoring with feedback, direct challenging of irrational beliefs by the therapist, cognitive rehearsing of rational statements, and behavioral testing of both the validity of irrational beliefs and the effectiveness of rational thinking through the use of homework assignments (Newell & Dryden, 1991).

CT shares constructs with RET, although it was developed independently of RET. Beck stressed the presence of "automatic thoughts," which are of particular significance in depression and anxiety disorders (Thase & Beck, 1993). Automatic thoughts are types of self-statements, private thoughts, or internal dialogues that occur without deliberation over them. Unless these thoughts are challenged, they are believed unquestionably. As the thoughts increase in frequency and intensity, so does the level of emotional distress. The course of treatment in CT involves monitoring automatic thoughts, recognizing their relationship to behavior and mood, testing their validity, generating alternative thoughts, and identifying and modifying the dysfunctions underlying the assumptions that predispose a depressed person to such thoughts (Newell & Dryden, 1991).

SIT is similar to RET and CT in that emphasis is placed on underlying cognitive structures that cause uncomfortable feelings and inappropriate behavior. Treatment involves identifying and modifying negative self-statements, training in a range of coping and problem-solving skills, and coaching and reinforcement from the therapist (Newell & Dryden, 1991).

All three treatment models advocate an individualized approach to treating maladaptive thoughts and behavior (Newell & Dryden, 1991). One of the primary differences among the models involves the role of the therapist (Yost, Beutler, Corbishley, & Allender, 1986). The therapist using RET plays an active role in challenging clients' irrational thoughts, frequently using a confrontational style. In SIT the therapist assumes the role of educator, helping clients to challenge their thoughts and observe the processes governing their behavior in order to provide systematic self-instruction and self-direction. RET defines 11 basic irrational attitudes that are the foundation of most adjustment problems, whereas CT and SIT do not emphasize a specific number of inappropriate or irrational attitudes (Yost et al., 1986).

Behavior therapy refers to the application of a variety of procedures that are rooted in learning theory. No single underlying theoretical model in behavior therapy exists other than the assumption that self-limiting behavior is learned behavior. In many cases self-limiting behavior represents a habitual response pattern that may be maintained indirectly by cognitions of or events in the environment. The goal of treatment in behavior therapy is to learn adaptive behavior to take the place of the self-limiting behavior. Behavior therapy has been used extensively with older adults to correct a wide range of problems (Mosher-Ashley, 1986–1987; Wisocki, 1991). Behavioral approaches are particularly useful in altering some of the common sources of depressive feelings. The frequency of pleasurable events can be increased, meaningful activities sought out, and greater control of the environment established.

Because typically the cognitive therapies include behavioral strategies to treat affective problems, they have come to be called *cognitive-behavioral approaches*. Other cognitive-behavioral therapies have been developed by adapting Beck's CT and expanding the range of behavioral procedures used. Cognitive-behavioral therapy is a highly effective treatment that has gained widespread acceptance. Part of its appeal lies in its highly structured, time-limited format. Cognitive-behavioral therapy has also been used effectively by people who are not mental health specialists (Thompson, Gallagher, Nies, & Epstein, 1983).

Cognitive-behavioral therapy has been effective in reducing depression in older adults. This finding is reflected in the work conducted by Gallagher and Thompson (Gallagher, 1981; Gallagher & Thompson, 1982; Thompson, Gallagher & Breckenridge, 1987; Thompson, Gallagher, Nies, & Epstein, 1983). Endogenous depression (i.e., depression arising from a disordered biology rather than from an external stressor) has been treated effectively in older adults using short-term cognitive-behavioral psychotherapy alone (Gallagher & Thompson, 1983) or in combination with medication (Rodman, Gantz, & Schneider, 1991). DeVries and Gallagher-Thompson (1993) also found cognitive-behavioral therapy of benefit for caregivers of frail older adults to manage the anger and frustration they feel in providing care.

The cognitive-behavioral approach featured in this chapter was developed by Yost et al. (1986) specifically for use with older adults. This approach is an extension of Beck's CT, incorporating many of its concepts and procedures. Cognitive-behavioral therapy is effective in reducing depressive symptoms in older adults who are experiencing a wide range of problems, including chronic disabling illness and early-stage dementia.

USE OF COGNITIVE-BEHAVIORAL THERAPY WITH OLDER ADULTS LIVING INDEPENDENTLY

It is somewhat difficult to provide cognitive-behavioral therapy to older adults living independently. The amount of preparation and time needed to cover the therapeutic principles and apply them make it infeasible for medical and social services professionals to engage in cognitive-behavioral therapy on an individual basis. A group approach is more cost-effective and can be offered through senior centers, acute care hospitals, adult day centers, and community service programs provided by long-term care facilities. Because older adults and their families are not attuned to seeking psychological services, much effort to advertise the group and what it can do will be needed. Additional effort must be expended to transport older adults with physical impairments to their groups.

Maggie was a 67-year-old woman who had spent 2 years caring for her cantankerous husband, Fred, who had multiple health problems. Maggie was in good health, and, until Fred became disabled, she had been socially active. Although Maggie belonged to a church group and charitable organizations, she had few close friends. Much of her life had been centered on her role as mother and homemaker. She and Fred had three sons, all of whom had families of their own. Fred's medical condition, which included severe disabling arthritis, made him dependent on Maggie. She felt overwhelmed by the numerous caregiving tasks she faced. These tasks included helping Fred to bathe and dress, fetching items he needed, and keeping him company, in addition to her usual chores of preparing meals, housekeeping, and marketing. In response to the increasing demands on her time, Maggie withdrew from her social activities. Going out to dinner or a movie, which she had previously enjoyed, was complicated by Fred's use of a wheelchair and reluctance to leave home.

Maggie began to spend much of her time obsessing over how much work she faced. She would make mental lists of everything she needed to do and would find herself overwhelmed by the length of the lists. She had difficulty sleeping, which increased her anxiety about accomplishing everything on her mental lists. Maggie began to complain of low energy and an inability to start on daily tasks after assisting her husband with morning care.

Although Maggie felt compelled to give up many of her social contacts, some of them had not given up on her. A member of her church group informed Maggie of a group designed to help older adults cope with depression. The group intervention emphasized a cognitive-behavioral approach. In the group Maggie began to identify negative thoughts indicative of her tendency to expect that her situation would continue to worsen and that she would be forced to manage alone. She also came to identify her tendency to expect too much of herself and to not give Fred a chance to participate in meaningful activities. Through individual homework assignments, Maggie was encouraged to allow Fred to do what he was still capable of doing, which would lighten her load and help him to feel less of a burden to her. He took on the tasks of managing the household finances, keeping track of investments, and making investment decisions. Fred also worked out a financial plan to cover the cost of hiring household help for Maggie.

Maggie was required by the group to increase her participation in pleasurable activities and work toward reestablishing her social network. As a result, she scheduled periodic breaks during the week to attend church and social functions. Fred agreed to stay home alone if he did not wish to accompany her. Maggie arranged for a local senior van service to transport Fred to social occasions that he was willing to attend. As things began to change, Maggie began to feel that she had more energy. Her spirits lifted, and her outlook on the future brightened.

USE OF COGNITIVE-BEHAVIORAL THERAPY WITH OLDER ADULTS LIVING IN LONG-TERM CARE FACILITIES

Because cognitive-behavioral therapy is best provided in a group format, it is particularly well-suited to older adults living in congregate settings. However, Hayslip and Caraway (1989) caution that some environments for older people do not encourage rational thinking. Depressed older adults residing in long-term care settings usually lack peer models who are in control of their lives and who are coping effectively with the losses they are experiencing. In addition, many residents tend to be passive. Typically, few individuals make productive use of their time.

Abraham, Niles, Thiel, Siarkowski, and Cowling (1991) found that group interventions using cognitive-behavioral therapy helped nursing facility residents reduce depressive symptoms and increase pleasurable activities. Even residents with mild cognitive impairment were able to participate in and benefit from the therapeutic approach. (Individuals with mild memory impairment do need a slower-paced therapy, with considerable repetition of concepts [Steuer & Hammen, 1983].) The therapeutic approach can be modified for older people who have difficulty with abstract reasoning. Greater emphasis can be placed on the behavioral aspects of the therapy.

An advantage to using cognitive-behavioral therapy in long-term care facilities is that caretakers can be trained in the cognitive principles and can cue their use by the residents. The behavioral assignments can be incorporated into the residents' daily schedule (Casey & Grant, 1993). The practical nature of the cognitive-behavioral approach is usually appealing to residential care staff. Its directive approach also fits the medical model, making it easier for staff members to follow recommended procedures.

Casey and Grant (1993) recommend that when working with psychiatric inpatients, therapy sessions be time-limited, averaging about 20 minutes, and that they be offered five or more times each week because of the severity of disorders experienced. Whenever possible, family members should be included in the work. Family members can be provided instruction and handouts on cognitive-behavioral principles with specific strategies for countering negative thoughts and behavior.

Ruth was a 74-year-old woman residing in a retirement facility for women. She was a widow with one daughter, Sally, who had an extensive history of psychiatric hospitalization for schizophrenia. Ruth's involvement with Sally was limited to periodic visits to a community residential program in which Sally had been living for 8 years. With increasing age and physical limitations, Ruth became depressed. She showed little interest in social functions, preferring to spend her time alone in her room. When she did venture out, usually for meals, Ruth would ruminate about her unfair life. She would describe at length how she had lost her husband, who was her main source of support, to cancer. She was particularly bitter about the amount of pain he experienced after living a moral and just life. She would add that Sally had been lost years earlier to mental illness and would describe the difficulties her illness had presented. She would complain about how unfair it was that people who had done bad things in their lives ended up having many advantages.

Ruth was referred to a group therapy program offered through the local mental health center by one of the clinicians who worked with her daughter. At first, she was reluctant to attend but was persuaded to do so for the sake of her daughter, who relied on her mother's visits and needed her support. The group therapy consisted of a highly structured cognitive-behavioral program. Ruth was instructed in how to monitor her feelings and the thoughts that drove them. Her underlying belief in a fair and just world was uncovered, and Ruth was instructed to keep a record of unfair events that happened to good people. Ruth's tendency to perceive her past as bleak and dismal was challenged by requiring her to record events and experiences that were especially important in her life. This assignment led to discussions about Ruth's relationship with her husband. The discussions revealed that Sally's illness had actually drawn the parents closer together. Ruth was asked to compare her marriage with that of others she knew. The comparative process made Ruth reevaluate her judgment of the past.

Ruth was also instructed to increase her participation in pleasurable activities. This was a particularly difficult part of the treatment because she was convinced there was little pleasure open to her. After much exploration, she settled on scheduling simple activities such as walking through the greenhouse at a nearby college, attending a free music recital, and helping out at a local senior meal site. The latter proved to be a rich source of potential friends, which she capitalized on toward the end of treatment, when she was required to work on increasing her social network. Ruth's feelings of bitterness continued to haunt her, but through cognitive-behavioral therapy she developed a palette of strategies to help her cope with them.

Precautions to Take and Accommodations to Make in Implementing Cognitive-Behavioral Therapy

As some people age, their ability to analyze and synthesize abstract material decreases. They may have difficulty focusing attention for long periods of time and may be easily distracted. Some older people may need more time to organize their thoughts and may have difficulty retaining material from week to week (Yost et al., 1986). It should be noted that there is considerable variability in intellectual skills among older adults. For example, many older people had limited formal education, a fact that accounts for a lack of interest in and experience with abstract reasoning. When working with older adults on an individual basis, the therapist can present concepts in a manner that matches the cognitive abilities of the client. When working with older adults in a group setting, it is wiser to follow a therapeutic format that meets the cognitive level of the group. Yost et al. (1986) have constructed a model of cognitive-behavioral psychotherapy for implementation in a group format that compensates for some of the cognitive changes associated with increasing age. The modifications they made to accommodate the needs of older adults include the following:

- Sessions that consist of several short segments, each with a definite beginning and end, accompanied by verbal and visual cues that hold the participants' attention
- Techniques to cue participants' attention and memories
- Provisions to "warn" participants of tasks to be accomplished (to give participants time to organize their thoughts)
- Techniques to assist members in retaining concepts and to practice strategies between treatment sessions

Older adults tend to have less knowledge of and experience with psychological interventions than do younger adults, and they are less likely than younger adults to ascribe a psychological cause to their affective state. Consequently, older adults in therapy need to be educated about the purpose of therapy and the procedures involved (Knight, 1992). Older adults tend to be passive in therapy (Steuer & Hammen, 1983). This passivity has been attributed to years of relying on the help of experts, particularly those in the medical system. Other differences in conducting therapy with older adults as compared with younger adults also exist. In traditional psychotherapy the therapist tends not to disclose personal information. This approach is not advocated in the treatment of older adults (Yost et al., 1986). Sharing some general information about one's personal life helps to put older adults at ease, increases trust, and decreases the perceived distance between therapist and client. Many older adults are somewhat skeptical about the therapist's ability to help them. This distrust may be accentuated by the age of the therapist, which is usually younger than that of the client. It is best to raise this issue and discuss it openly. Yost et al. (1986) point out that even if doubts linger in participants' minds, the therapist's openness will set a precedent for airing issues that may affect the group.

A trusting relationship between therapist and clients is critical. Change in the participants' condition is usually facilitated by the positive characteristics of that relationship. Consequently, it is important for participants to feel accepted by the therapist and by other group members. (See Chapter 11 for an examination of group cohesion and strategies to facilitate it.) When events occur that can threaten the acceptance of an individual member, the therapist should intervene. Yost et al. (1986) found that empathically reframing or recasting participants' concerns or self-limiting behaviors helps to facilitate group member acceptance. They provide two examples of reframing: 1) an attention-seeking group member was recast as a person who was lonely and in need of human contact, and 2) a

Table 3.1. Common problems presented by participants during cognitive-behavioral therapy

Problem	Definition	Possible solution
Attention seeking	Uses up group time and does not permit coverage of therapeutic principles; facilitator will be viewed as ineffective	Point out importance of information but ask for a summary; point out time limitation and ask to table issue until next meeting
Lengthy expression of emotion/problem	Uses up too much of group's time	Empathic statement should be followed with a request to focus on change
Multiple problems	Presentation of several problems or shifts from one to another blocks treatment efforts	Ask which problem takes precedence; place other problem on hold; point out need to work on one problem at a time
Dependency	Will not be able to take on active role to resolve problems; may not do homework; will rely on facilitator to plan interventions	Work on negative thoughts indicating helplessness; shift dependency to the group
Depression blamed on external events (e.g., poor health)	Condition will feed depression and feel insurmountable; facilitator will not be effective	Gently point out that other people with similar problems cope; reframe situation as one governed by underlying negative beliefs
Bring up ideas out of sequence	Undermines step-by-step structure of cognitive-behavioral intervention	Ask if situation can be put on hold until topic is covered; if feasible, present topic out of sequence
Inability to grasp concepts	Understanding of the conceptual framework is necessary to do the homework and effect change in depressive symptoms	If limited to 1 or 2 people, keep to the structure while providing support and assistance; if experienced by most of the group, cover less of the planned material

Adapted from: Yost et al. (1986).

group member who complained frequently of physical disabilities was recast as a person with low self-esteem because of lost capabilities.

It is critical that the therapist's feelings about the aging process and negative stereotypes about older adults be explored (Steuer & Hammen, 1983). Otherwise, the hopelessness and helplessness characteristic of depression may be confused with limitations that are perceived to be realistic. The therapist also should be familiar with community services available to older people (Knight, 1992; Steuer & Hammen, 1983). Kemp, Corgiat, and Gill (1991–1992) advocate the development of a supportive environment for the expression of emotional experiences. Burnside

(1986) points out the importance of not using a confrontational style with older adults, who will simply retreat and not disclose personal information in future sessions.

It is important to begin and end therapy sessions on time because, frequently, older adults are dependent on others for transportation. Yost et al. (1986) report that many older adults arrive early for group sessions. Arrangements should be made to accommodate these early arrivals. For example, group members can socialize a bit before the session, which will reduce their desire to do so during the session. The therapist would also have a chance to interact with some members on an individual, personal level. Members should be greeted with a handshake on arrival, a comfortable social pattern for older adults (Yost et al., 1986).

Several problems can arise in conducting cognitive-behavioral therapy with older adults in a group format. Yost et al. (1986) have outlined the most common problems and have suggested possible solutions (Table 3.1). When attempting to respond to any of these problems, it is important that the older adults believe that the group facilitator is sympathetic and understanding. Even participants who are annoying to other group members should be treated with sensitivity.

Cognitive-behavioral therapy has been found to increase the frequency of participation in activities that older adults are able to perform (Kemp, Corgiat, & Gill, 1991–1992). Therefore, it is important to determine whether the functional limitations of older adults with disabilities are truly a manifestation of their physical conditions or are extensions of depressive symptomology.

When conducting individual work using a cognitive-behavioral approach, therapists sometimes find it difficult to motivate depressed older adults. Spiegler and Guevrement (1993) recommend starting with a simple task that is rewarding—one that the individual feels cannot be accomplished—and working toward accomplishing it.

IMPLEMENTATION OF COGNITIVE-BEHAVIORAL THERAPY WITH HEALTHY OLDER ADULTS[1]

Cognitive-behavioral therapy[2] is a highly structured and directive therapeutic approach. It is unlike a support group, which is nondirective and actually strives to avoid having the group facilitator take control. The cognitive-behavioral therapy approach described in this chapter involves a group format, although modifications can be made so that a therapist can carry out the procedures in an individual context. The treatment model developed by Yost et al. (1986) involves four

---

[1]Health care and social services professionals who have little experience in conducting group therapy sessions are advised to consult Chapter 11. Unless supervision is available, the group facilitator would also be wise to limit initial experiences in carrying out cognitive-behavioral therapy to older adults with mild forms of depression. Group facilitators who plan to implement cognitive-behavioral therapy with severely depressed older adults and those who wish to read an in-depth explanation of how to implement this therapeutic approach are advised to consult Yost et al. (1986).

[2]The procedures described in this section stem primarily from the model of Yost et al. (1986), which has been used by many researchers investigating the use of cognitive-behavioral therapy with older adults (e.g., Hamblin, Beutler, Scogin, & Corbishley, 1993; Kemp, Corgiat, & Gill, 1991–1992) and may become the standard in the field. The purpose of this chapter is to introduce professionals to the therapeutic approach. It is not meant to replace the original work.

phases, which are preparation, collaboration/identification, change, and consolidation/termination (further detail is available in Table 3.2).

Cognitive-behavioral psychotherapy is a psychoeducational approach; Yost et al. (1986) employ a blackboard or large newsprint pad, handouts, and homework assignments in therapy sessions. Group facilitators using this model should follow the four recommended procedural phases as described by Yost and associates; not following the prescribed structure will reduce the effectiveness of the therapeutic approach. Alternatively, an overly strict reliance on the structure can lead to a routine style of presentation that will make the participants feel that they are attending a class, not engaging in therapy. In order to be responsive to group members, the therapist can be flexible in the manner in which some of the information is presented or in the procedures to be carried out. Not all members of the group will achieve the same level of change. Some participants may achieve a great deal, others much less. This differential pattern should be expected.

Preparation Phase

Selection of Group Members

In selecting members of a cognitive-behavioral therapy group, specific criteria should be established for the inclusion of potential candidates. Consideration should be given to the level and type of depression individuals experience, the amount of psychological distress and physical impairment with which individuals cope, and whether individuals who are abusing medications and alcohol should

Table 3.2. Four sequential phases of treatment in cognitive-behavioral therapy

Phase	Tasks to be accomplished	No. of sessions
Preparation	Client selection and screening process, which permits group facilitator to explore clients' specific problems and thought patterns to teach them what to expect in therapy	2
Identification/ collaboration	Clients are helped to identify problems in their lives that can be changed to reduce depressive symptoms; emphasis is placed on active participation and social support	5–8
Change	A move away from an educational process to one that emphasizes practicing changes in cognitive, affective, and behavioral experiences	9–14
Consolidation/ termination	Preparation for the end of treatment: expanding social support networks, inoculating the client against future stress, and learning methods of self-evaluation	15–20

Adapted from: Yost et al. (1986).

be included (Yost et al., 1986). To benefit from a cognitive-behavioral approach, participants must be able to openly discuss their problems and actively collaborate in problem-solving strategies (Yost et al., 1986). Prospective participants must also be able to accept some direction in resolving their problems. Highly autonomous individuals can be helped through this treatment modality, but they may need individualized treatment and a skilled therapist. These individuals require an approach emphasizing increased facilitator inquiry into their problems and self-discovery. Individuals with severe medical problems can be included, but their inclusion will present challenges to the cohesiveness of a group format (e.g., frequent absences, possible early termination because of hospitalization, possible death). Once these individuals are included, the group facilitator has an ethical responsibility to maintain contact with them on some level for the contracted period of time (Burnside, 1986).

Individuals who are at risk for suicide should not be included in the group (Yost et al., 1986). Client safety is the priority. The amount of time needed for cognitive-behavioral changes to take place and the tendency of suicidal individuals not to disclose their problems in a group format make them inappropriate candidates. Severely depressed older adults should be referred to more experienced personnel.

Participants who are impulsive, non–self-reflective, or prone to acting out and projecting their feelings and problems onto others usually are not good candidates for cognitive-behavioral therapy (Yost et al., 1986). Participants who are experiencing hallucinations and possess strong delusional systems should be considered with caution.

Interest in therapy is important, but lack of interest should not be used as a criterion for exclusion from the group. Knight (1986) has pointed out that older adults who are not psychologically minded (i.e., familiar with the concepts and procedures of psychotherapy) need to be educated concerning the purpose and procedures of therapy as well as its benefits. The benefits should be described as realistically as possible. Yost et al. (1986) found that some participants expected widely different outcomes, many of which could not possibly be met by therapy. An initial screening session of at least 1 hour in length should be conducted. This period offers an excellent opportunity to determine what the person expects from therapy and whether the criteria for inclusion have been met. Older adults who are not considered to be appropriate candidates for the proposed cognitive-behavioral intervention should be referred to a more appropriate source of help. Whenever possible, the referral should be specific (Yost et al., 1986). Many older adults have difficulty negotiating the bureaucracy of the numerous clinical and social services agencies. A clear, tactful explanation of the reasons that the individual is being excluded from the group should be provided to the person.

Group Size

The number of participants in the group depends on the physical and cognitive conditions of the older adults being considered. Even with cofacilitators and an able group of participants, the number should not exceed 12 because each member is expected to participate several times in each session. Kemp, Corgiat, and Gill (1991–1992) limited group size to nine when working with people with physical disabilities.

Preparation of Group Members for Therapy

Yost et al. (1986) recommend that participants be prepared for cognitive-behavioral therapy using a two-step method. The first step involves seven tasks to be carried out with participants on an individual basis. The amount of time needed to accomplish the tasks in the first step depends on the participant. The seven tasks are as follows:

1. Establish rapport with and reassure participants about the therapeutic process and the hope of recovery. Older adults who are unfamiliar with the therapeutic process often hold exaggerated beliefs about it. Group facilitators should explore these beliefs by specifically asking about them rather than waiting for them to surface in conversation. Two commonly held beliefs are that people in therapy are crazy and that they are forced to discuss topics they do not wish to. The participants should be reassured that these stereotypes are not true.

2. Educate participants about depression. Some information about causative factors—particularly losses; a sense of helplessness; and a negative view of the past, present, and future—should be presented. Listing and explaining the symptoms associated with depression help participants to understand that their situation is not unusual. (See p. 16 for a list of these symptoms.) Many participants are relieved when they realize they do not possess all of the symptoms. Understanding that fatigue, lethargy, and memory losses are symptoms of depression rather than a bellwether of Alzheimer's disease, for example, can provide hope to some older adults.

3. Familiarize participants with the basic principles and procedures used in cognitive-behavioral therapy. The explanation should emphasize that depression can produce negative thoughts; these thoughts can exacerbate depression. Participants should be informed that the strategies to be learned in therapy will help them to reduce these thoughts, which in turn will diminish their depression. Participants also should be assured that the procedures will be tailored to their individual needs and that clear guidance will be provided to help them accomplish the tasks in the therapy. A brief overview and rationale should be provided about homework assignments, with examples.

4. Explain the roles of the group facilitator and the participants in cognitive-behavioral therapy. The facilitator's function is to help participants understand the cognitive-behavioral principles and apply them to everyday experience. Participants should be informed that they will be playing an active role in dealing with their depression. Some personal problems that contribute to their depression must be selected and worked on, and the process that they will undertake is collaborative and will not consist of a "cookbook" solution to be followed.

5. Establish and discuss reasonable expectations for the outcome of cognitive-behavioral therapy with participants. Participants who have been depressed for a long time cannot expect total recovery at the end of treatment. It is important to keep therapy outcomes in perspective while not discouraging participants from believing that change can take place. An effective approach is to explore what the participants would like to see happen at the end of treatment and how they will know that they have accomplished their goal or goals (e.g., experiencing fewer crying episodes, attending more social activities, participating in volunteer activities).

6. Assess the participants' motivation for therapy. Participants must be willing to commit to the duration of the treatment program. Yost et al. advise that participants not attend initial sessions on a trial basis because it can have a deleterious effect on group cohesion.

7. Refer participants who report suicidal ideation for more skilled treatment. Individuals who are not at immediate risk for suicide but have contemplated it can be included in the group provided they agree to a no-suicide contract. (A no-suicide contract is a verbal promise that these participants will not attempt suicide during the course of treatment.)

The second step in preparing participants for cognitive-behavioral therapy involves a group meeting with the participants, as detailed in the section "Initial Group Meeting."

Duration and Length of Group Sessions

Yost et al. (1986) advocate a 20-session format in order to cover all of the treatment phases adequately. Other researchers have found that gains can be achieved with shorter session lengths, but these intervention programs have addressed a limited number of cognitive distortions (i.e., maladaptive thought patterns) and focused on specific problems such as living with a chronic illness or disability (e.g., Kemp, Corgiat, and Gill used a 12-session format). The cognitive-behavioral session designed by Yost et al. is 2 hours long, with the first 10 minutes devoted to preliminary activities such as social time and description of the agenda. Preliminary activities are followed by a 50-minute review of the homework assigned at the previous session. This review is followed by a 5-minute lecture ("lecturette") and a 45-minute period during which feedback, personal applications of the material, assignment of the new general homework assignment, contact work and individual homework, and feedback on the contact work take place. The last 10 minutes are devoted to a final review of the homework to ensure that everyone understands the assignment and the feedback on the session. In general, older people who are cognitively intact do not have difficulty tolerating the lengthy sessions. Even older adults with physical disabilities have been found to tolerate 2-hour-long sessions (Kemp, Corgiat, & Gill, 1991–1992). People with cognitive impairments and older adults with psychiatric problems tend to require shorter but more frequent sessions.

Initial Group Meeting

Although the first group meeting is considered a part of the preparation phase, it is structured in a way similar to the subsequent treatment sessions. All treatment sessions follow a six-step sequence (Yost et al., 1986).

Step 1 consists of abbreviated introductions. The group facilitator begins the introductions in order to model for participants the kind of information expected and its brevity. Introductory information focuses on nonthreatening material such as marital status, children's names, and hobbies. Then, each participant introduces him- or herself. At the conclusion of this step, the group facilitator informs group members that they have just completed a "round." A round is a brief, focused canvassing of each member of the group on a specific issue, usually preceded by a question posed by the group facilitator. Each group member is given a chance to speak. A member can elect to "pass" if he or she chooses not to speak. Several rounds should take place in the first session in order to give participants experience in completing rounds and in speaking in the group. Possible questions for rounds in the first session include Where do you live? How long have you lived there? What do you like to be called? How many children do you have? Where do they live? How do you like to spend most of your time?

Step 2 is a review of what is expected of the participants in therapy—specifically, that they will be discussing their own problems as well as those of others and that they will be working actively toward change, rather than looking to the group facilitator to devise potential solutions. It should also be made clear that members are expected to attend each session, even when they may not feel like doing so. Rules regarding self-disclosure and confidentiality should be discussed with participants, particularly these two points: 1) although members are expected to discuss personal problems, they are not to be coerced into disclosing more information than they wish to; and 2) so that members feel secure about the material they disclose, no information is to be shared with people outside of the group. (The reader is advised to review Chapter 11 for an in-depth examination of confidentiality issues.)

The outcomes of treatment should also be reviewed with participants. The group facilitator should ask each member to set personal goals related to resolving his or her depression. This request serves two purposes: It encourages members to discuss their depression in a structured manner in the group, and it permits the group facilitator to ascertain whether the goals are realistic. Goals that are vague or too general can be transformed into goals that are more specific by asking participants how their goal would manifest itself at the end of treatment. Unrealistic goals can be revised by asking whether the proposed goal is likely to occur. It is essential that the participants not set themselves up for failure and disappointment with unattainable goals.

Step 3 involves a formal presentation of about 5 minutes in length, covering one aspect of a cognitive-behavioral therapy concept. The presentation is followed by a group discussion. Whenever possible, the lecturette should include examples from the group members' experiences. A handout summarizing the main points of the lecturette should be provided to the participants and mailed to members who were absent.

The group facilitator can forgo presenting a lecturette during the first session. If one is given, the most appropriate place to begin is with the relationship between thoughts and emotions, which is the cornerstone of cognitive-behavioral therapy. However, the group facilitator should not assume that all members will have understood or retained the information covered. The connection between thoughts and emotions is a fundamental aspect of treatment and will require more coverage in later sessions. Yost et al. (1986) suggest that if group members do not respond well to the presentation of concepts, the lecturettes should focus on behavioral techniques. These techniques are discussed in the section "Collaboration/ Identification Phase."

If a lecturette is presented during the first session, the homework assignment (*Step 4*) that follows it should be an extension of the material covered. Participants can be asked to self-monitor behavior related to their depression if a lecturette is not presented. A rationale should be provided for assigning homework. Details provided about how the assignment is to be carried out should be clear and fall within the members' abilities. The group facilitator should ask participants to air any concerns they may have. Participants should also agree to at least attempt the homework assignment. This aspect is described in greater detail in the section "Collaboration/Identification Phase."

Feedback (*Step 5*) is provided after the lecturette and at the end of each session. The group facilitator should also prompt feedback during other steps. During this part of the session participants are asked to list their reactions to any aspect of the therapy (e.g., homework, part of a session, impact of the session on individuals). Asking participants to provide feedback empowers them and permits the group facilitator to tailor the therapeutic procedures to the specific needs of the members. All concerns expressed by the members of the group should be addressed before the end of the session. If time does not permit this, some concerns can be tabled until the next session.

The group facilitator should conclude the first session by providing an overview (*Step 6*) of the upcoming sessions. This overview should provide a brief description of each of the four treatment phases (see Table 3.2). Participants should be told they will examine the situations, thoughts, and emotions related to depression that can be experienced in different ways by different participants. They should also be asked to make some small changes in their everyday activities that may reduce some of their depressive symptoms. Toward the middle of treatment, they will make other types of changes in the attitudes and thoughts that tend to influence their level of depression. Toward the end of therapy, they will discuss strategies for managing their lives once the group disbands so that they can continue to cope effectively with depression. As the session concludes, the group facilitator should stand by the door, formally shake each member's hand, and make a personal comment as the individual leaves.

Collaboration/Identification Phase

The aspect of treatment known as *collaboration* refers to the therapeutic relationship between the group facilitator and group participants. This relationship is facilitated by creating an environment of acceptance on the part of group members and facilitators. A working relationship develops through the group facilitator's solicitation of feedback and through his or her response to concerns expressed by the participants. Additional strategies that can be used to facilitate collaboration include active listening, attentiveness, and encouragement to openly express concerns and difficulties about the therapy.

The *identification* aspect of treatment involves self-monitoring feelings of sadness, hopelessness, and helplessness along with the thoughts and situations that precede and cause those feelings. The task of recognizing and labeling maladaptive thoughts is not easy for adults of any age to learn and can be even more problematic for older adults who have not been exposed to psychotherapeutic concepts and who do not have insight into their behavior and that of others. The method employed by Yost et al. (1986) to identify dysfunctional thoughts is the use of an observational record (using either two or three columns) of events that precipitate thoughts, which in turn trigger negative feelings.

Initially, participants are taught to monitor their depressive feelings using a two-column record of situations and their corresponding emotions (Table 3.3). The participants are asked to identify times during the week when they experience depressive feelings and are instructed to define the situation that preceded it or that they believe prompted the emotional state. Some participants will report that they feel depressed constantly. In such cases the group facilitator should probe for times of the day when the participants feel particularly low and for events that increase feelings of sadness and worthlessness. Participants who are able to complete a two-column record can be encouraged to share theirs as examples for the rest of the group.

Participants should not progress to three-column records (Table 3.4) until they have mastered two-column records, as reflected in their completed homework assignments. Inducing participants to identify the thoughts that precede their depressive feelings will require much direction on the part of the group facilitator. These thoughts tend to be habitual and occur so automatically that they may be experienced as fleeting events. Encouraging participants to describe aloud a distressing situation in detail while the group facilitator asks what the event meant to them can help to clarify the thought pattern involved. Yost et al. (1986) recommend the use of questions such as "And what does that prove?" "How do you interpret that?" "What does it mean when. . .?" (p. 58) in motivating par-

Table 3.3.   Sample two-column record used in the identification/
collaboration phase

A Situation	C Mood/feeling
Forget teakettle on stove, water boils away	Stupid, afraid
No phone call during evening	Alone, unloved
Light bulb burns out, can't reach it	Useless, worthless

Adapted from: Yost et al. (1986).

Table 3.4.   Sample three-column record used in the identification/
collaboration phase

A Situation	B Thought	C Mood/feeling
Sees a TV commercial picturing an attentive son and his mother	"My children don't call. They don't love me."	Worthless, depressed
Neighbor passes by without saying hello	"People are cold and uncaring. Things aren't the way they used to be. I don't belong here anymore."	Alone, old, empty
Kitchen looks dirty	"I don't have any energy. I just can't get things done anymore."	Useless, worthless
Aches and pains on arising from sleep	"The pain feels worse. What will happen if I can't get around on my own?"	Worried, afraid

Adapted from: Yost et al. (1986).

ticipants to attend to thought patterns. If a participant cannot identify an automatic thought, other members of the group can be asked to guess at his or her possible fears, worries, expectations, or other responses to a situation that can produce the feelings involved.

Homework

The purpose of homework assignments is for participants to practice the skills learned during the therapy session and generalize what is learned to the setting in which depression is experienced. General homework and individualized homework are the two types of homework assigned. *General homework* is assigned to all members of the group and is an extension of the material presented in the lecturette. It consists primarily of monitoring and recording emotional reactions to and thoughts about events and applying behavioral techniques to reduce depressive symptoms. Homework assignments can vary in complexity or amount depending on the abilities of the group members. *Individualized homework* is undertaken by participants as part of contact work, which is examined in the following section. The homework assignment pertains to a specific problem that is not experienced by all members.

Depressive symptoms such as apathy, loss of energy, and feelings of hopelessness can lead to noncompliance with homework. Providing rationales and explaining clearly how the assignment is to be carried out can help to increase compliance. The participants' focus should be on efforts to do the assignment, not on its successful completion. Participants should be told that it will take time to master the task and that practice is needed. If participants do not complete the homework assignment, the reasons for noncompliance can become aspects to be discussed during the session (Kemp, Corgiat, & Gill, 1991–1992; Yost et al., 1986). Special attention should be paid to participants' negative thoughts surrounding the assignment or its perceived lack of helpfulness. When participants have difficulty with a homework assignment and require a simpler variation, they frequently experience negative thoughts that they are less capable than other members or that their depression is much worse than others and will be more resistant to treatment. It is important to reassure these participants that depression assumes different forms in different people and that each person must work at his or her individual pace. When a participant is having difficulty undertaking a homework assignment, asking other group members to offer suggestions for how to induce the participant to try it can help. Yost et al. (1986) recommend asking the following questions: "Can anyone think of a way that might help John try this assignment?" "Is there a better way to explain it?" "How can we help you to overcome your difficulty with this assignment?" (p. 24).

Homework assigned in the previous session should be reviewed at the beginning of each session. Reviewing the completed tasks will enable the group facilitator to monitor the symptoms of depression, clarify concepts, and prepare group members to provide feedback. When reviewing homework, the group facilitator should emphasize successes. The focus should be on the positive aspects of the response, not on the negative aspects. All members should be encouraged to positively reinforce any achievement, even when success in accomplishing the task is limited. The function of the procedure is to model setting realistic goals and accepting less-than-perfect performance. Before a participant progresses it is critical that he or she fully understands the relationship between thoughts and emotions, the cornerstone of cognitive-behavioral therapy (see Step 3 of the section "Initial Group Meeting," and the section "Relationship Between Thoughts and Emotions" later in the chapter).

Contact Work

Contact work usually arises out of difficulties a participant is experiencing, either in carrying out homework assignments or in learning a concept. When an appropriate situation or problem presents itself during the group session, the group facilitator offers to engage in a one-to-one minisession of up to but not more than 20 minutes' length. The participant is free to decline. Other members are asked to refrain from making any comments during contact work. At the end of the minisession, group members are asked to provide feedback on the meaning of the interchange and its impact.

During the identification phase of treatment, contact work helps participants who are experiencing difficulty identifying thoughts. (Later in therapy it is used to facilitate change.) In contact work undertaken during this phase, the participant is asked to recall a situation in which his or her depressive feelings were particularly noticeable. Then, using the three-column record (see Table 3.4), the group facilitator probes for the thoughts that give rise to the feelings. The group facilitator is free to solicit help from group members, but they must refrain from making any comments that have not been requested. At the end of contact work, the group facilitator and participant may collaborate on designing an individualized homework assignment. It is important that contact work be used appropriately from the beginning because it will become a major feature of treatment in the change phase. Participants who tend to digress need to be reminded of its purpose and gently kept on track.

Group facilitators should keep lists of the type of situations and dysfunctional thoughts that are common to each member of the group. As the participants conduct the homework assignments and examine their thoughts, repetitions and patterns will begin to emerge. Certain words will be found to be connected to some of the thought patterns. The lists will enable the group facilitator to individualize the therapy in contact work during the change phase of treatment.

Lecturettes

Yost et al. (1986) have developed a three-part format for the lecturettes, as follows, but caution that rigid adherence to the outline is not necessary:

1. The group facilitator provides an explanation of the main point using clearly presented examples, preferably drawn from the experiences of the members, in the two- or three-column record format. To ensure understanding, participants should be able to apply the concept of the main point to additional examples provided by the group facilitator.
2. The group members apply the concept presented to their own experiences. Specific examples can be analyzed on the board.
3. The group facilitator outlines on the board an assignment based on the lecturette. Members can be assigned different levels of the task if the participants vary in their understanding of the material.

Five areas are commonly covered in the lecturettes during the collaboration/ identification phase: relationship between thoughts and feelings, relationship between depression and pleasant activities, relationship between mastery over activities and depression, scheduled activities, and social activities. With the exception of the first area, relationship between thoughts and feelings, which is critical to the treatment of depression and is covered here in depth, the amount of time and the degree of coverage of the other areas are generally tailored to the needs of the particular group. The areas may need to be presented in more than one lecturette. Several examples should be given within each area.

Relationship Between Thoughts and Emotions

The relationship between thoughts and emotions may need to be presented in several different ways before everyone understands the concept fully. The following example is drawn from Yost et al. (1986, p. 64). Write on the board:

Situation	Thoughts	Feelings
Letter from son	Mother:	
	Father:	

Explanation: In general, people assume that emotions are caused by others' behavior or by things that happen to them. This belief leads to an underlying assumption that people do not have any control over their emotions, that their emotions are controlled by outside forces. In reality, emotions are caused by the thoughts and beliefs that have been learned about an event or about someone's behavior.

Example: A mother and father receive a letter from their son, from whom they have not heard in many years. The mother experiences great joy while the father feels anger. Because both parents are reading the same letter, the letter itself does not cause the different emotions. (Under "Emotions," the group facilitator should list "joy" and "anger.") When the mother reads the letter, she thinks about the fact that her son is alive. When the father reads the letter, he concentrates on how their son has worried them and should have written earlier. (Under "Thoughts," the group facilitator should list the respective thoughts for each parent.) Thus, it is the way each parent thought about the letter that was responsible for the emotions experienced. The letter itself did not cause the different reactions. Additional examples based on this format should be provided.

Practical application: Group members should be asked if they can think of a situation in which they experienced sadness, anger, or another emotion. Several examples should be solicited and written on the board under the headers "Situation" and "Emotions." Each participant who offers an example should be asked to supply thoughts that could have given rise to the emotions. If someone is unable to generate these thoughts, group members can be asked to offer suggestions. Next, the participants should be asked what different, less distressing emotion could have been experienced in the situation. They should be asked if they have experienced an initial negative emotion about a situation that changed to a more positive emotional state. It will be necessary for the group facilitator to probe for the different underlying thoughts. (Examples should be written on the board under the respective header.)

Homework: The group facilitator should point out to group members that emotions are so strong and occur so quickly that it is often difficult to recognize or even believe that thoughts are involved. When certain emotions are experienced frequently, the thoughts that precede them become automatic, so much so that they are not experienced consciously. Thus, efforts need to be made to "catch" them. To accomplish this, unpleasant emotions need to be examined carefully as they happen in order to elicit the thoughts that precede them.

The homework that accompanies the early lecturettes should focus on completing the two-column record. After recording several situations and their associated emotions, the participants should be asked to identify the thoughts involved. Then, three-column records should be assigned to monitor future thoughts. Participants who move quickly through the records' sequence should be asked to include occasions on which a change for the better in their thoughts and resultant emotions took place.

The structure described for the preceding lecturette can be used in preparing additional presentations on this topic and in the following four areas.

Relationship Between Depression and Pleasant Activities

One of the common symptoms of depression is loss of energy or motivation to carry out normal activities. Over time, depressed people even stop doing the things that used to bring them pleasure. With few pleasurable activities in their lives, depressed people feel like doing less, and the situation worsens.

Relationship Between Mastery over Activities and Depression

Another symptom of depression is an individual's belief that he or she is inadequate. This belief is reinforced by other depressive symptoms, such as the decreased ability to concentrate, retardation in speech and movements, and negative comparisons with one's previous level of functioning. In time, the person's sense of mastery over activities begins to erode. Because the depressed person is cutting back on the number of activities engaged in, opportunities to reestablish his or her sense of mastery are limited. Self-blame and raised expectations about what the person should be doing increase the depression.

Scheduled Activities

Scheduled activities bring structure and a measure of self-control into the lives of depressed people. For depressed people, being able to accomplish the activities provides a sense of achievement and challenges their inertia and the belief that they cannot do anything at all. Structured days are also less boring, pass more quickly, and give the depressed person less time to brood.

Social Activities

Frequently, depressed people withdraw into themselves and lose contact with others who were once sources of pleasure. Without someone with whom to interact on a regular basis, people's social skills deteriorate. Depressed people begin to lose whatever social confidence they felt and to withdraw even more. Eventually, friends drift away and the person's social circle constricts. This situation is not automatically reversed when the depression lifts. The need for depressed people to slowly but actively increase social contacts should be addressed in the group setting.

Behavioral Techniques

As previously mentioned, the identification of dysfunctional thoughts does not in itself lead to changes in depressive symptoms. Changes in symptoms are effected through the use of behavioral techniques, or modifications in the behavior that fuels the depression. Behavioral strategies have the added advantage that, once engaged in, they can challenge the beliefs that group participants may hold about their inability to function and overcome depression. Yost et al. (1986) propose using four behavioral techniques in the collaboration/identification phase: activity scheduling, activity mastery, graded task assignment, and pleasure in performing activity.

Activity scheduling Participants are asked to schedule a variety of activities for the following week, make an effort to keep to the schedule, and record their successes. Participants are given a blank schedule of hourly blocks for the week and asked to fill in their usual activities. Difficult periods and long periods in which little scheduled activity takes place are identified and suitable activities to be engaged in are explored. Participants are asked to make an effort to engage in the activities at their scheduled time each day. Performing even part of the activity at the scheduled time is more important than how well it was done or for how long. Success in the activity should be defined in terms of the ability to take control, not in terms of a reduction in depressive symptoms. Schedules are reviewed during the following session.

Activity mastery The activity mastery technique is designed to help participants set realistic goals and evaluate their successes positively. Participants are asked to select one or two tasks of some importance that reasonably could be completed before the next group session. If the task appears too difficult or beyond a participant's resources, input from the group facilitator and other group members can help the participant adjust the task to a realistic level. A rating system should be developed to indicate the level of mastery. Yost et al. (1986) used the following system: 1 = got started, 2 = finished about half the task, 3 = completed what was planned.

Graded task assignment The goal of the graded task assignment technique is to help participants perform more complex, challenging tasks. With assistance from the group facilitator, each participant identifies a desired task that is realistic but is felt to be too difficult to undertake. Negative thoughts about the task should be explored. Then the task should be broken down into small, manageable steps, beginning with the easiest steps to complete. Possible strategies to make the task pleasant and easy should be explored (e.g., asking for help or advice, listening to favorite music while working).

Pleasure in performing activity The goal of the pleasure technique is to help participants relearn how to have fun and increase the range of pleasant activities in which to engage. Participants are asked to identify one or two activities that gave them pleasure in which they engaged before the onset of the depression. The activities should be available and should not require much time or energy. The participants are then asked to fit the activities into their weekly schedule, choosing convenient times in order to facilitate success. A rating scale for pleasure should be developed (e.g., 1 = very small, 2 = noticeable pleasure, 3 = more pleasure than expected). Participants who have difficulty identifying pleasurable activities can be helped by suggestions from the group facilitator or the other participants.

When introducing each of the behavioral techniques the group facilitator should clearly establish the purpose and benefit of the technique, inquire for negative thoughts associated with carrying out the tasks, and clearly explain how to carry out the technique. Special attention should be paid to negative self-statements, which can indicate cognitive distortions.

Change Phase

Any improvement in depressive symptoms observed up to the change phase is probably the result of the group therapy process and the participants' sense that measures beyond the identification of dysfunctional thoughts are being undertaken to handle their depression. In the change phase participants are taught how to evaluate their dysfunctional thoughts, generate more realistic and adaptive thoughts, and practice these alternative thoughts as homework assignments. The basic format of the group session remains the same as in the collaboration/ identification phase, although the steps do not occur in the same order. The use of contact work is increased and emphasis is placed on individual change in the lecturettes. The one-to-one contact work enables the group facilitator to help individual participants move through the sequence of the therapeutic steps at different rates, depending on their understanding of the concepts.

One of the critical factors contributing to change in participants is their ability to perceive the cognitive errors in the thoughts they produce. The group facilitator should use a questioning approach rather than a listing-of-explanations approach to help participants to understand the concepts presented. A group facilitator's reliance on explanations framed as statements does not usually result in comprehension by group members. The participants simply acquiesce and accept the group facilitator's viewpoint. Without a fundamental understanding of the concept presented, they are not able to generalize it to new situations. The questions posed by the group facilitator also serve as a model of the questions the participants should pose to themselves when challenging their cognitive errors.

Lecturettes

In the change phase lecturettes focus on the cognitive errors in depressive thoughts and the ways to challenge them. The homework assignments involve asking participants to identify their errors and to implement ways to counteract them. Once the majority of the participants have completed the process of identifying their thoughts, the process of classifying the thoughts into categories of cognitive errors should take place. Yost et al. (1986) selected seven categories that are common in older adults: overgeneralizing, "awfulizing," mind reading, self-blaming, being demanding of others, harboring unrealistic expectations of self, and exaggerating self-importance. The researchers caution that these categories are neither mutually exclusive nor exhaustive. Rather, the categories represent a useful way of interpreting thoughts that, once identified and classified, can be targeted for change. Therapeutic questions are posed by the facilitator to help participants recognize the distortions in their cognitive processes.

Overgeneralizing The tendency of some participants to equate one event with all subsequent events is the most fundamental of the cognitive distortions. In overgeneralizing, a participant assumes that one unpleasant event applies to all similar situations for all time. The group facilitator should focus on exceptions that demonstrate the error in this type of thinking.

Homework In the recognition part of the homework assignment participants should look for distressing incidences in which they use the key words that indicate an overgeneralization. Incidences should be monitored using a three-column record. In the identification part of the homework assignment participants should look for evidence that contradicts the overgeneralization. A fourth column (D) should be added featuring the evidence as a "corrective technique" to counteract the negative thoughts.

Key Words all, never, always, everyone, no one, nobody

Therapeutic Questions   Is there an exception to your belief? Is it true that you can't do anything right? What have you been able to do recently?

"Awfulizing"   "Awfulizing," the tendency to exaggerate the negative aspects of present or anticipated events, is a form of overgeneralizing. Participants who awfulize attach great importance to unpleasant events, permitting these events to overshadow and destroy good things that may be happening. To counteract awfulizing, the participants should 1) distract themselves from negative thoughts by turning their attention to a positive aspect of their life, 2) ask themselves if there is a "silver lining" to the unpleasant situation or any way that it can be made less negative, 3) decide that the event is not going to ruin the day, or 4) accept the negative aspect of the situation but minimize it. The group facilitator should avoid discussing major situations such as death.

Homework   In the first part of the homework assignment participants should monitor their thoughts using a three-column record to note incidences during which they used any of the key words. In the second part of the assignment the fourth column should be added, featuring the use of one of the corrective techniques to counteract each negative thought.

Key Words   awful, terrible, devastating, dreadful, tragedy, catastrophe, my day/ life is ruined

Therapeutic Question   How much importance do you want this incident/person to have in your life?

Mind Reading   The tendency of some participants to make assumptions about the internal states of others leaves these participants open to potential misunderstandings. Participants should be asked to provide examples of recent incidences in which they assumed what someone else thought, felt, or believed. To counteract this cognitive error, participants should inquire about the assumption with the person whose mind is being read. If this is not possible, they should look for evidence of a more positive assumption or imagine other possible explanations for the person's response.

Homework   Participants should be asked to spend some time each day evaluating whether they have engaged in mind reading in their interpersonal interactions. The thoughts should be monitored and challenged using the four-column record.

Key Words   he, she, you, followed by feel, think, believe

Therapeutic Questions   What is your evidence? Is there any other way to explain. . .?

Self-Blaming   Depressed people tend to blame themselves for mistakes or unpredicted and negative outcomes of behavior. To challenge this type of cognitive error, participants should ask themselves two questions: Would the blame being ascribed to the self be reasonable if someone else was engaging in self-blame in a similar situation, and is someone else, in addition to the self, to blame? If so, how much is the self to blame legitimately? Exaggeration has been found to be a useful strategy to challenge the tendency to engage in self-blame.

Homework   In the first part of the assignment the participants should make a list of all daily negative occurrences and find a way to blame themselves for each item. If they have few items on their list, they should be told they are not trying hard enough to do the homework. In the second part of the assignment the participants should make lists of all past incidences for which they blame themselves, other people who could share in the blame, and other factors that could have influenced the situation.

If the participants continue to accept more blame than can be reasonably expected, other group members should be consulted for a realistic appraisal.

Key Words *bad, wimp, crazy, stupid, dope, S.O.B.,* and personal statements in which the participant frequently uses name calling

Therapeutic Questions How much are you really to blame for? Is there anyone else who might share the responsibility? Are there any factors that could have affected the outcome?

Being Demanding of Others Many depressed people use exaggerated performance criteria for others. People who make unreasonable demands on others are unable to accept weaknesses or to realize that another person may have different values. As a result negative conclusions are frequently made about that person's character. To challenge their tendency toward unreasonable demands, the participants should recognize that there are many different standards in the world and that no measure exists to identify which is the right one, talk with others to determine whether the expectations that they have are reasonable, and examine the conclusions drawn when others do not do what they wish.

Homework In the first part of the assignment participants should monitor their feelings about the ways in which others treat them or believe toward them using the three-column record. Any incidences in which key words appear or are implied should be examined. In the second part of the assignment participants should determine whether the standard they hold for others should be maintained or discarded. Role-playing within the group may be helpful for participants having difficulty with this type of cognitive error.

Key Words *has to, have to, must, need to, can't, should, shouldn't* preceded by *he, she, they*

Therapeutic Questions What can you reasonably expect? Is there another way to explain the behavior? Does one act mean that the whole person is worthless?

Having Unrealistic Expectations of Self Some depressed people employ exaggerated criteria of performance, frequently comparing the self to an unrealistic view of others. They are unable to generalize the weaknesses of others to the self and do not take into account uncontrollable circumstances. They are also unforgiving when they cannot meet their unrealistic expectations. Many of these standards are a product of lifelong learning and may be difficult to change. A more effective goal may be to reach a compromise. To challenge this type of cognitive error, participants should ask others whether they maintain the same rules of behavior and whether exceptions play a role, whether they feel that breaking one rule means that one has not lived up to the personal standard, and whether the rule applies to others as well as to oneself.

Homework In the first part of the homework assignment participants should record in a three-column record each incidence in which they feel disappointed, upset, angry, or frustrated with themselves. Participants who are experiencing difficulty identifying their unrealistic standards should make a list of their roles with appropriate definitions (e.g., a good parent loves his/her children, a good wife/husband is faithful). In the second part of the assignment participants should explore whether the standards are realistic. In some cases they may need to work on whether occasional failures are acceptable and on methods of compensation for failures.

Key Words *have to, must, need to, can't, should,* in reference to the self

Therapeutic Questions Is your standard too high? Are you being too hard on yourself? Are you doing your best, even if you make mistakes?

Exaggerating Self-Importance Depressed people who exaggerate their self-importance think that others are watching or thinking about them. Any social errors made are perceived as monumental, with everyone noticing and being shocked. To challenge this type of cognitive error, participants should think of a social situation in which they felt embarrassed or were the object of everyone's attention regarding a social mistake. They should then review the situation and ask themselves if everyone actually noticed and, if they did, how important it was. They should also examine how much time they spend looking at others and criticizing their behavior.

Homework Participants should be asked to evaluate any incidences in which they felt a social error had been made and whether they have engaged in exaggerated self-importance in their interpersonal interactions. The thoughts should be monitored using a three-column record and challenged using a four-column record.

Key Words *most, biggest, worst,* when referring to the self

Therapeutic Questions What is your evidence that. . .? So what if they noticed?

Behavioral Techniques

Two behavioral techniques are used in the change phase: stimulus control and behavioral rehearsal. The goal of stimulus control is to rearrange specific environmental features that often trigger or exacerbate depressive symptoms in order to effect positive changes in these symptoms. Participants are asked to identify a depressive thought, action, or feeling that is prompted by an environmental feature. Then they are asked to narrow the targeted thought, action, or feeling to one specific situation (e.g., an older woman may think about suicide when she sees the clothes worn by her deceased husband hanging in a closet). The participants are asked to keep a record of which stimuli trigger the targeted response and which inhibit it. A plan is worked out with each participant to rearrange features in the environment in order to eliminate or reduce the cues that trigger the targeted response. A deceased loved one's favorite chair could be moved to a guest bedroom. The furniture could be moved so that the missing chair is not as noticeable. Clothing can be moved from a frequently used closet to one less frequently used or even given away to someone in need.

The goal of behavioral rehearsal, or role play, is to help participants create appropriate responses to problematic situations by building effective interpersonal skills. Before designing the rehearsal, the group facilitator must make the participants understand the need for new responses. Once they understand the necessity, a situation that is likely to occur during the week is targeted. The targeted situation must be responded to by a course of action initiated by the participants so that they will feel in control. When selecting a situation it is important to determine whether the underlying difficulty in the person is a lack of interpersonal skill or a cognitive distortion (i.e., dysfunctional thinking). If it is the latter an intervention dealing with the dysfunctional thinking should be developed. If the situation involves a problem in interpersonal communication, the behavioral rehearsal approach should proceed. The situation is clarified as to where and when it will take place and with whom. Participants are asked how they have handled similar situations. Based on their responses, they are asked to specify the desired (new) response and any concerns they may have about what may happen during the situation.

The behavioral rehearsal should contain sufficient details to represent the targeted situation as accurately as possible. Other group members assume the roles of significant individuals involved in the situation, and the group facilitator directs the role play. The participant with difficulty in interpersonal communication acts out the desired response and is then asked to evaluate his or her behavior. If the participant appears anxious or reports feeling considerable anxiety, additional rehearsal should be conducted. The homework assignment asks the individual to carry out the desired response in real life.

Contact Work

During the change phase individual participants who are experiencing a problem can ask for or be invited to engage in contact work. Contact work is carried out in a group session, with other members as observers but not as participants. The participant who is the recipient of contact work benefits from individualized attention and the other members gain insight into the intervention process. Participants who elect to engage in contact work add their names to the agenda at the beginning of the session. The work follows the A-B-C format used in the three-column record (see Table 3.4). The participant describes the situation and his or her feelings about it while the group facilitator records them on the board or on a notepad. Then the group facilitator helps the participant to identify the thoughts that precede the feeling. Together they determine which pattern of thinking is responsible for the distressing feelings and accompanying problem behavior. Using a rating scale of 1 (lowest)–10 (highest), the participant rates the degree to which he or she believes in the maladaptive thought pattern. An intervention is then undertaken in which the group facilitator uses open-ended questions to help the participant uncover conclusions about the thought pattern. The questions concern the exceptions to the pattern (if any), alternative views, or realistic assessments of the anticipated consequence or other possible results, as well as the likelihood of the occurrence of the consequence. Group members provide feedback, the thought pattern is rated by the participant a second time, and homework is designed to evaluate the existing pattern or to practice a new, more adaptive pattern.

Consolidation/Termination

Preparation for termination of therapeutic treatment should not be left until the final session, but should begin approximately three fourths of the way into treatment. The termination date should be specified at the beginning of treatment and referred to periodically in subsequent sessions. Some group facilitators find that spacing out the sessions in the last phase of treatment (e.g., every other week or every third week) helps prepare participants to cope on their own. Follow-up sessions several months after termination are advantageous in assessing participants and ensuring that they are still employing the strategies learned in treatment.

Group members can also be encouraged to stage a reunion of sorts. Participants should be informed that if they encounter serious problems, they should contact the group facilitator for consultation. Preparing for termination involves three goals:

1. *Consolidation of gains made during therapy* Two processes must be learned to achieve this goal: recognizing and specifying the gains made in treatment, and anticipating situations that could lead to depression after the group sessions are terminated. Both goals can be accomplished by helping participants to identify the prevailing cognitive errors governing their thoughts and subsequent feelings. Although all depressed people tend to engage in a variety of maladaptive thought patterns, an examination of the records will uncover one or two that appear with regularity and must be watched for. The recurring distortions should be described as generalized life attitudes that may have been but are no longer beneficial.

2. *Maintenance of gains made in therapy* To achieve this goal, participants should be asked to describe the gains they have made to date. The gains can be listed on the board and group members asked how these gains can be maintained after therapy is terminated. The group should generate numerous practical ideas that can then be typed into a list and distributed at the next session. The following represent some strategies to look for (Fishback & Lovett, 1992):

   - Avoid people, events, or situations that have triggered depression in the past.
   - Seek out people and activities that engender good feelings.
   - Keep a notebook containing hints and plans that have effectively managed the depression in the past and refer to it frequently.
   - Make a list of negative thoughts from the three-column records and devise successful rebuttals that have been found to be effective.
   - Keep the group facilitator's written summary of the cognitive-behavioral principles and techniques for future reference.
   - Set small, attainable goals for the period following termination of therapy.
   - Identify potential problems that may be encountered once the group ends. Identify the cognitive errors that could be influential and think about how they can be handled. (This item is the most important in the list.)
   - Remember that depression tends to recur, so prepare for the possibility of relapse.

3. *Separating from the group* Many participants experience an increase in their depressive symptoms as they anticipate the end of treatment. The group facilitator should inquire as to whether anyone is experiencing this increase and point out that this is a temporary phenomenon. Separation issues should not be left to the final session because some participants may feel overwhelmed by separating from the rest of the group. Individuals experiencing strong reactions to the end of treatment can be helped through contact work.

In addressing separation issues participants should explore other support systems available to them. The group facilitator should present a lecturette on this topic. Some members may wish to hold informal group meetings following termination. This support option can be explored, focusing on who would like to participate and who would take responsibility for finding a location and coordinating the meetings.

It is critical that all participants leave the final session on a positive note. No participant should feel abandoned, and all participants must be clear about the gains they have made and the skills they have acquired.

COGNITIVE-BEHAVIORAL THERAPY WITH CHRONICALLY ILL OLDER ADULTS

Chronic illness that results in functional disabilities can cause psychological distress, decrements in enjoyable activities, loss of independence, and lowered self-esteem (Kemp, Corgiat, & Gill, 1991–1992). Depression in chronically ill older adults can manifest itself in noncompliance with rehabilitative efforts as well as in personal distress (Lopez & Mermelstein, 1995). Cognitive-behavioral therapy has been found to be effective in treating medically ill older adults. The cognitive aspects of the therapy can help chronically ill older adults put aside negative thoughts and compare themselves to others less fortunate, whereas the behavioral component can help them to manage the pain and anxiety, increase pleasurable activities, and reduce the difficulties that accompany chronic illness (Rybarczyk et al., 1992).

Kemp, Corgiat, and Gill (1991–1992) were able to ameliorate significantly depression in older adults with chronic disabling illness using a 12-week cognitive-behavioral program based on the approach of Yost et al. (1986). Lopez and Mermelstein (1995) reported on an individually administered approach in an acute care hospital. A team approach was used, incorporating nurses; physical and occupational therapists; and, in some cases, social workers, physicians, speech-language pathologists, recreation therapists, and chaplains. The participants were seen 3–4 times a week for 30-minute sessions. The interventions consisted of the following:

- Making graphs of progress and goals and having team members reinforce the participants' progress
- Encouraging participants to seek information about their conditions and to talk more openly and realistically about their diseases and disabilities
- Training in relaxation techniques where appropriate
- Helping participants to make positive social comparisons and in developing perspective
- Increasing participants' pleasant activities (e.g., involving them in unit social activities and events)
- Training in coping skills, in which setting realistic goals, taking one step at a time, and rewarding oneself were stressed
- Cognitive restructuring to realign expectations and increase confidence (e.g., promoting a "survivor" self-concept)

Rybarczyk et al. (1992) have identified five treatment issues to be addressed in working with older adults who are chronically ill (Table 3.5). In addition to the cognitive errors described by Yost et al. (1986), Rybarczyk et al. have identified two cognitive errors made commonly by older adults who are chronically ill:

1. Negative filtering—This error involves focusing solely on the problem at hand as a measure of happiness. In the case of people who are chronically ill, this problem is their lowered health status. Without good health, happiness is not believed to be possible.

2. Negative forecasting—This error involves anticipating events that have not yet taken place, and may not, with the expectation that the results will be negative.

Gains obtained by older adults with disabilities may not be as dramatic as those obtained by older adults without disabilities. Kemp, Corgiat, and Gill (1991–

Table 3.5. Common treatment issues in cognitive-behavioral therapy with chronically ill older adults

Issue	Description
Resolving practical barriers to participation	Enable people who have physical disabilities to participate; need to compensate for disabilities that can interfere with therapeutic procedures (e.g., inability to write, which can limit homework); shorter, more frequent sessions for participants who have difficulty concentrating because of pain
Accepting depression as a separate and reversible problem	Need to separate symptoms of depression from those of chronic illness; need to challenge acceptance of depression as a realistic outcome of chronic illness and belief that illness equals inevitable misery
Limiting excess disability	Disability that is not a direct result of chronic illness needs to be separated and reduced (e.g., withdrawal from activity because of embarrassment, anxiety, depression or misinformation); inactivity reduces access to pleasant events and fuels depression
Counteracting loss of social roles and autonomy	Need to challenge belief of worthlessness by asking client to "check the data" on whether belief is valid, and eventually to have client clarify responsibilities and choices that are available
Challenging perception of "being a burden"	Need to challenge perception by examining underlying cognitive errors (e.g., mind reading, negative filtering, negative forecasting); check with family as to accuracy of perceptions; explore actual losses experienced and the contributions provided by client to others

Adapted from: Rybarczyk et al. (1992).

1992) found that older adults with disabilities are more likely than older adults without disabilities to experience worsening health problems, difficulties with family members, and a change in residence, all of which can result in increased stress. As long as the therapy continues, these issues can be handled. Once on their own, people tend to revert to maladaptive cognitions. Periodic follow-ups with at-risk older adults may be needed. Training caregivers to prompt corrective techniques may also be helpful.

COGNITIVE-BEHAVIORAL THERAPY WITH OLDER ADULTS WITH COGNITIVE IMPAIRMENTS

Depression and anxiety can cause temporary impairments in thinking. The symptoms of cognitive impairment associated with depression and anxiety (e.g., slower thought processing, difficulty in concentrating, easy distractibility, preoccupation with sad or anxious thoughts), combined with the cognitive losses resulting from a dementing illness, can cause even greater declines in cognitive functioning. Treating the depression can lead to improved cognitive functioning and can prolong the remaining capacities of the person with cognitive impairment (Cohen, 1990; LaBarge, Rosenman, Leavitt, & Cristiani, 1988; Thompson et al., 1990). In the scant literature that exists on counseling interventions for older adults who have a dementing illness, cognitive-behavioral therapy has been found to reduce depressive symptoms measurably (Teri & Gallagher, 1991). Cognitive-behavioral therapy is well-suited for use with older adults in the early phase of a dementing illness because it is time-limited, highly structured, focused on current problems, involved with helping people to relearn basic problem-solving skills, and a therapy in which a variety of different strategies are used to accomplish goals (Thompson et al., 1990).

Functional Level

For cognitive-behavioral therapy to be effective, older adults with a dementing illness must demonstrate sufficient insight and some basic cognitive abilities. Thompson et al. (1990) recommend that potential participants in therapeutic support groups score at least at the mild dementia phase on the Clinical Dementia Rating Scale (Hughes, Berg, Danzinger, Coben, & Martin, 1982) or a 3 on the Global Deterioration Scale (Reisberg, Ferris, DeLeon, & Crook, 1982). Snyder, Quayhagen, Shepherd, and Bower (1995) propose that potential participants with cognitive impairment score 20 or above on the Mini-Mental State Examination (Folstein, Folstein, & McHugh, 1975) or score 100 or above on the Dementia Rating Scale (Mattis, 1988).

Treatment Issues

Thompson et al. (1990) recommend that persons beginning work with older adults with cognitive impairment review the older adults' neurological assessments in order to design an effective individualized cognitive-behavioral intervention. Knowledge of specific cognitive deficits and strengths also helps professionals to determine whether a client's negative thoughts or self-appraisal is accurate or is the result of a cognitive distortion.

Adhering to the structure of cognitive-behavioral therapy is critical for people with cognitive impairment. For them, discovering the ability to respond well to the structural tasks included in therapy reestablishes hope and a sense of accomplishment. Participants also learn how to break down their problems and solve them in an incremental fashion, which will permit them to generalize the strategies after treatment has ended (Thompson et al., 1990).

Approaches

Thompson et al. (1990) recommend using the following approaches in conducting cognitive-behavioral therapy with older adults with cognitive impairment:

- Schedule frequent but brief (30-minute) therapy sessions to compensate for declines in attention.
- Involve family members so that they can prompt their loved one to use the strategies learned in the sessions.
- Repeat therapeutic themes and interventions frequently during the sessions.
- Ask that the person with cognitive impairment keep a simple record of key issues worked on in therapy, homework assignments and their results, and important information for future sessions.
- Provide audiotapes of the sessions for the person with cognitive impairment to play between sessions to facilitate learning and remembering.
- Encourage the person with cognitive impairment and his or her family members to use the external prompts and aids introduced during therapy whenever possible (e.g., keeping a diary, asking people to speak slowly or to repeat information).

Participants with cognitive impairment are unlikely to accomplish all of the treatment phases, nor will they be able to explore all of the concepts usually covered in each phase. It is best to limit the intervention to a prominent dysfunctional thought or cognitive error that is employed frequently by the participant (Thompson et al., 1990). Less emphasis should be placed on questioning the participant and more on instructing him or her. The therapeutic techniques should not rely much on information-processing abilities. For example, Thompson et al. recommend the following for use with people with cognitive impairment:

Prompts. Participants are to write numerous positive thoughts, many involving the self, on 3" × 5" cards (one thought for each card). The cards are kept in a pocket and referred to during the day. Participants are instructed to pay particular attention to the cards' content. People with severe memory impairment are to display the cards in places where they are likely to cue reading (e.g., taped to the refrigerator). The cards should prompt or prime the creative pump of the individual and facilitate a flow of positive thoughts.

Thought Interruption. Participants are instructed to tell themselves when experiencing a persistent negative thought, "I am going to stop thinking about that now." Then, without becoming upset, the participants are to shift their thoughts to nonnegative ideas. If this approach is not effective, the participants are to be instructed to practice gaining control over negative thoughts. Participants are asked to conjure a negative thought and then yell STOP! as loudly as they can in a private setting. The procedure is to be practiced for 3 days. As participants gain expertise in dispelling the negative thought, the STOP! command is stated with force but volume is reduced until the command can be executed mentally (Lewinsohn, Munoz, Youngren, & Zeiss, 1986).

Worry Time.   Participants who believe that they need to process certain negative thoughts can elect to set aside a period of time to mull them over. In this way the negative thoughts can be confined to a specific time and will not interfere with their mood and other activities. If the participants are concerned that a certain thought must be dealt with when experienced for fear it will be forgotten later, the thought can be recorded, then dispelled. A half hour of worry time each day is usually sufficient (Lewinsohn et al., 1986).

Blowup.   Blowup is used to exaggerate a disturbing thought to the point at which it becomes ridiculous. This is accomplished by asking the participant to describe the recurring fear, escalating what could happen. A fear of being embarrassed in public could be exaggerated to the point at which bystanders are staring with mouths open, pointing at the participant. The participant is then asked to picture him- or herself wearing a sign announcing the faux pas to the world (Lewinsohn et al., 1986). In using blowup with clients, Mosher-Ashley found another useful result. Often, before the thought could be carried out to its ridiculous conclusion, clients would discover that the fear was not realistic. For example, a client with cognitive impairment had a recurring fear that she had left the television set or radio on when away from home. She was asked to describe what would happen if she did leave them on. She described how hot these items could become. When prompted as to what would happen then, she said that the curtains nearby could catch fire. When asked if she had fire detectors in the apartment and whether they could be heard by others tenants, she admitted that her landlord lived below her apartment and that he was always home. The client was confident that he would hear the alarm and notify the fire department. This procedure required several repetitions over the next few sessions, but its use significantly reduced her anxiety about leaving electronic equipment on.

Realistic Goal Establishment.   Participants are asked to identify activities that are satisfying and pleasurable. The activities may need to be evaluated in terms of whether individuals can still reasonably engage in them. Participants can be encouraged to focus on activities that are equally enjoyable but easier to manage.

"Reality Check"

At times, people with cognitive impairment will confront losses that are both evident and real. These losses should be acknowledged and individuals permitted to grieve the loss. Gentle redirection to existing abilities and specific advantages in individuals' lives will help them to keep things in perspective. Shifting the focus to what can be changed (i.e., how one thinks and feels about what is happening) is critical. Pointing out that others persevere under very difficult conditions and that there are skills that enable these people to do so can help.

REFERENCES

Abraham, I., Niles, S., Thiel, B., Siarkowski, K., & Cowling, W.R. (1991). Therapeutic work with depressed elderly. *Nursing Clinics of North America, 26,* 635–650.

Burnside, I. (1986). *Working with the elderly: Group process and techniques* (2nd ed.). Monterey, CA: Wadsworth Health Sciences.

Casey, D.A., & Grant, R.W. (1993). Cognitive therapy with depressed elderly inpatients. In J.H. Wright, M.E. Thase, A.T. Beck, & J.W. Ludgate (Eds.), *Cognitive therapy with inpatients: Developing a cognitive milieu* (pp. 295–314). New York: Guilford Press.

Cohen, G.D. (1990). Psychopathology and mental health in the mature and elderly adult. In J.E. Birren & K.W. Schaie (Eds.), *Handbook of the psychology of aging* (pp. 359–371). San Diego, CA: Academic Press.

DeVries, H.M., & Gallagher-Thompson, D. (1993). Cognitive/behavioral therapy and the angry caregiver. *Clinical Gerontologist, 13*(4), 53–57.

Fishback, J.B., & Lovett, S.B. (1992). Treatment of chronic major depression and assessment across treatment and follow-up in an elderly female. *Clinical Gerontologist, 12,* 31–40.

Folstein, M.F., Folstein, S.E., & McHugh, P.R. (1975). Mini-Mental State: A practical method for grading the cognitive state of patients for the clinician. *Journal of Psychiatric Research, 12,* 189–198.

Gallagher, D. (1981). Behavioral group therapy with elderly depressives: An experimental study. In D. Upper & S. Ross (Eds.), *Behavioral group therapy* (pp. 187–224). Champaign, IL: Research Press.

Gallagher, D., & Thompson, L. (1982). Differential effectiveness of psychotherapies for the treatment of major depressive disorders in older adult patients. *Psychotherapy: Theory, Research, and Practice, 27,* 482–490.

Gallagher, D., & Thompson, L. (1983). Effectiveness of psychotherapy for both endogenous and nonendogenous depression in older adult outpatients. *Journal of Gerontology, 38,* 707–712.

Hamblin, D.L., Beutler, L.E., Scogin, F., & Corbishley, A. (1993). Patient responsiveness to therapist values and outcome in group cognitive therapy. *Psychotherapy Research, 3,* 36–46.

Hayslip, B., & Caraway, M.L. (1989). Cognitive therapy with aged persons: Implications of research design for its implementation and evaluation. *Journal of Cognitive Psychotherapy: An International Quarterly, 3,* 255–271.

Hughes, C.P., Berg, L., Danzinger, W.L., Coben, L.A., & Martin, R.L. (1982). A new scale for the rating of dementia. *British Journal of Psychiatry, 140,* 566–572.

Kemp, B.J., Corgiat, M., & Gill, C. (1991–1992). Effects of brief cognitive-behavioral group psychotherapy on older persons with and without disabling illness. *Behavior, Health, and Aging, 2,* 21–28.

Knight, B. (1992). *Older adults in psychotherapy.* Beverly Hills, CA: Sage Publications.

LaBarge, E., Rosenman, L., Leavitt, K., & Cristiani, T. (1988). Counseling clients with mild senile dementia of the Alzheimer's type: A pilot study. *Journal of Neurological Rehabilitation, 2,* 167–173.

Lewinsohn, P.M., Munoz, R.F., Youngren, M.A., & Zeiss, A.M. (1986). *Control your depression: Revised and updated.* Englewood Cliffs, NJ: Prentice Hall.

Lopez, M.A., & Mermelstein, R.J. (1995). A cognitive-behavioral program to improve geriatric rehabilitation outcome. *Gerontologist, 35,* 696–700.

Mattis, S. (1988). *Dementia rating scale: Professional manual.* Odessa, FL: Psychological Assessment Resources.

Mosher-Ashley, P.M. (1986–1987). Procedural and methodological parameters in behavioral-gerontological research. *International Journal of Aging and Human Development, 24,* 189–229.

Newell, R., & Dryden, W. (1991). Clinical problems: An introduction to the cognitive-behavioral approach. In W. Dryden & R. Rentoul (Eds.), *Adult clinical problems: A cognitive-behavioral approach* (pp. 1–26). New York: Routledge.

Reisberg, B., Ferris, S.H., DeLeon, M.J., & Crook, T. (1982). The global deterioration scale for assessment of primary degenerative dementia. *American Journal of Psychiatry, 139,* 1136–1139.

Rodman, J., Gantz, F., & Schneider, J. (1991). Short-term treatment of endogenous depression using cognitive-behavioral therapy and pharmacotherapy. *Clinical Gerontologist, 10*(3), 81–84.

Rybarczyk, B., Gallagher-Thompson, D., Rodman, J., Zeiss, A., Gantz, F.E., & Yesavage, J. (1992). Applying cognitive-behavioral psychotherapy to the chronically ill elderly: Treatment issues and case illustrations. *International Psychogeriatrics, 4,* 127–139.

Snyder, L., Quayhagen, M.P., Shepherd, S., & Bower, D. (1995). Supportive seminar groups: An intervention for early stage dementia patients. *Gerontologist, 35,* 691–695.

Spiegler, M.D., & Guevremont, D.C. (1993). *Contemporary behavior therapy* (2nd ed.). Pacific Grove, CA: Brooks/Cole.

Steuer, J.L., & Hammen, C.L. (1983) Cognitive-behavioral group therapy for the depressed elderly: Issues and adaptations. *Cognitive Therapy and Research, 7,* 285–296.

Teri, L., & Gallagher, D (1991). Cognitive-behavioral interventions for treatment of depression in Alzheimer's patients. *Gerontologist, 31,* 413–416.

Thase, M.E., & Beck, A.T. (1993). Overview of cognitive therapy. In J.H. Wright, M.E. Thase, A.T. Beck, & J.W. Ludgate (Eds.), *Cognitive therapy with inpatients: Developing a cognitive milieu* (pp. 3–34). New York: Guilford Press.

Thompson, L.W., Gallagher, D., & Breckenridge, J.S. (1987). Comparative effectiveness of psychotherapies for depressed elders. *Journal of Consulting and Clinical Psychology, 55,* 385–390.

Thompson, L.W., Gallagher, D., Nies, G., & Epstein, D. (1983). Evaluation of the effectiveness of professionals and nonprofessionals as instructors of "coping with depression": classes for elders. *Gerontologist, 23,* 390–396.

Thompson, L.W., Wagner, B., Zeiss, A., & Gallagher, D. (1990). Cognitive/behavioral therapy with early stage Alzheimer's patients: An exploratory view of the utility of this approach. In E. Light & B.D. Lebowitz (Eds.), *Alzheimer's disease treatment and family stress: Directions for research* (pp. 383–397). Rockville, MD: National Institute of Mental Health.

Wisocki, P.A. (Ed.). (1991). *Handbook of clinical behavior therapy with the elderly client.* New York: Plenum.

Yost, E.B., Beutler, L.E., Corbishley, M.A., & Allender, J.R. (1986). *Group cognitive therapy: A treatment approach for depressed older adults.* New York: Pergamon.

When to the sessions of sweet silent thought
I summon up remembrance of things past . . .
William Shakespeare, Sonnet 30

Journey Through Time

Reminiscence Therapy

Reminiscence refers to the recalling or remembering of past events, experiences, people, and places. This activity can be mental or verbal and can bring about both negative and positive emotions (Kovach, 1991). Therapeutic benefits range from an improved ability to cope with aging and death to an improved self-concept. By sharing recollections with someone willing to listen, an individual can build his or her self-esteem by demonstrating current or past personal worth (Romaniuk & Romaniuk, 1981). Under the direction of a sensitive and caring guide, older individuals can recall accomplishments and past pleasures, gaining a sense of the meaningfulness and purpose of the lives they have lived.

Reminiscence therapy has been used effectively to reduce the anxiety associated with medical treatment. For example, Gropper (1991) described how discussing past successes with surgical operations and other medical interventions helped trauma victims to cope effectively with their injuries. Rybarczyk and Auerbach (1990) were able to reduce anxiety and enhance coping mechanisms in 104 older male patients undergoing surgery by instructing them to focus on positive life events and challenges that they had met effectively in the past.

Although its effectiveness as a therapeutic intervention to reduce anxiety has been demonstrated, the effectiveness of reminiscence as a therapeutic intervention to reduce depression is controversial. Part of the controversy is related to the lack of standardization in the provision of reminiscence therapy and the lack of controlled studies. Since 1987 the lack of empirical evidence concerning the effectiveness of reminiscence therapy has been noted (Burnside & Haight, 1992), but this has not had an impact on the frequency of its use. Reminiscence therapy has been used primarily by professionals who are not mental health specialists (e.g., nurses, social workers). In past years the type of training they received was different from that of mental health specialists in that, in general, empirical evidence is not stressed. Consequently, nurses and social workers tend to use different criteria in selecting a treatment approach. These practitioners learn to rely more heavily on intuitive common sense and logic. Few mental health specialists (e.g., psychologists, psychiatrists) use reminiscence as an intervention; however, these practitioners traditionally have not treated older adults.

The term *reminiscence therapy* has been used interchangeably with the term *life review therapy* by some researchers, while others differentiate between the two terms (Lashley, 1993). Burnside and Haight (1992) made an important distinction between the two therapeutic approaches. They view reminiscence as a psychosocial intervention that emphasizes positive memories, whereas they view life review as a form of psychotherapy in which the client reflects on life experiences in order to come to terms with past guilt, to resolve intrapsychic conflicts, to reconcile relationships, and to find meaning in past events. Recognizing these differences has important therapeutic implications and clarifies an otherwise confusing body of research on the effectiveness of reminiscence as a treatment modality. According to Thornton and Brotchie (1987), differences in definition and measurement of reminiscence have made it largely impossible to compare studies that have assessed its effectiveness. As a consequence no consensus on its adaptational value or therapeutic benefits has been reached. Burnside and Haight (1992) proposed that practitioners establish clearly which of the two treatment modalities they are using and carefully clarify the goals and procedural approach. They also recommend that greater emphasis be placed on evaluating the results of the therapeutic intervention.

According to Burnside and Haight (1992), reminiscence and life review have been used differently and have different consequences. Some of the uses and consequences reported by Burnside and Haight have been reformulated into a set of goals that are presented in Table 4.1. Although some of the goals are similar, there are important differences. For example, both reminiscence and life review therapy have been used to increase self-esteem. Reminiscence has been more clearly linked with increased socialization and communication when conducted in a group format, whereas life review has been associated with the working through of past events and with decreasing depression. It is logical that life review

Table 4.1.　Differences in goals and procedural components between reminiscence therapy and life review therapy

Reminiscence therapy	Life review therapy
Goals	
Increase socialization	Increase life satisfaction
Improve quality of life	Work through past issues
Reduce isolation	Improve affect
Increase self-esteem	Decrease depression
Provide a basis for other treatment groups	Increase self-esteem
Improve communication skills	Increase ability to handle present problems
Change overall affect	Increase sense of accomplishment
Produce memoirs for relatives	
Procedural components	
Can be performed in an individual and a group format	Be performed between a reviewer and a therapeutic listener on a one-to-one basis
Be an interaction that involves recall or telling of early events or a memorable early experience	Contain an evaluative component
Not concern recent events or experiences	Recall the entire life span
	Use memory/recall for both recent and remote events
	Address both sad and happy times
	Have a willing person who wants to share his or her past
	Take a period of time (at least 4–6 weeks), dependent on the life reviewer's needs
	Contain the element of self

Adapted from: Burnside & Haight (1992).

therapy would reduce depression more effectively than would reminiscence because life review involves a reconceptualization of events that may have been interpreted in a negative manner initially. Because an evaluative process is lacking in reminiscence, a cognitive reinterpretation of past events is less likely to take place. Unlike life review, reminiscence involves the recall of positive memories and is perceived generally as an enjoyable experience. Teri (1991) has pointed out that increasing pleasant interactions and decreasing negative ones is part of the process of treating depression in older adults. Although this component alone may not lead to long-lasting changes in people with depression, it appears to have the potential to alleviate depressive symptoms temporarily. Incorporating reminiscence therapy into the ongoing general care of an older client may be particularly helpful.

Differences also have been noted in the procedural components of reminiscence and life review therapies (see Table 4.1). This chapter focuses on reminiscence as a treatment modality because it is supportive in nature and the facilitator skills are easy to acquire, unlike life review. Life review therapy is a complex process requiring some training, and the reader is advised to consult Sherman (1991) and obtain supervision in carrying out a session initially. Reminiscence has been implemented by a range of professionals, many of whom are not mental health specialists. It has been used widely by nurses (Burnside, 1990; Oleson, 1989), occupational therapists (Stevens-Ratchford, 1993), and social workers (Sherman, 1991).

Reminiscence therapy can be implemented on an individual or a group basis. Experts disagree as to which format is the most beneficial (Cook, 1991; Haight, 1988; Watt & Wong, 1991; Youssef, 1990). Although individual therapy is more intimate than group therapy, sharing personal experiences with a group of peers may be easier for some older adults. The benefits of socialization associated with reminiscence groups can be therapeutic, particularly for older adults living alone. New residents of congregate housing or nursing facilities can become acquainted with others quickly in group situations, and a sense of affiliation is gained (Cook, 1991; Watt & Wong, 1991).

USE OF REMINISCENCE THERAPY WITH OLDER ADULTS LIVING INDEPENDENTLY

Mrs. Kaufman was 82 and had been living alone in her own home since her husband's death 16 years earlier. Her only living child, a 54-year-old daughter, was recently divorced, worked full time, and was experiencing emotional problems. Mrs. Kaufman's son had died in an automobile accident 35 years earlier. She had two grandsons, ages 28 and 31. Although they lived near her, both were employed and busy in their careers. The oldest was married but did not have children.

A reminiscence group had been established at a local senior center in an effort to help older adults who lived alone to socialize. Mrs. Kaufman was invited to join the group by the case manager who visited her every other month to coordinate her chore service and find out how she was doing. Mrs. Kaufman was reluctant to join the group but agreed to do so, as she said later, out of a sense of gratitude for the services she received. The group met on Tuesday afternoons. The case manager made arrangements for transportation via a senior van. The first Tuesday arrived, and Mrs. Kaufman, wearing one of her best dresses, attended. At the senior center, she met the 11 other participants. During the first session, all of the members provided some background information and described some favorite activity in which they used to engage. Mrs. Kaufman described how she had been a housewife and mother and had enjoyed making a home for her family. She described how she enjoyed baking and how she had always kept a cookie jar full of home-baked cookies. Her husband's favorites were Toll House chocolate chip cookies, and she had made a special effort to keep some on hand for him. Several other participants mentioned that Toll House cookies were among their favorites as well and agreed that store-bought cookies never tasted as good as homemade. Mrs. Kaufman offered to make some cookies for the next meeting although she had not yet decided whether she would continue attending the group. However, because she had promised to bring the cookies, she decided to "give it one more week."

On Monday of the following week, Mrs. Kaufman made two batches of Toll House cookies and packaged them for the trip to the senior center. The cookies were enthusiastically received, and Mrs. Kaufman reported feeling delighted at having an appreciative group for which to bake. Basking in their enthusiasm, she asked the group members to call her Sarah. During the session, the group was directed to discuss childhood memories. Sarah recalled that, in her childhood, children's toys were expensive and that most people made their own. She described how her parents had made a doll for her. Her father had carved the head out of wood and had painted the hair and facial features. Her mother had made a cloth body and dressed the doll in an elegant dress with bits of lace and velvet ribbon. Other participants described toys they had as children and games they played. This first true reminiscence session left everyone feeling upbeat and provided the participants with a sense of camaraderie. Sarah eagerly looked forward to the next session.

The following two sessions were devoted to discussions of late childhood and early adolescence. Sarah described how, at age 14, she was encouraged by a girlfriend to cut her hair, an act that angered her parents, who were very conservative. She pointed out that girls in those days wore their hair long, frequently coiling it into pugs (small buns) at the ears or braiding it over the top of the head. Sarah described how her friend bobbed her hair just below her ears. Her parents punished her by not permitting her to attend the end-of-school socials. She was also forced to stay indoors most of the summer until her hair grew out a bit so she could coil it, stuffing bits of rags in to make her hair appear longer. This recollection led other members to share rebellious acts they had engaged in. One participant, a frail-looking man, described having jumped a railroad car and traveled with hobos for 2 months. Once again, the participants left feeling enthused. Several participants commented that the sessions had made them feel as though they had traveled back in time for awhile.

Over the next several weeks, the reminiscence discussions addressed adult themes of courting, starting families, and parenting. Sarah described her son's death. He had been only 23 years old and was engaged to be married. He had been celebrating with two friends when they hit another car on a curve in the road about a mile from home. Questions arose about how much beer the young men had drunk. Although so many years had passed, Sarah still thought of her son frequently. As she left the center, another woman, Ethel, hugged her, telling her that she had also lost her son. He had died the year before, and she had never realized how fortunate she had been to have had him as long as she had. Ethel and Sarah talked about how difficult it was for family members to hear about the impact their sons' deaths had had on them, and they decided to meet for coffee and a good heart-to-heart chat.

The reminiscence sessions lasted another 3 weeks, during which time the participants shared good and bad memories. After the sessions concluded, Sarah found herself missing the Tuesday afternoon meetings. She and Ethel continued to meet, usually going to a small local restaurant for tea and ice cream. Sarah's case manager also encouraged her to attend some of the senior center functions. Sarah decided that because she had enjoyed the reminiscence sessions so much, she would no doubt enjoy attending the center once a week to play cards and meet new people. Getting out of the house and meeting others gave her something pleasant to think about and to look forward to. She also mentioned feeling that she had more energy and generally felt better.

It is feasible to provide reminiscence therapy in several different settings. For older adults who live independently, access to reminiscence therapy groups through senior centers and adult day centers may be possible. Obtaining the consent, cooperation, and support of the center's director and staff is essential when proposing a reminiscence therapy group in these settings (Blackman, 1980). Implementing reminiscence therapy in a group format, which is the most commonly used approach, has special advantages. A group approach provides older adults living independently with an opportunity to socialize. Hearing others share personal experiences can act as a stimulus to evoke memories in participants. Hearing how others interpret their experiences can help some individuals reinterpret personal events.

Individuals who are homebound can be provided with individual reminiscence therapy with a 1-hour weekly visit to their homes. An in-home facilitator can guide older people through their memories by asking certain questions and listening attentively (Haight, 1988). This work can be combined with other therapies, such as medical treatments and physical or occupational therapy.

USE OF REMINISCENCE THERAPY WITH OLDER ADULTS LIVING IN CONGREGATE HOUSING OR LONG-TERM CARE FACILITIES

Miss Sally Lavoir was a 69-year-old woman who had experienced a cerebrovascular accident (stroke), with some resultant paralysis on her left side. For 2 years following the stroke, she had lived with her widowed sister, Mrs. Martha Masters, until Sally's difficulty in ambulating and her incontinence made it difficult for her sister to continue to care for her. With some reluctance, Sally moved into a nursing facility. Over the course of the following year, she grew progressively despondent. She showed no initiative in self-care and would sit in her own body wastes, not even asking to be cleaned up. Sally rarely spoke and would not usually respond if staff members spoke to her. She experienced crying jags, during which she exhibited what staff described as "heartrending sobs."

Martha visited about three times a week. During these visits, Sally refused to speak with her sister and would simply weep. Martha confided to the charge nurse that she and her sister had been very close and that she felt very guilty about placing her sister in the nursing facility, but she could no longer care for her at home. The nurse referred Sally for counseling in the hope that her depression would lessen and she would be more responsive to Martha. Sally was seen by a therapist who met with her on an outreach basis at the nursing facility. During the first and second sessions, Sally responded little to the therapist. Martha joined her sister and the therapist for the third session. Sally became more attentive, but began to weep. Martha introduced herself and began to relate some of the family history. Sally was described as having been a very shy and reclusive person most of her life. In childhood, she had found refuge in books and school work, and as an adult had worked as a librarian. In contrast, Martha, who was 2 years younger than Sally, was outgoing and lively. She had married and had three children. The two women had an older brother, Ian, who had moved out of the area shortly after he married; they had rarely seen him after their parents died. Martha noted that she and her sister had lived in close proximity all of their lives. They had spoken to each other over the phone several times a week and had seen one another frequently. At one point in the conversation, Martha began to cry, saying it was hard to see her sister so unhappy in the nursing facility and reiterating that she could not care for her at home.

Given Martha's feelings of guilt and Sally's responsiveness to her, Martha was invited to join the therapy sessions. Reminiscence as a therapeutic modality was selected, with the goal of exploring feelings and establishing more effective communication patterns between the sisters. Martha was instructed to bring photographs of the two sisters when they were children. During the next session, the therapist and the sisters met in the empty dining room. The childhood photograph album was placed on the table in front of the two older women. They were instructed to describe the people in the photographs and any memories associated with them. The sisters took turns describing the photographs. Soon they were discussing the photographs together as though the therapist were not present. They described family vacations and how as children they would terrorize Ian, playing numerous practical jokes on him. On one occasion, they had written a note to one of his girlfriends, inviting her to dinner on the same evening he had invited another girl. The sisters described how both girls came to dinner and became angry with Ian, breaking off their relationships with him. He chased his sisters around the house, but was admonished by his father not to hurt the little girls. During the recounting of this event, the sisters were laughing so hard that tears flowed down their faces. Sally became alert and laughingly asked Martha if she remembered the time they put lipstick on and kissed the collar of one of Ian's shirts before he went out. Unknowingly, he had put the shirt on and gone to pick up a date in whom he was particularly interested. They described hiding in an upstairs closet when he came home, once again very angry and ready to throttle them.

Over the next several sessions, the sisters continued to review the photographs of their childhood, reminiscing about past events. Sally became somewhat more cheerful during these sessions, although she still exhibited considerable depression during the week. When the sisters began to review the photographs of their late adolescence and early adulthood, Sally began to weep. She admitted that she had envied her sister's appearance and ease with people. Martha quietly acknowledged that she was aware of her sister's feelings but never knew what to do about them. Sally also said that she felt that life was unfair, that her sister had been the lucky one, and even now she had her health and lived on her own rather than in a "home." Martha agreed that life was not fair and said that she sometimes wished that she could trade places to give her sister a break. Martha said that she missed their old relationship, that no matter how stressful her family became at times or how she would feel taken for granted, she could always turn to her sister. She said that not having had her to confide in and to spend a few pleasant hours with over the past year had been difficult.

The two sisters talked at length about life's inequities and about how they had always relied on each other to face adversities. They resolved to put their differences aside and work at getting along better during their visits. Sally talked about her feelings of resentment over not being able to continue living together. She said that she would try to get over it, but admitted that it was hard to do so. Martha offered to visit regularly and bring her sister anything that she needed. She also offered to take her sister on an occasional excursion. This delighted Sally, who asked if it would be possible to join the family for holiday events. Martha said she would "work on it."

The sessions continued for 6 more weeks, during which time Sally and Martha shared more memories, looking through two additional photograph albums. Two follow-up sessions, one at 1 month and another at 6 months, found the two sisters relating well. At the first follow-up session Sally reported that she had spent the afternoon at Martha's with the assistance of one of Martha's sons. The sisters reported that they had written to Ian and were encouraging him to correspond with them.

Older adults living in both congregate housing and long-term care facilities can benefit from reminiscence therapy. The most cost-effective format is to form a group. Regular sessions can be held once or twice a week in a quiet room away from interruptions. Sessions should be scheduled such that consistent attendance is possible. Staff should be consulted in order to avoid periods of time when other activities are planned (Blackman, 1980).

Individuals in long term care facilities who, in extreme cases, are bedridden or restricted to their rooms because of severe medical problems may benefit from individual reminiscence therapy as well. As mentioned previously, regular visits from the staff social worker or occupational therapist to help guide the resident into his or her past can be therapeutic (Haight, 1988). Even informal visits by nurses or other staff members during which recollections of family, hobbies, and careers are shared may brighten a resident's spirits (Watt & Wong, 1991). Before implementing either format, it is important to gain the support of the staff and administration of the facility (Blackman, 1980).

PRECAUTIONS TO TAKE AND ACCOMMODATIONS TO MAKE IN IMPLEMENTING REMINISCENCE THERAPY

Before implementing a reminiscence therapy group, certain factors should be taken into account. First, an appropriate site for the group must be chosen. Privacy is a necessity, and the site must be large enough to accommodate the group members comfortably, preferably with enough room for them to form a circle. Second, some supplies are necessary. A tape recorder is recommended to record each session for later evaluation (Blackman, 1980). Old photographs and scrapbooks, recordings of old songs and radio shows, and any other items that may evoke memories may be helpful but are not usually necessary (Cook, 1991; Youssef, 1990). However, these items may be valuable when conducting reminiscence therapy with older adults who have memory impairments. Props are particularly helpful when the person conducting reminiscence is young and has little experience. Group facilitators who employ items such as antique jewelry, old newspapers, old photographs, and old magazines tend to be more enthusiastic about their therapeutic efforts and feel that they gain as much from the experience as do their clients (Burnside, 1990). Third, there is the need to acknowledge that not everyone is comfortable engaging in reminiscence and that this form of intervention should not be assumed appropriate for all older adults (Burnside, 1990). Reminiscence therapy should not be conducted with individuals who are reluctant to disclose personal information or who display paranoid behavior or thoughts. This form of intervention could lead to increased suspiciousness and guarded behavior on the part of participants. Although experienced professionals can effectively probe for memories without increasing paranoid tendencies, it is easier to select an alternative treatment modality for these individuals. Health care and social services professionals who are not trained in psychotherapy should be cautious in pursuing the discussion of painful events, especially those that have led to psychological trauma. Emphasis should be placed on traditional reminiscence, which is emotionally supportive and not intrusive. Participants' attention should be directed to victories over life's challenges.

Some researchers have reported that reminiscence can lead to depression. However, if properly directed by a qualified listener, there is less chance of this outcome. The responsibility for observing the participant and determining the impact of the intervention lies with the facilitator (Haight & Burnside, 1993). In general, it is best to follow the lead of the participant, permitting him or her to decide what to share. Keeping questions focused on positive aspects and not probing negative issues unless the participant clearly wishes to do so will help to avoid increasing his or her depression.

Group Attendance and Size

Consistent member attendance is important in forming and maintaining group identity. Lack of consistency may negatively influence participation and the intimacy of the group. However, attendance may be difficult to ensure. Preselecting individuals for a "closed" group may be one solution (Blackman, 1980). This involves limiting the group to a select number of older adults for a specified period of time. Later, the group could elect to invite additional residents to join.

Effective Group Facilitators

It is important to find a facilitator for the group who is willing to make a long-term commitment (Blackman, 1980; Burnside, 1990). The stability of the group lies with the facilitator, who ensures that sessions take place and encourages participants to attend. It is important to note that the role of a group facilitator or individual guide is that of a supportive listener, encouraging an older individual's self-expression. Psychic probing, confrontation, and interpretation are not advised without proper training. In fact, these methods are unnecessary to achieve the therapeutic benefits of reminiscence therapy (Blackman, 1980).

Accommodation of Participants

Often, older people living in long-term care facilities have multiple problems that can interfere with their ability to participate in a reminiscence group. Problems can result when participants have difficulty hearing or speaking clearly or loudly enough for others to hear. Accommodations may be needed to include participants with disabilities. Special microphones are available to make speech audible, and most adults who are hearing impaired own hearing aids, even if they do not use them regularly.

Certain strategies can be used to facilitate effective sessions and to address specific problems:

1. Warming-up phase. Because of the personal nature of reminiscence, older participants may be hesitant initially to share memories. Time should be allowed for individuals to warm up to each other. Patience on the part of the group facilitator or individual guide is essential (Blackman, 1980; Youssef, 1990). It is wise to introduce easy and nonthreatening topics in the early sessions (e.g., food preparation, holidays, church organizations) before moving to personal topics such as family and friends (Youssef, 1990).

2. Coping with obsessive recall episodes. When conducting reminiscence therapy, the facilitator may encounter a form of obsessive recall that is characterized by a repetitive pattern of negative statements. These statements, which Sherman (1991) has termed *reparative reminiscence*, are directed at making amends or reparations. This type of morbid and obsessional rumination can lead to panic attacks or clinical depression if not handled properly. Although little attention has been paid to this type of reminiscence, the facilitator is advised not to dwell on the rumination itself. The facilitator and other members (if a group format is involved) should point out strengths, recall positive experiences, and provide positive interpretations associated with reparative reminiscence. For example, during a reminiscence group one of the authors conducted in a nursing facility, a participant, Joe, mentioned that he had not been a good father. When his three children were young, he and his wife lived on a houseboat, moving frequently from place to place. Although his wife and children lamented leaving friends behind and complained of not having a real home, Joe pursued his desire for a free and rootless existence. The author pointed out how many other men with similar yearnings simply abandoned their families. The group members praised him for finding a way to keep his family together and support them, while still meeting his own needs. When Joe repeated his negative evaluation of himself as a father, some group members commented on how his children must have had an interesting childhood and had a constant source of conversation. Had Joe persisted in his negative evaluation of himself and concerns over his children, he would have been referred for individual counseling.

Unverbalized Imagery

Imagery is a common experience in reminiscence. While recalling an event, many older adults experience brief, partial images (pictures, smells, sounds) of persons, places, and things that are frequently difficult to put into words. These images arise unexpectedly and spontaneously. Most of the time, the images are self-contained, enjoyable or aesthetic experiences that are sufficient unto themselves. Images are frequently elicited when one person's words describe an event that triggers the recollection of a similar event in the listener's experience (Sherman, 1991). Simply informing participants about imagery during the first session and how it may be experienced will help them understand that the inability to put some of these recollections into words does not make them unsuitable for reminiscence therapy.

IMPLEMENTATION OF REMINISCENCE THERAPY

Implementing reminiscence therapy involves numerous steps, which are delineated in the following sections.

Define Goals

A specific, measurable goal should be established at the beginning of the therapeutic process. Specific outcomes should be predicted and a means of assessing them established. The goals of the therapeutic intervention determine the amount of structure used in eliciting memories during reminiscence sessions (Haight & Burnside, 1993). If increased socialization is the goal, relatively little structure is needed. If self-discovery is the goal, considerably more structure is needed to help participants develop a life-span perspective. For example, the development of a specific strength can be explored across different phases of the individual's life. The goal also determines the type of reminiscence therapy to be implemented and whether an individual or group approach should be used. For example, if increased self-esteem is the goal, an individual approach focusing on the participant's strengths and accomplishments is advisable. Alternative approaches are an oral history or a written record of one's life experiences.

The format for reminiscence therapy tends to vary, depending on the goal of the intervention. The traditional format is chronological in nature, with 2 weeks devoted to each period: childhood, adolescence, early adulthood, middle age, old age. If increased self-esteem is the goal, then a topical approach is used instead of a chronological approach. For example, the focus could be on accomplishments—in work, relationships, contributions to others—and on positive experiences having great meaning for the individual.

Decide on Individual or Group Approach

The decision to engage in individual as opposed to group intervention is based on a number of factors. These factors include the functional ability of the client and his or her social skills, degree of withdrawal, and potential for hostile behavior or paranoid ideation, as well as the availability of a group. The specific benefits of each treatment modality also must be considered. The benefits of an individual format are

- Individual treatment permits the client's specific needs to dictate the type of reminiscence engaged in.
- The pace is tailored to the client, permitting more time for personally meaningful recollections.
- The client captures the full attention of the guide, who can validate or reinforce even subtle insights achieved through reminiscence.
- Even the most reticent client is required to participate actively.

- Participation is not dependent on the ability to travel to a communal setting.
- The treatment can be carried out during other treatment modalities or even over the phone during periods of illness.

The benefits of a group format are

- The group format affords an opportunity for increased socialization.
- Recollections presented by other group members can elicit memories.
- Other members can provide alternative interpretations of difficult past experiences.
- The group setting provides for the possibility of validation by a greater number of individuals.
- Exposure is greater to different ways of coping with feelings or problems.
- Opportunities are increased for an individual member's values to be shared by others, which is less likely when the health care professional or social worker is much younger.

More specific details regarding individual or group reminiscence therapy are examined in the sections "Individual Reminiscence Therapy" and "Group Reminiscence Therapy."

Assess and Evaluate Participants

The progress of individuals undergoing reminiscence therapy must be formally evaluated using an appropriate form (sample forms can be found in Chapter 14). Staff members and family may be enlisted to assess observable social behavior before and after reminiscence therapy sessions as well (Blackman, 1980). Formal pre- and posttesting are important aspects of evaluation; various depression and life satisfaction scales are available, as noted in Chapters 1 and 2, respectively.

An evaluation of group progress must also be conducted. Two sample forms that can be used or adapted to evaluate a reminiscence program are provided. The first (see p. 104) is designed to monitor the clients' progress at the end of each session in a group intervention. The second form is used to evaluate a client who is participating in an individually tailored program (see p. 105). Keeping track of each member's participation in each session is helpful in directing future sessions. Noting the amount and nature of each participant's contribution to the group discussion can lead to strategies for encouraging a reluctant participant or quelling an overly forthcoming one who tends to dominate the sessions. Similarly, an assessment of the predominantly positive or negative nature of each participant's contributions to the group discussion can lead to adjustments in strategy, helping an individual to gain more from the experience and enhancing the comfort level for all participants. Tape recording or videotaping each session is an easy method for maintaining a log of participants' contributions. However, it may be difficult to judge the degree of involvement of each participant from an audio- or videotape alone. Most professionals use a record in checklist form, which is completed following each session. Careful record keeping can help to validate the facilitator's perception of the relative effectiveness of the therapy, as well as pro-

Reminiscence Record Form

Client_____ Date _____

General Impressions

Responded to reminiscences shared by others _____ Many _____ Some
_____ None

Shared reminiscences with the group _____ Many _____ Some
_____ None

**In the space below, record "pos" for positive memories shared,
"neg" for negative memories shared.**

Reminiscences Shared

Personal

_____ Childhood experiences _____ Adolescence _____ Early adulthood
_____ Middle age _____ Post-middle age _____ Currently

Family (spouse, if any)

_____ Dating [_____ Adolescence _____ As adults]
_____ Marriage [_____ Early _____ Middle _____ Currently]

Family (siblings, if any)

_____ During childhood _____ Adolescence _____ Early adulthood
_____ Middle age _____ Post-middle age _____ Currently

Social and Animal Relationships

_____ Friends _____ Neighbors _____ Acquaintances _____ Support staff
_____ Pets

Abilities

_____ Job related _____ Community involvement _____ Hobbies/crafts _____
Helping others _____ Parental role _____ Artistic _____ Volunteer

Support Received (check one in each category)

Positive feedback from peers ___ Much ___ Some ___ None

Negative feedback from peers ___ Much ___ Some ___ None

Positive feedback from facilitator ___ Much ___ Some ___ None

Insights Shared (check one in each category)

Positive self-assessment ___ Many ___ Some ___ None

Negative self-assessment ___ Many ___ Some ___ None

Gained new understanding of self ___ Positive ___ Negative ___ None

Specifically mentioned enjoying the group discussion ___ Yes ___ No

A Life Worth Living: Practical Strategies for Reducing Depression in Older Adults, by Pearl Mosher-Ashley and Phyllis Barrett. ©1997 Health Professions Press, Inc., Baltimore.

Reminiscence Progress Form

Client_____

Date_____

Estimated length of intervention_____

Date started_____

Type of Reminiscence Activity

❏ Individual ❏ Group ❏ Discussion ❏ Autobiography
❏ Photographs ❏ Genealogy ❏ Family History
❏ Videotape ❏ Oral History ❏ Other_____

Short-term goal_____

_____

Long-term goal_____

_____

Progress on activity since last session

Insights obtained from activity

Activity to be engaged in during the next week

Questions to pose to client

Are you enjoying the reminiscence project? Yes_____ No_____

What aspect of the activity do you enjoy?_____

_____

Are you experiencing any problems with the project?_____

_____

Would you like other people/relatives to become more involved?_____

If yes, explore how others could be involved_____

_____

A Life Worth Living: Practical Strategies for Reducing Depression in Older Adults, by Pearl Mosher-Ashley and Phyllis Barrett. ©1997 Health Professions Press, Inc., Baltimore.

vide insights into improvements that might be made in the format or goals of future reminiscence therapy groups.

INDIVIDUAL REMINISCENCE THERAPY

Once the initial steps to implementing a reminiscence therapy program for an older adult living independently or in a long-term care facility have been taken, a therapy schedule should be arranged. Family members and/or nursing staff may be consulted to determine the optimal time to fit in one or two 1-hour sessions a week (Haight, 1988). A 1-hour session may be too tiring for individuals with cognitive impairment, so shorter sessions may be needed.

Sessions may be structured in several different ways. They may be informal, allowing the older adult to choose the topic to be discussed. A more formal method is to predetermine the weekly topics, wherein the therapist guides the older adult through his or her positive and negative experiences (Arean et al., 1993). The therapist may also use a predesigned set of questions to help guide the older person through his or her memories:

Life span experiences[1]
1. What is your earliest childhood memory?
2. What pleasant things do you remember about your adolescence?
3. What was your life like in your 20s and 30s?
4. What was the hardest thing you had to cope with during your life?

Work experience[1,2]
1. Talk about your work. Did you enjoy it?
2. What kinds of jobs did you work at?
3. What was it like for you when you worked as a _____?
4. What gave you the greatest satisfaction while you were working at _____?

Relationships[2]
1. When did you get married? Were there other big moments in your married life/single life?
2. How would your relatives describe you as a mother? Father? Grandmother? Grandfather? Aunt? Uncle?
3. Who were your closest friends? How would they describe you?
4. Did you have neighbors or people in your community whom you came to know fairly well?

Accomplishments[2]
1. What are some of the milestones in your life?

---

[1]Questions recommended by Haight (1988).
[2]Questions recommended by Peachey (1992).

2. What one thing (object, person, idea, event, achievement) do you prize most at this time in your life?
3. What do you like most about yourself?
4. What do you see as your most significant contribution to your family and the next generation?

The individual's responsiveness to the questions should direct the reminiscence work. If the individual appears reluctant to pursue a topic, it should be dropped. Melia (1995) has developed a useful manual designed for college students featuring 52 questions that they can choose from to structure reminiscence interviews with older adults.

Active listening is the key to reminiscence therapy. The older individual should feel that the listener is interested. Novice facilitators all too often want to solve problems before they hear what the client is really saying. Effective use of attending skills by facilitators enables clients to fully air their concerns before action is taken. These skills also help to focus the content of the material being covered and, consequently, permit more rapid coverage of critical information. Most important, the attending skills facilitate the client's perception of being heard as well as promoting discussion. Attending skills include questioning, encouraging, paraphrasing, reflecting feeling, and summarizing (Ivey, 1983; Ivey & Authier, 1978; Ivey, Ivey, & Simek-Downing, 1987).

In *questioning*, two types of questions are employed: closed and open questions. *Closed questions* are those that can be answered "yes," "no," or in a few words. Such questions usually begin with "is," "are," "do," or "did." A closed question is used to gather information, clarify, gain focus, and narrow the area of discussion. It can also be used to stop a client from continuing to speak if he or she is digressing or straying from the topic. It is important to use closed questions judiciously because they can discourage the client from speaking freely. A question that can be answered in one or two words does not provide much interpersonal communication or material with which to work. Also, using a series of closed questions can result in disempowering the client. If used extensively, closed questions can overwhelm the client and cause him or her to fall silent.

Open questions are those that must be answered with an explanation, require discourse, and cannot be answered with "yes" or "no." An open question serves as an invitation to talk. Often, these questions begin with "what," "how," "why," "could," or "would." "What" questions solicit facts and information (e.g., "What did you decide to do?"). "How" questions are most typically associated with process (e.g., "How did this affect you?") or emotion (e.g., "How did you feel about that?"). "Why" questions concern reasons (e.g., "Why do you think this happened?") and intellectual history (e.g., "Why did you turn out the way you did?"). "Could" or "would" questions encourage the client to explore issues (e.g., "Could you elaborate on that a little?"). It is important for facilitators to use different types of open questions. The type of question used depends on the needs and particular concerns of the client. Many facilitators develop a habit of asking only one type of question, thereby limiting the client's therapeutic experience as well as the material that can be covered. For example, facilitators who ask only "what" questions tend to focus sessions on facts and information. The facilitator who focuses primarily on "why" questions can cause clients to become defensive and look to the past to explain present behavior. "Why" questions should be used with caution because they can lead to extended discourses on history that may not generate the desired range of reminiscences. "Could" and "would" questions tend to be the most open, allow for the most discussion, and allow the client to refuse to talk about a subject he or she is uncomfortable discussing.

Encouraging is a direct repetition of what the client has said or a brief comment that punctuates the discussion, providing smooth flow (e.g., "Uh-huh," "So . . . ," "Tell me more . . .). This skill is often overlooked because it is so simple. A facilitator who uses "encouragers" keeps the client talking, once started, and this enhances reminiscence. Encouragers provide a means by which to demonstrate facilitator involvement with minimal intrusion into the client's conversational flow. Encouragers also represent the facilitator's selective attention to key utterances of the client and influence what the client talks about in more detail. For example, a client reports the following: "My life has been so difficult. My husband got hurt on the job when the kids were little. There wasn't much money for extras. We never went on vacations, and we couldn't afford a decent TV for a long time. I made some money making Christmas wreaths and other crafts. My husband was good at carpentry. He made the girls fancy doll houses." If the facilitator were to pick out the words "difficult," "vacations," or "a decent TV," the client could be expected to continue talking about the struggles endured and the things the family lacked. If the facilitator were to pick out the phrase "hurt on the job," the client could be expected to describe the injury in detail. If the facilitator were to pick out the phrase "making Christmas wreaths and other crafts," the client could be expected to recount her resourcefulness and skills. If the facilitator were to pick out the words "carpentry" and "fancy doll houses," pleasant memories may be triggered for the client.

Paraphrasing is an encapsulated repetition of the client's key words and thoughts. Selective attention is given to the content, which is then restated in the facilitator's words. It is not a parroting of what was said by the client—it is a means of providing a more complete understanding of what was said. Often, it is helpful to use the words that the client stresses most. The paraphrase is used by the facilitator to clarify; to bring together threads of discussions; and to present concisely the client's ideas, thoughts, and issues. Paraphrasing provides the client with the opportunity to reexplore old issues, to establish new connections between events/issues, and to speak in greater depth about issues. In addition, paraphrasing helps clients who are evaluating events or actions taken (or not taken) in their lives. The client is freed to make clearer assessments.

Reflecting feeling is similar to paraphrasing. In practice, however, fine distinction between the two skills is not often possible or desirable. Whereas the paraphrase is primarily concerned with cognitive content, reflecting feeling is focused on the client's emotions and affect. Emotions are basic to cognitive and intellectual life, and a clear understanding of the client's feelings provides an important baseline for comprehending the client's decisions, thoughts, and attitudes. In learning to reflect feelings, it is helpful to be able to label emotions (e.g., "angry," "sad," "glad," "cynical," "joyful"). Once a facilitator is able to label another person's emotional experience accurately, he or she can master the skill of reflecting feeling easily. Reflecting feeling often consists of three or four parts, as follows: the pronoun "you" or the client's name (this personalizes the reflection), the labeled emotion, a sentence stem (e.g., "You seem to feel . . ."), and a context to provide a setting for the emotional experience (e.g., "You feel sad when your son doesn't visit you").

Adding the context or situation to the reflection transforms the statement into a paraphrase as well as a reflection of feeling. Pure reflections of feeling tend to include only the first three parts. Intentional reflections of feeling give the client a feeling of collaboration with the facilitator and of being understood by him or her. More powerful reflections tend to focus on the feelings that the client is experiencing at the moment rather than on those in the past. The statement "You appear to be sad about your lack of visitors" has greater impact than "All of your life you have been unhappy about the few friends you had." It should be noted that for some clients the present experience may be too painful, and asking for past reflections may be more appropriate. (Frequently, clients describe mixed emotions during a therapy session. It is typical for people to feel both love and hate toward family and friends. As the facilitator's skills develop, he or she uses these ambivalent feelings as markers to help clients reassess past and present experiences.)

Summarizing is the gathering together of a client's verbalizations, behaviors, and feelings and presenting them to the client in an abstracted form. Summarizing involves attending the client, experiencing the feelings and thoughts of the client, and integrating and ordering the content of the session. The summary reviews the content of the session to bring order to and clarify the content. Summarizing also provides the facilitator with an opportunity to hear whether his or her thinking is accurate and the client with a "breather" before continuing.

Many researchers (e.g., Burnside [1990], Gropper [1991], Peachey [1992]) have recommended that reminiscence be coupled with direct care, such as bathing, grooming, dressing, or medical treatments. They also recommend that reminiscence be encouraged by initiating memory-evoking questions involving family, friends, occupation, living arrangements, and past challenges. Special attention should be focused on significant achievements and relationships established during the individual's lifetime. Even individuals who report having accomplished little in their lives can be encouraged to describe how they have contributed to society by raising children who became productive adults and by working hard to create tidy, attractive homes that have enriched the lives of their children and neighbors.

The use of cues can encourage staff to use reminiscence in direct care. Burnside (1990) describes how the director of nursing in a long-term care facility developed information cards for each resident. The cards, which were hooked to the head of each of the residents' beds by a metal ring, provided background information on the older adult that staff members could use to expand on in reminiscence during direct care.

One of several reminiscence activities can take place during the week, and progress can be reviewed during the weekly visit. The following is a list of sample reminiscence activities that can be conducted with participants:[3]

- Search through old photographs/perform tasks
    - Place photographs in sequential and historical order
    - Label the back of each photograph with the year and people and/ or places depicted
    - Separate and place the photographs in albums to be given or left to specific family members or even to future generations
- Prepare a historical account for future generations emphasizing early recollections (e.g., where the family originated, where different branches of the family settled, family stories and myths, autobiographical information)
    - Write a descriptive account in the form of a journal, profile of individual family members, or both
    - Prepare an oral history in the form of video- or audiotape recordings; each cassette should be labeled with content and date of recording
    - Enlist someone to videotape family photographs, perhaps adding reminiscence narration
    - Write an autobiography
- Prepare a family tree or genealogical record
- Write letters to other family members and share common memories (inexpensive copies of old photographs related to the memory can be made on a copy machine and enclosed with the letter)
- Visit places from the past (e.g., first school attended, summer camp attended)
- Host or attend reunions (e.g., family, school)
- Prepare a cookbook of family recipes, with comments on who originated the dish and when it was most frequently served (e.g., Thanksgiving, family picnics, Passover)
- Teach traditional crafts to young people

It is best to ask the older adult to select one of these tasks and complete it over a period of time that is agreed on beforehand (the time can be extended by mutual agreement at the end of the originally specified period). In working through any of the tasks, the older adult should also be encouraged to contact other family

---

[3]Additional activities can be found in the book *To Our Children's Children: Preserving Family Histories for Generations to Come,* by Bob Greene and D.G. Fulford. Available from Wireless, Minnesota Public Radio, P.O. Box 64422, St. Paul, MN 55164-0422. Phone (800) 669-9999 (item #46614, $15.95). This book is a step-by-step guide to recording personal history. Suggestions and questions help readers to recall and share information about the people, places, and events that have been significant in their lives.

members to obtain additional information. These contacts may help to create emotional connections as well as social opportunities.

GROUP REMINISCENCE THERAPY

Burnside's pioneering work in the 1970s identified a number of behaviors believed to be important for a successful facilitator of a group of older adults (Botella, 1991):

- Flexibility—Ability to incorporate the participant's system (i.e., the facilitator must somehow incorporate the participant's way of doing something—in this case, reminiscing—into the overall approach being used in the activity; hence, flexibility)
- Warmth—Ability to be caring, friendly, and sympathetic; to chat; and to shake hands or pat someone on the shoulder
- Perseverance Ability to focus on a given issue until everyone seems to understand it
- Patience—Ability to work calmly and not become angry or anxious
- Active listener—Ability to allow older people to feel that they are understood and valued as human beings

When implementing a group reminiscence therapy program in a senior center, an adult day program, congregate housing, or a long-term care facility, the facilitator must schedule sessions so that they do not conflict with other activities. Directors, family members, and staff should be consulted to determine the optimal times. Again, sessions should last no longer than 2 hours because some participants may become too tired and feel that they cannot keep up with the rest of the group.

The structure and type of session should be described to the participants at the first meeting (Youssef, 1990). Time must be allowed for individuals to open up to the group facilitator and other group members (Blackman, 1980). One way to "break the ice" is for the group facilitator to encourage each participant to share information from his or her past or present with the group (Watt & Wong, 1991). It is important to address older adults by name (Blackman, 1980). Asking participants to wear name tags may be helpful.

An effort must be made to maintain group cohesion (Haight & Burnside, 1993). Beginning with a closed group of selected participants and not including new members for a period of time may help. The facilitator should contact any members who have failed to attend one of the sessions, encouraging them to come to the next meeting. At the end of the first session, it is a good idea to provide a handout that lists the dates and times of the sessions to follow. This memory aid is helpful for both the older adult participants and their caregivers (Blackman, 1980; Youssef, 1990).

Topics in the early sessions should be easy and nonthreatening (e.g , food, movies, music). When the older participants become comfortable with the group facilitator and each other, more personal topics can be introduced (e.g., family, friends) (Youssef, 1990). Items such as photographs, scrapbooks, and recordings of old songs may be brought in to help stimulate reminiscence (Youssef, 1990). Andrada and Korte (1993) used visual, tactile, gustatory, and olfactory senses to stimulate reminiscences in a group of older adult Hispanics. The sensory stimuli consisted of ethnic foods, folklore, household items, and photographs of past community events representative of Hispanic culture. A similar approach can be employed with most older adults. Group members can be requested to bring in an item from the past that other members may also have used. This item can be a tool, souvenir of a local historic site, food, household goods, or any other memorabilia. It is possible that as the members of a reminiscence therapy group become more experienced with reminiscence techniques, they will not need to have a topic introduced and will be able to lead themselves (Watt & Wong, 1991). The facilitator should avoid probing or pushing for insight. A supportive environment encouraging positive memories should be emphasized.

The goals of the group facilitator include encouraging each member of the group to speak and to listen attentively during each meeting (Youssef, 1990) and reducing feelings of loneliness and isolation in participants. The weakest members of the group need to be encouraged to speak. The facilitator can gracefully shift the conversation away from individuals who monopolize the discussion. The group facilitator should also become somewhat tolerant of silence. A usually hesitant member of the group may jump at the chance to make a comment (Blackman, 1980). Also, pointing out similarities between group members' experiences often helps to diminish feelings of loneliness and isolation (Blackman, 1980).

GUIDED AUTOBIOGRAPHY

Reminiscence therapy in the form of guided autobiography incorporates autobiography writing with therapeutic recollections. The purpose of writing an autobiography is to share the events of one's life. Although the process is frequently therapeutic, the primary focus is on producing a product, a record of the past to share with others (Birren & Deutchman, 1991). The most common format in guided autobiography groups involves 10 sessions in which members read aloud and discuss one another's autobiographical statements. Topics are assigned at the end of each session and the essays are written between sessions to be presented at the following session (Birren & Hedlund, 1987). Botella (1991) used a 90-minute session divided into 30 minutes of lecture by the group facilitator followed by 60 minutes of autobiographical texts produced by group members. The topics selected emphasized self-discovery and represented important relationships (e.g., History of My Family of Origin, History of the Family I Created, History of My Friendships, History of My Loves) and experiences (e.g., History of My Hobbies, History of My Positive Experiences, History of the People Who Most Influenced Me).

Individual Intervention

Health care providers and social workers who wish to direct individually administered autobiography writing can easily modify the group format by meeting with a client weekly and asking the client to write an autobiographical passage, which is then reviewed in the individual session. Older adults who hope to prepare an autobiography as a record for family members may benefit from a guidebook by Daniel (1985) on how to write a life story. The book is written for nonprofessional writers and features clear step-by-step instructions.

Group Intervention

According to Botella and Feixas (1992–1993), there are three important goals in guided autobiography groups. These goals are used to help group members gain an improved sense of self:

- Promotion of self-awareness, in which the group facilitator questions the self-perceptions of members during the sessions to expand their understanding of themselves
- Promotion of self-disclosure, in which the facilitator encourages members to share life experiences
- Promotion of an alternative view of the autobiography, in which the facilitator assists members in expanding their views of their experiences and their meanings

Self-Awareness

Self-awareness can be encouraged by asking participants questions that help to define the self. Botella and Feixas (1992–1993) used the personal construct technique of *laddering* to accomplish this goal. In laddering, the client is asked to describe him- or herself. Then questions are asked to determine why the individual prefers to be described by one pole of a construct instead of the other. For example, a person who describes herself as being outgoing can be asked why she prefers to be considered an outgoing person as opposed to someone who considers him- or herself introverted. The response should help her uncover insights about herself (e.g., enjoying others, being friendly, having others to rely on, giving support as well as receiving it). These statements can then be validated by group members or by the facilitator.

Self-Disclosure

Self-disclosure can be encouraged by asking group members to write a personal secret on a slip of paper (Botella & Feixas, 1992–1993). The secrets are gathered, shuffled, and anonymously presented one at a time to the group for discussion. Another strategy that can be carried out in a group setting involves the sharing of autobiographical writing on an assigned topic between two paired members. Over time, new pairs are formed between group members on a rotating basis, until all members have been paired with each other. It is important to educate group members about the need to keep confidential information presented in the sessions. Confidentiality is particularly critical when the focus of the session is on self-disclosure. The facilitator should also foster a nonjudgmental attitude and encourage empathy for the problems of others. Self-disclosure can be promoted in an individually administered autobiography by the facilitator disclosing some personal information. This information need not be sensitive material. Simply sharing personal information or experiences related to the topic being addressed is sufficient.

Awareness of Alternatives to Current Thinking

Promoting alternative viewpoints can be encouraged using strategies borrowed from personal construct theory (i.e., a therapeutic modality that focuses on how the individual defines the self and can be guided to form new insights). Existing interpretations represented in the autobiographical writing can be expanded by using the technique of *loosening*. The older adult generates alternative solutions or different interpretations. For example, a woman who complains that her husband never helps her in the kitchen can be helped to loosen this construct to "If I ask him to help when he has not started to watch TV, he may help" (Viney, 1993, p. 41). The facilitator or other group members may offer alternative interpretations. However, Botella and Feixas (1992–1993) caution that some alternative interpretations may threaten an individual's core view of self. If an older adult becomes upset by an interpretation offered by the facilitator or another member of the group, the facilitator should reframe the interpretation in a more acceptable but still meaningful format.

Role-playing can be employed to encourage alternative viewpoints. Requiring older adults to adopt different roles in a given situation may help them to understand different points of view (Botella and Feixas, 1992–1993). *Tightening* is another technique employed by personal construct theorists to encourage alternative views. When older adults propose maladaptive interpretations, they can be encouraged to focus consistently on the other pole of the construct (Viney, 1993). For example, a person who complains of being dependent on others could be refocused onto areas of independent functioning of which he or she is still capable.

Psychological and Historical Autobiography

Wacks (1989) believes that there are two types of guided autobiography: psychological and historical. Psychological autobiography emphasizes self-discovery. For example, Botella's approach would be representative of the psychological autobiography. Historical autobiography focuses on helping participants prepare memoirs with less emphasis on exploring the self. An example of historical autobiography is to have an older adult describe his or her life during the Great Depression. Historical autobiography is particularly well suited for people with a strong interest in history or who are uncomfortable disclosing highly personal information.

Oral History

Oral history is an in-depth process in which information is gathered to help participants gain a greater understanding of past events and in order for them to speculate on how those events shaped the lives, values, attitudes, and expectations of the people who lived through them (Newbern, 1992). The format employed emphasizes storytelling as a means of unearthing or verifying facts or trends. Oral history has been used primarily as a means of collecting historical information, but the therapeutic value of participating in this activity has also been recognized (Watt & Wong, 1991). An oral history can be conducted in one session or over several sessions, depending on the goals of the facilitator, and on an individual or a group basis. Health care professionals or social workers who visit older adults in their homes can combine their usual duties with oral history gathering. High school or college students can be assigned oral history projects that require that they visit older adults to collect information. Oral history tends to be a less intrusive approach to reminiscence than group therapy for example, permitting the older adult more control over the information shared. Individuals who are reluctant to share highly personal information in an oral history can simply rely on a description of events as they applied to people in general.

Oral history groups can be offered through senior centers, college or high school extension programs, adult education programs, and even libraries. The information gathered through oral history groups or projects can be written down, compiled, and made available to historical societies. These compilations can provide useful information about personal experiences. Topics for oral history projects can address a broad range of areas—everything from how people met their health care needs to what they did for fun. Participation in compiling an oral history can be a source of increased socialization and self-esteem for older adults because they are making a valuable contribution to society.

Newbern (1992) interviewed 60 older adults living independently in the southern United States about how their health care needs were met in their youth. Although Newbern did not specifically prompt for reminiscences, many of her subjects spontaneously produced them. Newbern's work, like that of many other researchers, demonstrates how oral history can be used to foster productive reminiscence.

ASSISTANCE FOR OLDER ADULTS COPING WITH PAINFUL MEMORIES DURING REMINISCENCE THERAPY

Although discussions that evoke painful memories should be avoided in reminiscence therapy, occasions will arise during which an older adult will share painful experiences. Therefore, individuals planning to implement reminiscence therapy should be prepared to deal with painful disclosures (Haight & Burnside, 1993). Preliminary preparation should focus on a private exploration of the facilitator's response to painful memories. Sample questions to prompt such an exploration follow (Lashley, 1993):

- What does the story of my life reveal to others about who I am as a person?
- What happens to me when I reflect on the painful parts of my life?
- What can I discover about others from listening to their stories?
- How can the process of reminiscence evoke painful memories?
- What impact does remembering painful events have on an individual? On a group?
- How do people cope with the pain of reflecting on their experiences?

The purpose of this exploration is to help the facilitator empathize with the individual who is recalling something painful. Individuals participating in reminiscence therapy should be monitored for markers or indicators of emotional discomfort. These indicators may include verbal statements, emotional responses (e.g., tearing up, choking up, speaking difficulty, wavering voice), and facial expressions. When a participant recounts a painful memory, other members of the group may experience discomfort as well. Signs of their discomfort are

- Lack of attentiveness
- Avoidance of eye contact with the reminiscing group member
- Nervous shifting of the body in a chair
- Closed protective body posture—arms crossed in front of chest, body faced away from group, legs crossed

An effort should be made to distinguish between responses to descriptions of painful experiences and feelings of boredom, fatigue, illness, or physical discomfort.

In dealing with painful recollections, the facilitator should listen actively to the individual experiencing the painful memory by maintaining eye contact, leaning forward in a listening posture, and not glancing at his or her wristwatch. While listening, the facilitator should prevent other group members from drawing attention away from the speaker and to themselves. The facilitator should reflect what was heard back to the speaker by repeating the information to demonstrate that it has been heard and by recognizing and commenting on the feelings underlying the painful experience. The facilitator should also provide support physically, such as a gentle pat (care should be exercised because some individuals may not wish personal contact), and verbally.

Despite the problems inherent in calling up memories of things past, there is considerable potential for positive and even exceedingly pleasurable experiences through the vehicle of reminiscence. Handled carefully, in either an individual or a group setting, reminiscence can result in, at the least, some very happy hours in an otherwise routine or even difficult day; at best, it can lead to long-term improvement in an older person's sense of connectedness, of self-worth, and of life satisfaction.

USE OF REMINISCENCE THERAPY WITH OLDER ADULTS WITH COGNITIVE IMPAIRMENT

In reminiscence therapy the focus of the work is on remote memories, which makes this form of intervention particularly suitable for individuals with dementing illnesses (Burnside, 1990) because their long-term memory is more intact than is their short-term memory. In fact, reminiscence may serve an important purpose in maintaining a sense of self in these older people (Sherman, 1991). However, it is best not to use the word "memory" frequently during reminiscence sessions with participants with dementia because they may believe their memory is being tested (Haight & Burnside, 1993).

A form of reminiscence therapy developed by Lowenthal and Marrazzo (1990) for older adults with mental illness living in a psychiatric hospital holds promise for older adults with dementia. The procedure, called *milestoning*, is designed to stimulate the retrieval of positive experiences from a period in the older persons' life before they became demented. This therapeutic intervention is highly structured and directed by a facilitator who assists the participants in retrieving positive memories. In addition, role-modelling techniques such as cueing and coaching are used to activate the appropriate words and gestures for social interaction. Lowenthal and Marrazzo report that the most effective discussions involved childhood memories. They recommend incorporating the actual poetry and music from the participants' school days. Additional strategies to evoke memories include enlarged reproductions of photographs, artwork, and printed materials. The memories discussed and shared should be positive in nature. Discussions that may lead to negative self-evaluations should be avoided. Also, cognitively impaired individuals with memory loss tend to become agitated when prodded to supply more details of events they have difficulty remembering.

REFERENCES

Andrada, P.A., & Korte, A.O. (1993). En aquellos tiempos: A reminiscing group with Hispanic elderly. *Journal of Gerontological Social Work, 20*(3/4), 25–42.

Arean, P.A., Perri, M.G., Nezu, A.M., Schein, R.L., Christopher, F., & Joseph, T.X. (1993). Comparative effects of social problem-solving therapy and reminiscence therapy as treatment for depression in older adults. *Journal of Consulting and Clinical Psychology, 61*, 1003–1010.

Birren, J.E., & Deutchman, D.E. (1991). *Guiding autobiography groups for older adults*. Baltimore: The Johns Hopkins University Press.

Birren, J.E., & Hedlund, B. (1987). Contributions of autobiography to developmental psychology. In N. Eisenberg (Ed.), *Contemporary topics in developmental psychology* (pp. 394–415). New York: John Wiley & Sons.

Blackman, J.C. (1980). Group work in the community: Experiences with reminiscence. In I.M. Burnside (Ed.), *Psychosocial nursing care of the aged* (pp. 126–144). New York: McGraw-Hill.

Botella, L. (1991). Psychoeducational groups with older adults: An integrative personal construct rationale and some guidelines. *International Journal of Personal Construct Psychology, 4*, 397–408.

Botella, L., & Feixas, G. (1992–1993). The autobiographical group: A tool for the reconstruction of past life experience with the aged. *International Journal of Aging and Human Development, 34*, 303–319.

Burnside, I. (1990). Reminiscence: An independent nursing intervention for the elderly. *Issues in Mental Health Nursing, 11,* 33–48.

Burnside, I., & Haight, B.K. (1992). Reminiscence and life review: Analyzing each concept. *Journal of Advanced Nursing, 17,* 855–862.

Cook, E.A. (1991). The effects of reminiscence on psychological measures of ego integrity in elderly nursing home residents. *Archives of Psychiatric Nursing, 5,* 292–298.

Daniel, L. (1985). *How to write your own life story: A step by step for the non-professional writer.* Chicago: Chicago Review Press.

Gropper, E.I. (1991). Reminiscence therapy as a nursing intervention. *Advancing Clinical Care, 6*(6), 26, 41.

Haight, B.K. (1988). The therapeutic role of a structured life review process in homebound elderly subjects. *Journal of Gerontology, 43,* 40–44.

Haight, B.K., & Burnside, I. (1993). Reminiscence and life review: Explaining the differences. *Archives of Psychiatric Nursing, 7,* 91–98.

Ivey, A. (1983). *Intentional interviewing and counseling.* Monterey, CA: Brooks/Cole.

Ivey, A., & Authier, J. (1978). *Microcounseling: Innovations in interviewing, counseling, psychotherapy and psychoeducation* (2nd ed.). Springfield, IL: Charles C Thomas.

Ivey, A.E., Ivey, M.B., & Simek-Downing, L. (1987). *Counseling and psychotherapy: Integrating skills, theory, and practice* (2nd ed.). Englewood Cliffs, NJ: Prentice Hall.

Kovach, C. (1991). Reminiscence: Exploring the origins, processes, and consequences. *Nursing Forum, 26*(3), 14–20.

Lashley, M.E. (1993). The painful side of reminiscence. *Geriatric Nursing, 14*(3), 138–141.

Lowenthal, R.I., & Marrazzo, R.A. (1990). Milestoning: Evoking memories for resocialization through group reminiscence. *Gerontologist, 30,* 269–272.

Melia, S.P. (1995). *Life review interviews: A manual to help students understand, conduct and analyze life review interviews with older people.* Worcester, MA: Author. (Available from Susan Perschbacher Melia, Department of Sociology, Assumption College, Worcester, MA, 01609. $5.00)

Newbern, V.B. (1992). Sharing the memories: The value of reminiscence as a research tool. *Journal of Gerontological Nursing, 18*(5), 13–18.

Oleson, M. (1989). Legacies, reminiscence, and ego-integrity. *Nurse Educator, 14*(6), 6–7.

Peachey, N.H. (1992). Helping the elderly person resolve integrity versus despair. *Perspectives in Psychiatric Care, 28*(2), 29–30.

Romaniuk, M., & Romaniuk, J. (1981). Looking back: An analysis or reminiscence functions and triggers. *Experimental Aging Research, 7,* 477–489.

Rybarczyk, B.D., & Auerbach, S.M. (1990). Reminiscence interviews as stress management interventions for older patients undergoing surgery. *Gerontologist, 30,* 522–528.

Sherman, E. (1991). *Reminiscence and the self in old age.* New York: Springer Publishing.

Stevens-Ratchford, R.G. (1993). The effect of life review reminiscence activities on depression and self-esteem in older adults. *American Journal of Occupational Therapy, 47,* 413–419.

Teri, L. (1991). Behavioral assessment and treatment of depression in older adults. In P.A. Wisocki (Ed.), *Handbook of clinical behavior therapy with the elderly client* (pp. 225–243). New York: Plenum.

Thornton, S., & Brotchie, J. (1987). Reminiscence: A critical review of the empirical literature. *British Journal of Clinical Psychology, 26,* 93–111.

Viney, L.L. (1993). *Life stories: Personal construct therapy with the elderly.* New York: John Wiley & Sons.

Wacks, V.Q. (1989). Guided autobiography with the elderly. *Journal of Applied Gerontology, 8,* 512–523.

Watt, L.M., & Wong, P.T.P. (1991). A taxonomy of reminiscence and therapeutic implications. *Journal of Gerontological Social Work, 16,* 37–57.

Youssef, F.A. (1990). The impact of group reminiscence counseling on a depressed elderly population. *Nurse Practitioner, 15*(4), 32–38.

I wandered lonely as a cloud
That floats on high o'er vales and hills,
When all at once I saw a crowd,
A host of golden daffodils . . .
William Wordsworth, "Daffodils"

Reaping What You Sow

Horticulture Therapy

When an individual enters residential care or becomes physically disabled or isolated because of the loss of a spouse or family, activities once enjoyed may not seem possible. These individuals are hindered by the passivity, dependency, and noninvolvement associated with living in a residential facility, in isolation, or both and become ideal candidates for depression (Szekais, 1985). In order to counteract the onset of depression it is important for older adults to engage in activities that are stimulating and challenging. Gardening or horticulture therapy[1] is an activity with which many older people are familiar, and it can be integrated into many different settings to provide an outlet for creative self-expression. If horticulture therapy is appropriately tailored to its older adult participants and is well supervised but not dictative, positive reactions are likely to result.

Horticulture is the art of cultivating fruit, flowers, vegetables, and other plants. Horticulture therapy is the application of horticultural activities, specifically gardening, to people with special needs in an attempt to meet those needs (Burgess, 1990). Gardening is one of the most common leisure activities in the United States, particularly among older adults (Burgess, 1990). It provides excellent opportunities for self-expression and creativity, mental stimulation, and exposure to variety and change, as well as an opportunity for physical activity. Whether practical or simply beautiful, the products of gardening are reassuring evidence of the natural cycles of life and of the interconnectedness of all living things.

Gardening can be a therapeutic experience for older people. Few of life's labors are as cathartic as the pulling of an interloping weed or as gratifying as the harvesting of homegrown vegetables or a lovely bouquet. A heightened self-awareness can result from taking time to sit back and enjoy the beauty of a lush, green garden, knowing that one has participated in its growth and development (Burgess, 1990). Gardening also provides older adults with an opportunity to care for living things, removing themselves from the "sick role" (i.e., overdependence on others because they cannot do for themselves) if only temporarily (Goodban & Goodban, 1990a). Variety and change are essential to worthwhile and interesting living, and gardening provides exposure to many different types of activities that vary with the seasons. For example, everyone looks forward to the emergence of spring blooms, the first summer fruits and vegetables, autumn pumpkins and chrysanthemums, and poinsettias, along with preparation for the coming spring. In addition, gardens and plants bloom and grow daily and the variety of plants available to cultivate is extensive (Burgess, 1990). Indoor plants or window boxes are an excellent alternative to outdoor gardening for frail, homebound older adults. Bulb plants are particularly cheering during the winter months.

Gardening has special appeal for older people of color. For example, Allison and Geiger (1993) found that older Chinese adults rated gardening as one of their

---

[1]Professionals electing to implement horticulture therapy with several individuals or to make this therapeutic intervention a primary part of their work with older adults should consider membership in the American Horticultural Therapy Association. The association publishes a newsletter that updates information about this therapeutic approach, provides information about additional sources of ideas and support, and assists in answering questions or solving problems. Their address is 362A Christopher Avenue, Gaithersburg, Maryland 20879. Phone (800) 634-1603. The membership fee is $35.00.

most frequently engaged in leisure activities. This activity was viewed as one of the ways these older people maintained their cultural identity. Several of them spoke of gardening as a chance to grow Chinese plants and vegetables and familiar flowers and fruits. The products of their gardens also enabled them to cook special meals for their families.

Horticulture therapy can also lead to activities such as arranging dried flowers, bird watching, researching/growing specialized plants, taking field trips to gardens or nurseries, flower and leaf pressing, and cooking jams and pies from the produce grown (Burgess, 1990; Goodban & Goodban, 1990a). Surplus produce and plants may be grown and sold to friends and family, nursing facility staff members, or even the public, generating an income that could be used to support or supplement the therapy program (Burgess, 1990; Goodban & Goodban, 1990a).

Use of Horticulture Therapy with Older Adults Living Independently

Mrs. Mulligan was a 79-year-old woman caring for her husband, who was exhibiting severe cognitive losses. Caregiving was taking a toll on her, and she was experiencing symptoms of anxiety. She had difficulty making decisions; choosing what to wear in the morning took hours. She was also reluctant to leave the house. Mrs. Mulligan was referred for outpatient counseling to help her cope with these signs and symptoms. During the course of counseling, Mrs. Mulligan explored her concerns over the progress of her husband's dementia and her feelings of being overwhelmed by the care he needed. For years, he had taken care of the finances and made most of the major decisions. His cognitive losses forced her to assume all of these responsibilities. Although Mrs. Mulligan had three adult sons, she did not feel comfortable asking them for help because they were involved with their own families and she did not want to burden them.

Most of the counseling sessions took place in Mrs. Mulligan's home because finding someone competent to stay with her husband was difficult. During counseling, the therapist explored past activities that had been pleasurable for Mrs. Mulligan. Several activities were mentioned, including reading and gardening. Mrs. Mulligan said that reading had become difficult. Her ability to concentrate on printed material was limited. She felt she needed to constantly see what her husband was "up to." Mrs. Mulligan told her therapist that before Mr. Mulligan developed dementia, they took walks through their vegetable garden every evening to discuss the day's events and how well the vegetables and herbs were growing. She also described how she and her husband used to pour over seed catalogs in February, picking out the vegetables and herbs to be grown that summer. Once the seeds were selected, her husband would create a detailed plan of the garden. As she described these accounts, her face lit up and the muscles in her face and hands visibly relaxed. The therapist was encouraged and explored the possibility of Mrs. Mulligan growing a garden. During the discussion, Mrs. Mulligan admitted that she missed growing fresh herbs and salad vegetables.

A small garden was planned outside her back door, off the kitchen. One of her sons brought over his rototiller and tilled the area. His wife took the Mulligans to a garden center to pick out plants. She walked with Mr. Mulligan, giving Mrs. Mulligan time to wander about and select the plants she wanted. Although her sons offered to plant the items she chose, Mrs. Mulligan decided to "put them in" herself. In the next counseling session Mrs. Mulligan described how pleasant it felt to work the soil. Mr. Mulligan sat on the back stoop while she planted, and she reported that it "felt like old times" to reminisce with him. She planted chives, thyme, basil, rosemary, lettuce, cucumbers, and two tomato plants. The fresh herbs encouraged Mrs. Mulligan to cook more elaborate meals. She also spent less time trying to decide what to make. She reported that working in the garden relaxed her and was one of the few times during the day when she forgot her troubles.

Mrs. Mulligan's family was so pleased with her interest in and enjoyment of the small garden that they bought her some chrysanthemums to plant for fall harvesting and bulbs to put in for spring flowering. Gardening did not change the course of Mr. Mulligan's dementia nor did it alleviate the many real problems that the caretaker of an older person with cognitive impairment faces. It did, however, prove to be a distraction and a source of relaxation for Mrs. Mulligan, enabling her to cope more effectively. Over the next year, her family was encouraged by the therapist to provide Mrs. Mulligan with occasional bouquets of fresh flowers, which were readily available at the supermarket, and to continue to bring her bulbs to be planted and grown indoors. These gifts provided cheerful reminders of her family's affection and concern for her.

Involvement in gardening usually begins as a means of making one's home more attractive. In many cases it becomes an intrinsically rewarding experience for older people. Some older adults may have abandoned gardening because of a prolonged period of poor health, apathy, or depression, or the responsibility of caring for an ill spouse. Others never gardened and have not experienced the joy of growing flowers, vegetables, and other plants. In either case horticultural activities can provide unexpected pleasures and benefits. Working in a garden is good exercise and the extra movement and bending involved (if properly executed) can increase the flexibility of muscles and joints. The process of growing flowers and vegetables can also lead to a greater sense of control over the environment, reducing the negative thoughts that can lead to depression.

Gardening can take many forms for older adults living independently. Gardens can vary in size from large, open areas in a backyard to small containerized gardens the size of a dutch oven. It is best to start small, expanding the project if the person wishes to do so. The older person's physical condition should be taken into consideration. Older people with pronounced impairment can benefit from gardens planted in window boxes or planters designed for use on patios. Local high schools may be willing to build a box or planter as part of their woodworking shop classes. A surprising number of items can be used as planters: One of the authors' clients used an old tire from her garage to make a raised bed for a salad garden.

In addition to improving mood and mobility, gardening can improve an older person's nutrition (Weatherly & Weatherly, 1990). Older adults who grow vegetables are more likely than those who do not to eat nutritionally balanced meals. If vegetables are grown in a person's garden, they are more likely to be eaten. A garden gives a person incentive to eat the products of his or her labor. Older adults who were raised during the 1930s and 1940s remember their parents' "victory gardens" and may grow a garden out of nostalgia for that "simpler time." People living on a fixed income can supplement it by selling their surplus produce.

Socialization with neighbors can begin or be expanded by sharing the horticultural bounty with them. Older individuals living independently who report a lack of social involvement or who do not have space available for a personal garden can become involved in a horticulture program developed by local churches or senior centers. Becoming a member of a senior garden club, which offers guidance on starting a garden and possibly nutritional information, can result in both mental and social stimulation. Local retirement or horticultural associations may be interested in funding a program or in providing raised garden beds for home use or use at a retirement center, as well as seeds, plantlets, and tools (Burgess, 1990).

Family members can be encouraged to give plants as gifts rather than the usual perfume, bath powder, candy, or knickknack. Some companies provide a plant-of-the-month or flower-of-the-month gift package (see appendix at the end of the chapter). For some older adults, monthly plants or flowers may represent a gift the recipient may otherwise never receive and give them something to look forward to. (Prepackaged kits of paperwhites and tulips often are available at garden centers and are usually half the price of those sold in catalogs or through florists.)

USE OF HORTICULTURE THERAPY WITH OLDER ADULTS LIVING IN CONGREGATE HOUSING OR LONG-TERM CARE FACILITIES

Dr. Lampher was a 74-year-old physician residing in a nursing facility. Despite cognitive impairment he had insight into his condition. On two occasions he indicated his despair over his condition to his family: "I feel like a burden" and "I wish I were dead." His cognitive impairment was diagnosed as the result of Alzheimer's disease, and he functioned at the moderate level of intellectual decline that is characterized by memory losses for current events and some aspects of personal history. His ability to travel alone, handle finances, and perform other complex tasks was impaired. Dr. Lampher was married, but his relationship with his wife had been strained for many years because of numerous extramarital affairs in which he had engaged. Although Mrs. Lampher was not willing to become his caregiver, she did visit him occasionally out of a sense of duty. His sons were both professionals who lived a considerable distance away. Consequently, he received few visitors.

Dr. Lampher was a proud man who quickly took offense at any perceived lack of respect. His pride and depression combined into considerable alienation and isolation from other residents. He did interact with facility staff, however. Because of his professional background, Dr. Lampher was given permission to visit administrative offices freely. During these visits, the director of nurses observed him tending the plants in her office. He would admonish the director for neglecting the plants and would wipe the leaves clean of dust and debris, remove dead leaves, and water the plants. The director described these events to a therapist, who had been asked to evaluate and treat Dr. Lampher for depression. The clinician approached Dr. Lampher and asked him if he would like to explore the reasons for his depression, which he agreed to do. In addition, the therapist worked with the facility social worker to implement a horticulture therapy program for Dr. Lampher, feeling that this could benefit other residents as well.

A section of the large day room was designated as the area in which the horticulture therapy would take place. Dr. Lampher was assigned the responsibility of caring for plants in the area and making the unit a more attractive, homelike place to live. A heavy-duty 5 × 8 foot rubberized mat was purchased and placed in front of a window that faced south. A notice requesting gardening materials placed at the facility entrance resulted in donations of 7 large, attractive planters; 2 plant stands; and 10 plants. A layer of small rocks was placed at the bottom of each planter (the rocks compensated for Dr. Lampher's tendency to overwater the plants), the potted plants placed on them, and the plants and stands arranged on the mat. A calendar was posted on a cork board near the plants noting when the plants were to be watered and fertilized. Dr. Lampher was asked to check off on the calendar when he completed these tasks. When staff members noticed that he had not checked off a day, he would be subtly reminded to water or fertilize. Dr. Lampher also repotted plants when necessary under the direction of one of the maintenance men, who had grown particularly close to Dr. Lampher.

The number of plants in the day room increased, and soon there were more than the area could accommodate. The social worker who met with Dr. Lampher regularly suggested that he consider preparing plants for residents who needed cheering up. He decided to start small and distributed two plants. He was so encouraged by the response to his plants and visits that the project expanded beyond the day room plant area. He contacted his wife and requested that she obtain some bulbs that he could grow indoors. On one of her infrequent visits she brought in a bulb catalog and together they selected a variety of flowers that would cheer the residents and make the unit more attractive.

When the bulbs arrived, Dr. Lampher planted them carefully and placed them in the plant area. By this time most family members were aware of his efforts, and several had contributed additional plant containers; one person brought in a large bag of soil. When the bulbs began to sprout, Dr. Lampher placed the plants on the windowsills of individual residents. Periodically, he visited the residents in order to check on the plants. In about 8 weeks the unit was full of flowers. Residents' spirits soared as they watched the plants blossom. Paperwhites and hyacinths, with their large blooms, were particularly popular.

Over the course of his therapy, Dr. Lampher's mood improved considerably. His work with the plants kept him as busy as had his medical practice. His interactions with staff continued but became less geared to seeking attention. He developed relationships with other residents, and during these interactions he was always consulted about plants—a role with which he was comfortable.

As in the vignette, in order for a horticulture therapy program to succeed there must be some interest on the part of residents and staff members of the facility must cooperate (Burgess, 1990). Depending on the location of the facility and the availability of the grounds, there are several different options from which to choose. If sufficient land is available, developing outdoor gardening plots for each participant is optimum. If the setting does not permit such an arrangement, a greenhouse can be constructed on a rooftop or connected to the existing facility. If there is an extra community room available, some seedlings may be grown indoors under fluorescent lights. An area of the unit or lobby can be set aside for plantings. Finding funding is an issue and the amount of available financing may dictate the choice of gardening site. In situations in which none of these constructs is feasible, furnishing a small window box in which residents can cultivate their favorite plants or vegetables in their room can be therapeutic.

A horticulture therapy program can be incorporated as part of the regular in-facility recreation activities. An easy activity is for residents to pot bulbs that can be grown indoors. Residents with impairment can be encouraged to pot their own bulbs, while people without impairment can be asked to assume the extra responsibility of potting bulbs for older people who are unable to participate in the activity. The individual pots could then be placed on windowsills in the residents' rooms. The advantage of bulbs is that they grow rapidly (in about 8 weeks), require little effort to plant, require almost no maintenance, and result in blooms that are usually spectacular and fragrant. One of the authors' clients, who was dying, experienced great pleasure in watching three hyacinths grow on her windowsill during February. The flowers were not only a visual and olfactory delight but provided staff and visitors with a cheerful topic to discuss. Forcing branches of forsythia, pussywillow, and flowering shrubs is another relatively simple activity, the result of which is considerable given the amount of energy expended.

Gardening is an excellent activity for older people living in congregate housing and long-term care facilities. Many of the activities provided for residents tend to have a feminine quality to them (e.g., arts and crafts, knitting, bingo). The authors' experience has been that men are particularly responsive to horticultural activities involving the actual growing of plants and vegetables. Many male participants in horticulture therapy describe how they used to grow a vegetable garden every summer.

In any situation in which a horticulture therapy program is being implemented, one should keep in mind that the competencies of each older person should be matched to the demands of the program. If a program is too large in scope and requires the completion of too many complex tasks, staff members may be left with the burden of the upkeep. However, if the program is not challenging and interesting, boredom will result (Blumenthal & Kupfer, 1990).

PRECAUTIONS TO TAKE AND ACCOMMODATIONS TO MAKE IN IMPLEMENTING HORTICULTURE THERAPY

Certain precautions must be taken before implementing a horticulture therapy program. If an outdoor gardening site is chosen, weather will be a factor. Precautions should be taken to prevent damage to plants from frost, excessive sun, and high winds. Sunlight can also be a hazard for residents taking medications that have photosensitivity-related side effects. Sun hats, long-sleeve shirts, and sunblock are necessities (Goodban & Goodban, 1990a). By planting early in the spring, the heat and extended exposure to the more direct sun of summer months may be avoided. Planning maintenance tasks to be conducted during cooler morning hours in the summer is recommended (Burgess, 1990).

Chemicals and sharp tools can be dangerous if not handled properly (Goodban & Goodban, 1990a). Retaining sufficient staff with knowledge of the necessary precautions, storing fungicides and insecticides in a safe place, and posting signs as to when the plants have been sprayed are important ways to avoid accidents (Burgess, 1990). Finding alternative methods for preventing pests and weeds that do not require dangerous chemicals, such as organic pesticides, and are environmentally friendly may be a viable option.

Horticulture therapy requires both fine and gross motor movements, utilizing muscles from all parts of the body. Although this total body workout can be beneficial to older participants, moderation is a necessity (Burgess, 1990). Participants and staff members should also be screened for allergies before implementing horticulture therapy. Staff members should know the emergency procedures for allergic reactions and bee stings (Alvarez, 1992; Burgess, 1990).

Wheelchair accessibility to the gardening site is essential to ensure that no participants are excluded. An ideal setting for horticulture therapy is an outdoor patio with ramps that are accessible by wheelchair. It is important to include a shaded area with places for sitting and taking a break, transplanting, or socializing. Portable seating ensures that participants can escape the sun in hotter months or sit in the sun's warmth during cooler months (Burgess, 1990). The greater the beauty of the area, the more residents it will lure outdoors. The patio should be designed to house soil beds of varying sizes and heights. Burgess (1990) suggests using a sawhorse on which is placed a 4- × 4-foot shallow box, built at a height at which it would be accessible to older adults in wheelchairs. In addition to these boxes, ground beds and planters can provide plentiful garden space that is accessible to many people.

Any gardening program setting should include access to a telephone (e.g., cordless, cell phone) and a first aid kit in case of emergencies. A nearby toilet and live electrical outlets are recommended (Goodban & Goodban, 1990a).

Considerable supervision is necessary in conducting horticulture therapy with older people with cognitive impairment. Although this therapeutic intervention is effective for some individuals (e.g., Smith, 1992), the authors' experience is that older adults with cognitive impairment eat plants and soil. A client in a therapy group quickly consumed an entire plant, leaves and stem, even with two staff members in attendance. Although the incident was met with laughter, the authors became cautious about the types of plants selected for the horticulture group. Caution should also be exercised as to the type of plants used to decorate special care units.

When implementing horticulture therapy in long-term care facilities, the coordinator must not violate state licensing regulations. Long-term care facilities are licensed in most states, and there are strict rules against employing residents at them. One of the authors encountered this problem when a client planted a large garden at a nursing facility and asked that the vegetables he grew be served to the other residents at mealtimes. Facility administrators were concerned about being cited for violating regulations and would not permit the vegetables to be served during regular meals. Although alternative uses were developed (e.g., a small vegetable stand with a cash box was established in front of the facility, vegetables were shared with neighbors, special cooking projects involving other residents were arranged), the authors' client was somewhat discouraged. Preventive measures, such as making the client aware of the regulation, should have been taken before the garden was planted.

Depending on the setting, special accommodations must be made and certain materials must be acquired. If the site of the garden is to be outdoors, it must be located where an ample amount of sun (at least 6 hours a day) and running water are accessible. The soil should be checked for fertility and necessary topsoil and fertilizer should be added. A storage area keeps necessary materials such as tools and equipment, seeds, plantlets, pots, planters, fertilizers, insecticides, and chemicals organized. Many of these necessary items may be obtained through donations or at a discount price from local businesses, nurseries, farmers, staff, families, and friends.

Sufficient staff, the training of whom can be mainly experiential, are also necessary for adequate safety and supervision. Advice from family and friends may be helpful. Goodban and Goodban (1990a) suggest establishing an advice and assistance hotline with local growers. Additional volunteer help, if necessary, may be acquired through local high schools, job centers, or probation services. Burgess (1990) recommends that the gardening area be highly visible to encourage participation and increase motivation to keep it looking aesthetically pleasing. Blumenthal and Kupfer (1990) warn that the size of and demands placed on individuals by the garden should be compatible with the participants' abilities, requiring only minutes of maintenance a day. The gardening program must remain a leisure activity, not become a work detail.

IMPLEMENTING HORTICULTURE THERAPY

Prior to implementing a horticulture therapy program, several criteria must be met. The following sections describe those criteria.

Establishing Feasibility

Before initiating any horticulture therapy program, it should be determined if it is feasible in the particular situation. Residents or community members should be surveyed as to whether they are interested and to what degree they feel they could be involved. Holding a meeting may be a way to determine if sufficient interest exists (Burgess, 1990). It is also necessary to survey staff members who may be affected, participating, or both. If the proposed site is a senior center, then the director of the center and other staff members should be consulted. If the proposed site is a congregate living situation or a long-term care facility, the administration, nurses, and other staff members should be included in the determination process.

Defining Goals and Objectives

Goals with clearly stated objectives should be established. These objectives may include regaining and maintaining musculoskeletal integrity, enhancing self-esteem and self-sufficiency, reducing loneliness and stress, promoting cooperation among residents and staff, and strengthening personal creativity (Catlin, Milliorn, & Milliorn, 1992). Defining the goals for the therapeutic intervention provides some direction for developing the treatment plan. For example, Weatherly and Weatherly (1990) wanted to increase socialization, improve nutrition, and increase self-worth in eight homebound older adults through horticulture therapy. Nutritional considerations influenced the type of plants to be grown. Although some flowering plants were included, emphasis was placed on growing vegetables that would stimulate interest in eating a well-balanced meal. Volunteers were directed to visit the older adults periodically and spend time with them in order to meet their need for increased socialization.

Orienting Involved Individuals

Staff and family should be informed about the horticulture therapy program and invited to contribute ideas to its development. An atmosphere of humor and a willingness to try something new and learn by making mistakes should be fostered (Goodban & Goodban, 1990b). Failure to include family members in the horticulture therapy program described by Weatherly and Weatherly (1990) led to its demise in one of the eight cases when the son-in-law of one older woman refused to mow the lawn around the planters. Reportedly, the woman was disappointed because she lived alone and looked forward to the visits from the volunteer.

Choosing a Site

In selecting an appropriate site for horticulture therapy, the physical abilities of older adult participants must be taken into consideration. Independent-living healthy older adults can cultivate a garden in an area at or near their home. Older people with some physical impairment can cultivate plants in tubs, troughs, or window boxes. Plants can also be grown on porches or inside the home.

Older adults residing in long-term care facilities have several site options from which to choose, depending on the setting of the facility and the available resources and funding. The site should be compatible with the interest expressed by the participants and the level of involvement of which they are capable. If the gardening project exceeds their capabilities, it will likely become a burden for staff members. Important features to include when selecting a site are wheelchair accessibility; storage areas for tools and supplies; access to running water, telephone, toilet, and electricity; and sufficient sunlight (if outdoors). Pathways should be at least 1 yard wide for wheelchair access (Goodban & Goodban, 1990b). Indoor settings can include a section of the unit, recreation area, or other part of the long-term care facility.

Gathering Supplies

Once a site has been selected, supplies must be assembled. Local nurseries, horticulture groups, and farmers may be willing to donate used equipment, and local businesses may be willing to offer substantial discounts. Depending on the type of garden, an assortment of hoes, rakes, spades, forks, shears, wheelbarrows, sieves, and buckets is necessary. All must be of various sizes to accommodate various physical abilities. Recyclable materials, such as plastic beverage containers, cups, and milk cartons, can be used as pots (Catlin, Milliorn, & Milliorn, 1992). Kneeling pads or wheeled seats make many gardening tasks easier and more comfortable (Goodban & Goodban, 1990b).

Seeds, plantlets, and cuttings should be collected for a range of plants. Local businesses can be approached to provide donations or discounts. Also, family members, visitors, and staff members can be asked to donate these items. A notice requesting gardening supplies placed near the entrance of an adult day center, elder housing complex, or long-term care facility can result in numerous donations, particularly if a list of specific items needed is included. Involvement in the planning stages is important for their creative self-expression. The participants should be involved as much as possible in deciding which varieties and color schemes of plants should be grown (Burgess, 1990). If space permits, individuals who want their own garden space can be given their own plot in which to grow what they please (Burgess, 1990).

Unusual planting containers should be considered. Old wooden tool boxes, watering cans, baskets, and bowls make attractive garden containers. Many of these items can be donated by family members and staff, who may find them in their attics or cellars. Once the plants are grown, some can be sold in an effort to fund other gardening projects.

Seating in the garden is also recommended (Burgess, 1990) so that gardeners can rest and other residents and visitors can enjoy the results of the gardening effort.

Selecting Plants

Plants should be selected on the basis of geographic location and their ability to provide interest and color year round. Most plants require specific climates. A local nursery can help identify plants that will grow in the area. Also, numerous books describe plants and the areas for which they are best suited (e.g., Taylor, 1987a, b, c; see also appendix at the end of the chapter). In general, evergreen shrubs and rockery plants (i.e., succulents and cacti, which grow among rocks), although easy to grow, tend to stimulate little interest and should not be considered for horticulture therapy (Goodban & Goodban, 1990b).

Flowering shrubs and bulb flowers planted the previous autumn are impressive and cheering in spring. In many areas, crocuses poke through February and March snows, and daffodils and tulips provide bright color on overcast days. During February the branches of flowering shrubs can be brought indoors and "forced." The procedure for forcing a plant is simple: Branches should be cut in 3- to 4-foot lengths and placed in a vase or container of water. Move the vase or container to a warm area, preferably in a window that receives some sun, and left there. The branches will sprout in approximately 2–3 weeks. As spring progresses, summer bedding plants and flowers, either perennials or annuals, can be planted. In autumn, chrysanthemums and sedum blossom until a hard frost, and the bright red foliage of burning bush and the berries of firethorn and holly herald the end of the season.

During winter, house plants are an excellent alternative to outdoor gardening, as are bulbs, which can be forced to provide spectacular blooms. An easy method for forcing bulbs is as follows: (Bulbs should be kept in cold storage—refrigerator, unheated basement—until planting or forcing.) Place bulbs in a shallow clay pot or pot liner, the bottom of which has been lined with small white stones or gravel. Then place the pot in a sunny window. Regular watering will produce blooms within a few days or weeks, depending on the plant. Among the popular bulbs are paperwhites, which have fragile white flowers and a distinctive aroma; tulips, which are available in a rainbow of colors; hyacinths, an aromatic flower; daffodils, harbingers of spring; and the spectacular amaryllis. The appendix at the end of the chapter lists the addresses and phone numbers of several catalog companies dealing in bulb flowers, plants, and gardening supplies.

Incorporating Related Activities

In addition to the actual planting and harvesting, many activities such as field trips to nurseries and gardens, craft projects (e.g., pressing flowers, making potpourri), and plant or fresh-cut flower sales can be incorporated into a horticulture therapy program. These activities can be organized by a committee comprising the horticulture therapy participants. Their duties would be to plan and implement the activities. This democratic operation can elevate the sense of control over their lives that older individuals often feel has been diminished by the regimentation of facility life or their physical disabilities (Burgess, 1990). The sale of some of the products can provide supplementary income for independent-living older adults or funds for additional group projects.

Other activities that can be incorporated into horticulture therapy include making hanging baskets, terrariums, bonsai, dried flowers for arranging, seasonal crafts such as wreaths and garland, seed pictures, and culinary items (jams and pies), and holding gardening contests (Burgess, 1990). "Garden" can be the theme of an endeavor in which residents work together to decorate an area of the unit or the recreation area with flowers, leaves, trees, and items such as butterflies and birds made in arts and crafts sessions (Gilmour, 1988).

Assessing and Evaluating

Conducting an assessment before and after a course of horticulture therapy is important in determining the effectiveness of the intervention. The assessment devices described in Chapters 1 and 2 may be helpful in identifying pre- and posttreatment levels of depression in participants. Ongoing monitoring of the program is also critical and can be facilitated by maintaining detailed, quantitative records (see Chapter 14 for more detailed information on record keeping and for sample forms). Monitoring the program can provide guidance to facilitators in helping participants reach the goals of the treatment plan. In many cases early improvement in depressive symptoms can be followed by a plateau, or a period in which little improvement occurs. Recognizing a plateau and making necessary adjustments can lead to further improvement. For example, if an older adult who is engaged in a solitary gardening activity shows some initial relief in symptoms but feels the activity is not resulting in continued improvement, alternatives involving a group activity or sharing the product of the activity can be explored.

Maintaining detailed, quantitative records can also provide support for expanding the program to include other older participants or in seeking funding. The exhibit on page 132 provides a sample form that can be used to monitor the effectiveness of a horticulture project. The form may be adapted for use with older adults who reside independently by substituting "staff" and "other residents" with "neighbors" and "friends."

INTERESTING VARIATIONS ON HORTICULTURE ACTIVITIES

There are many alternatives to implementing a horticulture therapy program featuring traditional gardening; several are described in the following sections.

Horticulture Therapy Progress Form

Client: _____   Date:_____

Gardening activity: ____ Individual ____ Group

Location of project: ____ Indoors ____ Outdoors ____ Combination

Description of project:

Short-term goal (e. g. , improved mood):

Long-term goal (e.g., increased socialization with staff and other residents):

Behavioral indicators
_____ Establishes eye contact _____ Initiates conversation
_____ Responds to questions _____ Speaks in single-word responses
_____ Speaks in short phrases ____ I full sentence ____ 2 to 3 sentences
_____ More than 3 consecutive sentences

Able to carry on conversation for ___ 30 seconds ___ I minute
___ 2 minutes ___ 3 minutes ___ 4 minutes ___ 5 minutes
___ More than 5 minutes

Smiles: _____ Once _____ 2 to 3X _____ 4 to 6X _____ More than 6X

Laughs: _____ Once ____ A few times _____ A great deal

Speaks more frequently with ___ staff _____ with other residents

Behavior recorded was observed by ___ respondent ___ reported by staff

Questions posed to client
Are you enjoying the gardening activity? _____ Yes _____ No
What aspects of the gardening project do you enjoy?

Are you having any problems in the gardening project?

Evaluator comments:

A Life Worth Living: Practical Strategies for Reducing Depression in Older Adults, by Pearl Mosher-Ashley and Phyllis Barrett. ©1997 Health Professions Press, Inc., Baltimore.

Hydroponic Gardening

Hydroponic gardening is a method of growing plants in mineral solutions rather than in soil. Some individuals believe that this method of gardening may be safer than traditional gardening for older individuals because no bending is involved and few tools are required that could cause injury (Alvarez, 1992). The cost of setting up a hydroponic gardening program is low. Recycled plastic, boxes, or even tires can be used to construct beds, as long as they provide excellent drainage and the beds are placed at a height that is comfortable for gardeners to work either sitting or standing. Another advantage to this type of gardening is that it can be located in virtually any sunny spot, even on rooftops. A potential drawback to a hydroponic garden is that it requires technical skill and constant care in order to correctly mix and apply specific mineral solutions to individual plant species (Alvarez, 1992).

"Midget" Vegetables

One promising avenue that has opened for gardeners is the development of midget vegetables. Although some of these vegetables are novelty items, such as the tiny pumpkins available at Halloween, others are practical for gardeners with limited space. These vegetables are well-suited to growing in window boxes, large pots, or even hanging baskets. Midget vegetables are also popular with gourmets. Varieties of midget vegetables include 'Little Ball' beets, 'Short n' Sweet' carrots, 'Little Leaguer' cabbage, 'Patio Pik' cucumber, 'Modern Midget' eggplant, 'Tom Thumb' lettuce, 'Minnesota Midget' muskmelon, 'Baby Crookneck' summer squash, and 'Small Fry' tomato. These vegetables are suited for older people who are living alone and cooking for one, such as independent-living older adults who reside in their own homes or in congregate housing as well as those with impaired mobility. Most of these vegetables can be grown in a window box or in containers. The plants pose little risk to older adults with cognitive impairment living in long-term care settings, who may eat the plants.

Volunteer-Staffed Containerized Gardening

When participation in conventional gardening is limited or terminated, many older adults can engage in containerized gardening. Weatherly and Weatherly (1990) describe an effective horticulture program designed for homebound older adults that is staffed entirely by volunteers from the Tuscaloosa (Alabama) County Extension Service. The program served eight older people who were living on low, fixed incomes. Part of the goal of the program was to improve their nutrition because often, older adults substitute less expensive canned fruits and vegetables for fresh produce. Vegetables were selected that provide vitamins A and C, often missing from older people's diets. A $500 grant from a nearby university was used to purchase the following supplies: 16 whiskey barrel planters, 8 watering cans, 8 hand cultivators, vegetable dust, fertilizer and lime, tomato cages, vegetable plants, and grow mix. A memorandum was sent to staff field nurses explaining the program and asking them to identify patients from their case loads who could benefit from the program, would enjoy growing vegetables, would be able to observe the growth process, and would be receptive to visits from volunteers. The Tuscaloosa County Extension Service provided horticulture sessions and required participants to contribute time to the community through service projects.

Gardens were planted in late April and early May. The participants could choose to plant tomatoes, sweet or hot peppers, squash, and eggplant or any combination. Several of the volunteers contributed flowering bedding plants and vegetable plants. The volunteers provided an opportunity for the participants to socialize as well as their assistance in gardening. The nurses monitored the progress of both the older adults and the vegetables. Many positive responses were reported by family members, who described how the gardens had improved the mood of their loved ones.

The program was expanded the following year despite the fact that the original funding came from a one-time grant. Donations were solicited, and, to reduce costs, the volunteers made planters of treated lumber 18 × 18 × 22 inches and 24 × 24 × 22 inches. One volunteer started the plants from seeds, and a load of topsoil was donated. Volunteers also provided fertilizer and tomato stakes as needed.

Weatherly and Weatherly (1990) suggest that a similar program can be established using volunteers from a senior citizens organization or from youth groups such the 4-H Club or a scouting organization. They also propose contacting county or state extension service offices, which have developed many resources and would help with suggestions and possibly with organization.

Living Wreaths

Although making dried flower wreaths has been a popular craft for several years, two gardeners, Beth Holland and Donna Wright, have been experimenting with wreaths made of live ivy and succulent plants (Brandsen, 1995; Crandall, 1995). The wreaths are made by wrapping moss and soil around a flat wreath form or by mounding the moss and soil in a concave form and tucking transplanted ivy and succulents from $\frac{1}{2}$- and $\frac{3}{4}$-inch pots into the moss and soil. Holland has added flowers to create living wreaths of vibrant color. Wright proposes that anyone following her simple directions can create a beautiful wreath at reasonable cost in 45 minutes or less. At least two methods can be used to create the wreaths. Instructions for the easiest-to-make wreaths are available by consulting Brandsen (1995).

Completed wreaths must be placed in an area protected from wind and direct sun. Because the plantings sit in shallow soil, they must be watered daily. Living wreaths also must be taken down every 10 days and thoroughly soaked to ensure that the soil is absorbing water. Wreaths can be survive unwatered for a few days if placed on the ground, soaked well, and left alone until daily watering can be resumed.

Dried Wreaths

Dried wreaths can be made from a variety of materials to reflect the different seasons of the year. Four types of wreath frames on which to build a wreath are available: wire, foam, straw and natural vine or branches. The materials needed are approximately six lengths of natural vine (amount and length depends on how large a wreath is desired; grapevine is readily available in autumn and is pliable), craft wire, dried flowers, artificial fruit, assorted pics, and fabric bow. To create a vine wreath (Sterbenz, 1991), start with equal lengths of natural vine. Bend one length of vine into a hoop of the desired size, overlapping and intertwining the ends. Temporarily secure the overlapping ends of the vine with craft wire. Intertwine two or three more vines around the main vine in the same way. Continue to add new lengths of vine and weave the loose ends into the main vine until the wreath is the desired thickness. Remove the wire.

Vine wreaths can be decorated with dried flowers or items purchased from local craft stores and florists. For example, several strands of eucalyptus can be poked between the vines at the top center of the wreath and wired or hot-glued in place. Artificial grapes can be drooped down from the top of the wreath and secured with wire. A soft bow can be added to the top. Decorative material such as dried flowers or herbs can be used to cover the foam or straw frames, which can be purchased at craft shops. Wire frames can also be purchased, or, in the case of the Christmas wreath, can be made by hand. Instructions for making a Christmas wreath follow.

The materials needed are three wire clothes hangers, metal cutters, craft wire, fishing line, evergreen bunches or boughs, pine cones, plastic berry pics, a fabric bow, and a small bell. Make a ring using three wire clothes hangers. Use metal cutters to cut the top hook and its stem off each hanger. Take one length of hanger wire and form a ring of the desired size by twisting the two ends. Twist the excess wire around the sides of the circle. Using the second and third lengths of hanger wire, lay one length of wire over the other, twisting it around the ring. The twists provide sturdiness and prevent the evergreen material from sliding down the ring. Form a hook from which to hang the wreath by looping craft wire through the top twist.

Take small bunches of evergreen material (princess pine or tree boughs) and attach them to the ring with fishing line or craft wire. Each successive bunch of material should overlap the previous one so that the section attached is not visible. Turn the ring over after adding each bunch of material so that the front and back are completed together as you work around the frame. When all of the evergreen material has been added to the ring, use scissors to trim the irregular bits.

Decorate the wreaths with pine cones and plastic berries, attaching them with fishing line or craft wire. Place a bow at the top center of the wreath. A small bell hanging from the bow is an optional touch.

Herbs

Herbs are undemanding plants, easy to grow, and require only occasional watering (Boxer & Back, 1988). These hardy plants can be used in a variety of ways: in fresh herb baskets or dried arrangements, in cooking, and in potpourri. Herbs can be grown outdoors or indoors. Most herbs need a considerable amount of sun during the growing season—about 7 hours a day. Plants requiring partial shade need up to 4 hours of sun a day. Herbs should be grown in an area protected from cold winds. Outdoors, herbs can be grown in a small garden, in raised beds, or in containers; indoors, herbs can be grown in window boxes. Raised window boxes placed around a patio or outdoor sitting area is an effective strategy for older adults in wheelchairs. Growing herbs indoors requires treatment different from that for outdoor growth, but most of the herbs that can be grown successfully in containers outdoors also grow well indoors. Pots containing herbs should be placed on trays or in saucers of gravel to allow for drainage of excess water and to provide humidity around the plants (Boxer & Back, 1988).

The selection of herbs to grow depends on the intended use (e.g., cooking, decoration). Herbs can be grown from seeds, cuttings, or small plants, most of which can be obtained at modest cost at any garden center. The appendix at the end of the chapter provides a list of herb suppliers, if transportation is a problem for an interested older adult.

Herb Baskets

Herbs can be grown for decorative purposes or for use in cooking. Hanging baskets of three or four herbs hung by wires from ceiling hooks or brackets attached to the wall can be attractive and useful. Once established, marjoram, thyme, and sage trail downward. Kitchen baskets should feature individual pots of herbs commonly used for cooking, including tarragon, thyme, chives, dill, salad burnet, and summer and winter savories, which are attractive and aromatic (Boxer & Back, 1988).

Dried Herb Arrangements

Dried herbs are aromatic and attractive and can be combined with dried flowers and displayed in baskets, wreaths, and garlands. Herbs should be picked when dry, after the dew has dried but before the heat of the sun has fallen on them, and just before they flower, when buds have begun to form but before they actually open (Boxer & Back, 1988). The flavor of an herb lies in its leaves, but once the plant produces seeds, much of its flavor is lost. The tips of the branches should be picked along with about 7–8 inches of stem. Instructions for drying herbs and flowers follow.

Herbs should be dried either by tying the stems together into small bunches that allow air to pass through or by placing individual stalks in a single layer on racks or trays. The racks are covered with a sheet of cheesecloth and placed in a warm, airy location. Herbs should not be placed in the sun to dry or they will burn (Boxer & Back, 1988).

For best results, flowers should be dried in the same manner described for herbs. Dried flowers can also be removed from floral arrangements received as a gift or solicited from family and friends when their gardens are in full bloom. The fresh-cut blooms can be left in place until they dry. The water must be removed early in the process.

Dried herbs can be displayed in a variety of containers. Baskets tend to be the most popular, although interesting and decorative effects can be achieved using crockery, tin containers, and other items commonly found in attics, flea markets, and thrift shops, and left over from holidays. It is best to begin with easily accomplished tasks, such as arrangements in baskets or containers, before progressing to the somewhat more complex but still easy-to-make wreaths and garlands.

An herbal basket or container arrangement can be made by placing a block of florist's foam into the basket or container. The block should be cut and shaped so that its surface is slightly higher than the container's rim. After the corners have been rounded off, the block should be secured in place by stringing a wire over it or gluing it in place using a hot glue gun. Small flowers and leaves should be used as the base by sticking stems into the foam block around the sides, with a few on top. Height and texture can be achieved with larger seed heads and flowers. Artemesia, thyme, lavender, and melilot are easy herbs to grow and dry. Other interesting herbs are teasel, alexanders, yarrow, red bergamot, and fennel (Bremness, 1988). Garlands can also be made with dried herbs and dried flowers. The procedure for creating a garland follows (Bremness, 1988).

The materials needed are fine reel wire, scissors, string, and assorted dried herbs and flowers. Cut the string to a desired length of one swag. Knot a loop at one end. Take a length of fine reel wire and attach one end to the string loop by wrapping it around a few times.

Gather a small bunch of herbs and flowers and lay it on the string to hide the loop. Bind in place with wire. Turn the arrangement so that the first bunch lies under the string. Position a second bunch so that it overlaps the stems of the first bunch and covers the string loop. Bind the second bunch in place by wrapping over the wire, always pulling it tight from underneath after each turn.

Continue to turn the arrangement and secure bunches, always covering the string and the stems of the bunch above. This procedure should be followed until the end of the string is reached.

Connect swags to the desired length and effect, adding a ribbon or other decorative touch to the finished garland.

Pressed Flowers

Pressed flowers can be used to decorate everything from bookmarks to placemats, candlesticks to notions boxes, as well as notecards and pictures for framing and displaying. The pressing can be done in any season, and many plant materials, including petals, stems, and leaves, are suitable. Regardless of the object being made, the materials and technique are standard. Materials include blotting paper; dry, clean newsprint; artists' card (i.e., acid-free matte board, which can be purchased at artists' supply stores or frame shops); adhesive (Elmer's or multipurpose glue, or a hot glue gun, but the person using the gun must work quickly); small watercolor brushes; sharp scissors; tweezers; a razor blade; toothpicks; and a nail file. The process includes choosing flowers and leaves that will retain their color fairly well and complement each other, pressing them to remove moisture, cutting so that all flower materials lie flat, arranging, mounting, and, when applicable, framing the finished product. Patience is also required because the project must be placed under heavyweight objects, such as a pile of books, or in a flower press for about 10 days before it can be completed (*The Beautiful Naturecraft Book*, 1979).

Potpourri

Potpourri is an aromatic mixture of flowers, leaves, fruit peels, nut husks, and other objects. The dry method of mixing flowers and leaves is the most popular because it is easier than the wet method and the colorful result can be displayed in bowls or potpourri balls and used in sachets and pillows (Bremness, 1988). The basic ingredients can be organized into four categories: flowers for scent, color, or both; aromatic leaves; spices and peels; and fixatives to preserve the scents of the blend. Fixatives (e.g., orris root, gum benzoin) are used to absorb and hold the other scents so they will last longer and are available in powder form. Orris root is a vegetable fixative with a violet fragrance that does not affect a blend strongly. Gum benzoin has a sweet vanilla fragrance (Bremness, 1988). Many herbs are available as essential oils, which can substitute for herbs that may be expensive or difficult to locate, as well as rejuvenate mixtures that have lost their scent. These oils must be used cautiously to avoid dominating subtler scents. The act of creating the mixture, in which one concentrates on scent and color, provides as much pleasure as does the finished product. As older adults become familiar with herbs and flowers and their seasons, leaves and blossoms can be stored and a catalog of aromatic ingredients for potpourri built up. When blending potpourri, ingredients are selected on the basis of a recipe (Boxer & Back, 1988).

The materials needed are dried rose petals; lemon verbena; lemon thyme; lavender flowers; rind of one orange and one lemon, finely grated; orris root and gum benzoin; container with lid for potpourri; and essential oils (optional). Add four parts of dried rose petals to one part each of lemon verbena, lemon thyme, and lavender flowers. Combine gently by hand. Mix in the finely grated rind of an orange and a lemon. Cover the container and leave for 2 days.

Add $\frac{1}{2}$ ounce each of the fixatives orris root and gum benzoin to 20 pints of petals, flowers, and leaves. Stir the potpourri every day for 1 week; then seal and store in a warm, dark, dry location for 6 weeks to cure. After curing, place in open glass or china bowls (a lid will prolong the scent). The container can be left open for a few hours a day. Essential oils can be applied a drop at a time, stirring the potpourri between each drop.

Potpourri can be used to scent rooms or clothing. The latter can be accomplished by making small sachets. Sachets can be made by taking two squares of fabric of approximately 2–3 square inches, sewing them together on three sides, stuffing the fabric with potpourri, sewing closed the open side, and adding lace or other trim around the edges.

Terrariums and Bottle Gardens

Terrariums and bottle gardens may be an option for older adults who were avid gardeners but who are now frail and experience mobility problems. These self-contained gardens are advantageous in that they require little maintenance once they have been planted (Hessayon, 1986). Several varieties of plants are recommended for these environments. The most common include *Hypoestes phyllostachya*, *Dracaena sanderiana* (palm), *Hedera* (ivy; miniatures), *Saintpaulia* (African violet; miniatures), and *Maranta leuconeura* (maranta).

Before planting, clean the terrarium thoroughly with a solution of 1 teaspoon of bleach to 1 quart of water to avoid contamination with algae and fungal diseases, which thrive in enclosed, humid environments (Goold-Adams, 1993). A 1- to 2-inch layer of drainage material (e.g., turface, gravel, pebbles) should be added, along with horticultural charcoal to absorb any gaseous by-products and maintain the freshness of the soil mix. Add 1 inch of moist potting mix. Young plants with root systems that are sufficiently small to establish easily in shallow soil mix should be used. Soak the plants thoroughly before planting, and remove dead foliage that might encourage rot. Insert the plants into the soil mix, allowing space for them to spread. Cover bare areas with moss or pebbles to prevent the soil mix from drying out. Water lightly before replacing the lid. If excess condensation appears on the glass, leave the lid off until there is only a slight misting of the glass in the morning.

A bottle garden is similar to a terrarium but uses smaller plants. Any clean clear or slightly colored glass bottle can be used (Goold-Adams, 1993). If the neck is too narrow to insert plants by hand, a dessert fork or teaspoon can be used. Pour the drainage material into the bottle with the aid of a funnel. Cover the material with moist potting mix. Begin planting at the sides of the bottle and work toward the center. Carefully lower each plant into a hole using tongs or tweezers or a length of wire twisted into a noose. Space the plants at least $1\frac{1}{4}$ inches apart to allow for growth. The roots should then be covered with soil mix and tamped down gently. A cupful of water should be trickled down the sides of the bottle to dampen the soil mix and bare areas covered with sphagnum moss to keep the mix moist. Clean the inside of the glass with a sponge fixed to a length of stake or stiff wire. If the garden is not sealed after planting, it should be watered occasionally. Be careful not to overwater.

REFERENCES

Allison, M.T., & Geiger, C.W. (1993). Nature of leisure activities among the Chinese-American elderly. *Leisure Sciences, 15,* 309–319.

Alvarez, E.A. (1992, June). A hydroponic garden in the Hospicio San Vicente de Paul: A productive aging project. *Ageing International,* pp. 22–24.

The beautiful naturecraft book. (1979). New York: Sterling Publishing.

Blumenthal, S.J., & Kupfer, D.G. (1990). *Suicide over the life cycle: Risk factors, assessment, and treatment of suicidal patients.* Washington, DC: American Psychiatric Press.

Boxer, A., & Back, P. (1988). *The herb book* (2nd ed.). New York: W.H. Smith Publishers.

Brandsen, L. (1995, Summer). Living wreaths. *Country Gardens,* pp. 103–106. (A copy of the magazine can be obtained by writing to Country Gardens Back Issues, 1716 Locust Street, Des Moines, IA 50309-3515. The issue must be specified and a prepayment of $4.95 should be sent with the request.)

Bremness, L. (1988). *The complete book of herbs: A practical guide to growing and using herbs.* London: Penguin Books.

Burgess, C.W. (1990). Horticulture and its application to the institutionalized elderly. *Activities, Adaptation & Aging, 14*(3), 51–61.

Catlin, P.A., Milliorn, A.B., & Milliorn, M.R. (1992, July). Horticulture therapy promotes 'wellness,' autonomy in residents. *Provider, 18,* 40.

Crandall, C. (1995, Summer). A living wreath. *Woman's Day, 5,* 62–65.

Gilmour, J. (1988, January). Gardening with Grant. *New Zealand Nursing Journal, 81,* 29–30.

Goodban, A., & Goodban, D. (1990a). Horticulture therapy: A growing concern. I. *British Journal of Occupational Therapy, 53,* 425–431.

Goodban, A., & Goodban, D. (1990b). Horticulture therapy: A growing concern. II. *British Journal of Occupational Therapy, 53,* 468–470.

Goold-Adams, D. (1993). The indoor garden. In C. Brickell (Ed.), *Encyclopedia of gardening* (pp. 426–457). London: Dorling-Kindersley Limited.

Hessayon, D.G. (1986). *The armchair book of gardening.* London: Century.

Smith, V. (1992, April 1). Flowering potential. *Nursing Times, 88,* 48.

Sterbenz, C.E. (1991). *Wreaths.* New York: Dorset Press.

Szekais, B. (1985). Using the milieu: Treatment-environment consistency. *Gerontologist, 25,* 15–18.

Taylor, N. (1987a). *Taylor's guide to bulbs.* Boston: Houghton Mifflin.

Taylor, N. (1987b). *Taylor's guide to shrubs.* Boston: Houghton Mifflin.

Taylor, N. (1987c). *Taylor's guide to perennials.* Boston: Houghton Mifflin.

Weatherly, L., & Weatherly, K. (1990, September). Containerized vegetable gardening for homebound patients. *Caring,* pp. 52–54.

Appendix
Horticulture Materials/Information

Bulbs

Breck's
U.S. Reservation Center
6523 North Galena Road
Peoria, Illinois 61632
Phone (800) 722-9069
Fax (309) 691-9693

Burpee
W. Atlee Burpee & Co.
Warminster, Pennsylvania 18974
Phone (800) 888-1447
Fax (800) 487-5530

Michigan Bulb Company
1950 Waldorf, NW
Grand Rapids, Michigan 49550
Phone (616) 771-9500
Free catalogs are available from all of the companies, which offer reasonably priced bulbs and plants; sales are frequently available on all bulbs purchased during the spring or summer months; bulbs are shipped in the fall; some can be placed in cold storage (e.g., home refrigerator) for winter projects

Plants, Shrubs, and Trees

Alpine Garden Society
AGS Centre
Avon Bank
Pershore, Worcestershire, WRPIN3JP, England

American Horticultural Society
7931 East Boulevard Drive
Alexandria, Virginia 22308
Membership is $35.00 a year; extensive catalog; offers free seeds to members

American Rock Garden Society
Post Office Box 67
Millwood, New York 10546
The American Rock Garden Society offers seeds for 6,500 different plants, some of which are rare; the seed lists are sent out each December; membership in the society is $25.00, and local meetings are offered

Brooklyn Botanic Garden
1000 Washington Avenue
Brooklyn, New York 11225
The Brooklyn Botanic Garden's Signature Seed program is available to members who join for $50.00; seeds are offered in the autumn and winter

Burpee
W. Atlee Burpee & Co.
Warminster, Pennsylvania 18974
Phone (800) 888-1447
Fax (800) 487-5530

Cook's Garden
Phone (800) 457-9703
Offers a line of seeds called "The New American Kitchen Garden"

Ferry-Morse Seeds
Phone (800) 283-3400

Johnny's Seeds
Phone (207) 437-4395

Meyer's Seed Company
Phone (410) 342-4224

New England Wildflower Society
Garden in the Woods
180 Hemenway Road
Framingham, Massachusetts 01701
Membership is $35.00 a year for individuals, $45.00 for families; members receive a free catalog and a 40% discount on seed orders; nonmembers can send a check for $2.50 to the address above; offered more than 200 species of plants in their 1997 catalog; their 45-acre living collection is open to visitors

Ronninger's Seed Potatoes
Post Office Box 1838
Orting, Washington 98360

Seeds of Change
Phone (505) 438-8080

Shepherd's Garden Seeds
Phone (806) 482-3638

Southern Exposure Seed Exchange
Phone (804) 973-4703

Spring Hill
110 West Elm Street
Tipp City, Ohio 45371
Phone (800) 582-8527
Fax (309) 689-3817

Thompson & Morgan
Phone (800) 274-7333

Tomato Growers' Supply
Phone (914) 768-1119

Thomas Jefferson Center for Historic Plants
Twinleaf '97 Orders
Post Office Box 318
Charlottesville, Virginia 22902
The Thomas Jefferson Center for Historic Plants has an interesting seed list, which includes flowers and plants that Jefferson himself grew in his extensive gardens at Monticello

Herb Suppliers

Caprilands Herb Farm
Silver Street
Coventry, Connecticut 06238
Phone (860) 742-7244

Garden Solutions
617 Garden Terrace
Holland, Michigan 49422-9030
Phone (616) 771-9540

Hilltop Herb Farm
Box 1734
Cleveland, Texas 77327
Phone (281) 592-5859

Merry Gardens
Camden, Maine 04843
Phone (207) 236-9064

Nichols Garden Nursery
1190 North Pacific Highway
Albany, Oregon 93721
Phone (541) 928-9280

Rosemary House
120 South Market Street
Mechanicsburg, Pennsylvania 17055
Phone (717) 697-5111

Well Sweep Herb Farm
Mount Bethel Road
Port Murray, New Jersey 07965
Phone (908) 852-5390

Midget Vegetables

Thompson & Morgan, Inc.
Post Office Box 1308
Jackson, New Jersey 08527-0308
Phone (903) 363-2225
Free catalog available

Florists

Calyx & Corolla
1550 Bryant Street
Suite 900
San Francisco, California 94103
Phone (800) 800-7788
Free seasonal catalog that features
long-lasting fresh flowers, dried
arrangements, herb baskets, and prepotted bulb kits; provides one-time de-
liveries or 3, 6, or 12 months' worth
of flowers

White Flower Farm
Litchfield, Connecticut 06759-0050
Phone (800) 822-9600
Free catalog; specializes in a variety
of prepotted bulbs for forcing, indoor
seed gardens, wreaths, potted herbs,
and hanging baskets

Harry & David
Bear Creek Corporation
2578 South Pacific Highway
Medford, Oregon 97501
Phone (800) 547-3033
Primarily a supplier of high-quality fruit, Harry & David also carries various
flowers (a flower-of-the-month club is available) and plants

Garden Supplies

Gardener's Eden
Post Office Box 7307
San Francisco, California 94120-7307
Phone (800) 822-1214
Free catalog that features upscale garden equipment, decorative items, and some
plants and bulb kits

Smith & Hawken
Two Arbor Lane, Box 6900
Florence, Kentucky 41022-6900
Phone (800) 776-3336
Smith & Hawken offers a beautifully illustrated catalog of tools; plants and flowers (including bulbs); wreaths; goods such as commercial-grade greenhouses, grow lights, and birdbaths; clothing, and furniture

General Information

Garden Catalog Guide
Mail Order Gardening Association
Post Office Box 2129
Columbia, Maryland 21045
Offers a complete listing of more than 100 gardening catalogs for $2.00

HGTV (House & Garden Television network)
A cable channel devoted to issues surrounding home and garden. Numerous gardening programs, including "The Victory Garden," are broadcast and are usually repeated during the week. Check local listings for channel and times.

Bibliography for Creating a Garden

Better Homes & Gardens complete guide to gardening. (1979). Des Moines, IA: Meredith Corporation.

Burpee complete gardener. (1995). New York: Macmillan.

Bush-Brown, L., & Bush-Brown, J. (1996). *America's garden book*. New York: Macmillan (in print since 1939).

Landscape Contractors Association Consumer Service Guide. Rockville, MD: Author. (The guide is available free from the LCA at 15245 Shady Grove Road, Suite 130, Rockville, Maryland 20850. Phone (301) 948-0810, Fax (301) 990-9771, e-mail lca@mgmtsol.com.)

MacCaskey, M. (1997). *Gardening for dummies*. Foster City, CA: IDG Books Worldwide.

Oehme, W. (1995). *Gardening with water*. New York: Random House.

Oehme, W., & Van Sweden, J. (1996). *Process architecture: New world landscapes*. New York: Process Architecture, Ltd.

Reader's Digest illustrated guide to gardening. (1978). Pleasantville, NY: Author.

Stewart, M. (1996). *Martha Stewart's great American wreaths*. New York: Clarkson Potter Publishers.

Stewart, M. (1993). *Martha Stewart's holidays*. New York: Clarkson Potter Publishers.

Stewart, M. (1991). *Martha Stewart's gardening month by month*. New York: Clarkson Potter Publishers.

Wilson, J., Thomson, B., & Wirth, T. (1990). *The Victory Garden: The essential companion*. New York: Black Dog & Leventhal.

I think I could turn and live awhile with the
animals. . . they are so placid and self-contained . . .
Walt Whitman, "Song of Myself"

Man's Best Friend

Animal-Assisted Therapy

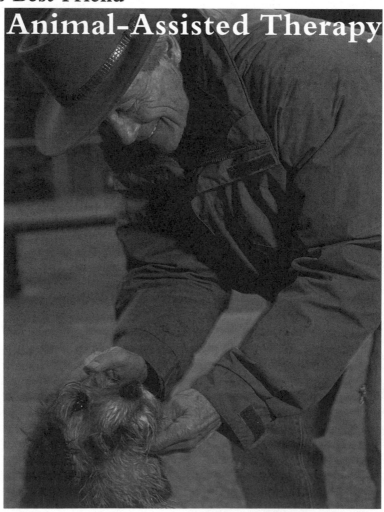

Feelings of depression in older adults frequently result from enforced isolation and loneliness. Whether older people live independently or in long-term care, these feelings are in part a symptom of the losses that accompany normal aging. Loneliness stems primarily from a person's awareness that he or she is isolated from other caring people (Kehoe, 1991) and has been reported by many older adults (Mosher-Ashley, 1994). One therapy that has had a surprisingly restorative effect on depressed and lonely older people is animal-assisted therapy.

My (Mosher-Ashley) own first experience with animal-assisted therapy occurred while preparing to be married and giving away my collection of stuffed animals. My mother gave my 4-foot-tall stuffed St. Bernard to a newly widowed uncle. I believe he took the toy in order not to hurt my mother's feelings. Several weeks later, he confided to her that he found the stuffed animal to be a comfort and, embarrassed, described how he would find himself talking to it. I remember thinking that if a stuffed animal could produce such an effect, how much more valuable a live pet might be.

Pets have a boundless capacity for acceptance, adoration, attention, forgiveness, and unconditional love (Bustad & Hines, 1983). They may serve as love objects to whom unlimited affection may be given without the fear of desertion or lack of reciprocation (Levinson, 1972). In interventions with older adults, however, one must keep in mind that pets are not a replacement for contact with other people; priority should be placed on providing human supports (Goldmeier, 1986). Pets are not a solution to the thought patterns that result in depression. If the structure of the emotional defenses of a lonely person is such that other people, including health care professionals, are routinely rejected, then attempting to foster a relationship with a nonthreatening pet may help to relieve some symptoms of depression (Goldmeier, 1986). For example, Winkler, Fairnie, Gericevich, and Long (1989) described how, in a long-term care facility, one woman with clinical depression and another with cognitive impairment who was isolated from other residents were able to form strong attachments to a resident dog, an attachment that considerably improved their daily functioning.

The beneficial effects of pets on human health are demonstrable (Schellenberg, 1993). Simply watching or petting and talking with an animal can lower blood pressure and heart rate. Interacting with animals can also reduce mental distress by reducing anxiety levels. Pet owners make fewer visits to their physicians than do people without animal companions. Pets also tend to serve as a "stress buffer" during difficult periods, such as coping with illness or the death of a loved one. Because of the healthful effects of pets on their owners, the use of animals to remediate physical or psychological problems has been explored. One of the earliest investigators was Boris Levinson, who in 1969 used a dog in psychotherapy sessions with children. Levinson's work and that of others (e.g., Brickel, 1980–1981; Lawton, Moss, & Moles, 1984) was subsequently expanded in the 1970s and 1980s by researcher Alan Beck (head of the Center for Applied Ethology and Human–Animal Interaction at the Purdue University School of Veterinary Medicine, Indianapolis, Indiana), and psychiatrist Aaron Katcher (Schellenberg, 1993). Their work, along with that of numerous others, led to the development and formal recognition of animal–assisted therapy as an applied science and therapeutic intervention (Culliton, 1987). Animal–assisted therapy differs from simply owning a pet or using a pet as entertainment in that it involves assessments and evaluation procedures (Gammonley & Yates, 1991). This form of intervention has been implemented by a range of professionals working with older adults, including nurses (Harris, Rinehart, & Gerstman, 1993), occupational therapists (Taylor, Maser, Yee, & Gonzalez, 1993), activity directors (Savishinsky, 1992), and speech–language pathologists (Smith, 1995).

Five forms of animal–assisted therapy have been proposed (Nebbe, 1988, unpublished data cited in Gammonley & Yates, 1991). Each type is defined by the manner in which the therapy is presented and the effect the treatment exerts on the individual. The forms and their benefits are as follows:

Functional—The primary focus of this form is responsibility. An animal's care is assigned to a specific individual. Exerting control over the animal's well-being results in increases self-esteem, self-confidence, or mobility.

Relationship—The primary focus of this form is the affective component of the intervention. Opportunities are provided for close interaction between the individual and the animal. This interaction results in the possibility of free expression of affection and sensory stimulation.

Passive—The primary focus of this form is relaxation. Animals are introduced for their ability to entertain. The experience results in enjoyment, stimulation, relaxation, and, when conducted within a group format, increased social interaction.

Cognitive—The primary focus of this form is increased knowledge of the animal. Animals are introduced in an effort to stimulate and expand knowledge, which leads to increased self-respect and feelings of increased control over the environment.

Spiritual—The primary focus of this form is developing a sense of oneness with life and creation. Introduction of an animal is designed to stimulate memories of past experiences with pets or interactions with animals in nature.

For older people living independently, a pet can provide opportunities for meeting new friends; for example, walking a dog can provide a ready introduction to people, and casual conversation about pets may kindle new interests. These new interests may provide the depressed older person with a reason for living (Levinson, 1972). In addition, maintaining the health of a pet requires interaction (e.g., feeding, exercising, proper grooming). The desire to care for the pet's needs may stimulate or facilitate otherwise neglected self-care (Levinson, 1972). Women more than men report associating pets with uplifted emotions, freedom, and positive use of leisure time (Miller, Staats, & Partlo, 1992).

For older adults living in congregate housing, a pet may ease the emotional transition from a home in which the individual may have lived for many years and even shared with loved ones to a place where everyone is a stranger. A pet may also serve as a means of becoming acquainted with neighbors and may provide the older person with a structured activity in which to engage.

For older people living in long-term care settings, animal–assisted therapy can supplement the recreational and occupational activities normally provided.

Although these activities are extremely worthwhile and beneficial to residents, they do not resolve the basic dilemma of nursing facility life: the tremendous psychological need for unlimited affection, constant companionship, and opportunities to do something for other people (Levinson, 1972). Pets can help to meet the dependency needs and increase the responsiveness of depressed older adults (Brickel, 1985). Also, pets can confer a sense of normalcy and promote the involvement of community members in long-term care facilities (Haughie, Milne, & Elliott, 1992). An animal's need to be fed, groomed, exercised, and nurtured, even its need for a daily schedule, can remind people of the comfortable routines of independent living. Caring for an animal can also provide a sense of being needed, of having responsibility for a life other than their own, and of being grounded in the realities of time and place.

Animal-assisted therapy can be provided effectively for depressed older individuals living independently, in congregate living situations, and in long-term care facilities. Although the therapeutic needs of these individuals are somewhat similar, there are significant differences, warranting different methods of organization and implementation of an animal-assisted therapy program.

At its best, animal-assisted therapy can help a person cope with some of life's greatest hurdles. A friend of one of the authors' became extremely attached to an emaciated stray cat that he named Abby. During the last year of the friend's life, Abby was a constant source of comfort. He often described the feeling of closeness he experienced each night when Abby curled up near his pillow. As he prepared himself for death from cancer, he told everyone of his wish to be cremated and, once Abby died, for her ashes to be mingled with his and scattered over the land he loved. It should be noted that the friend had a loving family and many friends who visited him frequently. Abby, however, shared his everyday existence, and his feeling of companionship with her was special. When people die, they usually hope to leave behind family and friends who will remember them. The author's friend wanted Abby to continue to share his existence in whatever form it would take.

Use of Animal-Assisted Therapy with Older Adults Living Independently

Mrs. Gallano had been widowed for 4 months. One afternoon a neighbor informed her over tea that she had decided to move into a nursing facility because she was losing her vision. The neighbor described her concern over what would happen to her dog, Daisy, a Pekingese. In what she later described as a generous but rash and impulsive move, Mrs. Gallano offered to take Daisy. Although Mrs. Gallano immediately regretted making the offer, the visible relief on her neighbor's face prevented her from retracting it. The next several weeks were anxious ones as Mrs. Gallano fretted over how she would care for Daisy. Numerous issues came to mind: Where would Daisy sleep? How could she afford to feed her? How often would she need to see a veterinarian? How much would that cost? How would they get there? Mrs. Gallano chastised herself constantly for her impulsiveness. During that time Daisy came for several visits. Mrs. Gallano's misgivings increased as she watched Daisy roam about the parlor between the legs of fragile, Chippendale pie-crust tables laden with treasured porcelain figurines and photographs.

The fateful day arrived, and after a tearful parting with her former owner, Daisy moved in. Almost immediately, Daisy appeared to take over the apartment, jumping onto Mrs. Gallano's favorite chair and making herself comfortable. The resentment Mrs. Gallano felt over Daisy's presumptiveness began to fade that night when she awoke to find Daisy's warm little body sleeping beside her in bed. Daisy's presence in the bed unleashed strong memories of Mr. Gallano. For the first time, his memory brought a sense of comfort rather than the usual sense of insurmountable loss. Mrs. Gallano softly stroked Daisy, who awoke and began to lick her fingers. Over the following days, the relationship between Mrs. Gallano and Daisy grew. Mrs. Gallano found herself chatting to Daisy as she did household chores and watched the local news. Daisy's interest in and play with the toys Mrs. Gallano purchased at the supermarket provided an endless source of entertainment. Everyday activities became intertwined with Daisy, who listened patiently to commentaries on the weather and the benefits of a new skin lotion or dish detergent. Daisy changed Mrs. Gallano's life in other ways as well. When Daisy had a small accident near the front door, Mrs. Gallano realized she needed to take the dog for walks more often, which led to chats with other neighbors, who stopped to admire the dog. Mrs. Gallano and Daisy became a staple of the neighborhood, as they took their late afternoon constitutional together. One of the neighbors they met offered to take Daisy and her mistress to the nursing facility to visit Daisy's former owner. Periodic phone calls enabled the two women to keep in touch and discuss Daisy's needs and progress.

Regrettably, Daisy died 2 years after moving in with Mrs. Gallano. This loss was extremely difficult for Mrs. Gallano, who reported that Daisy's death was even more difficult to bear than the loss of her husband. Because Mr. Gallano was still working at the time of his death, there were numerous activities Mrs. Gallano engaged in that did not immediately bring him to mind. The compounded effect of the two losses, coupled with the manner in which Daisy had become part of her everyday experiences, made this loss even more painful. All activities in the small apartment were now reminders of Daisy.

Six weeks later, Mrs. Gallano's neighbors combined their resources to purchase a Pekingese puppy for Mrs. Gallano. The neighbor who had given Mrs. Gallano and Daisy a ride to the nursing facility obtained an agreement with the local pet store that the puppy could be returned in 3 weeks if Mrs. Gallano found the new dog too burdensome. Luckily, Mrs. Gallano and Iris are doing well, and Mrs. Gallano is happily complaining about the energy needed to raise a puppy.

Most older adults live independently outside of residential care facilities. For many of these individuals, loss of significant loved ones and physical or mental health, in addition to increased dependence on others, may precipitate depression. Women living alone are particularly vulnerable to feelings of isolation, as are older adults who do not have children or who live alternative lifestyles, such as homosexuals (Kehoe, 1991). An animal companion may provide comfort to the bereaved, companionship to the lonely and isolated, and may help to prevent complete social isolation (Struckus, 1991). Pets also demand attention from older people, instilling a sense of responsibility and purpose: They can take care of something rather than be taken care of, while reaping the benefits of appreciation that the pet reciprocates (Brickel, 1985). Although caring for pets can incur considerable cost for older adults on a limited budget and add responsibilities that can feel burdensome, Miller, Staats, and Partlo (1992) found among a group of 250 pet owners (50–90 years old) that pets provided more uplifts than problems.

The options for interaction between animals and older adults who live independently are many. One option is the "individual companion," or the owned pet, that is placed with the older person on a full-time basis (McCulloch, 1983). A pet may be obtained from a pet shop or provided by a pet adoption agency in cooperation with local humane societies or interested volunteer groups. A pet may even be selected from animals destined to be euthanized. The feeling that the animal selected was saved from death by the older person can increase his or her perception of being needed. Also, animals can be utilized on a part-time basis (a pet-loaning service), being left with an older individual for a period of time (e.g., several hours a week), but ultimately being the responsibility of someone else (McCulloch, 1983). This arrangement may be more feasible for older people who either are not capable of or do not wish to take on the responsibility of a full-time pet. Many types of pets would be appropriate for this type of program, ranging from the most popular, a dog or cat, to birds, rabbits, or guinea pigs. The need for ease of transport should be considered, and only animals that are comfortable being handled by strangers should be selected. Private pet owners and possibly humane societies may be willing to participate in a pet-loaning service. A neighbor may welcome an older person taking responsibility for regularly walking a dog or feeding a pet while he or she is away. Groups of volunteers that visit with the animals may be organized through local churches, schools, or senior centers. Youth organizations (e.g., Girl Scouts) also may be interested in participating, making pet care an intergenerational project.

One of the authors' clients was quite unhappy when a young family with a golden retriever moved into the neighborhood. The client complained about the prospect of hearing the dog bark endlessly. After 2 months, he began to visit the dog and ended up taking the dog for a half-hour walk every day. Although he became extremely attached to the dog, he did not want the responsibility of owning and housing it.

USE OF ANIMAL-ASSISTED THERAPY WITH OLDER ADULTS LIVING IN CONGREGATE HOUSING

Following the death of her husband, Mrs. Richardson moved into a high-rise elder housing complex. She moved from a large, spacious apartment to a two-room apartment with a bedroom and combination living room-dining area that had a small galley kitchen at one end. Her greatest pleasure came from a 12-foot-long glass wall in the living room, which overlooked a common area with about six trees. She would spend hours watching squirrels moving from limb to limb. Eventually, she purchased shelled nuts at the supermarket and began to throw nuts to the squirrels from the bedroom window.

An increasing number of older people live in congregate housing. Although this environment may be conducive to social interaction, the residents are not immune to the problems of social alienation and depression. The losses of loved ones, social contacts, and independence are often intensified by the transition to a new living situation. Leaving a beloved home and neighborhood after residing there for many years can be painful. Animal–assisted therapy can help older adults overcome some of the losses associated with relocation.

Several different options for implementation in congregate living arrangements are available. One possibility is the individual adoption of a pet, as previously mentioned. The type of pet that may be appropriate depends on the regulations and the accommodations of the housing complex. If an older person owned a pet prior to relocating, it may be possible to bring that pet to the new home. Although some congregate housing complexes prohibit pets, increasing numbers are becoming sensitive to the need some residents have for pets. Some states have enacted legislation that prevents discrimination against residents with pets living in congregate settings. For those facilities that prohibit cats and dogs, adopting a fish or a bird may be an alternative. Attaching a clear acrylic bird feeder to the outside of a window or a sliding glass door may be a viable alternative in more restrictive settings.

Another option for implementing animal–assisted therapy in congregate living settings is pet visitation. "Pet mobile" programs bring puppies or kittens to entertain residents in a central area so that all can enjoy them. A variation on this is the acquisition of a mascot, or group pet, which would reside in the complex and provide companionship to all of the residents (McCulloch, 1983).

USE OF ANIMAL-ASSISTED THERAPY WITH OLDER ADULTS LIVING IN LONG-TERM CARE FACILITIES

Sam had been living in a nursing facility for 18 months. He spent much of his day either wandering about the facility or sitting in a chair in the day room facing away from the other residents. The medical staff would attempt to cheer him up, chatting with him in a teasing and familiar manner and trying to interest him in television programs, but his apathy continued.

On the recommendation of the social service staff, the administrators contemplated the purchase of a pet for the facility. A bird was mutually agreed on and a cage was placed across from the nurses' station. Prior to the bird's arrival, Sam was asked to care for it. His duties would include feeding the bird and changing the cage twice a day. In an effort to increase his involvement with the bird, the charge nurse asked Sam to spend some time each day with the bird to help it to adjust to moving into the nursing facility. Sam approached the duties initially with reluctance and little interest. To increase his level of interest the charge nurse requested a formal report from Sam on the bird's status and how other residents were relating to the new pet. Over the following weeks, as Sam cared for "Belle" and reported on her condition, his energy level increased noticeably. He now spent much of his day hovering around the bird cage, talking to Belle. Less time was spent sitting by himself in the day room. He began to circulate through the unit talking to residents. As with the charge nurse, Sam would report to them on Belle's condition. He also began to discuss with staff the possibility of installing outdoor bird feeders to involve other residents in caring for birds. The social worker contacted the local high school to inquire whether the students would consider making and installing birdhouses outside of the nursing facility. The school administrators agreed to sponsor the project and offered the task of building and installing the birdhouses as a possible club activity. A local church was contacted to inquire whether a charitable group would be willing to absorb the cost of birdseed.

A large bird feeder was installed outside of the main windows of the day room. Sam selected a few residents to have feeders placed outside their windows. The residents were selected on the basis of their inability to engage in many activities, ability to see the feeder, and Sam's feeling that they needed "sparking up."

Although individual adoption of pets in long-term care facilities is not common, with the appropriate accommodations and the cooperation of administration and staff it is feasible and has been successful in alleviating even deep depression in some residents (McCulloch, 1983). A common option is pet visitation, in which volunteers, often with the cooperation of humane societies, bring animals to visit residents either privately or in a group setting for several hours each week. In fact, a survey conducted by Behling (1990) of 233 skilled and intermediate care facilities found that 58% had regularly scheduled animal visitation programs. Pets are now permitted in nursing facilities in most states (Schantz, 1991). Animal-assisted therapy programs have even been implemented with older residents of psychiatric hospitals (Haughie, Milne, & Elliott, 1992). Long-term care facilities may also be appropriate settings for the mascot option of animal-assisted therapy, in which all residents can participate in the companionship with and care of a single group pet (McCulloch, 1983). Whichever option is selected, it is important that sufficient opportunity exists for residents to interact with the pet and form an attachment to it. Again, bird feeders placed outside, visible from residents' rooms or attached to a window, may be an effective alternative.

A particularly exciting animal-assisted therapy program, A Birds-Eye View to Watch Wildlife, was developed by the Department of Environmental Conservation (DEC) in New York State (Matthews, Ritchie, & Farrell, 1993). The program was established in 18 nursing facilities and retirement centers around the state in an effort to restore to residents the pleasure of viewing wildlife. The DEC provided each long-term care facility with a start-up kit that included a tube feeder, a platform feeder, a $25 gift certificate for birdseed, a garbage can for storing the seed, a how-to video, and a bird identification poster. These few items resulted in a greater variety of wildlife species attracted to the areas and increased viewing opportunities for residents.

An especially interesting kind of bird feeder is one that fits into and takes up the lower half of a window. The feeder extends into the room about 6 inches and has one-way glass. The bird cannot see into the adjacent room, but people inside the room can see the bird clearly. Birdseed can be added from a circular lid at the top of the feeder so that it is not necessary to go outside, and the feeder needs cleaning only once or twice a year. This type of feeder should be placed in a window that is not accessible from the ground to ensure against break-ins. A cautionary note: Any bird feeder attached to a window or sliding glass door should be placed out of the reach of cats. One visitor to a nursing facility reported that while she was admiring a bird perched at a vinyl feeder attached to a window, she saw a cat jump from the ground to the windowsill, which was close to the feeder, to catch the bird. The visitor was philosophical, noting, "It helps to be a Buddhist." For other older adults, this incident may be truly upsetting.

An aquarium can provide hours of relaxing stimulation, particularly for residents in wheelchairs. Male blowfish (betas) are colorful, and some frail residents who rarely leave their rooms find them appealing. One blowfish can be placed in a brandy snifter for several hours during a visit.

Individuals contemplating an animal-assisted therapy program in a nursing facility need not worry about finding volunteers willing to work with frail or cognitively impaired residents. Savishinsky (1992) found that the volunteers who had participated in a pet visitation program for the greatest length of time and who had most consistently attended sessions were those who regularly visited the individuals with profound impairments: people who were bedridden, people in wheelchairs, or people with advanced Alzheimer's disease or communication disorders. These volunteers reported feeling a special satisfaction in helping individuals who were especially in need of contact because they received less attention and entertained fewer visitors. The potential for volunteers to experience prolonged and intense interaction with these residents was greater, which led to more effective results for resident and volunteer.

It is important to keep in mind that the social context in which the animals are present could mediate their impact on the targeted individuals (Taylor et al., 1993). If the goal of the intervention is to increase socialization, efforts should be made to ensure others are present to discuss the animals and reminisce about past experiences.

PRECAUTIONS TO TAKE AND ACCOMMODATIONS TO MAKE PRIOR TO IMPLEMENTING ANIMAL-ASSISTED THERAPY

The implementation of animal-assisted therapy can give rise to certain complications, as enumerated below. Taking appropriate steps to ensure both safety and convenience should be considered when implementing this type of therapy in any of the three settings mentioned previously.

One environmental adjustment that may be helpful in either congregate housing or in long-term care facilities is the preparation or construction of an area where animal–older person interaction can take place. Items to be considered include an entry wide enough to admit wheelchairs, provisions for wind and rain protection, and proper lighting, if the area is outdoors. Adequate fencing or barriers and a double-door entrance to prevent the escape of the animal may also be necessary. The optimal placement of the area would be one that is visible to as many residents' rooms or apartments as possible (Levinson, 1972). Other considerations include rules and provisions for the proper sanitation and maintenance of the pets, adequate kennel facilities, proper immunization, and insurance against any possible damage done by a pet (McCulloch, 1983; Struckus, 1991). In situations in which a pet (or pets) is being adopted by independent-living older persons, accommodations must be made for the pet's (or pets') need for food, medical care, exercise, possible house-training and behavioral training, and the like. Follow-up visits ensure that proper care is being taken of the pet and that the pair is compatible (McCulloch, 1983).

Although animal-assisted therapy has a good safety record, it is important to identify the potential hazards and plan how best to minimize the risks to older adults. Obviously, disease transmission or bite/scratch injuries during the trial stages could jeopardize the potential value of the program (Schantz, 1991). Various other problems, examined in the following sections, must also be anticipated.

Avoiding Unsuitable Matches

Each individual has a unique history of experiences with animals as well as individual perceptions of and attitudes toward certain types of animals (Struckus, 1991). This history must be considered when selecting a pet. Problems may result if the selection of a pet is inappropriate. Timing must also be considered. If a person is not physically capable of caring for or appreciating the animal, then animal-assisted therapy is not an appropriate therapeutic intervention (McCulloch, 1983). Serious evaluation of the emotional status and physical condition of the person must be made before arranging for his or her participation in the care and maintenance of a pet (or pets) (Levinson, 1972). For example, an individual with an impaired immune system is particularly vulnerable to certain infections, and the need to share one's life with a pet must be balanced with the risk involved (Schantz, 1991; Schellenberg, 1993). Involved staff members must also be aware of the increased vulnerability experienced by depressed people and how detrimental the loss of a pet may be (McCulloch, 1983). Once owning a pet is deemed feasible, it is important to involve the older adult in the decision-making process as much as possible. In a best-case scenario he or she should be the one to select the new pet.

Exploring Health Issues

It is important for animals to be given a thorough physical examination. They should be evaluated for temperament and possible behavioral problems, dewormed, spayed or neutered, and immunized. Some pet adoption agencies provide appropriate obedience training and licensing of pets, in addition to physical examinations (Struckus, 1991).

Injury may result if the pet is handled improperly, if the pet selected is not appropriate, or if staff supervision is not adequate. It is necessary to carry insurance against any type of damage or injury that may occur (McCulloch, 1983). Screening for allergies to animals should be part of every potential owner's medical records. Proper immunization, veterinary examinations, and sanitation procedures are necessary to prevent any transfer of disease from animals to older adults. Table 6.1 provides a list of the potential health risks animal-assisted therapy poses to older adults and their possible preventive measures. Dogs present the greatest risk for bite injuries, whereas cats (the allergen is located in cat saliva, which, when dry, becomes airborne dander), guinea pigs, and horses, in that order, appear to be the most allergenic of species (Schantz, 1991). Dogs and pet birds have been known to trigger allergic responses as well (Marks, 1984; Schantz, 1991). Most

Table 6.1.   Potential health risks posed by animal-assisted therapy

Risk	Preventive measures
Animal bites	Careful selection of appropriate species and temperament of individual pet
	Use of trained dogs in long-term care facilities
	Appropriate supervision of residents who are handling animals
	Older adults living independently should keep antiseptic substances (e.g. hydrogen peroxide) on hand and be instructed in wound care
Infectious diseases	Initial veterinary screening of pet; vaccinate pet
	Eliminate fleas by periodic treatment of pet and environment
	Frequent handwashing
	Keep pets away from food preparation and consumption areas
	Frequent removal of bird droppings and animal wastes
	Resident animal rather than visitations for units with older adults with physical or cognitive impairments
Animal allergies	Medical records should be reviewed and residents questioned concerning possible allergies
	Skin-prick tests or serologic tests (e.g., RAST) may be used to rule out clinical allergy diagnosis
	Efforts should be made to avoid exposing animal-allergic residents to pets

Additional considerations

- Pet policies should be developed with advice from public health veterinarians, physicians, and administrators.
- Plans should be designed to provide and maintain surveillance and response to emergent problems.
- Training should take place in long-term care facilities to educate staff members and residents about potential dangers and how to avoid them.

Adapted from: Schantz (1991).

animals can transmit infectious diseases. The pathogens can be transmitted by direct contact; by animal bites; in food; or via bedding, carpets, and other items with which the pet has come in contact (Schantz, 1991). Schantz (1991) has pointed out how children are particularly vulnerable to pet-related transmission of disease because of their tendency toward pica (the eating of inedible objects) and oral exploration of the environment. This may also be true of older adults with cognitive impairment.

Tackling Financial Issues

For older persons living independently who wish to adopt a pet, alleviating certain financial concerns may be helpful. More older adults are likely to accept an animal companion in the following instances (McCulloch, 1983):

- If offers are made for some type of financial aid for veterinary care and other expenses
- If offers are made for help with the major grooming and training tasks
- If pet-sitting arrangements are available for times of sickness or travel
- If they can be assured of proper care of the animal in the event of their death or their relocation to a facility that does not allow pets

One option for helping an older person to adopt a pet may be to suggest to family members and friends that they present certain pet supplies or possibly gift certificates in lieu of impractical items (e.g., perfume, aftershave, knickknacks) at the holidays or for birthdays and anniversaries.

Considering Liability Issues for Damage or Injuries

Long-term care facilities may be vulnerable to legal liability for injuries to residents caused by animals. Also, there may be legal obstacles to permitting animals in the facilities at all. Although legislative changes have been made, some state regulations prohibit animals completely or permit only visiting but not housing of animals on the premises (Bustad & Hines, 1983).

Involving Caregivers

Caregiving routines, which are often precious, may be interrupted when implementing animal-assisted therapy (Levinson, 1972). Caregivers must be properly oriented to this therapy and included as much as possible in the decision-making and pet selecting processes. Levinson (1972) found that their lack of involvement may result in them undermining the program. Many long-term care staff are hesitant about the prospect of pets entering the facility. It is interesting that studies that have explored staff concerns found that few of their worries materialize (Winkler et al., 1989). Caregivers are also subject to the same hazards, such as injury and allergies, if proper selections are not made (McCulloch, 1983).

Losing the Pet

The impact of the death of a pet should be taken into consideration when implementing animal-assisted therapy. All animals will die eventually, but the pain of the loss should not cloud the gains that may be achieved through involvement with the pet. Should death occur, older people should be supported during the grieving process. A small, formal ceremony marking the passing of the pet is advisable, and after a short time, a replacement should be discussed. A sympathy card and a card on the anniversary of the pet's death can be comforting to the person. For many individuals, pets become members of the family and their passing can be as painful.

Summary

It is essential that animal-assisted therapy is not viewed as a "cure-all" or a panacea. The needs and limitations of the individual should be considered. Both the animal and the older person should be prepared carefully. The research has been supportive of this type of therapy, yet much needs to be done to determine the problems in and limitations of this form of treatment (Struckus, 1991). It is also important to remember that animal-assisted therapy is not appropriate for all older adults. Certain people will not welcome animals into their home. (Note: There seems to be much less appreciation for animals by older adults of color, especially Asian Americans [Kehoe, 1991], but this should not be construed to mean that minority involvement in animal-assisted therapy should be avoided altogether.)

IMPLEMENTING ANIMAL-ASSISTED THERAPY WITH HEALTHY OLDER ADULTS

Preliminary Analysis

A review of the institutional structure and a study of the caregivers, individuals, and families is the first step in the preliminary analysis. A survey of capabilities and attitudes of the caregivers and family is necessary in order to rule out or handle any adverse feelings. In-resident programs should properly prepare for housing and feeding the pet (or pets). Contacting colleges, churches, animal-training classes, and community service organizations in the area can help to build a corps of volunteers willing to help out in establishing and maintaining a pet visitation program (Savishinsky, 1992).

An interest inventory is provided on page 157 for use with independent-living older adults to determine their interest in and ability to care for a pet. It is important to remember that a pet should not be forced onto someone who does not wish the responsibility of caring for an animal. Readers who need more specialized information or who have questions about implementing animal-assisted therapy programs may find the resources listed in the appendix at the end of the chapter helpful.

Proper Selection

A carefully executed match between the needs and limitations of the older client and the characteristics and temperament of the animal must be attempted (Struckus, 1991). This process is not easy. The animal must meet the social, emotional, and physical needs of its human companion and the facility or home in which it will live (Levinson, 1972). No strict guidelines have been established. Some studies suggest that small, sedate dogs (e.g., beagles, Pomeranians, Boston terriers, pugs) or toy or miniature poodles are more appropriate than large dogs for older people, whereas others maintain that large dogs (e.g., German shepherds, golden retrievers, Labrador retrievers) are easier for people who are less ambulatory or in wheelchairs to communicate with because they do not have to bend down to meet them (Fick, 1993). It is important to remember that dogs used for therapeutic interventions are not breed specific; proper upbringing and training are more critical factors. Puppies should be avoided because of their tendency to be frisky and playful. In general, mature female dogs are preferable, and spaying is a necessity (McCulloch, 1983). The animal should be interesting to the older person, and it should not present a financial burden. Investigating whether the older person has owned pets in the past and what his or her experiences have

Animal-Assisted Therapy Interest Inventory

Client _____ Date _____

Functional Skills

Would you be able to purchase food for pet? ___ Yes ___ No

Would you remember to feed pet regularly? ___ Yes ___ No

Would you be able to provide proper sanitary conditions for pet

(e.g., walking dog, cleaning cat box or cage)? ___ Yes ___ No

Background Information

1. Have you ever had a pet? Yes ___ No ___ (If no, go to Question 6)
2. When did you have a pet?

3. What type of pet did you have?

4. What did you enjoy the most about the relationship?

5. What did you not enjoy about having a pet?

Present Concerns

6. Would you consider having a pet at this time? Yes ___ No ___
7. What problems are running through your mind as you think about this?

   ___ Against housing rules ___ Will make a mess ___ Too much work

   ___ Will trigger allergies ___ Other_____
8. Do you think these problems can be overcome?

9. What type of pet would you like if you could have one?

10. Would you like to own a pet ___ or simply visit with one regularly ___ ?
11. If a dog or cat does not appear to be feasible, explore the following options:

    ___ Bird ___ Fish ___ Guinea pig ___ Gerbil ___ Turtle(s)

Evaluator Comments

A Life Worth Living: Practical Strategies for Reducing Depression in Older Adults, by Pearl Mosher-Ashley and Phyllis Barrett. ©1997 Health Professions Press, Inc., Baltimore.

been may aid in determining an appropriate match (Levinson, 1972). For placement in a facility, Winkler et al. (1989) recommend a gregarious animal that seeks the company of many people. They do not advise adopting an animal that will form an attachment with only a few individuals. Their survey of the residents of a long-term care facility 22 weeks following the introduction of a resident dog found that two thirds of the residents reported that the dog was either indifferent to them or disliked them. In-facility pets should be fed by the residents, not the staff, in an effort to foster attachments between residents and pets (Kalfon, 1991).

Matching older persons living independently with a sponsor who shares an interest in the pet and can help with education and orientation as well as follow-up visits is suggested (Struckus, 1991). A mature spayed or neutered cat can offer close companionship to an older person living alone without making demands for constant care or regular exercise (Levinson, 1972). It is important to allow time for the older person and the animal to become acquainted and form an attachment. Providing a probationary period is advised.

Birds seem to pose the fewest problems as in-facility pets in terms of cost, care, and maintenance. They can contribute beauty; cheer; and a warm, homelike feeling. Birds require little care, yet can be amusing and relaxing to watch (Levinson, 1972). An aquarium may be the logical choice for old-old nonambulatory older adults, particularly those residing in long-term care facilities (Hoffman, 1991). In fact, the relaxation-inducing qualities of watching colorful fish have led many dentists and physicians to install aquariums in their waiting rooms (Schellenberg, 1993).

The older person's preference for a particular type of animal must be adhered to as much as possible. Potential companions may be referred from shelters, kennels, and private donors (Struckus, 1991). Possibilities include dogs, cats, birds, fish, caged mammals (e.g., rabbits, guinea pigs), and reptiles (e.g., iguanas, nonpoisonous snakes). Certain types of animals are more receptive to people and better reciprocate affection than others, and are more appropriate for an animal-assisted therapy program.

Pet visitation programs often use the services of animal welfare, 4-H, or other animal-related volunteer programs to provide visiting animals on a regular daily, weekly, or monthly basis (Fick, 1993). The pet should be allowed to relieve itself before visiting with residents, and proper education of animal care and handling techniques should precede pet visitation (McCulloch, 1983). It may be appropriate to gather residents in small groups for these visitations, or incorporate the visits into other, preexisting therapy or activity groups. The animal should be introduced in the presence of or through a staff member. Residents who have never owned pets may need considerable time to learn how to handle them so as not to hurt them or themselves (Levinson, 1972).

Another option is to stage a dog show in collaboration with dog clubs (Bumanis, 1991). A local veterinarian should be able to provide a list of dog clubs in the area. Club dogs are well-groomed, trained, and accustomed to traveling and socializing. Most clubs can provide between 10 and 30 dogs, allowing each resident a dog with which to interact. Also, clubs usually carry insurance that covers their participation in club-sponsored events. Many dog clubs are interested in conducting dog shows in long-term care facilities as part of their community service.

Other animal-oriented activities include petting zoos, special outings to view animals, and photographic displays showing the residents with visiting pets (Savishinsky, 1992). Supplementary materials (e.g., bird identification poster, books describing different breeds or types of animals) should be made available to interested older adults.

Definition of Goals

It is important that the specific goals of an animal-assisted therapy program be determined. The staff, volunteer group, and/or family should be informed of the goals, the intent, and the procedures of the program (Struckus, 1991). Goals should be *operationalized,* that is, they should be defined in strictly behavioral terms that are clear to all involved (e.g., "Mrs. Stinefelt will increase the frequency with which she speaks to staff or other residents"). Although group goals are frequently selected, it is best to target one or only a few individuals who are depressed and who are most in need of treatment. Operational goals should be established and a treatment plan developed for each individual targeted.

Proper Orientation

It is essential to "sell" facility staff, volunteer groups, and families on animal-assisted therapy and to assess the degree of opposition and resistance to the program. Implementation of an animal-assisted therapy program often involves a reorganization of routines, and negative attitudes may undermine possible therapeutic benefits (Levinson, 1972; McCulloch, 1983).

Volunteers should be provided with training to prepare them for the varied experiences that they would be fielding. Training should include an orientation to the kinds of residents they would be encountering, the types of communication problems that tend to arise during sessions, the range of positive and negative reactions they can expect from residents, and the nature of life and routine in long-term care settings (Savishinsky, 1992). Special emphasis should be placed on describing the likely reactions of older adults who are frail, impaired, or both.

Volunteers should also be prepared to understand the limits of what they can accomplish with animal-assisted therapy—that they will not cure people, arrest their decline, or return them to the community. Some volunteers may not realize that they will be involved in an emotionally supportive role with residents, not simply be transporters of animals. Older volunteers may have difficulty working in a nursing facility. The sight of frail and impaired older adults may trigger feelings that they are viewing their own future. Discussion of some of these issues may prepare volunteers to cope with these feelings when they arise and may even immunize some against experiencing them. In addition, volunteers must be told of the importance of terminating with, or saying goodbye to, their clients when they end their volunteer service. Savishinsky (1992) has found that few volunteers formally terminated with residents, even after a prolonged series of visits. The lack of closure was attributed to feelings of guilt or embarrassment and a reluctance to admit the finality of their involvement. The volunteers should be assured during preliminary training that, although the residents will be saddened by the termination, they need to be informed of it. Formal goodbyes may be painful but they provide an opportunity for both individuals to express and share the pleasures obtained through the interaction. It is more difficult for residents and even staff members to continue waiting in the hope that the volunteer will return or to wonder why the individual never said goodbye.

Given the propensity for volunteers to encounter problems, Savishinsky also recommends that volunteers who visit the same facility be encouraged to form a cohesive and supportive group. This can be accomplished by holding occasional gatherings of volunteers following their visits to residents. A listing of volunteer names and phone numbers can be distributed so that one volunteer can arrange for another member of the group to visit his or her residents when the volunteer is ill or out of town.

Coordination with Other Therapies

Animal-assisted therapy should supplement rather than replace and be integrated into existing physical, occupational, recreational, group, or individual therapies. Animal-assisted therapy can facilitate motivation in other types of therapies as well (McCulloch, 1983). For example, Rosenkoetter and Bowes (1991) recommend that walking a dog can be used to motivate a resident with circulatory problems to increase ambulation. They further suggest that 5–10 minutes of stroking a dog may help to increase flexibility in a resident with shoulder mobility problems. Smith (1995) describes how a trained therapy dog can help older people with balance problems gain greater control over their gross motor coordination: The dog is placed on a leash and the person takes it for a walk. The dog is instructed by a physical therapist to walk fast or slow, to veer from side to side, and to pull against the leash with varying degrees of force. Clients also practice maintaining balance while sitting on the edge of a bed or mat and throwing objects for the dog to retrieve. Several items are laid out on the floor some distance in front of the person, who then commands the therapy dog to retrieve one of them. The dog's ability to recognize the desired item tends to foment delight and a feeling of accomplishment in the person. Animal-assisted therapy has also been employed to facilitate speech retraining in people with aphasia (Smith, 1995).

Feelings of being needed and loved by the pet can lead to increased energy to participate in recreational activities. One of the authors witnessed a neighbor, a frail 80-year-old man, walking his cat on a leash. It was a lovely spring day and the man was examining flowers and saying hello to neighbors as he walked by. A pet may also facilitate adherence to medical treatment. Gray (1988) reported withdrawing a man's dependence on sleep medication by having her own dog, who was familiar with the residents in her facility, sleep beside the man's bed. Over a period of 10 weeks, the man was able to increase the amount of time he slept by 90 minutes without medication.

Continued Supervision of Older Adults, Staff, and Animals

It is necessary to supervise the program continually, assessing potential problems and maintaining the focus of the goals. Periodic conferences may be necessary to alleviate any older adult–pet or staff–pet relationship problems (Levinson, 1972). Safety issues should not be ignored. It is important for everyone to avoid open-ended situations in which there is no supervision or in which problems have not been anticipated (McCulloch, 1983; Schantz, 1991). Ongoing supervision may be facilitated by formally integrating animal-assisted therapy into the targeted individual's overall care plan. Also, regularly scheduled team meetings should list the therapy on the agenda. An individual staff member could be assigned responsibility for the animal-assisted therapy program and given the duties of scheduling veterinary appointments and flea and tick treatments, assessing resident–pet interactions, and supervising the general care of the animal.

Evaluation of Progress

Analyzing the effects of the program and making changes accordingly is a necessity. Some trial and error may be necessary to mold the treatment to individual settings. It is important to maintain realistic expectations; pets should not be expected to execute permanent personality changes in individuals (McCulloch, 1983). However, if goals have been determined and a treatment plan developed, some reduction in symptoms can be expected. Conducting assessments before and after the introduction of the pet can establish whether improvement has taken place. Pre- and posttreatment assessments should consider behavior related to the goals selected. For example, if the goal was to improve the mood and level of social interaction in a depressed individual, assessment should focus on indicators such as smiles, laughter, and energy level for mood and amount of eye contact, amount of conversation, and length of communication for social interaction.

In addition to assessments, ongoing monitoring of the program should be part of the evaluation process. This type of monitoring can be facilitated by maintaining specialized records. Page 162 is a sample form that can be used to monitor a client's progress. By recording the successes and failures of animal-assisted therapy programs, building blocks are provided for future treatment plans.

IMPLEMENTING ANIMAL-ASSISTED THERAPY WITH OLDER ADULTS WITH COGNITIVE IMPAIRMENT

Particularly promising in animal-assisted therapy research is the work being conducted with nursing facility residents who have cognitive impairment (e.g., Dorn, 1985). Animals can trigger memories and can provide affection in the form of a safe and secure interaction. Animals are not judgmental and respond to minimal overtures, which is an important consideration when working with individuals experiencing advanced cognitive losses. Kongable, Stolley, and Buckwalter (1990) found the staff in a 20-bed special care unit to be receptive to a newly developed

Animal-Assisted Therapy Monitoring Form

Client _____ Date _____

Pet _____ Owned _____ Visitor _____ (Frequency _____)

Short-term goal (e. g. , improved mood):

Long-term goal (e.g., increased socialization with staff and other residents):

Behavioral Indicators

___ Establishes eye contact ___ Initiates conversation
___ Responds to questions ___ Speaks in single-word responses
___ Short phrases ___ Full sentence
___ 2 to 3 sentences ___ More than 3 consecutive sentences

Can carry on conversation for ___ 30 sec ___ I min ___ 2 min ___ 3 min
___ 4 min ___ 5 min ___ >5 min

Smiles ___ Once ___ 2 to 3X ___ 4 to 6X ___ >6X

Laughs ___ Once ___ A few times ___ A great deal

Speaks regularly ___ with staff ___ with other residents

Behavior recorded was ___ observed by respondent ___ reported by staff

Questions Posed Directly to Client

Are you enjoying the contact you have with the pet? ___ Yes ___ No
What aspect do you enjoy about the pet?

Are you having any problems with the pet? If so, what are they?

Would you like more involvement with the pet?   ___Yes ___ No
If yes, how much?

Would you like less involvement with the pet?   ___Yes ___ No
If yes, how much?

A Life Worth Living: Practical Strategies for Reducing Depression in Older Adults, by Pearl Mosher-Ashley and Phyllis Barrett. ©1997 Health Professions Press, Inc., Baltimore.

Table 6.2. Benefits and risks reported by staff in implementing animal-assisted therapy using a dog with people with Alzheimer's disease

Benefits	Risks
Improved psychological response	Hazard to the dog
Positive regard for self	Resident grabbed at dog's collar,
Affords a feeling of recognition	tugged dog's tail, and kicked dog
and attention	Produced a stress overload in the
Bolsters self-esteem	dog
Provides a sense of control over	
the environment	
Increased socialization	Hazard to the resident
Dog acted as a social catalyst	Resident fell over the dog
Dog provided the person with Alz-	Dog bit or nipped at the resident
heimer's disease an opportunity	Possible transmission of microor-
to display social skills in a non-	ganisms from dog to resident
threatening atmosphere	
Provided sensory stimulation	Sensory overload
Dog gave the resident something	Misperception of or inability of
to watch	resident to process stimuli from
Gave the person with Alzheimer's	the dog
disease an opportunity to touch	
and be touched	
Improved physiologic state	Potential dislike of pet by resident
Dog served as a physical outlet	No resident reported a dislike for
Dog produced a relaxing effect	pets
Fostered reminiscence	Added responsibility placed on staff
Residents shared some of their pet	
ownership memories	
Some residents mistakenly called the	
dog by the name of a previously	
owned pet	

Adapted from: Kongable, Stolley, & Buckwalter (1990).

program involving animal-assisted therapy. A dog that was brought to the unit initially for 3 hours 1 day a week became a permanent resident. Table 6.2 lists, in order of priority, the benefits and risks of the program reported by the unit staff. This list may help others who wish to establish an animal-assisted therapy program with older adults with cognitive impairment. It is interesting that two of the risks one may assume would be of utmost concern to staff were the least-frequently reported: Although staff members reported ethical concerns over residents who dislike animals being housed on a unit with one, they were quick to note that no such situation had occurred. Also, the extra work imposed on staff because of the pet's presence was the least-frequently reported concern.

Although five risk areas were mentioned by the staff, only one, hazard to the animal, posed a problem. Fortunately, the resident dog was well-trained and had little difficulty handling occasional rough treatment. Kalfon (1991) reported similar success in an animal-assisted therapy program for residents with cognitive impairment that involved a rabbit. More positive responses (e.g., smiles, laughter, attention, touch, verbalizations) were observed during animal-assisted therapy sessions than during other planned leisure activities.

REFERENCES

Behling, R.J. (1990). *Animal programs and animal assisted therapy in skilled and intermediate care facilities in Illinois*. Unpublished doctoral dissertation, The Union Institute, Cincinnati.

Brickel, C.M. (1980–1981). A review of the roles of pet animals in psychotherapy and with the elderly. *International Journal of Aging and Human Development, 12*, 119–128.

Brickel, C.M. (1985). The clinical use of pets with the aged. *Clinical Gerontology, 2*, 72–74.

Bumanis, A. (1991, September). Dog shows involve residents in pet therapy program. *Provider, 17*, 41.

Bustad, L., & Hines, L.C. (1983). Placement of animals with the elderly: Benefits and strategies. In A.H. Katcher & A.M. Beck (Eds.), *New perspectives on our lives with companion animals* (pp. 291–302). Philadelphia: University of Pennsylvania.

Culliton, B.J. (1987). Take two pets and call me in the morning. *Science, 137*, 237–238.

Dorn, J. (1985). *Love, goodwishes, and a warm puppy*. [Video]. (Distributed by the Orlando Alzheimer's Disease and Related Disorders Association, University of Central Florida, P.O. Box 160111, Orlando, Florida 32816-0111. Telephone (407) 823-3000.)

Fick, K.M. (1993). The influence of an animal on social interactions of nursing home residents in a group setting. *American Journal of Occupational Therapy, 47*, 529–534.

Gammonley, J., & Yates, J. (1991). Pet projects: Animal assisted therapy in nursing homes. *Journal of Gerontological Nursing, 17*, 13–15.

Gray, K.B. (1988, August 24–30). A man's best friend. *Nursing Times, 84*, 40–42, 44.

Goldmeier, J. (1986). Pets or people: Another research note. *Gerontologist, 26*, 203–206.

Harris, M.D., Rinehart, J.M., & Gerstman, J. (1993, October). Animal-assisted therapy for the homebound elderly. *Holistic Nursing Practice, 8*, 27–37.

Haughie, E., Milne, D., & Elliot, V. (1992). An evaluation of companion pets with elderly psychiatric patients. *Behavioural Psychotherapy, 20*, 367–372.

Hoffman, R.G. (1991). Companion animals: A therapeutic measure for elderly patients. *Journal of Gerontological Social Work, 18*, 195–205.

Kalfon, E. (1991, Winter). Pets make a difference in long term care. *Perspectives, 15*, 3–6.

Kehoe, M. (1991). Loneliness and the aging homosexual: Is pet therapy an answer? *Journal of Homosexuality, 20*, 137–142.

Kongable, L.G., Stolley, J.M., & Buckwalter, K.C. (1990, Fall). Pet therapy for Alzheimer's patients: A survey. *Journal of Long-Term Care Administration, 18*, 17–21.

Lawton, M.P., Moss, M., & Moles, E. (1984). Pet ownership: A research note. *Gerontologist, 95*, 307–312.

Levinson, B.M. (1972). *Pets and human development*. Springfield, IL: Charles C Thomas.

Marks, M.B. (1984). Respiratory tract allergy to household pet birds. *Annals of Allergy, 52*, 56–57.

Matthews, M.J., Ritchie, B.T., & Farrell, M. (1993, November). Watchable wildlife for nursing homes. *Conservationist, 48*, 23.

McCulloch, M. (1983). Animal-facilitated therapy: Overview and future direction. In A.H. Katcher & A.M. Beck (Eds.), *New perspectives on our lives with companion animals* (pp. 291–302). Philadelphia: University of Pennsylvania.

Miller, D., Staats, S.R., & Partlo, C. (1992, December). Discriminating positive and negative aspects of pet interaction: Sex differences in the older population. *Social Indicators Research, 27*, 363–374.

Mosher-Ashley, P.M. (1994). Diagnoses assigned and issues brought up in therapy by older adults receiving outpatient treatment. *Clinical Gerontologist, 15*, 37–65.

Rosenkoetter, M.M., & Bowes, D. (1991). Brutus is making rounds. *Geriatric Nursing, 12*, 277–278.

Savishinsky, J.S. (1992). Intimacy, domesticity and pet therapy with the elderly: Expectation and experience among nursing home volunteers. *Social Science and Medicine, 34*, 1325–1334.

Schantz, P.M. (1991). Preventing potential health hazards incidental to the use of pets in therapy. *Anthrozoos, 4*, 14–23.

Schellenberg, D. (1993, December). Pets and health. *Harvard Health Letter, 19*, 1–3.

Smith, R. (1995, August/September). Rehab's phdog. *Rehab Management*, pp. 49–53.

Struckus, J.E. (1991). Pet-facilitated therapy and the elderly client. In P.A. Wisocki (Ed.), *Handbook of clinical behavior therapy with the elderly client* (pp. 403–419). New York: Plenum.

Taylor, E., Maser, S., Yee, J., & Gonzalez, S.M. (1993). Effects of animals on eye contact and vocalizations of elderly residents in a long term care facility. *Physical & Occupational Therapy in Geriatrics, 11*, 61–71.

Winkler, A., Fairnie, H., Gericevich, F., & Long, M. (1989). The impact of a resident dog on an institution for the elderly: Effects on perceptions and social interactions. *Gerontologist, 29*, 216–223.

Appendix
Specialized Animal-Assisted Therapy Resources

A Birds-Eye View To Watch Wildlife Program (Joseph Pane)
Department of Environmental Conservation
47-40 21st Street
Long Island City, New York 11101
Phone (718) 482-4922
Provides brochures and loan of a video to long-term care facilities and others on how to select and set up bird feeders and seed to attract specific birds; also willing to provide information on how to set up pilot programs in other states

Canine Companions for Independence
Post Office Box 446
Santa Rosa, California 95402-0446
Phone (707) 528-0830
Provides information on how to obtain a trained pet for people with disabilities, including older adults in wheelchairs

Delta Society
Post Office Box 1080
321 Burnett Avenue South, 3rd Floor
Renton, Washington 98057-9906
Phone (206) 226-7357
Association for health professionals and mental health, social services, and long-term care staff, as well as laypeople; provides materials and consultation to members on issues related to implementation of animal-assisted therapy programs

Paws With a Cause
46-46 South Division
Waylen, Michigan 49348
Phone (616) 698-0688
Provides information and referral on the use of pets in rehabilitative treatment; mails literature on available services

Pet Loss Support Hotline
Tufts University
200 Westborough Road
Grafton, Massachusetts 01536
Phone (508) 839-7966
Hotline designed to help individuals cope with feelings of grief over the loss of a pet; service is available from 6 P.M. to 9 P.M. Tuesdays and Thursdays

7

*Outside of a dog, a book is man's best
friend—and inside of a dog, it's too dark to read.*

Groucho Marx

No Frigate Like a Book

Bibliotherapy

D uring the 2 years before my (Mosher-Ashley's) mother passed away from cardiovascular disease, one of the activities she most enjoyed was to lie in bed reading a good, "trashy" book. She looked forward to the publication of every Danielle Steel novel. Her difficulty in ambulating, coupled with ever-present fatigue, made few activities truly enjoyable for her, but books provided her with a temporary means of escape from physical discomfort and the knowledge that her life was coming to an end. Years earlier, she had established an extensive book trade with a circle of relatives. They frequently discussed the plots, and, on one occasion, I truly believed that they were discussing real people rather than the characters in a book they had particularly enjoyed. The last time I saw my mother in the hospital, she had three books with her, all carefully selected: a favorite novel set in Venice, which she had once visited; the biography of Danielle Steel; and a Harlequin romance. These books had been among her last companions and had served an important purpose in her life.

Books can provide a pleasant way to while away idle hours, lift spirits, and genuinely enhance the quality of life of people who are coping with the challenges of aging. Books allow us to escape from our daily cares and preoccupation with physical pain and limitations. When carefully chosen, they can even speak to the specific conditions or concerns of the older adult reader. One of the authors' clients gained great comfort from reading former U.S. Senator Paul Tsongas'[1] autobiography, *Heading Home*. The book describes Tsongas' reevaluation of his life after a diagnosis of lymphoma. The client's mother had also been diagnosed with lymphoma, and reading about Tsongas' experience gave him hope and reduced his anxiety level considerably.

Bibliotherapy, "the therapeutic use of literature with guidance or intervention from a therapist" (Cohen, 1994a, p. 40), is not a new idea. The ancient Greeks recognized the value of reading and referred to their libraries as "places of healing for the soul" (Brown, 1975, p. 13). Regrettably, little attention has been paid to the role that reading for entertainment plays in helping people cope with life's problems. Both Brown (1975) and Hynes and Hynes-Berry (1986) have pointed out that reading can serve as a distraction and a pleasurable pastime. Increasing pleasurable activities has been recognized as an effective means of reducing depressive symptoms.

To gain optimal therapeutic benefit, the use of books, poetry, magazine articles, or other literary materials must be supplemented by the guidance and advice of a trained mental health professional. However, the principles of bibliotherapy may be adapted for use by professionals who are not specialists in treating mental health problems, and this form of therapy is particularly well suited for implementation by health care providers (Cohen, 1994b). In fact, librarian training programs now include bibliotherapy as a part of the educational process. Bibliotherapy differs from general reading in that a third party (a therapist or facilitator) is involved and the general principles of therapeutic intervention—including assessment, treatment planning, and evaluation—are part of the

---

[1]Tsongas died of complications from chemotherapy in January 1997.

process. The amount and the format of the guidance is flexible so that bibliotherapy can be modified and implemented in many different settings for individuals with varying needs.

Bibliotherapy can be categorized into two main forms of treatment: interactive bibliotherapy and reading bibliotherapy (Hynes & Hynes-Berry, 1986). The latter is also called *self-help bibliotherapy* (Cohen, 1989). *Interactive bibliotherapy* involves a therapeutic interaction between a facilitator and a participant. *Reading bibliotherapy* is an individual pursuit in which the person reads material recommended by an advisor; the reader has little contact with the therapist, and the response of the reader to the reading material is not generally discussed. A variation on reading bibliotherapy has been proposed by Cohen (1994a, b, c), in which a variety of therapeutic readings, including fiction and nonfiction, are used to resolve difficult life situations.

Two specialized forms of interactive bibliotherapy exist: poetry therapy and group bibliotherapy. *Poetry therapy* involves a combination of silent reading and recitations of poems to elicit feelings and gain therapeutic insight (Heller, 1987). Poetry therapy may also involve the client writing poetry in response to readings (Cohen, 1994b). Some people perceive poetry therapy and bibliotherapy as synonymous because poetry and prose are integrated frequently in the readings and both are literary forms that comprise the core of the discussions (Hynes & Wedl, 1990). In group or developmental bibliotherapy therapeutic factors for group psychotherapy are integrated into the process of interactive bibliotherapy (Cohen, 1989). *Group bibliotherapy* can be broken down further into two types: clinical and developmental bibliotherapy (Hynes & Wedl, 1990; O'Dell, 1986). *Clinical bibliotherapy* is a form of group therapy conducted by a mental health professional, which usually takes place in psychiatric units, day treatment programs, community mental health centers, and chemical dependency programs. *Developmental bibliotherapy* does not involve clinical contact or formal psychiatric evaluation. It is designed to be used with healthier individuals to foster enjoyment, stimulation, socialization, and positive self-esteem and self-image, and to encourage growth by working through problematic feelings and by discovering personal strengths, talents, and accomplishments (O'Dell, 1986).

Frequently, creative writing is incorporated into bibliotherapy as a means of discovering the self and expanding on the readings (Hynes & Wedl, 1990). The writing is assigned following the reading. A specific type of therapeutic writing is called *scenario writing*, which is a description of a current issue or problem (Haddock, 1989). Hynes and Wedl (1990) recommend this type of writing when an older adult is facing a difficult life situation, such as moving to a retirement center or nursing facility.

Although limited, the research on bibliotherapy indicates that it holds much promise as a therapeutic intervention. The self-help approach, which calls for little or no contact with a therapist and involves the use of a single, nonfiction work or book of programmed instruction, has been the focus of some well-designed research and has been found to improve emotional health (Scogin, Hamblin, & Beutler, 1987; Scogin, Jamison, & Davis, 1990; Scogin, Jamison, &

Gochneaur, 1989; Wollersheim & Wilson, 1991). The support for interactive bibliotherapy tends to be anecdotal in nature but has been influential in directing clinical interventions.

Most of the research on bibliotherapy has focused on outcome measures. With the exception of Cohen's work, little attention has been directed to understanding the reader's experience of therapeutic reading in favor of an effort to study the process underlying bibliotherapy. Cohen (1994a, b, c) conducted a qualitative study involving in-depth interviews with eight people on their experience with therapeutic readings. The material was self-selected and included a variety of readings. All participants purposefully sought out the readings to help them cope with difficult life situations. An examination of the participants' experiences in therapeutic reading uncovered a basic structure to the process and some experiential characteristics. The readers' ability to recognize themselves, significant others, and their situations in what they read was found to be the underlying component in the process (Table 7.1). This recognition of self evolved into ways of feeling and knowing that assisted them in coping with difficult personal situations. Cohen (1994b) uncovered other important elements of therapeutic readings, which she called *characteristics of therapeutic readings* (Table 7.2). The structural components and experiential characteristics are useful factors that should be taken into consideration in recommending therapeutic readings and in monitoring the progress of the client.

It should be noted that the participants in Cohen's study differed in their need to discuss their reading. Some found that sharing and discussing the material enriched their understanding of the material; an equal number did not wish to share or discuss their reading. This finding suggests that facilitators should tailor the intervention to meet the needs of their clients. Some clients benefit from exploring their thoughts relative to the material read, although others may prefer to pursue the readings on their own. Either approach is appropriate. The temptation is to believe that interactive discussion is necessary. However, as the research on the self-help approach has shown, self-directed intervention is effective in reducing depression (Scogin, Hamblin, & Beutler, 1987; Scogin, Jamison, & Davis, 1990; Scogin, Jamison, & Gochneaur, 1989; Wollersheim & Wilson, 1991). Another of Cohen's findings has important implications for clinical practitioners: It did not seem to matter what type of reading material the participants read, provided they could perceive themselves or their situation in the reading. Cohen's work also suggests that the understanding gained from the therapeutic reading took place on both cognitive and emotional levels.

Bibliotherapy has been coupled with reminiscence therapy, which is covered in detail in Chapter 4. In this coupling the readings are used to elicit memories of the past, which are then related to the facilitator or to members of a group, or are experienced by the individual. O'Dell (1986) warns that direct questions about family may be painful to an older person who has little contact with family members. Readings about someone else's family experiences can generate strong memories, which can be discussed at the reader's own pace. Bibliotherapy may be a viable treatment alternative for these individuals because it is inexpensive and noninvasive (Mahalik & Kivlighan, 1988; Scogin, Jamison, & Gochneaur, 1989).

Table 7.1. Structure of the experience of therapeutic reading

Component	Definition
Recognition of self	Identification with literary characters
	Shock of recognition
	Sense of oneness with characters
	Ability to relate literary characters to significant others (e.g., family members, friends)
Ways of feeling	
Shared experience	Sense of not being alone with problems
	Problems were not isolating or unusual
Validation	Life experience perceived in some way as being acceptable
	Acknowledgment that the pain occurred and was real
Comfort	Sense of peace, well-being, serenity, confidence, or reassurance
Hope	Sense that their situation would improve because others experienced positive outcomes
	Sense that if other people found solutions to problems, so would they
	Gained information that could lead to solutions to problems
Inspiration	Gained energy, strength, and determination to take steps to improve their situation
Catharsis	Sense of release or relief, as if burdens had been lifted from their shoulders
Ways of knowing	
Understanding	Gained insight, brought feelings and ideas to surface, and clarified and crystallized ideas and feelings
Information gathering	Knowledge to deal with bureaucratic systems, including health care system
	Ability to speak intelligently with professionals
	Increased confidence in ability to make decisions

Adapted from: Cohen (1994c).

It is particularly well suited to some older adults who are plagued by feelings of sadness but who may be skeptical of traditional mental health services (O'Dell, 1986). Not only is bibliotherapy an effective method of treating mild and moderate depression but the effects are frequently long term, lasting upwards of 2 years (Scogin, Jamison, & Davis, 1990). For older individuals living independently in congregate housing or in long-term care facilities bibliotherapy is feasible and may fill otherwise lonely hours and stave off feelings of depression (Brown, 1975).

USE OF BIBLIOTHERAPY WITH OLDER ADULTS LIVING INDEPENDENTLY

Mr. Hance married late in life. His wife had been an office manager at the company for which he had worked. When they retired, they moved to a semirural area known

Table 7.2.   Characteristics of therapeutic reading

Characteristic	Definition
Intentional	
Purposeful reading	Identifying a problem and purposefully looking for reading material that would help
Rereading	Rereading specific articles or books to obtain added understanding or to revitalize positive feelings that readings produced
Recalled reading	Recalling reading in an effort to receive continuing help with difficult life situations
Relational	
Individual experience	Perceiving therapeutic reading as a personal, individual experience that could not be shared with others easily
Alternate form of therapy	Finding similarities between reading and attending a support group or seeing a psychotherapist
Like relating to a friend	Relating to a literary character as though he or she were a friend
Transporting	
Immersion	Losing oneself in reading
Escape	Using readings to escape from difficult life situations

Adapted from: Cohen (1994b).

for its beauty and numerous colleges. This area was particularly attractive to them because it offered many cultural activities, excellent libraries, and numerous bookstores. Both Mr. and Mrs. Hance were avid readers. Two years after they relocated, Mrs. Hance began to exhibit signs of cognitive losses. Initially, she became withdrawn, complaining of fatigue when she would forget appointments, make errors in judgment, or have difficulty in carrying out daily tasks. Mr. Hance was concerned and thought that she may be depressed. He tried to discuss the situation with her, but she always changed the subject.

Mrs. Hance continued to show a decline in mental functioning. Soon, Mr. Hance found that he was doing most of the cooking, cleaning, and general maintenance. Over time, his entire day began to center around doing household chores, supervising his wife, and helping her to wash and dress. This pattern continued until Mrs. Hance began to resist her husband's attempts to assist her. She would refuse to wash or dress. When he tried to encourage her, she would refuse loudly and frequently would strike him. After several months of this behavior, Mr. Hance, encouraged by his physician, elected to place his wife in a nursing facility.

Once she was admitted to the facility, Mr. Hance visited every day, spending 2–3 hours with her in the afternoon and another hour or two in the evening. During these visits, Mrs. Hance would occasionally make requests. When her husband was not able to comply with her wishes, Mrs. Hance would become angry and strike and scratch him. His response was to speak patiently to her and hold her arms down in an effort to defend himself. The nursing staff began to worry about Mr. Hance, fearing that he was exhibiting signs of a deepening depression. He was referred for outpatient counseling.

During counseling sessions, Mr. Hance reported that he had no close family, only a few distant relatives he rarely visited. He also had few friends, and he confided that he had difficulty establishing close, intimate relationships. In fact, one of his great hopes had been that his marriage would result in the type of intimacy that he had read about and seen in other couples. Sadly, it had not. He also felt guilty over his relief in placing his wife in long-term care, and believed that on some level he caused his wife's aggression in an effort not to be forced to care for her at home.

Part of Mr. Hance's treatment focused on bibliotherapy. He was assigned chapters in two books, *The Vanishing Mind* and *The 36-Hour Day* (Heston & White, 1991; Mace & Robbins, 1991), which explained the symptoms and behaviors associated with Alzheimer's disease. As Mr. Hance worked through the material, he began to understand how his wife's ability to reason was affected and that his emotional responses and hers were common. He began to perceive her aggressive behavior as a manifestation of the illness, not as a reaction to him or his handling of her illness. As a result, he was able to put aside his dream of the type of intimacy he had longed for with his wife and replace it with a more realistic view of what they shared: He was "there" for her regardless of her condition, and, he believed, she would have done the same for him.

Soon Mr. Hance began to demonstrate changes in his depressive symptoms, which delighted the staff. He continued to visit his wife every day, but only once a day. He attended the cultural activities that he had previously enjoyed and often told the nurses and nursing assistants about concerts, dance performances, and art exhibits he had attended.

Bibliotherapy can be implemented for older adults living independently in several different ways. Depending on the physical capabilities and preferences of the individual, a reading bibliotherapy program may be suitable (Scogin, Hamblin, & Beutler, 1987). After the older person is assessed, it may be helpful to prescribe a self-help or therapeutic book containing strategies for coping with unpleasant events, for gaining control over one's thoughts, and for building self-esteem (Mahalik & Kivlighan, 1988; Scogin, Jamison, & Gochneaur, 1989). Older adults engaging in self-directed readings should not simply be assigned or given the readings and then abandoned. Follow-up therapy in the form of weekly home visits or telephone calls, during which questions about the book's content may be answered and progress monitored, is essential (Scogin, Hamblin, & Beutler, 1987).

Another method of implementing a bibliotherapy program for older adults living independently is to form a group session in a nonthreatening environment such as a library, church, senior center, or community center. After becoming acquainted with the needs and desires of group members, the bibliotherapist selects material that can be either read aloud during group sessions or sent home with the client and discussed at the next meeting (Brown, 1975). Combining the benefits of reading at home and reading during group sessions may be the best option.

USE OF BIBLIOTHERAPY WITH OLDER ADULTS LIVING IN CONGREGATE HOUSING OR LONG-TERM CARE FACILITIES

Emma Terrell was a 72-year-old woman who had been residing in a nursing facility for over a year. She had been placed there as a result of her severe osteoporosis, which had led to a frail skeletal structure and numerous small fractures. Much of her day was spent in laborious and cautious preparation to move and ambulate. When she did not need to move about, she spent much of her time in a large easy chair in her room. Several types of activities were introduced to keep Emma busy: Her family provided a television set in her room, which she rarely turned on. The recreation staff encouraged and provided materials for knitting and needlepoint. Emma did not pursue the craft activities. A cassette player and an assortment of tapes were placed in her room. Emma enjoyed some Celtic music, but played it only in the morning, saying she preferred a quiet environment.

One afternoon, the facility social worker, Barbara, visited Emma as part of her duties in conducting psychosocial assessments of the residents. In the course of conversation Barbara described a book she was reading about developmental disabilities, which was helping her cope with her child, who had been diagnosed with attention-deficit/hyperactivity disorder. Emma commented that she would like to read about osteoporosis. Barbara offered to obtain some material on the topic, which she located at the library of a local community college. Although the two articles and book on the topic were academic in nature, Emma read them avidly. When her physician, Dr. Abbott, visited the following month, Emma discussed her condition with him. He subsequently provided her with additional material. Her physician's willingess to share information meant a great deal to Emma. She told Barbara that she felt Dr. Abbott was not "talking down" to her and was treating her with more respect than before. She also reported that it was easier to discuss her condition because she understood some of the physiological changes taking place in her body. The staff found her more tolerant of the need to be careful in moving and in taking time to ambulate.

Having discovered that reading was of interest to Emma, Barbara located other books that she might enjoy. Emma particularly responded to a book by comedian Gilda Radner on living with ovarian cancer. Emma began to compare her own invalid status with that of Radner. As Emma completed the book, she discussed insights she had obtained from it with Barbara. Most of all, Emma was struck by Radner's ability to experience pleasure in living despite the restrictions of her physical condition. Emma described her own ability to appreciate the sunshine and flowers she could see from her window and her morning music. Emma's pursuit of reading continued. She read poetry, developing a particular affinity for the work of Emily Dickinson. Through poetry, Emma looked for parallels in her suffering and insights into the beauties of the world. Barbara continued to meet with Emma for approximately half an hour each week to discuss the readings and Emma's thoughts. Reading seemed to provide Emma with both a distraction from her problems and an acceptance of the fact that suffering is part of every individual's life.

Bibliotherapy can be beneficial for older adults living in congregate housing and long-term care facilities as well as for those living independently. Several different possibilities exist for implementing a program. The physical limitations and emotional needs of residents will best define the appropriate bibliotherapy program. For older individuals who possess adequate visual acuity, reading ability, and concentration skills, simply providing a library on-site with a variety of subjects and materials may spark interest (Brown, 1975; Scogin, Jamison, & Gochneaur, 1989). Making someone available who is knowledgeable in many areas of literature and familiar with the backgrounds of the residents is essential to guide older adults toward choices that are therapeutically beneficial (Brown, 1975). Many public libraries offer bookmobiles that travel to certain facilities on a regular basis. However, it is still necessary to provide someone to guide the residents in selecting materials (Brown, 1975). Specific books recommended can be ordered from the library and obtained via the bookmobile staff. If facility staff members are not knowledgeable about potential reading material, a professional librarian may be helpful. Librarians, particularly those who have received training since the mid-1980s, tend to be familiar with bibliotherapy. Other potential resources include faculty at a local college or university. A good starting point is to write to the head of the language and literature or humanities department explaining the situation, with a request to be directed to a faculty member or representative. The letter should be followed by a telephone call. The psychology, social work, and social sciences departments are alternative sources of information. Most colleges and universities encourage their faculty to provide community service.

Many individuals residing in long-term care facilities have physical or cognitive limitations that prevent them from reading or even holding a book (Brown, 1975). In some cases adaptive devices may be used. In other cases bibliotherapy can be offered to these individuals in group form, with a facilitator reading aloud from literary selections that have some meaning for one or more of the residents present. The reading or readings can be followed by group discussion of the material. If the severity of the physical limitations is such that older adults are prevented from participating in a group, bibliotherapy can be provided individually, with a facilitator visiting residents in their rooms (Brown, 1975). Residents with visual impairments may be read to by another resident.

PRECAUTIONS TO TAKE AND
ACCOMMODATIONS TO MAKE IN IMPLEMENTING BIBLIOTHERAPY

When implementing a bibliotherapy program in a community setting, congregate living, or long-term care facility, certain accommodations should be made and precautions taken. Finding the appropriate individual to administer bibliotherapy is essential. Possessing a diverse knowledge of books—the product of many years of reading—is an important qualification. Other important attributes of the facilitator include emotional stability, ability to cooperate with others on a therapeutic team, respect for the older adult's wishes and rights, cheerfulness, patience, ability to communicate clearly, and a high degree of perceptiveness and sensitivity (Brown, 1975). Knowledge of the participant's physical and emotional conditions is a necessity. A facilitator must also know how an individual may react to certain types of literature (Brown, 1975). A skilled volunteer staff member or person in the field with a strong interest in reading may be the ideal candidate. Visiting health care or social services professionals are also in an excellent position to implement bibliotherapy. A local librarian or library assistant working under the direction of a librarian trained in developmental bibliotherapy are other options. The bibliotherapy facilitator must be an empathic listener and should project a nonjudgmental, accepting attitude (O'Dell, 1986). The facilitator should also avoid becoming the focus of attention. The goal of bibliotherapy is not to teach but to allow readers to share their insights from the readings. Consistent efforts must be made to shift interpretations of the material to the participants. Monitoring the client's progress can take place during weekly or even monthly visits.

It is necessary for the bibliotherapy facilitator to coordinate his or her schedule and efforts with family members, nursing staff, psychiatrists, and other professionals who may contribute to the therapeutic benefits of the program (Brown,

1975). More important, the facilitator must recognize that bibliotherapy is not suited for all older adults (Brown, 1975; Scogin, Hamblin, & Beutler, 1987). Individuals with severe cognitive impairment and those who are not interested in reading will not benefit from bibliotherapy. Many older people prefer to watch television or listen to the radio. Bibliotherapy should not be forced on these individuals (Brown, 1975).

Choosing appropriate material is necessary for the program to have therapeutic value. The content must be relevant and seem reasonable to older individuals (Scogin, Jamison, & Gochneaur, 1989). After gaining an awareness of the background of the older person or persons, the facilitator must carefully recommend a book, poem, or periodical that best suits the subject's or group's needs. One possibility is the self-help literature alluded to previously (Mahalik & Kivlighan, 1988; Scogin, Jamison, & Gochneaur, 1989). Brown (1975), who has communicated extensively with residents and staff of long-term care facilities, suggests that residents prefer a wide variety of books. Cohen (1994b) has pointed out that a range of literature can function as therapeutic reading. It may be best to ask the resident to work through a process of selecting the appropriate reading(s), a process that may involve trial and error. The bibliotherapy facilitator should avoid overly enthusiastically recommending a specific reading because it raises expectations and makes it difficult for the client to perceive him- or herself in the reading.

The appendix at the end of the chapter lists several categories of books that can serve as therapeutic readings for older adults. These readings can provide insight, result in improved coping skills, or provide mental respite. A growing number of books are offered in large-print format and on audiotape, many times read by celebrities or by the author. These books may be helpful for individuals with impaired vision, and often, public libraries stock a wide selection (Brown, 1975). Making arrangements with interlibrary loan services (offered by most state library systems and some professional schools, colleges, and universities) can help to broaden the range of materials available for use beyond that offered by public library bookmobile services (Brown, 1975). Establishing an on-site permanent library would be ideal in a residential setting. Collecting a wide array of materials through donations from family, local libraries, and businesses expands the offerings.

As important as it is for a facilitator to possess sufficient knowledge about an older person before recommending reading material, thorough knowledge of the material's content is even more important. If the facilitator's familiarity with the literature is superficial, he or she may suggest a book that provides an effect opposite from that desired (Brown, 1975).

Brown (1975) recommends careful use or avoidance of the following types of literature in bibliotherapy programs for older adults:

- Morbid or depressing novels (e.g., Sylvia Plath's *The Bell Jar*)
- Horror stories (e.g., Clive Barker novels, such as *Hellraiser*)

- Books containing obscenity or near-obscenity (e.g., Henry Miller's *Tropic of Cancer*, James Joyce's *Ulysses*)
- Books that may offend an individual's religious beliefs (e.g., Stephen Jay Gould's *Ever Since Darwin: Reflections on Natural History*)

Other precautions to keep in mind when selecting reading material include ensuring that it does not require too much mental effort—readers can become discouraged quickly—and that the amount of reading is appropriate for the individual. The amount should not be so great that the individual feels overloaded or becomes confused. The goal of bibliotherapy is to help the individual improve his or her coping skills (Brown, 1975). Finally, clients should not be forced to read material that is not interesting to them.

Audiovisual materials can be used to supplement a bibliotherapy program. Interest can be sparked by coordinating a table display of books of a certain theme with that of a weekly movie. For example, the film *A Woman's Tale* (1991) portrays a free-spirited octogenarian who takes charge of her life when she is diagnosed with terminal cancer. This fact-based film can be coupled with Wilfrid Sheed's book, *In Love with Daylight*, which deals with similar issues. Videotapes and books on tape are usually available free of charge through local libraries or schools. Recordings of television or radio programs may also provide a beneficial supplement to bibliotherapy (Brown, 1975). Television has been adventurous in portraying many difficult life situations. For example, *To Dance with the White Dog* effectively depicts the impact that death has on a surviving spouse. This remarkable film is available on videocassette and can be rented from video stores or borrowed from a local library.

Adaptive devices to aid in reading may be necessary for individuals with certain physical disabilities. Devices such as bookstands, books on tape, and page turners help older adults to compensate for their disabilities (Brown, 1975). A variety of tilting tables and book holders that reduce fatigue in holding books are available. These tables can be positioned over the individual who is seated in a chair or bed. Small, stationary holders are also available in many different forms. One is a pillow holder that holds open the pages of a book using braided cords and can be placed on a person's lap. Magnifying glasses are also available, ranging from small, round, handheld magnifiers to large, stationary magnifiers reminiscent of the type used by jewelers. The advantage of these large magnifiers is that they do not have to be held. The arm of the magnifier is positioned and the book placed beneath it. Full-page magnifiers have become popular with many older adults. Most adaptive devices are available through local department stores or catalogs (see appendix at the end of the chapter). If adaptive devices are not available, paperback books are a good alternative, provided that the smaller print is clearly visible (Brown, 1975).

IMPLEMENTATION OF BIBLIOTHERAPY

Several steps are involved in implementing bibliotherapy: determining the type of bibliotherapy, defining the goals of bibliotherapy, selecting therapeutic readings, and assessing and evaluating the participants and program.

Determine Type of Bibliotherapy

Reading Bibliotherapy

To implement a reading bibliotherapy program, certain preliminary steps should be taken. First, an individual or individuals must be chosen to administer the program. Second, candidates for the program must be screened. Participants must be able to read well, show interest, and be motivated to work on their problems (Scogin, Jamison, & Gochneaur, 1989). Third, literature is chosen based on the needs of the participants. Fourth, a meeting with each participant should be arranged to answer any questions and to provide a means of contact for him or her in the event of additional questions or concerns (Mahalik & Kivlighan, 1988). Fifth, each participant receives carefully selected literature and a reasonable time frame for when the book should be finished agreed on. Participants are contacted regularly, in person or by telephone, to monitor progress and answer any questions or clarify points in the text (Scogin, Hamblin, & Beutler, 1987; Scogin, Jamison, & Gochneaur, 1989).

The most effective therapeutic materials for self-help bibliotherapy are highly structured works oriented toward cognitive or behavioral issues (Scogin, Hamblin, & Beutler, 1987; Scogin, Jamison, & Gochneaur, 1989; Wollersheim & Wilson, 1991). Scogin, Hamblin, and Beutler compared a book by Dr. David Burns (1980) entitled *Feeling Good*, which is a pragmatic guide to reducing symptoms of depression, with Viktor Frankl's *Man's Search for Meaning* (1959), which provides a general perspective for coping with emotional difficulties but does not prescribe structured techniques for diminishing depressive affect. Burns's work, with its structured, practical steps, was found to be superior for use in bibliotherapy. The appendix at the end of this chapter lists suggested readings that have been used by Scogin, Jamison, and Gochneaur (1989) and found to be effective in reducing depressive symptoms.

Based on Cohen's work (1994a, b, c), it is conceivable that other general therapeutic readings can help older adults cope with problems. Regrettably, no research is available on which materials would be effective in meeting different goals. Requiring older adults to assume responsibility for selecting readings from a list of recommended alternatives may be advantageous in that it fosters in them a sense of control over the problems causing their emotional distress.

Group Bibliotherapy

Regardless of the setting—the community, congregate housing, or long-term care facility—preparations must be made when implementing a group bibliotherapy program. An appropriate site should be selected, and a group facilitator should be chosen.

The facilitator must consult with facility directors and staff members to arrange appropriate schedules and to be advised on prospective group members. Being aware of and understanding the goals of the setting in which the program is to be established is recommended (Brown, 1975). Successful groups tend to have no fewer than 5 and no more than 12 participants (Hynes & Wedl, 1990);

O'Dell (1986) proposes that the optimal range is 6–8 participants. Groups comprising too few participants places too much pressure on each participant to keep the discussion moving, whereas in large groups not all members may receive an opportunity to speak. Larger groups may profit by having cofacilitators, one of whom is an older adult. (See Chapter 11 for details on the advantages of and procedural issues in using an older adult peer as a cofacilitator.)

The group facilitator should gain as much knowledge as possible about each group member's interests, intelligence level, physical or mental abilities, and background (Brown, 1975). This information may be obtained in several ways. Family, staff members, the participant's records, and the participant may provide the information. Working with specialized groups of older adults, such as people with cognitive impairment or survivors of violence and abuse, is particularly challenging (Hynes & Hynes-Berry, 1986). Older people who have experienced years of abuse need help in reconstructing their lives and self-images through sharing their pain. Hynes (1987) recommends using newsletters from women's shelters in which the women write accounts of their experiences. People with Alzheimer's disease require more direction in discussing their reactions to the readings. Potenza and Labbancz (1989) report that a sense of achievement and well-being can be experienced by older adults with Alzheimer's disease who can remain focused and contribute even a little—a thought or a line— to a group poem.

The format of group bibliography sessions may vary. Materials may be read by the facilitator or by individual members. The selection of materials should be based on information gathered by the facilitator, consensus of the group, or both. Readings should be chosen so that benefit is provided to as many group members as possible, and precautions should be taken so as not to include material members may find offensive (Brown, 1975). The procedure recommended by Hynes and Wedl (1990) to facilitators for conducting group bibliotherapy follows:

Establish a welcoming atmosphere by playing appropriate selections of music and mounting magazine photos or objects related to the topic available for discussion.

Ask participants to identify themselves in the first meeting. In subsequent meetings each participant should add personal information (e.g., hometown, favorite movie, favorite foods) in an effort to gradually share his or her feelings about the reading.

Give a copy of the selection in large-print format to each member of the group.

Read the selection. Wenzel (1993) recommends asking participants to take turns reading part of the material: Each participant takes responsibility for reading a small part of the material. However, Wenzel cautions that no member of the group should be forced to read.

Allow a few moments for thought and reflection.

Allow approximately 15 minutes for discussion of the material read.

Suggest that participants write something on the general topic of the literary piece; feelings, memories, or any aspect may be expanded on.

Ask the participants to share what they have written with the rest of the group.

Another format is to provide participants with handouts or books of poems or short stories from which each person selects a poem or story that is meaningful to him or her. At the following session, poems or stories are read aloud and individuals are prompted to share their feelings about them (Brown, 1975; Hynes & Wedl, 1990). Another approach is to ask older adults without cognitive impairment to read the therapeutic selection on their own and discuss it during the subsequent group sessions.

The most important part of a group bibliotherapy program is the discussion that takes place after the reading is finished. During the discussion, the facilitator notes reactions, looks for areas of increased insight, and looks for misconceptions that need correction (Brown, 1975). It is from this information that the group facilitator is able to evaluate the group's progress and make appropriate material selections for the sessions to follow.

A variety of problems can arise for the bibliotherapist. The most common are (O'Dell, 1986) silence, emotional difficulties (e.g., crying, withdrawing, being angry), and illiteracy.

When encountering silence, the facilitator should not attempt to fill in the gap. He or she should sit back and allow some of the participants to feel the pressure to speak. This action shifts the responsibility for discussion onto the group members. If the facilitator takes the initiative and speaks first, he or she may set a pattern of facilitator-directed discussion and even encourage dependency. If no discussion ensues after a reasonable period, the facilitator should ask a specific, easy-to-answer question to encourage participation.

When encountering emotional difficulties, the facilitator should expect strong emotions to surface; this is part of the therapeutic process. These responses should be formally recognized and acknowledged rather than ignored or brushed aside. The facilitator should stop and mention to the participant that he or she appears to be upset and then wait for a response. A participant who is crying should be asked why he or she is crying and supported. If the participant wishes to leave the group, he or she should be allowed to do so but should be followed up with an individual visit from the facilitator. A person who is withdrawn should be encouraged gently to participate. If this is a new response in an otherwise gregarious person, he or she should be approached privately and concern expressed in a supportive manner. If the participant becomes angry, the outburst should be recognized as an honest reaction, but limits should be set if the anger is directed at another participant. The importance of treating each member of the group in a respectful manner should be stressed. A participant should not be permitted to verbally abuse or assault another member of the group. Acknowledgment of the anger and direction of attention toward analyzing the individual's response may help to contain the anger and manage it.

On occasion, someone with minimal reading skills will be referred to a bibliotherapy group (many illiterate people are able to hide their illiteracy from others successfully). Indicators of illiteracy include refusing to read, leafing through the material while reading is taking place, giving the material to someone else, complaining of headaches, and forgetting to bring glasses to the group (he or she may not own glasses). The facilitator should avoid confronting the individual. The person should be asked privately if he or she wishes to continue with the group. If he or she wishes to do so, the situation must be accepted. The illiterate person should be allowed to listen to the readings and participate in the discussions.

Individual Interactive Bibliotherapy

Many of the same preparations necessary for group bibliotherapy programs must be made for individual programs. Facilitators setting up bibliotherapy programs for individuals must consult with family members, and, in the case of residents in long-term care or those living in congregate housing, with both family and staff members. In residential settings the goals of the facility must be taken into account, in addition to the background and health of the individual (Brown, 1975). The selection of materials must be made based on these findings as well as on the goals of the intervention and the preferences of the participant.

The main difference between individual and group bibliotherapy is that in individual bibliotherapy there is a one-to-one relationship between facilitator and individual. Independent older adults should be provided with a choice of several different therapeutic readings and asked to select one. Older adults requiring more direction should be assigned a specific reading based on the goals for the intervention. The reading can then take place independently, followed by a therapy session in which the material is discussed by the facilitator and client. Older adults with visual impairment or those experiencing some cognitive impairment may require assistance in reading the material. The facilitator should read the selected material aloud in a clear and agreeable voice and then follow the reading with a discussion (Brown, 1975).

Define Goals

Some preliminary discussion should take place between facilitator and client concerning the client's objective in reading the therapeutic material. The client may wish to learn about a specific condition, to read about how someone coped with a similar illness or situation, to uncover strategies for coping with physical or emotional pain, or even to escape into a world of fiction or poetry that creates a pleasant diversion from problems. The facilitator should help the client to identify clear, well-defined goals. This step is critical because the goals that are established will direct the readings to be selected. Individual goals should be established for each participant in group bibliotherapy because more active members of the group tend to dominate the sessions, obscuring the level of participation of less-active participants (O'Dell, 1986). Setting individual goals enables the facilitator to monitor the progress of each member to determine if all are benefitting from the experience. Group goals should also be established (O'Dell, 1986). These goals tend to focus on reducing sadness, increasing socialization, or providing cognitive stimulation. Group goals provide the direction needed for structuring the intervention.

Select Therapeutic Readings

Therapeutic literature should be selected on the basis of the goals identified and the type of bibliotherapy in which clients are engaged. The literature should also be selected with an eye toward details that encourage maximum reader recognition of self (Cohen, 1994b). The appendix at the end of the chapter provides a list of appropriate readings to guide facilitators. It is critical, however, that facilitators read the materials before recommending them. Bibliotherapy should be designed to meet the needs of the indivdual or individuals involved. The facilitator should be familiar with the individual and the material before undertaking this form of treatment.

Selection of readings vary considerably depending on the functional level of the participants. Older adults who have been lifelong readers, who have more formal education, or both can handle longer selections. Older adults with physical or cognitive limitations or residents of long-term care facilities who have settled into a passive existence will respond better to short passages read during a group session. Older people who are engaged in a highly structured self-help form of bibliotherapy should be assigned short chapters or sections of approximately 8–12 pages (Maultsby, 1991). A minimum of 10–20 minutes of reading each day is recommended.

Careful selection of readings must take place throughout the intervention period, not only in the first few sessions (O'Dell, 1986). Many bibliotherapists develop a reference group of readings that they find useful in addressing common issues (e.g., family interactions, living with a chronic illness, feelings of loss) with a variety of individuals, but they should be mindful that the readings match the individuals' needs and interests. An assessment of functional skills and interests should take place in a preliminary interview with each prospective participant. A sample assessment form is provided on page 183.

The assigned therapeutic readings should be enjoyable, have some emotional content, and center on a common theme (O'Dell, 1986). Each theme should be explored fully before moving on to another. As the bibliotherapy sessions progress, more issue-oriented themes can be addressed. The participants will also be able to share more personal information. Much of this progression will depend on the level of trust developed between group members or with the facilitator, in the case of individual interactive bibliotherapy.

Bibliotherapists should keep in mind that readings that do not work for one person or one group may suit another. O'Dell (1986) proposes that a reading be tested in two to three groups before being discarded as unusable.

Assessment and Evaluation

Some type of evaluation is essential. Informal assessment tools can be used when the goal of the intervention is to increase social interaction and knowledge or insight into a condition or an event. Formal assessment tools should be used when the goal of the intervention is to reduce depression. One possibility is to administer self-reporting (informal) or formal pre- and posttests of depressive symptoms (Scogin, Jamison, & Gochneaur, 1989). Another possibility is to gather individuals together who have read similar material and hold a discussion in which individual contributions are recorded. This type of discussion can also be carried out on an individual basis. In addition to determining the effectiveness of the therapy in individual cases, careful monitoring allows for appropriate selection of subsequent

Assessment of Bibliotherapy
Functional Skills/Interest Inventory

Client _____ Date _____

Functional Skills

Can you read regular-size print in a book or newspaper? ___ Yes ___ No

Do you prefer a large-print format? ___ Yes ___ No

Do you prefer to use an adaptive device? ___ Book holder ___ Magnifying page ___ Other

Would you like to discuss readings with others? ___ Yes ___ No

Do you prefer solitary reading? ___ Yes ___ No

Life Experiences/Interests

Where were you raised? _____

How many siblings? ___ Sisters ___ Brothers Still living? ___ Yes ___ No

Did you marry? ___ Yes ___ No   Children? ___ Yes ___ No   How many? _____

Do your ___ siblings___ children ___ spouse live in the area?

What type of work did you do? _____

What type of hobbies did you enjoy? _____

Do you have any special interests? _____

What do you find yourself thinking about these days? _____

_____

Facilitator Observations

Attended to the topic without being prompted? ___ Yes ___ No

Responded to questions with ___ Gestures ___ Verbal comments ___ No response

Needed questions repeated? ___ Yes ___ No. needed (average) ___ No

Offered spontaneous comments? ___ Yes ___ No

Responded only to direct comments? ___ Yes ___ No

Sustained conversation for a period of time? ___ Yes ___ No

Appeared mentally confused? ___ Yes ___ No

Facilitator Comments

A Life Worth Living: Practical Strategies for Reducing Depression In Older Adults, by Pearl Mosher-Ashley and Phyllis Barrett. ©1997 Health Professions Press, Inc., Baltimore.

Bibliotherapy Progress Record Form

Client _____ Date _____ Week no. _____

Short-term goal

Long-term goal

Material read since last meeting

Summary of Discussion
Theme

Insights shared by client

Emotional reactions

Issues being dealt with

New reading assigned or selected by client

A Life Worth Living: Practical Strategies for Reducing Depression in Older Adults, by Pearl Mosher-Ashley and Phyllis Barrett. ©1997 Health Professions Press, Inc., Baltimore.

readings for an individual or group, while also making it possible to establish a list of appropriate and inappropriate readings for future readers whose circumstances are similar to those of former or current participants.

Record keeping is an important aspect of a therapeutic intervention and the evaluation process. Evaluation should be based on discrete indicators that reflect a participant's involvement and awareness. Hynes (Hynes & Wedl, 1990) and O'Dell (1986) have developed report forms that can be used by facilitators conducting group bibliotherapy (see p. 184 for a sample form that can be used for individualized therapeutic programs). The information recorded can assist other professionals in following the client's progress. The recorded degree of involvement of participants with cognitive impairment can serve as a measure of the course of the dementing illness (Hynes & Wedl, 1990).

References

Brown, E.F. (1975). *Bibliotherapy and its widening applications.* Metuchen, NJ: Scarecrow Press.

Burns, D. (1980). *Feeling good.* New York: Guilford Press.

Cohen, L.J. (1989). Reading as a group process phenomenon: A theoretical framework for bibliotherapy. *Journal of Poetry Therapy, 3,* 73–84.

Cohen, L.J. (1994a). Bibliotherapy: A valid treatment modality. *Journal of Psychosocial Nursing, 32*(9), 40–44.

Cohen, L.J. (1994b). Phenomenology of therapeutic reading with implications for research and practice of bibliotherapy. *Arts in Psychotherapy, 21,* 37–44.

Cohen, L.J. (1994c). The experience of therapeutic reading. *Western Journal of Nursing Research, 16,* 426–437.

Frankl, V. (1959). *Man's search for meaning.* New York: Pocket Books.

Haddock, B.D. (1989). Scenario writing: A therapeutic application. *Journal of Mental Health Counseling, 11,* 234–243.

Heller, P.O. (1987). The three pillars of biblio/poetry therapy. *Arts in Psychotherapy, 14,* 341–344.

Heston, L.L., & White, J.A. (1991). *The vanishing mind.* New York: W.H. Freeman.

Hynes, A.M., (1987). Biblio/poetry therapy in women's shelters. *American Journal of Social Psychiatry, 7,* 112–116.

Hynes, A.M., & Hynes-Berry, A. (1986). *Bibliotherapy: The interactive process.* Boulder, CO: Westview Press.

Hynes, A.M., & Wedl, L.C. (1990). Bibliotherapy: An interactive process in counseling older persons. *Journal of Mental Health Counseling, 12,* 288–302.

Mace, N.L., & Robbins, P.V. (1991). *The 36-hour day: A family guide to caring for persons with Alzheimer's disease, related dementing illnesses and memory loss in later life* (2nd ed.). Baltimore: The Johns Hopkins University Press.

Mahalik, J., & Kivlighan, D. (1988). Self-help treatment for depression: Who succeeds? *Journal of Counseling Psychology, 35,* 237–242.

Maultsby, M.C. (1991). Prescribed therapeutic self-help for the elderly: The rational behavioral approach. In P.K.H. Kim (Ed.), *Skills for practice: Modern applications of social work* (pp. 137–165). New York: Aldine de Gruyter.

O'Dell, L. (1986). A bibliotherapist's perspective. In I. Burnside (Ed.), *Working with the elderly: Group process and techniques* (pp. 410–425). Boston: Jones & Bartlett.

Potenza, M., & Labbancz, M. (1989). The use of poetry in a day care center for Alzheimer's disease. *American Journal of Alzheimer's Care and Related Disorders & Research, 3,* 10–12.

Scogin, F., Hamblin, D., & Beutler, L. (1987). Bibliotherapy for depressed older adults: A self-help alternative. *Gerontologist, 27,* 383–387.

Scogin, F., Jamison, C., & Davis, N. (1990). Two-year follow-up of bibliotherapy for depression in older adults. *Journal of Consulting and Clinical Psychology, 58,* 665–667.

Scogin, F., Jamison, C., & Gochneaur, K. (1989). Comparative efficacy of cognitive and behavioral bibliotherapy for mildly and moderately depressed older adults. *Journal of Consulting and Clinical Psychology, 57,* 403–407.

Wollersheim, J.P., & Wilson, G.L. (1991). Group treatment of unipolar depression: A comparison of coping, supportive, bibliotherapy, and delayed treatment groups. *Professional Psychology: Research and Practice, 22,* 496–502.

Appendix
Suggested Therapeutic Reading

Many books are available in large-print format. Also, many copy machines are equipped to make enlargements of printed material at a low cost.

Personal Experiences with Depression

Styron, W. (1990). *Darkness visible: A memory of madness.* New York: Random House.

Thorne, J. (1993). *You are not alone: Words of experience and hope for the journey through depression.* New York: HarperCollins.

Self-Help for Coping with Depression

Bloomfield, H.H., & McWilliams, P. (1994). *How to heal depression.* Los Angeles: Prelude.

Burns, D. (1980). *Feeling good.* New York: Guilford Press. (Recommended by Scogin, Jamison, & Gochneaur [1989].)

Carlson, R. (1993). *You can feel good again: Common sense therapy for releasing depression and changing your life.* New York: Dutton.

Hirschfeld, R. (1991). *When the blues won't go away: New approaches to dysthymic disorder and other forms of chronic low-grade depression.* New York: Macmillan.

Kimeldorf, M. (1994). *Serious play: A leisure wellness guidebook.* Berkeley, CA: Ten Speed Press.

Klein, A. (1989). *The healing power of humor: Techniques for getting through loss, setbacks, upsets, disappointments, difficulties, trials, tribulations, and all that not-so-funny stuff.* Los Angeles: Jeremy P. Tarcher.

Klein, D.F., & Wender, P.H. (1993). *Understanding depression.* New York: Oxford University Press.

Lewinsohn, P., Munoz, R., Youngren, M.A., & Zeiss, A. (1986). *Control your depression.* Englewood Cliffs, NJ: Prentice Hall. (Recommended by Scogin, Jamison, & Gochneaur [1989].)

LeShan, E. (1994). *I want more of everything.* New York: New Market.

Marmorstein, J., & Marmorstein, N. (1993). *Awakening from depression: A mind/body approach to emotional recovery.* Santa Barbara, CA: Woodbridge Press Publishing.

Maultsby, M.C. (1975). *Helping yourself to happiness through rational self-counseling.* New York: Institute for Rational Living.

Maultsby, M.C. (1986). *Coping better . . . anytime, anywhere.* New York: Simon & Schuster.

Maultsby, M.C., & Hendricks, A. (1974). *You and your emotions.* Lexington, KY: Rational Self-Help Aids, Inc.

Minirth, F.B., & Meier, P.D. (1994). *Happiness is a choice: A manual for the symptoms, causes and cures of depression.* Grand Rapids, MI: Baker Book House.

Minirth, F., States, S., & Meier, P. (1977). *100 ways to overcome depression.* Grand Rapids, MI: Baker Book House.

Preston, J. (1989). *You can beat depression: A guide to recovery.* San Luis Obispo, CA: Impact.

Ray, V. (1990). *Choosing happiness: The art of living unconditionally.* New York: HarperCollins.

Slagle, P. (1992). *The way up from down.* New York: Random House.

Life Experience and Reflections on Aging

Berman, P.L., & Goldman, C. (Eds.). (1992). *The ageless spirit: Reflections on living life to the fullest in our later years.* New York: Ballantine.

Cowley, M. (1981). *The view from 80.* Boston: G.K. Hall. (Available in large-print format.)

Downs, H. (1994). *Fifty to forever: The complete sourcebook for living an active, involved, and fulfilling second half of life.* Nashville: Thomas Nelson.

Downs, H. (1994). *Thirty dirty lies about old.* Boston: G.K. Hall. (Available in large-print format.)

Geller, D. (1979). *Living longer and loving it.* Maplewood, NJ: Hammond.

LeShan, E. (1994). *It's better to be over the hill than under it: Thoughts on life over sixty.* New York: New Market.

Robey, H. (1982). *There's a dance in the old dame yet.* Boston: G.K. Hall. (Available in large-print format.)

Wenzel, E.B. (1993). "It sure beats looking out the window": Literature for the elderly. *Activities, Adaptation & Aging, 17,* 63–79.

Collections and Stories Dealing with the Aging Process

Bloch, D. (1992). *I am with you always: A treasury of inspirational quotations, poems, and prayers.* New York: Bantam.

Buscalia, L. (1982). *The fall of Freddie the leaf.* Thorofare, NJ: Slack.

Cole, T.R., & Winkler, M.G. (1994). *The Oxford book of aging.* New York: Oxford University Press.

Fulghum, R. (1995). *From beginning to end: The rituals of our lives.* New York: Villard Books.

Kidder, T. (1993). *Old friends.* Boston: Houghton Mifflin.

Martz, S. (Ed.). (1991). *When I am an old woman I shall wear purple.* Watsonville, CA: Papier-Mache.

Self-Help in Coping with Aging Issues

Berman, P.L. (1989). *The courage to grow old.* New York: Ballantine Books.

Blythe, R. (1979). *The view in winter.* New York: Harcourt Brace.

Kaufman, S.R. (1986). *The ageless self: Sources of meaning in later life.* Madison, WI: University of Wisconsin Press.

Knopf, O. (1977). *Successful aging: The facts and fallacies of growing old.* Boston: G.K. Hall. (Recommended by Scogin, Jamison, & Gochneaur [1989].)

Pacheco, C.C. (1989). *Breaking patterns: Redesigning your later years.* Kansas City, KS: Andrews & McMeel.

Schachter-Shalomi, Z., & Miller, R.S. (1995). *From age-ing to sage-ing: A profound new vision of growing older.* New York: Warner Books.

Schmerl, E.F. (1991). *The challenge of age: A guide to growing older in health and happiness.* New York: Continuum.

Personal Experiences with Medical Problems or Coping Strategies (primary topic)

Cohen, D., & Eisdorfer, C. (1986). *The loss of self: A family resource for the care of Alzheimer's disease and related disorders.* New York: Norton. (Alzheimer's disease)

Glickfeld, C.L. (1991). *Useful gifts.* Athens: University of Georgia Press. (deafness)

Heston, L.L., & White, J.A. (1991). *The vanishing mind.* New York: W.H. Freeman. (Alzheimer's disease)

Kenney, S. (1987). *In another country.* New York: Viking Penguin. (cancer)

Kenney, S. (1991). *Sailing.* New York: Viking Penguin. (cancer)

L'Engle, M. (1987). *Two-part invention: The story of a marriage.* New York: Farrar, Straus & Giroux. (loss of spouse)

Mace, N.L., & Robbins, P.V. (1991). *The 36-hour day: A family guide to caring for persons with Alzheimer's disease, related dementing illnesses and memory loss in later life* (2nd ed.). Baltimore: The Johns Hopkins University Press. (Alzheimer's disease)

Matsakis, A. (1992). *I can't get over it: A handbook for trauma survivors.* Oakland, CA: New Harbinger Press. (death and other losses)

Oliver, R., & Bock, F.A. (1987). *Coping with Alzheimer's: A caregiver's emotional survival guide.* Boston: Dodd, Mead. (Alzheimer's disease)

Rice, R. (1991). *A time to mourn: One woman's journey through widowhood.* New York: NAL/Dutton. (loss of spouse)

Sarton, M. (1990). *After the stroke.* New York: Norton. (stroke)

Schreiber, L. A. (1991). *Midstream: The story of a mother's death and a daughter's renewal.* New York: Viking Penguin. (pancreatic cancer, loss of parent)

Sheed, W. (1995). *In love with daylight.* New York: Simon & Schuster. (cancer, depression, alcoholism, aging)

Sontag, S. (1990). *Illness as metaphor and AIDS and its metaphors.* New York: Doubleday. (cancer and HIV/AIDS)

Stone, B. (1994). *Cancer as initiation: Surviving the fire.* Chicago: Open Court. (breast cancer)

West, P. (1995). *A stroke of genius.* New York: Viking Press. (stroke)

Therapeutic/Meditation

Bennett, B. (1993). *Breathing into life: Recovering wholeness through body, mind, and breath.* San Francisco: HarperCollins.

Short Stories (Recommended by Wenzel [1993])

Brecht, B. (1961). "The Unseemly Old Lady," from *Tales from the calendar.* Translated by Yvonne Kapp. London.

Chekhov, A. (1915). "Grief," from *The steppe & other stories.* Translated by Adeline Lister Kaye. London: William Heinemann.

de Maupassant, G. (1945). "The Little Cask." In *The best stories of Guy de Maupassant.* New York: Modern Library.

Garcia Marquez, G. (1979). "Artificial Roses," from *No one writes to the colonel and other stories.* New York: Bernstein.

Mansfield, K. (1930). "Miss Brill," from *Stories by Katherine Mansfield.* New York: Knopf.

Paley, G. (1974). "A Conversation with My Father," from *Enormous changes at the last minute.* New York: Farrar, Straus & Giroux.

Porter, K.A. (1979). "The Jilting of Granny Wetherall," from *The collected stories of K.A. Porter.* San Diego, CA: Harbrace.

Welty, E. (1993). "A Worn Path," from *Thirteen stories.* Orlando, FL: Harcourt Brace.

Poetry (Recommended by Hynes & Wedl [1990])

Evans, M. (1970). "The Silver Cell," from *I am a black woman.* New York: William Morrow.

Faber, N. (1979). "Ponder of Learning," from *Something further . . . .* Ann Arbor, MI: Kylix Press.

Adaptive Devices to Facilitate Reading

Levenger
975 South Congress Avenue
Delray Beach, Florida 33445-4628
Phone (800) 544-0880
Free catalog that features a variety of tilting tables designed to hold hardbound books to reduce fatigue; book pillows, trays, and stands are also available; items are attractive but somewhat expensive

Reader's Window
192 Thomas Lane
Stowe, Vermont 05672
Phone (800) 867-7869
Overhead book holder $299.00

Books on Audiotape to Facilitate Reading

Audio Book Club
Post Office Box 986
Hicksville, New York 11802-0986
Phone (800) 422-2258

Bible Alliance, Inc.
Post Office Box 621
Bradenton, Florida 34206
Phone (941) 756-6846
The Bible and other religious material are available free of charge to older adults with visual or physical impairments; professionals may request material for their clients

Books on Tape, Inc.
Post Office Box 7900
Newport Beach, California 92658-9924
Credit card orders (800) 626-3733
Customer service (other than orders) (800) 252-6996
Fax orders (714) 548-6574
World's largest selection of unabridged books

Book Distributors

Amazon.com Books
www.amazon.com (Internet web site)
Billing themselves as "Earth's biggest bookstore," Amazon.com Books lists over 1 million titles. They offer 30% off the cover price of virtually every book reviewed that week in *The New York Times Review of Books* (discount period begins at noon on the Friday before the date of the review and expires 2 weeks from that date at midnight Pacific Standard Time).

Book Call
59 Elm Street
New Canaan, Connecticut 06840
Phone (800) 255-2665
Will locate any book

Daedalus Books
Post Office Box 9132
Hyattsville, Maryland 20781-0932
Phone (800) 395-2665
Offers recently published books at reduced rates; free annotated listing available

Edward R. Hamilton Bookseller
Falls Village, Connecticut 06031-5000
Offers inexpensive books on a wide variety of topics, including self-help books; free annotated listing available

Soda Creek Press
Phone (707) 463-1351
This catalog of publishers' overstock provides a listing of inexpensive books with reductions of up to 70% off publishers' prices.

He said he couldn't make the boy believe
He could find water with a hazel prong—
Which showed how much good school had ever done him.
He wanted to go over that. But most of all
He thinks if he could have another chance
To teach him how to build a load of hay—
Robert Frost, "The Death of the Hired Man"

Picking Up Where I Left Off

Role Replacement

L oss is a recurrent theme for many older adults. One of the most dramatic losses an individual can experience is the loss of life roles. Adelmann (1994) notes that in adulthood, individuals add new roles to those already held, and they replace lost roles with new ones. In later life role losses become more difficult to replace and in some cases may be irreversible (e.g., widowhood). In addition, the few remaining roles held by older adults undergo "shrinkage" (e.g., parenthood). Many older adults become roleless, and subsequently, their lives are devalued, unstructured, and deprived of social identity (Adelmann, 1994). To compensate for these changes, older adults must become involved or seek roles and activities such as paid work, creative leisure pursuits, volunteer work, grandparenting, education, and even household work to maintain optimal adjustment (Erikson, Erikson, & Kivnick, 1986). In fact, Adelmann (1994) found that older adults assuming multiple roles had higher levels of psychological well-being than those holding fewer roles. Also, Elwell and Maltbie-Crannel (1981) found that total role loss in both older men and women was associated with lower levels of life satisfaction.

Role loss in later life can result from retirement, reduced family obligations, or loss of control attributable to poor health or placement in a long-term care facility. Regardless of the circumstances, role loss may cause an older adult to feel unappreciated, isolated, lonely, bored, or depressed (Duncan & Whitney, 1990). Various studies have revealed that replacing a lost role with some type of part-time work or participation in volunteer activities can be effective. Role replacement can provide older individuals with an opportunity for social involvement and continuity, and increase their feelings of self-esteem, autonomy, and personal worth (Duncan & Whitney, 1990; Hayden, 1988; Kuehne & Sears, 1993; Okun & Eisenberg, 1992; Perkinson, 1992; Rife, 1992; Stevens, 1992; Voeks & Drinka, 1990).

Role replacement may be a suitable option for older adults living independently as well as for those living in long-term care facilities. However, certain types of role replacement are more appropriate than others in certain situations.

USE OF ROLE REPLACEMENT WITH OLDER ADULTS LIVING INDEPENDENTLY

Bernice, age 68, resided with her husband in a small New England town. While perusing the morning paper she saw a notice describing the formation of a peer counseling program and the need for older volunteers. Bernice was attracted to the notice because 2 years earlier, her family had weathered a difficult period: Bernice's husband was drinking heavily and his behavior, which had always been somewhat argumentative and solitary, intensified. This behavior placed considerable stress on their marriage and his relationship with their son, with whom they were in business. Fortunately, the family was able to obtain help through a mental health center, and over an 8-month period, they were able to resolve many of their problems. Bernice and her husband received couples counseling, which she credited with helping her husband to stop drinking. In reading about the proposed peer counseling program Bernice considered the number of older people she knew through her church who might benefit from peer intervention. Although Bernice had been a homemaker for most of her adult life, she had often worked in the family business. She was also college educated and had experience working in church-related activities. She felt she could learn how to help others.

Bernice contacted the peer counseling program and joined the first group of trainees. Over the next year, she learned how to listen effectively and give her "clients" time to understand their situation fully before beginning to explore possible solutions. She also became skillful at guiding individuals in generating and evaluating their own potential solutions rather than depending on her to advise them. Bernice also found that sharing her personal experience in living and coping with alcoholism made her particularly effective in encouraging older adults to discuss their drinking problem. Over the next 3 years Bernice worked as a peer counselor. She worked an average of 16 hours a week and carried a case load of 8–10 clients, whom she saw weekly or biweekly, depending on the person's problem. Bernice mentioned frequently that her work provided her with a sense of purpose and improved her own domestic situation. Exposure to the problems and concerns of others made her appreciate aspects of her own life. For example, her work with widows made Bernice more tolerant of her husband's moodiness; the financial limitations of many of her clients made Bernice enjoy her lovely home even more. Bernice's general mood became lighter and she became more cheerful through her work as a peer counselor.

Of the adults approaching retirement, 75% would prefer to reduce their work hours rather than retire completely (Forman, 1993). In fact, from 25% to 33% of retired workers return to work (Beck, 1986; Butler, Anderson, & Burkhauser, 1989; Myers, 1991). Interestingly, mandatory retirement has little influence on the decision to return to work. Individuals who elected to work following retirement were generally young-old, married, well-educated, and believed that they would never quit working (Myers, 1991). In contrast, most older adults who return to work tend to do so for economic reasons. Individuals who are more secure financially, eligible to receive employer pension and Social Security benefits, or both are less likely to obtain postcareer employment (Myers, 1991).

Older adults who continue employment or are active in volunteer work tend to feel more satisfied with their daily lives than those who are homemakers, retired but occasionally employed, or fully retired (Duncan & Whitney, 1990). Ruchlin and Morris (1991) attribute this finding to the importance these older adults placed on productivity and the need to feel useful. Older individuals who are employed or engaged in volunteer work are also likely to come into contact with other people, providing them with opportunities to socialize (Stein, Doress-Worters, & Fillmore, 1994).

Older people who live independently may find satisfaction working part-time in a variety of situations. These situations include "temping" (temporary employment through an agency), working at fast food establishments, clerking at a store, working in telemarketing, or doing clerical work. A job search club or counseling center can be developed through a community or adult day center, in which older people can find appropriate employment that utilizes their skills and meets their needs (Rife & Kilty, 1990).

Work programs have been established in some communities to assist older adults living on limited incomes. For instance, in 1989 the Board of Education in Littleton, Colorado, approved an innovative program that allowed low-income older people to work part-time in the school system in order to pay their property taxes. The success of the Colorado program prompted the development of three similar programs in Massachusetts. The Massachusetts programs were expanded to allow older adults to work not only in the school system but also in all of the town government departments and the senior center (McGrath & Mosher-Ashley, 1997). These programs were budgeted for $8,000–$10,000 and, like the Colorado program, paid older adults the equivalent of the federal minimum wage. Town attorneys determined that town finance laws and worker's compensation rules were not impediments to instituting the tax rebate programs. The program in Hopedale, Massachusetts, is administered by the Council on Aging. Older people can work a total of 100 hours within a fiscal year and receive a $500 credit toward their property taxes. Participants must be at least 60 years old and the property for which they receive the tax credit must be their principal residence.

Volunteer work is another role replacement for older individuals living independently. Volunteer employment includes helping out at local schools, adult day centers, or hospitals; reading to young children at a local library; offering clerical work or other services to a church or other favored organization; working as auxiliary police; completing income tax returns; working as consumer advocates; and engaging in lobbying and voter registration drives (Chambre, 1993). Even frail older people can become involved in volunteer activities (Perkinson, 1992). Transportation to the site can be arranged through a senior van service or the work can be done in the older person's home. Possible tasks include addressing and stuffing envelopes for charitable organizations, sewing or creating other skilled crafts, and making telephone calls to homebound older adults as part of an outreach program.

Older individuals who wish to volunteer may derive great benefit as well as great enjoyment in some type of intergenerational program. Intergenerational programs meet generativity needs and bring the older adult into regular contact with younger people, reducing ageism and providing stronger links to the community (Erikson, Erikson, & Kivnick, 1986; Strom & Strom, 1995). Some examples of intergenerational programs include child care centers that are staffed by older volunteers and/or housed in the same facility as adult day facilities; volunteer work in schools; and summer camps that use older people as camp counselors (Strom & Strom, 1995; Ventura-Merkel, Liederman, & Ossofsky, 1989).

Less formal volunteer work can also be beneficial for older adults. Simply by aiding neighbors, friends, or relatives, an older person can gain a sense of being needed and appreciated. Assisting with chores such as baby-sitting, cleaning or house repairs, making baked goods, and sewing or creating other craft items are all activities that may enhance an older person's life as well as that of the recipient. However, there is an advantage to being part of a formal volunteer or work program: The structure of complying with scheduled hours of activity prevents individuals from regressing into a passive state.

Little attention has been paid to the changes in roles older adults assume within their families. Most of the research has focused on the older relative as a recipient of assistance rather than as a provider of assistance. The thrust of the research has been on the burden of care experienced by children of older adults with physical or cognitive disabilities (e.g., Pruchno & Kleban, 1993; Stephens & Zarit, 1989). Even studies that stress the reciprocal nature of parent–adult child relationships emphasize the care provided to older adults by their adult children (e.g., Ingersoll-Dayton & Antonucci, 1988; Thomas, 1988). Although the pattern of exchanging support shifts heavily toward adult children as their parents age, many older adults can and do continue to assist their adult children in meaningful ways. For example, Glass, Seeman, Herzog, Kahn, and Berkman (1995) found that 25% of the older adults they defined as "successful agers" engaged in some grandchild care. Also, men engaged in grandchild care as often as did women, suggesting that grandchild care may be an especially important and significant social role for older people of both genders.

In general, both parents of school-age children are employed, with child care emerging as a primary concern. Strom and Strom (1995) propose that older adults should assume an active role in contributing to the welfare of their families, particularly in helping to raise grandchildren. Older adults already perform this role in many low-income or minority households. Although this goal is worthy, Strom and Strom (1995) recognize that there is a need to avoid exploiting older adults. Also, many young families need to establish autonomy from as well as interdependence with their parents (Thomas, 1988). To effectively resolve these issues, Strom and Strom (1995) advocate education for grandparents and have successfully taught a course entitled "Becoming a Better Grandparent." Outcomes of this course have included more effective definition of the grandparent role, maintenance of an optimistic outlook about family affairs, development of a sense of purpose, self-confidence, acquisition of communication skills for intergenerational dialogue, and the ability to build more mutually satisfying relationships (Strom & Strom, 1990).

Strom and Strom (1995) propose the formation of grandparent education councils that link families and schools. Such a council, which would be made up of grandparents, a volunteer coordinator, and the principal representing the school faculty, has two purposes: 1) to arrange opportunities for grandparents to learn how they can make a greater contribution to family harmony, and 2) to acquaint grandparents with ways in which they can enrich their grandchildren's school experience by volunteering and supporting them as students. Grandparent education councils can provide older adults with additional meaningful social roles. For example, grandparents can serve as teacher's aides and school representatives who acquaint newcomer families with community and social services. Also, they can pass on their cultural heritage through school-related activities (e.g., Black History Month celebrations).

Use of Role Replacement with
Older Adults Living in Long-Term Care Facilities

Alma Jenkins was an 81-year-old woman with advanced peripheral vascular disease, which severely impaired her ability to walk for distances greater than down the hallway to the nurse's station and back. Alma had been widowed early in her life and never remarried. She worked as a high school teacher until her retirement at age 65. Following her retirement, she traveled widely until medical problems forced her into a somewhat reclusive life. She had been admitted to a nursing facility a year earlier because of mobility problems and the need for medical supervision. Since her admission Alma had participated in most of the recreational activities offered to the residents. Although she was highly sociable and active, Alma frequently complained that she did not feel as though she was being productive with her time. The facility's social worker, who was concerned about several socially isolated residents, suggested to Alma that she become her assistant and encourage the isolated residents to attend some of the recreational activities. Alma was assigned six residents. She and the social worker developed a treatment plan whereby Alma would invite one of the isolated residents to a social function and stay with the person to acclimate him or her to the setting and to other participants. Alma accompanied each of the withdrawn residents to one of six recreational activities each week over the next 2 months. Once she was able to increase the residents' attendance without her constant presence, Alma and the social worker targeted other residents they felt would be receptive to peer invitations and accompaniment.

Alma's success with the withdrawn, socially isolated residents led the social worker to ask her to work with newly admitted residents to help them adjust to their new environment. During this time Alma's ability to walk deteriorated to the point that she needed a wheelchair. Each day, Alma could be seen wheeling down the corridors, checking on her "clients." On several occasions Alma described how her work at the nursing facility gave her the energy she needed to navigate the wheelchair. She pointed out that it was exhausting to wheel herself about, but that the needs of others kept her from dwelling on the difficulty.

Residents of long-term care facilities may also benefit from role replacement through work programs or volunteer activities. It is possible to establish a work program directly on the premises. Voeks and Drinka (1990) described a work therapy program established in a veterans hospital having a mean resident age of 71.5 years. A variety of tasks may be offered such as working at the reception desk, escorting other residents to appointments, delivering charts and mail, pushing wheelchairs, operating elevators, doing clerical work, and assisting with the preparation of recreational materials (Voeks & Drinka, 1990). Many volunteer activities are available to residents. They can make craft items to be sold at a facility tag sale or gift shop to raise money for a charitable cause or in-house project. Making treasured items for friends and family members, such as developing a family tree, writing descriptive accounts of the past, and reorganizing family photographs with detailed labels into albums for different members of the family are other possibilities. In addition, crocheting or knitting sweaters or afghans can be rewarding work. Writing to a person in the military or to a child in a foreign country who is learning English can provide a measure of purpose and socialization.

Older adult residents of long-term care facilities may find rewards in assisting residents with disabilities. Some suggestions include playing cards or other games with another resident who needs to increase socialization, reading to a resident with impaired sight, playing music and discussing favorite types of music with another resident who is isolated or visually impaired, and assisting at recreational activities.

PRECAUTIONS TO TAKE AND
ACCOMMODATIONS TO MAKE IN IMPLEMENTING ROLE REPLACEMENT

Certain considerations and necessary precautions must be addressed and heeded when implementing a role replacement program.

Work Programs

For any type of work program it is important to incorporate some type of counseling service or job search group. Information must be available to older adults about the options and opportunities available to them (Rife & Kilty, 1990). Counselors can assist older people in assessing their interests, needs, and abilities. Counselors may also be helpful in making any special arrangements for individuals with medical limitations (Cahill & Salomone, 1987). Another area in which counselors may be of help is coping with ageism. Often, older individuals who are entering or reentering the work force are confronted with bias from family, friends, themselves, or employers. Encouragement and support are essential to help them reach their goals (Brady, Palermino, Scott, Fernandez, & Norland, 1988; Cahill & Salomone, 1987; Rife & Kilty, 1990).

It is important to remember that participation is voluntary in any type of work therapy program (Voeks & Drinka, 1990). In some residential circumstances it may even be advisable to ask participants to sign a work authorization form. In any situation in which medical limitations are an issue, obtaining the approval of a physician is recommended (Voeks & Drinka, 1990). Tasks should be adapted, if possible, to accommodate older individuals with disabilities who wish to participate and should be approved by a physician (Cahill & Salomone, 1987; Voeks & Drinka, 1990). Specifically in long-term care it is important to carefully monitor the number of hours that a resident works, with over-performance rather than under-performance being of concern (Szekais, 1985; Voeks & Drinka, 1990).

Role-playing a job interview is a useful strategy to help an older adult practice projecting the appearance of confidence and competence. Also, developing and practicing a set of responses to questions and statements from others about the client's desire to return to work is helpful.

The therapist must be ready to deal with the frustrations a client may experience if he or she does not obtain the type of position or financial recompense sought. In addition, some positions may demand work hours that are not amenable to the older adult. When appropriate, the therapist should help the client develop more realistic expectations. Less important or less well compensating positions can be framed as an opportunity to demonstrate competence and potential to the employer.

It is possible that some older people will not obtain a position. This is likely to occur in areas with few jobs and high unemployment and with older adults who possess few marketable skills. Older people with obvious medical problems or physical disabilities are also vulnerable to being passed over for employment. In such cases therapists should advise clients to consider a temp agency or a volunteer position that has the potential to turn into paid employment.

Volunteer Programs

It is important in volunteer programs to incorporate some type of administration service, counseling service, or both to aid potential volunteers in their search for the appropriate position. As with work therapy programs, it is important to recognize and adjust for physical and mental disabilities in older individuals who wish to volunteer (Perkinson, 1992; Szekais, 1986). In long-term care situations caution must be exercised not to treat volunteers as though they were extra staff members (Szekais, 1985). In addition, monitoring the number of hours that an older person volunteers may be necessary in some cases because some older people will try to work to the point of sickness or exhaustion (Perkinson, 1992).

The recipient of the volunteer's work should show appreciation for the value of the services being rendered (Hayden, 1988). Also, individuals who are recipients of volunteer services occasionally need to be reminded to plan, assign, and provide meaningful tasks for older adults to perform (Tierce & Seelbach, 1987). One of the most common reasons that volunteers quit is that they do not feel as though they are being helpful enough or are needed enough (Kuehne & Sears, 1993). If handled appropriately, several factors may increase volunteer longevity (Chambre, 1993; Cohen-Mansfield, 1989; Herzog & Morgan, 1993; Kuehne & Sears, 1993):

Older volunteers tend to commit more of their time when they feel competent.

The volunteering opportunity should be located close to the older person's home, and transportation should be provided or expenses reimbursed by the organization.

The volunteer's work should be recognized publically.

Volunteers need peer group support, which should be provided by the organization.

Meal stipends should be provided to volunteers by the organization.

Szekais (1985) described several practical concerns in developing volunteer programs for long-term care settings or adult day centers. Participation in volunteer programs must be voluntary. Staff members must respect the right of older adults to refuse even if they believe volunteer work would benefit the older adult. Also, it is important not to treat volunteers as extra staff members. The goal of the volunteer effort is therapeutic and as such, ongoing efforts must be directed toward providing support to the volunteer in the form of physical assistance and encouragement. Volunteer programs must not turn into work programs. Work training or work carried out as part of a sheltered workshop program should include remuneration and should be organized differently. Staff should also respect client-initiated efforts and suggestions even when they appear impractical, impossible, or inconsequential. Clients' attempts to become involved must always be supported.

Intergenerational Programs

The points covered in the previous section apply to intergenerational programs, with a few provisions added. When intergenerational programs are being designed, the involvement of healthy older people as well as older people with disabilities must be ensured. If younger volunteers are exposed only to older people with physical and mental disabilities, a distorted perception of aging may result. Seefeldt (1987) found that after a year of visiting nursing facilities, preschool-age children appeared to hold more negative attitudes about the aging process than did children who did not participate in such visits. Weisburd (1992) recommends that only children who express an interest in visiting a nursing facility should be permitted to do so. The children participating should also be encouraged to ask questions and talk about their experiences.

It should not be assumed that older volunteers who work with children or teenagers will automatically enjoy them. Older adults with higher levels of education, frequent contact with children, and grandchildren of their own tend to hold favorable attitudes toward children participating in an intergenerational program (Seefeldt, Jantz, Serock, & Bredekamp, 1982). However, even these individuals have reported difficulties in coping with children who ask many questions or who are demanding. In general, older volunteers have expressed a preference for facilitators exercising strict discipline over the children, with an emphasis on having the children comply with rules without question. Efforts should be made to address these issues in ongoing in-service training sessions.

Proper screening of participants is essential. Personality assessments should be conducted to ensure that young person–older adult pairs are mutually compatible. In addition, activities should be structured in order to ensure that the interaction is purposeful. The activities will lessen feelings of discomfort and permit a relationship to develop spontaneously (Aday, Rice-Sims, & Evans, 1991).

Peer Counseling

Although training provides peer counselors with the opportunity to learn skills that can lead to increased competence, mastery, and control, the experience should not be used as a forum for the counselors to work through their own problems (Priddy & Knisely, 1982). Also, peer counseling is not always acceptable to or appropriate for older adults. Many of them will refuse counseling, even from a peer (Bratter, 1986). Others may have conditions (e.g., Alzheimer's disease and other forms of dementing illness) that require professional intervention. Older adults who assume the role of peer counselor need to be able to recognize their limitations and not become discouraged when their efforts are rejected.

IMPLEMENTATION OF A ROLE REPLACEMENT PROGRAM

Work Therapy Programs

The first step in implementing either a volunteer program or a work therapy program is to establish whether there is enough interest. If little or no interest is exhibited, no older person should be forced or coerced into participating in these voluntary activities. If sufficient interest exists, the second step is to define goals and set objectives, which also aid in later evaluation. Goals may vary with the different programs and participants. The emphasis of goal setting should be placed on fostering self-reliance, autonomy, and empowerment of the older individuals (Perkinson, 1992). The third step is to choose a director and job counselors. These individuals must be receptive to the idea of older individuals in the workplace or in volunteer activities, and any hint of ageism should be addressed (Cahill & Salomone, 1987). In addition, these individuals must be competent, committed, and sensitive to the needs and experiences of the older participants (Cahill & Salomone, 1987; Ventura-Merkel, Liederman, & Ossofsky, 1989). Individuals should be acquainted or reacquainted with job search techniques (Step 4). This familiarization process may take place in workshops (Rife, 1992) or individually. In Step 5 individuals should be invited to attend periodic (once or twice a week) job club meetings, at which job search goals can be set. These meetings may also be sources of job-seeking information, such as interviewing, writing resumes, completing applications, and gathering and following up job leads (Rife, 1992; Rife & Kilty, 1990). Critical issues such as transportation and the prospect of working weekends should be discussed. These two factors have been found to be common barriers to employment with older adults (Brady, Palermino, Scott, Fernandez, & Norland, 1988). Older applicants should be encouraged to point out to prospective employers that research has shown that older adults are reliable workers with low attrition and low absenteeism rates (Stein, Doress-Worters, & Fillmore, 1994).

Volunteer Programs

The first step in implementing a volunteer program is to appoint a volunteer coordinator. This person is responsible for recruitment, training, and placement of volunteers (Step 2). In addition, the coordinator is the person to whom the volunteers turn when they have questions or complaints and who represents them to others within the system. A trend in the 1990s has been to use an unpaid coordinator who is appointed by the volunteers or whose experience and expertise enables the person to rise from the ranks of the volunteers to a position of leadership. It is important for the director to establish a relationship with the volunteer coordinator of any organization in which older adults are placed (Tierce & Seelbach, 1987).

Step 3 is to draw up a list of prospective volunteers and then to informally interview each person. Application forms may be used that include a section in which the potential volunteer can indicate his or her preference for type of volunteer activity (Okun & Eisenberg, 1992). The applicant's resources and skills should be assessed and any special skills utilized, if possible (Hayden, 1988). The fourth step, orientation/training, can be accomplished in a workshop format, on an individual basis, or through the help of "veteran" volunteers (Okun & Eisenberg, 1992; Perkinson, 1992; Tierce & Seelbach, 1987).

Step 5 is to ask volunteers to choose their assignments and arrange their schedules, and be provided with several options to do so (Strom & Strom, 1995).

An initial trial period can help to determine whether the assignment fits the expectations and skills of the volunteer. Another option is to expose volunteers to several placements before asking them to decide where they would like to be assigned on a permanent basis. Step 6 is to determine the hours and schedules for individual volunteers. Ideally, the amount of time worked by older adult volunteers and the schedule of hours worked should be determined by the volunteer. It is sometimes difficult for paid staff members to keep in mind that older adults have other obligations in addition to their volunteer work. Also, older volunteers should be consulted periodically regarding their workload. It is not unusual for staff members to increase the workload of particularly competent volunteers, only to find them feeling overwhelmed. This maxim also holds for increases in responsibility, which may be interpreted as a promotion by the staff but may be viewed as overwhelming by the volunteer.

Finally, Step 7 is to follow initial training with periodic in-service training sessions. Through ongoing training volunteers can learn how to be more helpful and understand the standard operating procedures of the program or system in which they are working.

Intergenerational Programs

Intergenerational programs exist in many forms. Some of the programs were developed initially as opportunities for older adults to volunteer their time and expertise and were later recognized as "intergenerational" because they brought together different age groups. The most noteworthy of these programs is the Foster Grandparent Program, which was developed in 1965 to help low-income, lonely, older people earn a small stipend while helping children with special needs (Struntz & Reville, 1985). Applicants must be 60 years old or older with an income at or near the poverty level. After completing 40 hours of training, the foster grandparents work an average of 20 hours a week, usually focusing most of their time on two or three children. This work customarily takes place at facilities for children with disabilities, hospitals, Head Start centers, alternative schools, correctional facilities, special needs classrooms, or day centers. The primary role of foster grandparents is to provide the children assigned to their care with attention, affection, encouragement, and guidance (the appendix at the end of the chapter lists the address and telephone number of the Foster Grandparents Program).

Another important program is the National School Volunteer Program (NSVP), which was started in 1956 in the New York City schools and has expanded over the years to include schools throughout the United States (Tierce & Seelbach, 1987). Although the NSVP recruits adult volunteers of all ages, this organization is particularly well suited to older volunteers. Schools can benefit from the experience and skills of older adults. Also, increases in discipline problems, decreases in school budgets, and decreases in the number of younger volunteers (due largely to entry into the labor force out of economic necessity) make the older volunteer a particularly valuable resource. The skills and interests of the older adults are matched with the needs of a school and its teachers. Older volunteers can assist with tutoring and enrichment activities and serve as teacher's aides, library assistants, and living/oral historians (Ventura-Merkel, Liederman, & Ossofsky, 1989).

Intergenerational programs developed in the 1980s and 1990s differ somewhat from the traditional, long-standing programs in the way they view the relationship between older and younger people. Although both old and new programs emphasize the reciprocal nature of the relationship, the new programs tend to stress equality in the status of the two age groups (e.g., McGowan & Blankenship, 1994; Walsh, 1993).

A variety of programs have been developed that can serve as models for those wishing to start an intergenerational program. The appendix at the end of the chapter lists intergenerational programs, the source of information concerning each program, the younger cohort targeted, and a brief description of the method employed.

Numerous additional programs exist (see, e.g., Ventura-Merkel and Parks [1984] for a detailed profile of programs). Most of the intergenerational programs bring together people age 25 and younger with people age 60 and older (Ventura Merkel, Liederman, & Ossofsky, 1989). Both groups tend to have abundant leisure time that can be used in mutually rewarding recreational pursuits (Walsh, 1993). The advantages of intergenerational programs for very young children and older adults are believed to be especially important because many negative, stereotypic attitudes about older people and aging are said to develop during the early years of life (Aday, Rice, & Evans, 1991; Dellman-Jenkins, Fowler, Lambert, Fruit, & Richardson, 1994). For older children, older adults provide experience and a sense of continuity during an uncertain and frightening time (Roybal, cited in Walsh, 1993). Dellman-Jenkins et al. (1994) point out that positive and worthwhile interactions with older adults may be especially important in laying the foundations for career directions and choices that involve working with older people. The rewards for older participants are equally compelling. In addition to increasing the volunteers' well-being, level of life satisfaction, and self-esteem (Kuehne & Sears, 1993; Seefeldt, 1987), young people provide a resource for current ideas and impart a youthful energy and spirit to the joint enterprise (Walsh, 1993). Short-DeGraff, Spiegel-McGill, Diamond, and Brackett (1988) found that even older adults with cognitive impairment benefitted from involvement in intergenerational programs. These older adults displayed increased social interaction, greater mobility, higher levels of participation activities, and more joy (e.g., smiled and laughed more) during sessions with nursery school-age children. The benefits of intergenerational programs also extend beyond the immediate participants (Hegeman, 1985). Family members benefit from knowing their children and older relatives spend part of the day in a family-like setting. Also, staff morale has been found to increase in facilities in which intergenerational programs take place.

It should be noted that the practice of children visiting long-term care facilities has a long history. However, most of these visits were—and still are in many cases—a one-session event during which little interpersonal interaction takes place (Weisburd, 1992). For example, it is common for church groups, Girl Scouts, and school classes to visit a facility to entertain the residents with a few songs. Intergenerational programming extends this format, frequently pairing participants into dyads designed to enable a child and an older adult to get to know each other as individuals, with the goal that a friendship will develop. To accomplish this goal, the program must involve ongoing contact between the participants. If a dyad is not conducive to the type of program developed, efforts must be directed to provide numerous opportunities for open discussions among the same group of participants.

Intergenerational programs can also have a significant impact on society, when programs that address a major social problem or issue are designed (Ventura-Merkel, Liederman, & Ossofsky, 1989). Such a program was developed at Worcester State College in central Massachusetts by Maureen Power, who sought to connect pregnant teenagers with supportive older women. Funded through the Massachusetts Office of Elder Affairs, the Teen Parent Support Program provides education and training for a cross-section of college students ranging in age from 21 to 78 who work with teen parents. After the training period, the students are linked in service to teenage parents and their children through one of several cooperating agencies. The program provides support to and role models for teenage parents in nurturing their children and becoming economically independent through connection with a grandparent figure or college students working their way through school. It dispels both the myths of aging and myths about young people while launching older adults into new roles in the community and providing opportunities for college students to explore career pathways.

The Teen Parent Support Program at Worcester State College illustrates how older adults can assume supportive roles in relationships with children and teenagers who are particularly vulnerable because of abuse or neglect. Many of the teens involved live in poverty and have not had the benefit of effective parenting. Drawing on the life experience of an older adult may help to provide these young people with direction in life. Intergenerational programs that actually address a specific problem (e.g., working with juvenile offenders to keep them out of jail or provide support during interaction, strengthening the employment prospects of disadvantaged youths, helping foster families cope with the needs of the foster children, assisting child batterers in learning new ways to cope with the stresses and demands of parenting) tend to be the most effective.

Because much depends on the effectiveness of the intergenerational program, it is critical that the program be properly designed and maintained. Some of the steps critical to the design of an intergenerational program follow (Keller, 1990):

Step 1   Establish Goals and Objectives
A meeting should be held with the participants to discuss their needs and interests. These needs and interests should then be formulated into program goals and objectives specific to the group involved.

Step 2   Determine Roles and Responsibilities
The planners of the activity should determine clearly what needs to be done, the level of expertise that is necessary, the amount of time required, the qualities required of participants, and the level of commitment required by participants.

Step 3   Recruit Participants

Once the second step has been completed, appropriate participants with the necessary skills should be recruited to successfully implement the program. Personal interviews should be conducted with each potential applicant to determine interests, skills, attitudes, abilities, and suitability. Participants who can be matched for their mutual benefit should be evaluated. Size of the group should also be considered; too many or too few participants can inhibit success.

Step 4   Orient and Train Participants

Participants should clearly understand what is expected of them and how to carry out their roles and responsibilities effectively. The planners should discuss program policies and procedures, acceptable behaviors and appearance, participants' interests, expectations, attitudes, and skills. Training should be an ongoing process, with opportunities for group sharing of successes and failures.

Step 5   Manage and Coordinate Program

Ongoing management is essential in order to resolve problems and conflicts that arise during intergenerational exchanges. Planners must also provide for recognition of participants whose reasons and needs for participation change as time passes. Supervision of the program is vital during periods of change, such as death, relocation, lack of interest, and illness.

Step 6   Evaluate Program and Experiences

Each step of the program process should be thoroughly reviewed and critiqued as it occurs and after it has been completed. Participants, managers, coordinators, and administrators of the intergenerational program should be involved in the evaluation.

Strom and Strom (1995) effectively operationalized some of the principles listed above to the process of incorporating older adults into elementary and secondary schools as volunteers. They point out how the effectiveness and satisfaction of volunteers depends on the ability to provide clarity in the tasks to be undertaken, careful assessment and evaluation of the volunteers and their performance, and recognition of the volunteers for the assistance they provide. To accomplish these tasks Strom and Strom (1995) and Stevens (1992) developed four useful forms that can be used with school volunteers or adapted for use in other volunteer or intergenerational programs. The *Volunteer Assignment Request Form* is designed to help teachers identify the specific tasks the older adult is capable of completing. The form can be distributed to teachers, who can check off the tasks they feel can be entrusted to the volunteer. In addition, teachers can list other tasks that would be helpful to them but are not included on the form.

The *Grandparent Volunteer Information Form* simplifies the task of screening the applicant and identifying the older volunteer's skills and interests. Some of the information requested is also sought on any application for employment. For example, inquiring whether the applicant has a police record is in keeping with the provisions of the National Child Protection Act, which protects children from convicted abusers and pedophiles who seek to work in schools as volunteers or as staff members (Strom & Strom, 1995). (The prospective volunteers should be informed that similar investigations are required for the certification of teachers and should not be interpreted as a personal reflection on them.) Strom and Strom (1995) recommend that related issues be discussed during orientation. For example, many warm, nurturing older adult volunteers assume that part of their role will be to provide affection to children who they perceive as having neglectful parents. In addition, they may feel that physical contact with children and teenagers is acceptable as long as one's intention is appropriate. Both school policy and that of other programs involving children and teenagers must conform to public concerns over the potential for sexual misconduct. Establishing appropriate etiquette and regard for these concerns early in the process can eliminate problems or the potential for confusion later.

Periodic evaluations are essential to monitor the benefits of the placement to both the older individual and the recipient organization (Hayden, 1988; Szekais, 1985). Evaluations can be conducted through questionnaires (Kuehne & Sears, 1993). The *School Volunteer Report Card*, developed by Strom and Strom (1995), is designed to be completed by students as well as faculty or administrative staff members, and can be adapted to meet the needs of another type of program. Some programs may also wish to ask volunteers to rate the staff members to whom they have been assigned. Volunteer satisfaction can be measured using a form specifically designed for this purpose by Stevens (1992), the Senior Volunteer Satisfaction Scale. The Volunteer Assignment Request Form, the Grandparent Volunteer Information Form, the School Volunteer Report Card, and the Senior Volunteer Satisfaction Scale may be obtained by ordering the article listed in the references through the interlibrary loan system at any local college or university. In most cases no fee is associated with this process.

Volunteer effectiveness and satisfaction also relies on recognition of older volunteers (Chambre, 1987). Recognition can be given verbally (preferably, in the presence of their peers), through the presentation of certificates, or at a special luncheon (Szekais, 1985). One effective approach has been to link the recognition of volunteers with ceremonies to honor others in the system, such as students and faculty (Strom & Strom, 1995). Because the volunteers are not paid for their efforts, their rewards tend to be satisfaction and recognition.

Although much of the focus in intergenerational programming has been on bringing the skills of older adults to children and teens, some programs have been designed for young people to assist older adults. These young people provide a range of services, including friendly visiting and chore (e.g., seasonal yard work, shoveling, home repair), escort, and transportation services. Ventura-Merkel, Liederman, and Ossofsky (1989) recommend a variation on this approach in which the young person works either with or under the direction of a healthy older adult in providing services to people with physical disabilities. This approach is advantageous in that it exposes young people to older adults who have aged with little physical and mental impairment and those who incur considerable deficits and allows young people to develop new or improved work skills. Such programs should incorporate the same structural features as the programs designed for older volunteers.

Peer Counseling

Peer counseling for older adults was developed in the 1970s in an effort to compensate for the reluctance of many older adults to seek services from mental health professionals (Waters, Fink, & White, 1976). Interest in peer counseling was renewed in the 1980s because of cutbacks in mental health services budgets. The objective of peer counseling is to use the skills and life experiences of older adults in a self-help approach to restoring mental health (Bratter, 1986). Several advantages are inherent in older adults counseling older adults (Bratter, 1986): Peer counselors can serve as positive role models, they possess first-hand knowledge of the problems associated with aging, and their services can be provided at minimal cost.

Clients report increased self-confidence, a willingness to learn and try new behaviors, a sense of being connected to their community, and improved relationships with their families (Waters, Fink, & White, 1976). The peer counselors report enjoying the learning experience as well as deriving a number of personal benefits, including increased confidence in their abilities, increased tolerance of others, increased ability to make changes in their own lives, and a renewed focus for time and energies (Petty & Cusack, 1989). Older counselors have also acquired improved problem-solving and self-exploration skills in group programs (Waters, Fink, & White, 1976) and an increased ability to compensate for sensory losses (Petty & Cusack, 1989). Interestingly, peer counselors appear to gain as much from the peer counseling process as do their clients. Petty and Cusack (1989) found that peer counselors learned communication and social skills that were useful in their personal lives and increased their ability to be helpful and supportive to their peers. This finding supports France (1986), who suggested that in the process of helping others, peer counselors help themselves regain or renew their satisfaction with life.

Peer counseling has been found to be particularly effective in helping older adults recover from chemical dependency (Fuchs, Jacyk, Kostyk, Lindblom, & Tabisz, 1994). Counseling with a peer who has abused alcohol or drugs gives clients hope that they, too, can recover. Clients report feeling better understood and comfortable with a counselor from the same generation.

Older adults who elect to become peer counselors receive a considerable amount of training. Some programs require as many as 80 hours of instruction over a 1-year period (deVries & Petty, 1992). Often, the initial training program consists of learning active listening skills, how to keep empathy in its proper perspective, problem-solving skills, and ethical considerations. The second phase of training is a supervised practicum, which allows older adult trainees to practice the skills they learned in the first phase. The program also includes ongoing in-service training, which addresses aging-related issues such as sensory losses, relocation, bereavement, and community resources available to older adults.

Older adult peer counselors tend to be in their late 60s; to be well-educated; to perceive themselves to be interpersonally competent; to be somewhat dissatisfied with some aspect of their life situation (deVries & Petty, 1992); and to be mobile, healthy individuals with access to transportation. Much of the emphasis in training peer counselors has been placed on independent-living older adults; scant attention has been directed to those residing in long-term care facilities. Presumably, this oversight is attributable to the intense amount of training involved and difficulty in tailoring it to two or three individuals per long-term care facility. However, some cognitively intact but physically disabled older people who are living in residential care would make excellent peer counselors. The work would permit them to feel productive and of use to others, despite their own needs for assistance. Also, many residents of long-term care facilities are in need of mental health intervention (Mosher-Ashley, 1993) and would benefit from peer counseling, particularly because counseling by professional mental health therapists is rarely available (Brooks & Mosher-Ashley, 1996). Some success has been obtained in programs in which older adult residents of a nursing facility serve as peer counselors for newly admitted residents in order to help them adjust to their new setting (e.g., Scharlack, 1988).

Volunteer Programs

Perkinson (1992) recommends that health care and social services providers promote volunteerism among older adults as a means of empowering them to become active partners in making decisions about services and in the actual provision of services, which confers on them a significant social role. Providers may encounter some resistance in encouraging volunteer activities among individuals who lack self-confidence. Older adults who lack confidence or have no experience in volunteering their services may feel that they are not sufficiently competent or that potential recipients will not welcome their services. These older people need special encouragement. Directing someone from a volunteer organization to personally invite the reticent older adult may help to encourage him or her to become involved in the organization. Several invitations may be required before the person is able to overcome his or her fears (Perkinson, 1992). Tendering an offer to volunteer on a trial basis may also help to reassure insecure older adults. Efforts must be made to be encouraging without coercing the individual. Also, directions to complete any task should be understandable. Some volunteers drop out because they feel frustrated about lack of organization or that they are not using their time and talents fruitfully. Special efforts should be made to encourage frail older adults to volunteer (Chambre, 1993; Perkinson, 1992). Drewrey (1985) suggests that record keeping functions for volunteer social activities be carried out by a frail individual in an effort to provide all interested parties with opportunities to volunteer. The most promising program that enables homebound older adults to engage in community service is Linking Lifetimes. This program emphasizes telephone support to individuals of all ages in need of socialization or reassurance (e.g., latchkey children, nursing facility residents, people with developmental disabilities, homebound older adults).

Some older people do not wish to become volunteers. However, many of them may become interested if invited to volunteer. A survey found that almost 50% of older adults who volunteered did so because someone asked them (Independent Sector, 1990). Chambre (1993) points out that although the number of volunteer opportunities for older adults has increased, the means of recruiting them into these activities has not improved. Health care and social services professionals are well positioned to provide a link between older adults and volunteer organizations that can use their services. Local agencies should be contacted to determine the types of positions available. A clear picture of the available positions facilitates encouraging a client to assume the new role of volunteer. For example, some older adults who have no previous volunteer experience may be more interested in community service, which focuses on leisure activities, than they are in a work–role (Chambre, 1993).

Problems can arise in any volunteer program. Four of the most common problems, the behaviors associated with the problems, and the recommended interventions are listed in Table 8.1.

Novice facilitators may find John Krumboltz's writings on vocational decision making helpful in their work with older adults who are considering volunteer activities (Krumboltz, 1983; Krumboltz & Baker, 1973). The purpose of this form of behavioral counseling is to help the client reach a decision about which type of volunteer activity would best meet his or her needs. Krumboltz outlines seven steps to be followed by the client and the facilitator in counseling:

1. *Defining the problem and the client's goals.* The facilitator assists the client in clarifying his or her situation and objectives. The client needs to explore whether engaging in volunteer work is feasible and desirable. The client then generates a set of goals to be achieved as a result of the volunteer work. These goals are to be stated as clear, observable behaviors (e.g., "As a volunteer, I expect to come in contact with other people"; "I want to be doing something in a one-to-one situation"; "The work that I do must make me feel helpful"; "The volunteer work should be fun"; "The volunteer work should be important even if it makes me feel tired or feel sad at times"; "I want to do something that doesn't take up much of my time"; "I want to be kept busy").

2. *Agreeing to achieve goals.* As the client's problem and goals become clear, the facilitator must determine whether to assist the client in reaching his or her goals. Factors to be considered include interest, time constraints, and the facilitator's competency and knowledge about volunteer opportunities.

3. *Generating alternative volunteer activities.* The client needs to determine whether to engage in a structured volunteer activity in or out of the home. The client is free to defer this decision, if factors inherent in the volunteer opportunities seem likely to play a role. A variety of methods may be employed in generating alternative courses of action. The Appendix provides a list of some of the more common resources for older adults who wish to volunteer their services. The client should peruse this listing to determine whether any resource appears to meet his or her established goals. The facilitator and client should also engage in brainstorming different options and should try not to exclude or even evaluate any possibilities. It is important that the facilitator not reject any of the alternatives provided by the client, regardless of how unrealistic they may seem—the client needs support not discouragement. If the alternative is truly unrealistic, the client will be able to decide that for him- or herself.

4. *Collecting information about alternatives.* At this point in counseling the facilitator reviews with the client ways in which he or she has made decisions in the past. Decision-making processes that have led to satisfactory outcomes are contrasted with those that have not. The client is asked to review jobs or helpful

activities that have resulted in positive social interactions and feelings of satisfaction and purposefulness. These experiences are then compared with jobs and activities that have not resulted in positive interactions and feelings. The factors that contribute to positive outcomes are isolated. Once the client's past decision-making processes have been analyzed, he or she begins to explore what information is needed to make a decision concerning potential volunteer positions. The client is then encouraged by the facilitator to collect information in relation to the goals specified in the first step, the alternatives generated, and the client's limitations (e.g., transportation, disabilities, time constraints).

5. *Examining the consequences of the alternatives.* In order to narrow the number of possible volunteer opportunities, the client should examine the probability of outcomes in relation to certain information about him- or herself. For example, a client interested in volunteering in a school can review his or her experience in dealing with children, particularly those with behavior or emotional problems. It is important to note that experiences do not dictate what decisions the client should make. These experiences merely provide some indication as to whether the individual will find satisfaction in the volunteer position. It remains for the client to evaluate the probabilities for success in relation to his or her abilities, resources, and values.

6. *Reevaluating goals, alternatives, and consequences.* During the process of exploring different options for volunteering, the client may uncover new alternatives and may even discover values, qualities, and misconceptions previously unrecognized. The facilitator should understand these changes and encourage the client to reconsider the situation. For example, an older adult who is contemplating a volunteer position may come to the realization that he or she would prefer greater involvement with his or her grandchildren. In some cases increased grandchild care may be preferable to taking on a position working with others' children.

7. *Making the decision or tentatively selecting an alternative contingent on new developments and new opportunities.* The client selects a course of action based on the results of the preceding steps. The client is encouraged to consider the possibility that this plan of action may not work out as he or she hoped. The client should be open to opportunities as they become available. The new volunteer opportunities must be compared against the present plan of action to ensure that the client's basic needs are met. The client should be encouraged to attend to feedback from the postdecision experiences in order to assess the degree to which his or her choice is satisfactory.

Volunteerism in Congregate Housing

Drewrey (1985) suggests that a volunteer social activities program be organized within a congregate housing complex by making it an adjunct to the tenants' organization. The advantage of this type of program is that it can shift the customary complaint orientation of a tenants' organization to a constructive one. In addition to providing a way to focus the creative energies of some residents, this type of program can enhance the quality of life for all residents, especially for lower-income older adults, who may not be able to afford outside entertainment.

Drewrey (1985) proposes starting a program with a simple jointly produced activity such as a potluck dinner and progressing to more complex activities such

Table 8.1. Problems encountered among volunteers

Problem	Behavior	Intervention
Overzealousness	Volunteers place excessive demands on themselves and others to work harder; in extreme cases this behavior can lead to sickness and exhaustion and can alienate other volunteers	Place limits on the amount and type of involvement; try to understand the reasons underlying the disruptive behavior (e.g., illness, loss of spouse) and help others to understand the situation
Territoriality	Volunteers do not want to share tasks with others	Provide increased role clarification and reassign tasks periodically
Cliques	Some volunteers exclude others from the group	Encourage longtime volunteers to include others and mingle with newer participants; these individuals should be approached as knowledgeable veterans and be assigned tasks specifically include others
Role-exit	Volunteers experience burnout and are no longer able to carry out their responsibilities	Provide another volunteer to assist the older volunteer, who provides direction; role-exit should be a transitional process involving either supports or movement to a less-demanding position

Source: Perkinson (1992).

as pie baking contests and day trips. Drewrey points out that management and resident volunteers should take the lead in planning the first few activities for residents. The planning begins by appointing an activity director, who establishes written goals that provide direction and purpose for the social program. Notices announcing the date, time, and agenda of every planning committee meeting should be posted in convenient, conspicuous places. Ground rules should be established to minimize the potential for conflict between the residents and management. The rules proposed by Drewrey (1985) include the following:

- All activities must be approved by management and attended by the volunteer activities coordinator.
- All activities must be scheduled in advance to avoid conflict.
- Proper attire must be worn—no nightgowns and bathrobes.
- No alcoholic beverages may be served.
- All cleanup must be done by resident volunteers.
- Behavior at events should not offend other residents.

Evaluations both of the volunteer's performance and level of satisfaction with the assignment must be conducted. Stevens' Senior Volunteer Satisfaction Scale can be supplemented to assess volunteer satisfaction (Stevens, 1992). Evaluation is important because nearly 25% of older adults who volunteer drop out within the first year (ACTION, cited in Stevens, 1992). Any efforts expended toward decreasing the dropout rate can only benefit the volunteers and the recipients of their services. Recognition of the volunteers is critical to the success of the program.

Following the first or second activity, management should conduct a written survey of the entire resident population to garner suggestions for future functions and for availability of resident volunteers. Planning meetings should be encouraged to actively involve volunteers. Detailed record keeping of all events is recommended. These records help to shape the activity and allow for easier repetition of a successful event in the future. Management should work toward less involvement, turning over responsibility for planning and carrying out social functions to residents.

Volunteerism in Long-Term Care Settings or Day Programs

Like work therapy programs, volunteer activities in long-term care facilities must be structured carefully. Every effort must be made to avoid the potential for exploiting residents, especially those with cognitive impairment. One must keep in mind that residents in long-term care facilities and in day programs are vulnerable and may not feel that they can refuse staff recommendations. Szekais (1985) described a volunteer program for a large number of participants in two adult day centers. All of the residents were formally assessed as having moderate to severe impairment. The decision to institute the volunteer program stemmed from requests on the part of clients to take on more chores and hold more discussions concerning their responsibility, usefulness, and skill practice. Working together, clients and staff established goals of reducing helplessness and "sitting around doing nothing" and elected to work toward creating individual initiative and activity outside of formal treatment periods. Using a participant decision-making model, four categories of client involvement were identified: mealtime tasks, general cleanup, clerical tasks, and social and recreational activities. Client participation was voluntary. In some cases family consent was obtained.

Some of the tasks volunteers tackled included changing the reality orientation board information; distributing tea, coffee, and juice; passing lunch plates and silverware to other clients; clearing and wiping tables; emptying ashtrays; sweeping the carpet; watering plants; straightening games and bookshelves; calling bingo games; assisting with the monthly newsletter; and welcoming new clients. After 5 months, the volunteers were honored at a ceremony before the entire client group and formally thanked for their assistance with verbal thanks, a certificate of appreciation, a round of applause, and a brunch.

Other ways in which older, frail adults in long-term care settings and day programs can engage in volunteer activities include participating in participant/ resident councils, writing a newsletter, visiting with isolated or impaired residents, and writing to people in need of correspondents. The classified ads in literary magazines frequently carry listings of organizations that can provide a person with a pen pal. In addition, each November the Dear Abby newspaper advice column lists worldwide military addresses ("Operation Dear Abby") in an effort to provide military personnel who will not be home for the holidays with mail (see also the appendix at the end of the chapter). The U.S. Department of Defense also supplies Dear Abby with current addresses for lonely military personnel who are involved in peacekeeping operations overseas. For example, U.S. soldiers stationed in Bosnia in the mid-1990s had mail forwarded to them in the form of an "Any Soldier" correspondence.

Work Programs

Although volunteering provides an opportunity for older adults to replace lost roles, the primary reasons for engaging in this activity lie in helping others and filling leisure time with interesting activities (Cohen-Mansfield, 1989). In fact, studies have shown that involvement in volunteering in later life is more strongly related to previous volunteer experience than it is to retirement (Chambre, 1984; Cohen-Mansfield, 1989). Consequently, becoming a volunteer should not be recommended to older adults as a substitute for a missed work-role. These individuals may benefit from seeking reemployment. As Cohen-Mansfield (1989) points out, employment and volunteering may provide different options for different older individuals. Given the recognized association between life satisfaction and employment among older adults who wish to work (Duncan & Whitney, 1990; Soumerai & Avorn, 1983), every effort should be made to help those who desire to work to do so. Many communities have agencies that provide help to adults over age 55 who seek employment (Stein, Doress-Worters, & Fillmore, 1994).

Older individuals interested in working should be helped to assess their skills and vocational desires. A "skills resume," which focuses on abilities and accomplishments, may be more effective for older adults than the traditional chronological listing of paid employment (Stein, Doress-Worters, & Fillmore, 1994). Volunteer work should be listed as work experience. Special attention should be directed to older women, who constitute a growing segment of the American labor force. Women are less likely than are men to have earned enough money or accumulated enough pension credits to feel assured of an adequate retirement income (Stein, Doress-Worters, & Fillmore, 1994). They are also less likely to possess skills that will enable them to obtain jobs that pay well. One option to consider is higher education. Pursuing an advanced degree or certificate or simply taking courses can open up or create job opportunities as well as negate employer attitudes about the cognitive abilities of older people. Numerous positions are opening up in the field of gerontology. Obtaining a certificate in gerontology and being of advanced age may enable the older applicant to be competitive in the job market.

Lack of training and lack of necessary skills have been found to be among the major reasons that older adults have difficulty obtaining employment (Brady et al., 1988). Social services and health care professionals who work closely with healthy older adults should be familiar with job training programs in their local communities (Dorfman & Rubenstein, 1993; Rife & Kilty, 1990). These professionals should also encourage the formation of a job club among older adults in senior centers. Older adults who participated in such a club were found to be more successful in obtaining jobs than participants who used traditional services (Rife, 1992). Cohen-Mansfield (1989) found that among older adults the most effective strategy for finding a job was using one's social network, followed by direct application to an agency.

Alternative work models should be explored for older adults. Cahill and Salomone (1987) suggest that job sharing, which is currently used to integrate into the labor force women who are unable to work full-time, may be feasible for older workers. They also recommend that group work, in which workers perform duties as a team, would be beneficial for older people because it would compensate for their diminished physical abilities while allowing them to use their knowledge and experience. Self-employment may be another option (Cahill & Salomone, 1987; Stein, Doress-Worters, & Fillmore, 1994).

Follow-up is also important in work programs. Employed individuals should be contacted periodically so that they can be surveyed about their satisfaction with their position.

Work Therapy Programs in Long-Term Care Settings

Regulations for establishing work therapy programs in long-term care settings vary from state to state. Also, there may be problems in providing employment in settings such as nursing facilities, whereas in veterans hospitals, no such problems exist. Many states set strict rules to prevent the exploitation of residents. For example, in Massachusetts a resident who grows vegetables in a small garden cannot donate them to the nursing facility for use in patient meals. Although this situation may seem to be an example of a bureaucratic extreme, the underlying principle is sound—long-term care facilities should not profit at the expense of its residents. Consequently, work therapy programs must be developed with appropriate oversight and with the permission of regulatory boards.

Work therapy programs involving paid compensation have been established in veterans hospitals in Iowa, Washington, and Wisconsin. The program described by Voeks and Drinka (1990) was administered by a work therapy coordinator and was budgeted for approximately $20,000 a year to cover the employment expenses of about 250 residents in any given month. The rate of pay was half of the state's minimum wage, and a resident could work up to 5 hours a day or 112 hours a month. Resident participation in the program was strictly voluntary. Residents who elected to work signed an authorization to work, which was reviewed by the attending physician. The physician, staff, or both could include any restriction on activity felt to be needed to protect the individual resident. The physician also questioned the resident periodically to determine the individual's subjective experience of work therapy. The work assignments varied depending on the individual's abilities. External standards of productivity did not apply. Whereas some residents worked at a reception desk, mopped and swept floors, folded laundry, and pushed wheelchairs, others cut and sorted pictures for scrapbooks and placemats. No work assignment involved direct nursing care.

The advantages of the work therapy program were numerous. In particular, the residents pointed out that work therapy gave them something useful to do and distracted them from thinking about their problems. In fact, a considerable number of the participants were unable to think of other activities to occupy themselves were the work program to end.

It should be noted that the veterans hospital offering the work therapy program supported a fully operating therapeutic recreation and leisure activity program that provided one-to-one, small-group, and large-group activities. The residents participating in the work program can be viewed as representative of older adults who have had little experience with extended leisure or hobbies. Typical activity programs may not provide these individuals with opportunities for accomplishment and self-esteem building (Voeks & Drinka, 1990).

Residents of some nursing facilities may be too disabled for the type of work therapy program described by Voeks and Drinka (1990). A modified version with fewer work hours and less physically taxing work may be suitable.

Meaningful work is one of the cornerstones upon which rest self-esteem and feelings of self-worth and well-being for all people. Providing opportunities for older adults to continue to contribute to the people and institutions around them is a way of acknowledging that their productive lives do not end with retirement from their occupations or with the diminishing of family and household responsibilities. Given lengthening life spans and, in many cases, healthier retirement years, more older people should and will seek activities to replace those that occupied their time earlier in their lives.

References

Aday, R.H., Rice, C., & Evans, E. (1991). Intergenerational partners project: A model linking elementary students with senior center volunteers. *Gerontologist, 31*, 263–266.

Aday, R.H., Rice-Sims, C., & Evans, E. (1991). Youth's attitudes toward the elderly: The impact of intergenerational partners. *Journal of Applied Gerontology, 10*(3), 372–382.

Adelmann, P.K. (1994). Multiple roles and psychological well-being in a national sample of older adults. *Journal of Gerontology: Social Sciences, 49*, 277–285.

Beck, S.H. (1986). Mobility from preretirement to postretirement job. *Sociological Quarterly, 27*, 515–531.

Brady, E.M., Palermino, P., Scott, D., Fernandez, R., & Norland, S. (1988). Barriers to work among the elderly: A Connecticut study. *Journal of Applied Gerontology, 6*, 415–428.

Bratter, B. (1986). Peer counseling for older adults. *Generations, 10*(3), 49–50.

Brooks, J., & Mosher-Ashley, P.M. (1996). Resources for on-site mental health services: How private vendors are serving nursing homes in Massachusetts. *Nursing Homes, 45*, 26–28.

Butler, J.S., Anderson, K.H., & Burkhauser, R.V. (1989). Work and health after retirement: A competing risks model with semiparametric unobserved heterogeneity. *Review of Economics and Statistics, 70*, 46–53.

Cahill, M., & Salomone, P. (1987). Career counseling for work life extension: Integrating the older worker into the labor force. *Career Development Quarterly, 35,* 188–196.

Chambre, S.M. (1984). Is volunteering a substitute for role loss in old age? An empirical test of activity theory. *Gerontologist, 13,* 292–298.

Chambre, S.M. (1987). *Good deeds in old age: Volunteering by the new leisure class.* Lexington, MA: D.C. Heath & Co.

Chambre, S.M. (1993). Volunteerism by elders: Past trends and future prospects. *Gerontologist, 33,* 221–228.

Cohen-Mansfield, J. (1989). Employment and volunteering roles for the elderly: Characteristics, attributions and strategies. *Journal of Leisure Research, 21,* 214–227.

Dellman-Jenkins, M., Fowler, L., Lambert, D., Fruit, D., & Richardson, R. (1994). Intergenerational sharing seminars: Their impact on young adult college students and senior guest students. *Educational Gerontology, 20,* 579–588.

Dorfman, L.T., & Rubenstein, L.M. (1993). Paid and unpaid activities and retirement satisfaction among rural older adults. *Physical Therapy & Occupational Therapy in Geriatrics, 12,* 45–63.

Drewrey, F. (1985, November/December). An alternative approach to tenant organizations. *Journal of Property Management, 50*(6), 39–41.

Duncan, D., & Whitney, R. (1990). Work and the mental well-being of the elderly. *Psychological Reports, 66,* 882.

Elder, J.K. (1987). The role of intergenerational programs in the "Youth 2000" campaign. *Aging, 356,* 17–19.

Elwell, F., & Maltbie-Crannell, A.D. (1981). The impact of role loss on coping resources and life-satisfaction of the elderly. *Journal of Gerontology, 36,* 223–232.

Erikson, E.H., Erikson, J.M., & Kivnick, H. (1986). *Vital involvement in old age.* New York: Norton.

France, M.H. (1986). *People helping people: Peer counseling for older people.* Victoria, BC, Canada: British Columbia Ministry of Health.

Fuchs, D., Jacyk, R.W., Kostyk, K., Lindblom, L., & Tabisz, E. (1994). Chemical dependency in the elderly: Treatment phase. *Journal of Gerontological Social Work, 22*(1/2), 175–191.

Glass, T.A., Seeman, T.E., Herzog, A.R., Kahn, R., & Berkman, L.F. (1995). Change in productive activity in late adulthood: MacArthur studies of successful aging. *Journal of Gerontology, 50B,* S65–S76.

Greaves, G., & Lewis, P. (1995). Collaboration of seniors and faculty in an undergraduate program. *Educational Gerontology, 21,* 69–79.

Haber, E.A., & Short-DeGraff, M.A. (1990). Intergenerational programming for an increasingly age-segregated society. *Activities, Adaptation & Aging, 14,* 35–48.

Hamon, R.R., & Koch, D.K. (1993). The elder mentor relationship: An experiential learning tool. *Educational Gerontology, 19,* 147–159.

Hayden, C. (1988). Elder campers helping others—the ECHO project: A unique intergenerational model. *Activities, Adaptation & Aging, 11*(1), 11–19.

Hegeman, C. R. (1985). *Child care in long-term settings.* (Available from Carol R. Hegeman, Research Associate, Foundation for Long-Term Care, Inc., 194 Washington Avenue, Albany, New York 12210.)

Herzog, A., & Morgan, J. (1993). Formal volunteer work among older Americans. In S. Bass, F. Caro, & Y. Chen (Eds.), *Achieving a productive society* (pp. 199–142). Westport, CT: Auburn House.

Independent Sector. (1990). *Giving and volunteering in the United States.* Washington, DC: Author.

Ingersoll-Dayton, B., & Antonucci, T.C. (1988). Reciprocal and nonreciprocal social support: Contrasting sides of intimate relationships. *Journal of Gerontology, 43*, S65–S73.

Forman, J. (1993, June 18). In study, 3 of 4 prefer to work part-time rather than retire. *Boston Globe*, pp. 6–7.

Keller, M.J. (1990). Intergenerational sharing: Teens and Elderly for the Arts (TEA). *Journal of Applied Gerontology, 9*, 312–324.

Krumboltz, J. (1983). *Private rules in career decision making.* Columbus, OH: National Center for Research in Vocational Education.

Krumboltz, J.D., & Baker, R.D. (1973). Behavioral counseling for vocational decisions. In H. Borow (Ed.), *Career guidance for a new age.* Boston: Houghton Mifflin.

Kuehne, V., & Sears, H. (1993). Beyond the call of duty: Older volunteers committed to children and families. *Journal of Applied Gerontology, 12*(4), 425–438.

Lambert, D., Dellman-Jenkins, M., & Fruit, D. (1990). Planning for contact, between the generalizing: An effective approach. *Gerontologist, 30*, 553–556.

McGowan, T.G., & Blankenship, S. (1994). Intergenerational experience and ontological change. *Educational Gerontology, 20*, 589–604.

McGrath, L., & Mosher-Ashley, P.M. (1997, March). *Utilizing a valuable resource: The senior tax-rebate program.* Paper distributed in a program exchange at the American Society on Aging annual meeting, Nashville, TN.

Mosher-Ashley, P.M. (1993). Referral patterns of elderly clients to a community mental health center. *Journal of Gerontological Social Work, 20*, 5–23.

Myers, D.A. (1991). Work after cessation of career job. *Journal of Gerontology, 46*, S93–S102.

Okun, M., & Eisenberg, N. (1992). A comparison of office and adult day care center older volunteers: Social-psychological and demographic differences. *International Journal of Aging and Human Development, 35*(3), 219–233.

Perkinson, M. (1992). Maximizing personal efficacy in older adults: The empowerment of volunteers in a multipurpose senior center. *Physical Therapy & Occupational Therapy in Geriatrics, 10*(3), 57–70.

Petty, B.J., & Cusack, S.A. (1989). Assessing the impact of a seniors' peer counseling program. *Educational Gerontology, 15*, 49–54.

Priddy, J.M., & Knisely, J.S. (1982). Older adults as peer counselors: Considerations in counselor training with the elderly. *Educational Gerontology, 8*, 53–62.

Pruchno, R., & Kleban, M.H. (1993). Caring for an institutionalized parent: The role of coping strategies. *Psychology and Aging, 8*, 18–25.

Rife, J. (1992). Reducing depression and increasing the job placement success of older unemployed workers. *Clinical Gerontologist, 12*, 81–85.

Rife, J., & Kilty, K. (1990). Job search discouragement and the older worker: Implications for social work practice. *Journal of Applied Social Sciences, 14*(1), 56–73.

Rosenberg, M.K. (1994). The journal lab: Making friends at Friendship Corner. *Journal of Long-Term Care Administration, 21*(4), 4–6.

Ruchlin, H.S., & Morris, J.N. (1991). Impact of work on the quality of life of community-residing young elderly. *American Journal of Public Health, 81*, 498–500.

Scharlach, A.E. (1988). Peer counseling training for nursing homes. *Gerontologist, 28*, 499–502.

Seefeldt, C. (1987). The effects of preschoolers' visits to a nursing home. *Gerontologist, 27*, 228–232.

Seefeldt, C., Jantz, R.K., Serock, K., & Bredekamp, S. (1982). Elderly persons' attitudes toward children. *Educational Gerontology, 8*, 493–506.

Smith, C. (1995, May). Grandparent pen pals: Authentic writing at work. *Teaching K–8*, pp. 40–41.

Soumerai, S.B., & Avorn, J. (1983). Perceived health, life satisfaction, and activity in urban elderly: A controlled study of the impact of part-time work. *Journal of Gerontology, 38*, 356–362.

Stein, E., Doress-Worters, P.B., & Fillmore, M.D. (1994). Work and retirement. In P.B. Doress-Worters & D.L. Siegal (Eds.), *The new ourselves, growing older* (pp. 169–189). New York: Touchstone.

Stephens, M.A., & Zarit, S.H. (1989). Symposium: Family caregiving to dependent older adults: Stress, appraisal, and copy. *Psychology and Aging, 4*, 387–388.

Stevens, E. (1992). Senior volunteer satisfaction: A route to mental health in later life? *Clinical Gerontologist, 12*, 101–106.

Strickland, C. (1990, December). Intergenerational reading. *Wilson Library Bulletin*, pp. 46–48, 164–165.

Strom, R., & Strom, S. (1990). Grandparent education. *Journal of Instructional Psychology, 17*, 85–91.

Strom, R.D., & Strom, S.K. (1995). Intergenerational learning: Grandparents in the schools. *Educational Gerontology, 21*, 321–335.

Struntz, K.A., & Reville, S. (1985). *Growing together: An intergenerational sourcebook*. Washington, DC: American Association of Retired Persons.

Szekais, B. (1985). Using the Milieu: Treatment-environment consistency. *Gerontologist, 25*, 15–18.

Szekais, B. (1986). Therapeutic activities with the impaired elderly: An overview. *Activities, Adaptation & Aging, 8* (3–4), 1–10.

Thomas, J.L. (1988). Predictors of satisfaction with children's help for younger and older elderly parents. *Journal of Gerontology, 43*, S9–S14.

Tierce, J., & Seelbach, W. (1987). Elders as school volunteers: An untapped resource. *Educational Gerontology, 13*(1), 33–42.

Ventura-Merkel, C., Liederman, D., & Ossofsky, J. (1989). Exemplary intergenerational programs. *Journal of Children in Contemporary Society, 20*(3–4), 173–180.

Ventura-Merkel, C., & Parks, E. (1984). *Intergenerational programs: A catalogue of profiles*. Washington, DC: National Council on the Aging.

Voeks, S., & Drinka, P. (1990). Participants' perception of a work therapy program in a nursing home. *Activities, Adaptation & Aging, 14*(3), 27–34.

Walsh, E.R. (1993). A tie that binds: Intergenerational programming. *Parks & Recreation, 24*, 50–54.

Waters, E., Fink, S., & White, B. (1976). Peer group counseling for older people. *Educational Gerontology, 1*, 157–170.

Weisburd, S. (1992, April). Grandpals, link of ages. *Health*, pp. 82–84.

Weston, R., Owen, M., McGuire, F., Backman, K., & Allen, J. (1993). The intergenerational entrepreneurship demonstration project: An innovative approach to intergenerational mentoring. *Journal of Physical Education, Recreation and Dance, 64*, 24–26.

Appendix
Resources for Older Adults Wishing to Volunteer Their Services

American Association of Retired Persons (AARP) Talent Bank
601 E Street, N.W.
Washington, DC 20049
Phone (202) 434-2277
Matches older adults with volunteer positions

Foster Grandparents Program
1110 Vermont Avenue, N.W.
6th Floor
Washington, DC 20525
Phone (202) 678-4215
Provides a stipend to older adults who work with children who are autistic; have physical or mental disabilities; have been abused or neglected; and children, teenage parents, and adolescents who are substance abusers

Links
1200 Massachusetts Avenue, N.W.
Washington, DC 20005-4501
Phone (202) 291-7939
Organization of African American women; each chapter implements programs designed to provide enrichment experiences for those who are educationally disadvantaged and culturally deprived; numerous chapters in most states

National Association of Partners in Education
(formerly the National School Volunteer Program)
209 Madison Street
Suite 401
Alexandria, Virginia 22314
Phone (703) 836-4880
Recommends strategies on how to incorporate older adults as volunteers in schools

National Executive Service Corps
257 Park Avenue South
New York, New York 10010
Phone (212) 529-6660
Enables professionals amd business executives to provide consulting services to nonprofit organizations

Retired Senior Volunteer Program (RSVP)
1100 Vermont Avenue, N.W.
Washington, DC 20525
Phone (202) 205-6762
Offers a directory of different volunteer opportunities, including work with boarder babies, tax assistance, consulting assignments, and technical assistance

Senior Companion Program (SCP)
c/o ACTION
1110 Vermont Avenue, N.W.
Washington, DC 20525
Provides a stipend to older adults who visit older adults in their homes and provide them with social support

Service Corps of Retired Executives (SCORE)
409 3rd Street, S.W.
Suite 5900
Washington, DC 20024
Phone (202) 205-6762
Members provide management expertise to prospective or current small business owners

Intergenerational Programs

PROGRAM   St. Francis Gardens' Day Care (Weisburd, 1992)
AGES SERVED   6 weeks–6 years
DESCRIPTION   Day care center is located in a nursing facility and affiliated retirement center; the day care program offers five intergenerational activities every day (e.g., exercise class, rhythm band, gardening, reading stories together)

PROGRAM   Friendship Corner (Rosenberg, 1994)
AGES SERVED   Preschool-age children
DESCRIPTION   Day care program for employees' children is located in a long-term care facility; each day children interact with the residents in a structured activity for 30 minutes

PROGRAM   Grandparents and Books (Strickland, 1990)
AGES SERVED   Preschool- to elementary school-age children
DESCRIPTION   Library-based program in which older adults are trained in presenting stories with picture books, flannel boards, and puppets

PROGRAM   Family Friends (Kuehne & Sears, 1993)
AGES SERVED   Preschool-age children to teenagers with chronic illness
DESCRIPTION   Older adults are trained in medical and psychosocial aspects of chronic illness, and conduct weekly visits to the family; visits include play and educational activities with the child and support and respite for the parents

PROGRAM   Grandparent Pen Pals (Smith, 1995)
AGES SERVED   Children ages 6–10
DESCRIPTION   Elementary school children and nursing facility residents are matched on the basis of common interests; after several weeks of correspondence, the pairs meet; written communication continues on a weekly basis to improve writing skills in the children and socialization in the older adults

PROGRAM   Intergenerational Entrepreneurship Demonstration Project
(Weston et al., 1993)
AGES SERVED   6–19 years
DESCRIPTION   Children enrolled in a school for emotionally and behaviorally troubled youth were matched with retired older adults; they opened and ran a small business, a country-style market

PROGRAM   Elder Campers Helping Others (Hayden, 1988)
AGES SERVED   Preteens and teenagers
DESCRIPTION   An older adult volunteer is matched with a camp director; the older adult provides assistance in camp functions while informally sharing knowledge and skills

PROGRAM   Youth 2000 (Elder, 1987)
AGES SERVED   Teens and young adults
DESCRIPTION   Teens and young adults provide services to older people (e.g., making house repairs, doing chores, providing transportation, delivering meals, serving as nursing assistants and in-home services staff

PROGRAM   Teens & Elderly for the Arts (TEA) (Keller, 1990)
AGES SERVED   Teenagers
DESCRIPTION   Teenagers serve as apprentices to older adults in making candles, rugs, baskets, and soaps; caning chairs; weaving; and whittling

PROGRAM   Senior Guest Student Program (Dellman-Jenkins et al., 1994)
AGES SERVED   College students
DESCRIPTION   Students and older adults meet in six 1-hour sessions to discuss a 30-minute presentation designed to elicit reactions and opinions

PROGRAM   Elder Mentor Relationship (Hamon & Koch, 1993)
AGES SERVED   College students
DESCRIPTION   Single-semester relationship between a college student and an older student of their choosing (e.g., grandparent, neighbor, family friend, retired person who worked in their field of study, nursing facility resident, or homeless older adult)

PROGRAM   Life Histories Project (McGowan & Blankenship, 1994)
AGES SERVED   College students
DESCRIPTION   Students interview homebound older adults of a lower socioeconomic level regarding their lives and keep a journal on the information gathered

PROGRAM   Senior Advisory Committee (Greaves & Lewis, 1995)
AGES SERVED   Nursing students
DESCRIPTION   Older adults are recruited to serve as advisors on the gerontological content of an undergraduate nursing program; the older adults reviewed the courses, audiovisual materials used, advised the faculty, recruited other older adults, and actively participated in classes and seminars

Correspondence

(These addresses apply only to personnel serving in Bosnia)
Any Service Member
Operation Joint Endeavor
APO AE 09397
To write to a person in the Army, Navy, Air Force, or Marine Corps

Any Service Member
Operation Joint Endeavor
FPO AE 09398
To write to a person in the Navy or Marine Corps who is serving aboard ship

Resource Materials

Carroll, A. (1994). *Golden opportunities: A volunteer guide for Americans over 50*. Princeton, NJ: Peterson. $14.95. May be ordered by phone (800) 338-3282.

France, M.H. (1986). *People helping people: Peer counseling for older people*. Victoria, BC, Canada: British Columbia Ministry of Health.

I hear the violincello or man's heart complaint,
And hear the keyed cornet or else the echo of sunset.
Walt Whitman, "Song of Myself"

I Hear a Symphony

Music Therapy

On a Friday or Saturday night it is not unusual to find the parking lot full at the local inn. The crowd is predominantly older middle-class people out for the evening with spouses or old friends. The drinks are reasonably priced, dinner includes anything from full meals to lighter fare, and the popcorn is free. The main attraction, however, is the piano bar, where a young blond woman with an outgoing personality plays and sings popular songs from several decades. As the evening progresses, requests become more frequent, and many patrons begin to sing along. This is the generation that grew up before television and other modern distractions—people who very likely once sang in a church choir, played in their high school band, or gathered around the family piano to harmonize at holidays. Familiar tunes lift their spirits; bring back fond memories; and further cement relationships with family, friends, and neighbors. For this crowd, music is obviously therapeutic, taking their minds off their aches and pains and transporting them to happy moments of the past.

A growing number of older adults are participating in music programs in their communities, at churches and civic organizations, in continuing education classes, and in residential facilities (Bell, 1987). Although the recreational use of music can enhance the quality of life for many older adults, a formal program of music therapy can speak to the needs of individuals who suffer from many of the negative aspects of aging (Bright, 1987). Music therapy is a health service similar to occupational or physical therapy. Music is used therapeutically to address physical, psychological, cognitive, and social functioning. It is effective for individuals of all ages and abilities, including older people.

Music therapy is actually an ancient tradition. Egyptian priest-doctors used incantations to promote fertility, and Hebrew accounts suggest that music was employed in the treatment of both physical and mental illness in Biblical times (Shapiro, 1969). In Greek mythology Apollo was associated with both music and medicine, and in the Americas medicine men used songs in healing ceremonies (Lynch, 1987). Music therapy continues to be of worldwide interest; "surfing" the Internet turns up home pages offering news of national and international conferences, even one featuring a newsletter published by B.-C. Choi, a South Korean music therapist (Choi, 1995).

Music therapists are musician-counselors with specialized training in the use of rhythm and melody to enhance psychological and emotional well-being. Therapists work with individuals in many different circumstances and of all ages. They are skilled at improvising and arranging songs in many different musical styles and are generally accomplished in playing the piano or guitar and in singing. About 70 colleges and universities in the United States offer undergraduate or graduate degrees in music therapy, and national organizations have set standards for registered music therapists (R.M.T.), certified music therapists (C.M.T.), and board-certified music therapists (M.T.-BC) (Weiss, 1994). Although it is possible for laypersons to bring music into the lives of older people in informal ways, many applications require the expertise of a music therapist, working in conjunction with other health care providers or caregivers.

Whether they reside in long-term care facilities or are simply limited in their activities at home and in their communities, many older people are depressed as a result of the losses they have incurred and the monotonous structure and routine of their lives. Music therapy can be an outlet for creative expression and can help people cope with the losses that accompany aging. Music therapy can enable individuals to relive positive experiences, returning forgotten meaning to their lives (Blumenthal & Kupfer, 1990; Hanser, 1990). In addition, the stress and anxiety that often underlie depression can be diminished or alleviated with the use of music therapy (Blumenthal & Kupfer, 1990). The relaxing effect of music can clear the mind, preparing people to work through problems effectively (Hanser, 1990). Similar effects can be achieved for older individuals who have difficulty sleeping. Music therapy can provide a distraction from worries and disturbing thoughts, and possibly even from physical discomfort, allowing them to rest (Hanser, 1990).

The vast variety in style, instrumentation, melody, and music-related activities makes music therapy appealing to many older people (Hanser, 1990). It is also relatively inexpensive and requires a minimal expenditure of time, making it feasible in many different settings for older people with varying abilities (Gerdner & Swanson, 1993; Short, 1992). Even confused older adults living in nursing facilities can be inspired to participate in activities that are related to music, and the therapy sessions can improve their quality of life (Christie, 1992). Other research indicates that singing can substitute for speech, allowing people who experience difficulty expressing their feelings in spoken words to do so in song (Yon, 1984). One of the most interesting outcomes of one program of music therapy was that an aphasic woman, who had a stroke (cerebrovascular accident, CVA) 25 years earlier, made progress in her speech—actually forming several complete sentences—in response to imaging exercises she performed in the music therapy sessions (Short, 1992). Similarly, music has the power to "lift" people, including those with ambulation disorders, allowing them to experience mobility in feelings or spirit if not in body (Yon, 1984). Short (1992), working with a group of older adults who were in wheelchairs, found that most of them enjoyed freedom of movement while listening or keeping time to music.

People with Alzheimer's disease may also benefit from music therapy. It is estimated that 50% of older adults in residential care have Alzheimer's disease and the severe cognitive, physical, and social limitations it produces (Clair & Bernstein, 1990). Although there is no hope of remission or recovery from the disease, music therapy has been shown to promote behaviors that allow for some social interaction and nonverbal communication, even in advanced stages of the disease (Clair & Bernstein, 1990). For example, people with Alzheimer's disease frequently experience agitation, which is manifested in inappropriate verbal, vocal, or motor activity. This problem has a serious impact on health care providers, and, by extension, the quality of life for people with Alzheimer's disease (Gerdner & Swanson, 1993). While conducting individualized music therapy sessions with people with Alzheimer's disease, Gerdner and Swanson (1993) found that there was both an immediate and a 1-hour residual calming effect that may provide an alternative to pharmaceutical and physical restraints approaches to the management of agitation. Clair and Bernstein (1990) found that, despite marked deterioration in the cognitive, physical, and social abilities of a group of people with Alzheimer's disease during the course of a music therapy program, the participants continued to take part in the music activities in a structured group, sitting in chairs without the need for physical restraints during the 30-minute sessions. In fact, for most of them, this was the only time during the week when they could actually interact with others in an meaningful way.

Implementing music therapy in a group setting allows for the sharing of images and issues with peers. Music has been described as the most social of the arts, and it is the social aspects of life that are most frequently affected by aging or mental illness (Moore, 1986). Music therapy not only helps older adults cope with past, current, and future issues—including disability, bereavement, sexuality, and the aging process—but it also tends to buoy the spirits of group members via the possibility of sharing fears, concerns, and experiences (Short, 1992).

USE OF MUSIC THERAPY WITH OLDER ADULTS LIVING INDEPENDENTLY

Music therapy can also be implemented on an individual basis for older individuals who are homebound or too physically ill to participate in a group (Gerdner & Swanson, 1993; Hanser, 1990), as in the following example.

Mrs. Hanover, a widow in her 70s, is in good health and good spirits, and continues to live at home. While visiting one of her daughters, she enjoyed watching Woody Allen's *Mighty Aphrodite* on video. As the movie ends, a Greek chorus bursts into a lively rendition of a popular song from Mrs. Hanover's youth, "When You're Smiling." Mrs. Hanover immediately began to sing along. Her daughter reports that Mrs. Hanover often sings along with the car radio when they travel together; in fact, the two often sing together, with Mrs. Hanover taking the harmony.

When she was young, Mrs. Hanover and her sister performed as a song-and-dance team. Music has been an important part of Mrs. Hanover's life, and she is particularly proud of her ability to harmonize. This special talent has contributed to her self-confidence and self-esteem throughout her life. For Mrs. Hanover, music continues to be a source of fun, joy, and family connectedness.

Older people who live alone often feel isolated. Music therapy is feasible for these individuals in several different ways. The ease and relative inexpensiveness of implementing music therapy make it applicable to such venues as adult day centers, senior centers, and even an individual's home (Gerdner & Swanson, 1993). According to Hanser (1990), who has found music therapy to be particularly effective for people who are homebound, music allows older people to explore creative new directions and to relive past experiences; it is an appropriate activity for both healthy and impaired older adults and for older people who are musically talented or simply casually interested in music. Participation, whether by singing or playing an instrument or both, can lead to a sense of mastery or control over one's life; passive listening can result in relaxation and positive changes in mood (Hanser, 1990).

Involving the individual in some type of senior center or adult day program within which a weekly or biweekly music therapy group could be established is ideal because it offers an opportunity for socialization, in addition to the therapeutic benefits of music. Sing-alongs, musical quizzes, or participation in a jug-band are all fairly easily accommodated in the spaces normally provided, and the equipment need constitute little more than a record, cassette, or compact disc player, although a piano can be especially effective. Opportunities may arise for group participants to attend live musical performances. For example, since 1991 Evan Drachman and the other musicians in the Piatigorsky Foundation[1] have been performing at retirement communities and senior centers throughout the United States. The foundation is named for Drachman's grandfather, the legendary cellist Gregor Piatigorsky. Drachman plays his grandfather's 270-year-old cello, building each concert around one major piece of music and taking time to introduce the work and discuss his personal relationship to the music. From his student days at the Curtis Institute of Music in Philadelphia, he has been aware of the special reception he receives from older audiences. Says Drachman, "Here is a fantastic venue for concerts . . . people who really want to hear this music . . . [and] a growing number of musicians who have nowhere to play" (Noble, 1996, p. C5).

One of the most common barriers faced by group facilitators is transportation to and from a music therapy group—it may not be feasible for all independent-living older individuals. Bringing music therapy into the older individual's home is often an option for people who are homebound because of physical limitations and/or inclement weather. A weekly visit from a health care professional or case manager who combines his or her services with music therapy can have an impact on symptoms of boredom, sleeplessness, or depression. Often, the therapeutic procedure entails prescribing various homework exercises (specific examples can be found in the section on implementation variations) to be carried out daily, in addition to the work done in the therapist's presence (Hanser, 1990). Music selections are mutually agreed on and should be available either by looking through the older adult's existing collection or by borrowing library copies of cassettes, records, or compact discs; occasionally, donations may be obtained by contacting local churches, synagogues, or senior centers. Specific stressors are identified, such as difficulty in falling asleep at night or in becoming motivated in the morning, and listening and imaging exercises are prescribed. In some cases family members or friends are enlisted to assist in implementing the therapy (Hanser, 1990).

USE OF MUSIC THERAPY WITH OLDER ADULTS LIVING IN CONGREGATE HOUSING AND LONG-TERM CARE FACILITIES

Helena was a 92-year-old resident of a nursing facility who spent much of each day sitting in her room. Her sight was poor and television held little interest for her. The

---

[1]For more information on the Piatigorsky Foundation, write or call the Foundation at 90 West Street, Suite 1605, New York, New York 10006, (212) 732-8941.

staff would encourage her to attend activities and sit in the day room, but she refused, saying she preferred to stay in her room. During an assessment conducted by the social worker, Yolanda, it became clear that Helena did not engage in any activity in her room other than brooding. She would periodically comment, "I wish God would take me soon."

Yolanda developed a treatment plan that required Helena to sit each morning in the day room, where she could come in contact with other residents and staff as they passed by. Despite her reluctance to do so, Helena agreed to spend 1 hour in the day room, with the understanding that she could spend the remainder of her day in her room. Staff were instructed to pay special attention to her while she was out of her room in order to make the experience pleasant.

In addition to creatively motivating Helena to leave her room for a short period of time each day, Yolanda implemented a music therapy program for her. Yolanda discussed the plan with Helena, who did not respond enthusiastically. However, Yolanda was not deterred. They discussed musical preferences and Helena revealed a past enjoyment of polkas and Polish mazurkas. Her family was consulted, and they offered to make cassette tapes of some of Helena's old records. Yolanda requested that they make 90-minute-long tapes so that there would be 45 minutes of uninterrupted music before there was a need to turn the tape over. Each afternoon, the nursing assistant assigned to Helena would ask her to select a tape from the assortment provided by her family and to turn on the cassette player, which was usually kept at the nurses' station to prevent theft. The nursing assistant would return when the tape ran out. Helena was also free to turn the cassette over herself or to play additional tapes. After 1 month, Helena was encouraged to choose additional tapes for the collection and to play the tapes in her room as well as in the day room.

During an assessment of the program, Helena reported to Yolanda that she enjoyed the music and described memories of the many dances she and her husband had attended in their youth and of her childhood, when the family would sing together on winter evenings. The music coming from Helena's room also attracted several other residents, who would stop by to listen to the music. Helena continued to prefer to pass time in her room, but the music therapy program helped to make that time pass more enjoyably, replacing her depressive thoughts with pleasant memories.

An increase in life expectancy, attributable primarily to new drug therapies, means that the period between retirement and death has been extended 20–30 years for many people. According to Palmer (1977), society has a moral obligation to offer life, not just existence, to people during these later years. In fact, "quality of life" has become the major issue in the 1990s for health care providers. In congregate living arrangements and long-term care facilities, emphasis is placed more and more on the cleanliness and attractiveness of surroundings and on the possibility for residents to keep some of their personal effects in their rooms. Also, there is recognition that older individuals have physical, cognitive, emotional, and social needs. Music therapy can make a significant contribution to all of these areas (Christie, 1992).

Being part of a mariachi band, clapping to a German drinking song, or marching to band music provides distractions from pain for people with arthritis and stroke survivors, encouraging the physical exercise they need. Songs such as "Shine on, Harvest Moon" are useful as reality orientation for older adults with minor cognitive impairment because they reinforce concepts of season, day, year, and time (Palmer, 1977). Just hearing familiar music in an unfamiliar or seemingly hostile environment can transform that environment into one that feels safe and secure, facilitating conversation and interaction (McCloskey, 1985). Nurses in one study noted that participants in music therapy who used a popular karaoke format sometimes cried, perhaps because they reminisced about lost times and loved ones, but the nurses viewed this expression of emotion positively. In fact, the nurses found that one of the best by-products of the karaoke sessions was an enhanced sense of connectedness for both clients and staff: The atmosphere on the unit became more open and positive, clients seemed more cheerful and talkative, and some of them shared their thoughts and feelings in new ways (Mavely & Mitchell, 1994).

For individuals residing in congregate living situations and long-term care facilities, music therapy can be implemented fairly easily on both individual and group levels. A cassette player can be checked out from a central location (e.g., nurses' station, recreation room) and placed at a resident's bedside for use as needed. Music selections may be brought in by family members or obtained from libraries (Gerdner & Swanson, 1993).

Music therapy groups can be formed and sessions held regularly in a quiet room within the facility. The size of the group may vary; however, the possibility for intimacy is more likely within a small group of four to six older adults (Short, 1992). Music can be therapeutic in a group setting in many different ways. One possibility is to play one or more selections for a portion of the session and to follow that with a group discussion of the images and feelings that were experienced. Different themes can be chosen by the therapist or the participants, and the music selections can coincide with the particular theme. Another option is to ask group members to draw or paint during the music selection and then share their artwork with the rest of the group at the end of the session. Suggestions such as "draw to the rhythm of the music" or "choose a color that suggests the mood of the music" may encourage involvement and freedom of expression (Rosling & Kitchen, 1992).

PRECAUTIONS TO TAKE AND ACCOMMODATIONS TO MAKE IN IMPLEMENTING MUSIC THERAPY

Several important points should be considered when implementing a music therapy program. The most important is that music therapy is not suitable for all older individuals. Older people who have a severe hearing impairment may find this type of therapy frustrating. Individuals should be able to respond to musical stimuli, be able to comprehend simple instructions, and be able to demonstrate functional awareness of themselves and place. Participants in group music therapy should be able to attend a session of at least 45–55 minutes in duration without becoming restless and disruptive to others (Rosling & Kitchen, 1992; Short, 1992). A therapeutic technique that necessitates the ability to progressively relax the muscles, as with some therapies involving the use of imagery, is contraindicated for people with joint diseases. It should be noted that music therapy involving the evocation of imagery is usually inappropriate for people with psychosis (Hanser, 1990).

Adaptations may need to be made to compensate for some of the difficulties implicit in aging. For example, several music therapy techniques rely on the use of intact memory skills. However, some participants with memory impairment who are asked to discuss their feelings and images after the music has ended or after others have shared their ideas may have difficulty doing so. The result may be confusion, inaccuracies, and reduction in detail. Careful questioning by the group facilitator using cues and prompts during the postmusic discussion may be necessary to guide individuals with memory impairment. Another suggestion is to ask the participants to write down their ideas as they occur (Short, 1992), although this may not be feasible in some cases. Older adults with physical disabilities and those with dementing illnesses may be unable to keep a log of their thoughts. Interestingly, Hanser (1990) also points out that adaptations may be necessary when a music therapist works with musicians, as opposed to nonmusicians, because there is evidence that these individuals process music somewhat differently from the way a layperson does.

The length and nature of a music selection should be appropriate for the older individual or individuals for whom it is being played. Selections that are lengthy and repetitious may be inappropriate for music therapy sessions geared to evoking images and emotions but suitable for promoting relaxation and inducement of sleep (Short, 1992). It is important that each music selection be screened thoroughly before it is introduced to an individual or a group. Often, even after screening, selections may prove to be unsuitable in length. This problem can be controlled by monitoring the participants' nonverbal cues, such as yawns, restlessness, rate of breathing, and coughs. In addition, music selections with lyrics should be used with great care. On the one hand, vocal music is more frustrating than instrumental music for people with impaired hearing (Moore, 1986). On the other hand, depending on the content, the lyrics may elicit strong emotional responses from some participants, possibly counteracting the goal of the session (Short, 1992). For example, some songs may elicit memories of a lost child, spouse, or other loved one. Similarly, music therapy that encourages older adults to explore the imagery suggested by instrumental music can trigger unpleasant as well as pleasant images (Gerdner & Swanson, 1993). A music therapist who offers this kind of music must be clinically skilled in handling the great range of issues that may arise (Short, 1992).

When implementing music therapy in a group, the facilitator must choose a proper setting. A quiet, private room, free from interruptions, is preferable. Often, a lounge area or a recreation room can be used, provided that the music therapy sessions do not overlap other activities scheduled in those areas (Rosling & Kitchen, 1992; Short, 1992). Sufficient room for group members to form a circle, including room to accommodate wheelchairs, or for large tables, if artwork is to be included, is essential. It may be wise to use the room on a trial basis and move to another location if it proves to be unsuitable (Short, 1992).

For any type of music therapy, some form of equipment—cassette, record, or compact disc player—on which to play the music is necessary. It is important to avoid the use of poor-quality equipment, as poor sound is particularly irritating to older adults. It is best to keep the bass at a high setting, especially for people with hearing loss, and to keep the volume constant. Depressed individuals and people with brain injury, even if hard of hearing, can react strongly to increases in volume. Individuals who are particularly sensitive to variation in sound should be seated far from the speakers. Prerecording of the music for a session allows the facilitator more control (Moore, 1986). Biley (1992) suggests the use of a central system with remote speakers, both for sound quality and to safeguard against the theft of small, portable equipment.

The group facilitator should also have access to a wide range of music selections. Various instrumental selections, vocalists familiar to the participants, lively music, relaxing music, and different kinds of ethnic and folk music can be used. According to Moore (1986), the best choices tend to come from the participants' early life—childhood, adolescence, the early years of marriage. Regional, folk, pop, show tunes, spirituals, and patriotic songs can be effective, though the therapist should keep in mind the potential for strong emotional responses to some selections. Classical music also offers a wide range of selections, with certain pieces evoking imagery effectively (e.g., Beethoven's "Pastoral Symphony No. 6," Schumann's "Scenes from Childhood [Opus 15]") (Short, 1992). Familiar music has more penetrating power than that which is unfamiliar because people bring more of themselves (e.g., personal memories) to the encounter; familiar music can also create feelings of safety and protection (Moore, 1986).

It is possible to introduce music that is new to participants (e.g., the soundtrack from the movie *Jonathan Livingston Seagull*) and have it become familiar, provided that it evokes the desired mood in listeners. Moore (1986) notes that a cheerful song (e.g., "Mairzy Doats"), ironically, can be depressing if it is out of sync with the older adult's mood (i.e., too fast, too loud, too syncopated for someone who is depressed or too monotonous or mellow for someone who is hyperactive). The song's tempo is important, as are its rhythm, volume, and tone. For example, a high, shrill, or sharp tone is too stimulating for most older people; a mellow tone is usually better (Moore, 1986).

Whenever possible, participants should assist in the selection of music, possibly providing a favorite recording from their personal collection (Gerdner & Swanson, 1993). Family members may be helpful in remembering certain song titles, musical instruments, and performers favored by the older person if he or she has some memory impairment. Music may be obtained through libraries or donations can be sought from family, friends, staff, or philanthropic groups (Gerdner & Swanson, 1993).

By far the most important factor in the efficacy of music therapy is the proper selection of the music to be employed, and, particularly, the personal input of the older individual or of the group in the choice of that music. Still, mistakes can be made, by both musicians and nonmusicians, in using music in clinical settings. What is soothing to one person may be depressing to another. It is, therefore, important to request feedback and to learn from mistakes (Moore, 1986).

The practice of playing music continuously (e.g., as background, ambient noise; Muzak) in long-term care facilities is not a good idea. Neither should it be recommended to homebound older adults unless they have a clear preference for this format. Although Biley (1992) points out that soothing background music seems to be used effectively by dentists as a distraction from anxiety and pain, Clair and Bernstein (1994) contend that in most cases continuously played music simply fades into the background as the person habituates to the sound. Furthermore, their study, which looked at the effect of background music on 28 people with a severe form of dementia, found no difference in degree of agitation when no music, soothing music, or stimulative music was played in the background (Clair & Bernstein, 1994). It is more advantageous to feature regularly scheduled music periods of an hour or two during the morning, afternoon, and early evening. Music selections could be decided on by the residents' council or a music committee composed of residents. The committee could interview other residents to determine what they would like to hear.

Conducting individual music therapy sessions in long-term care facilities and possibly in congregate living situations may produce an effect on individuals within the immediate environment other than the individual for whom it is intended. This effect could well be positive. However, that may not be the case, and the privacy of other residents should be respected (Gerdner & Swanson, 1993).

IMPLEMENTATION OF MUSIC THERAPY

Initial Steps

The first step in implementing music therapy is to decide on the primary purpose of the therapy. Some possibilities include providing contact with music to enhance relaxation, reduce symptoms of depression, and access feelings (Rosling & Kitchen, 1992) or using music and imagery to address issues and difficulties of disability, bereavement, aging, and communal living (Short, 1992). Music-based life review allows for the recall and evaluation of earlier experiences and can lead to ego integrity, an acceptance of one's self and one's life in the face of death (Bennett & Maas, 1988). Reduction in belligerence, abusive behavior, or generalized agitation, behaviors that often arise because of stroke or such progressive disorders as Alzheimer's disease, may also be a goal of therapy (Palmer, 1977). Meddaugh (1987) began an exercise-to-music group for several extremely abusive residents in a long-term care facility primarily to improve morale among the nursing staff. Specific problems such as sleep disorders or lethargy associated with specific times of day can also be addressed by music therapy. In the case of individuals with Alzheimer's disease or other cognitive losses, a goal may be to improve attendance to surroundings and reality or to reduce stereotypical behavior such as hitting a chair or tabletop (Christie, 1992). Simply enhancing opportunities for socializing and for fun are also worthwhile and achievable goals. Obviously, there may be more than one purpose for the therapy. Formally acknowledging a purpose or purposes at the outset of therapy establishes a basis from which to evaluate its effectiveness. A sample form that may be used for this purpose is found on page 234.

With the purpose of the therapy in mind, the next step is to obtain information about an individual's or group's musical preferences. Information about musical likes and dislikes or about ethnicity and religious background that may indicate likely preferences could be included in an initial admissions assessment at a long-term care facility (Gerdner & Swanson, 1993). Specific information about what types of music the individual finds relaxing or enjoyable and even what specific pieces of music, composers, performers, or styles are favored is useful (Hanser, 1990). If the older person or persons are cognitively capable, this information can be accessed through interviews (see p. 235 for a sample form). If the older individual is unable to provide detailed information, family members can be asked to complete a brief questionnaire about the person's musical preferences and the relative importance of music in his or her life. This information is helpful in determining whether the individual is a viable candidate for music therapy and what types of activities would be the most helpful. Any severe hearing or advanced cognitive impairment will generally rule out the use of music therapy with such older adults in a group format (Hanser, 1990). However, individual therapy may be an option. Certain physical disabilities should be noted at this step as well, but in most cases these should not limit or prevent participation in music therapy (Short, 1992).

Once the initial steps have been taken, music therapy sessions can begin. The sessions can take many different forms. The appropriate format will depend on the purpose that has been established, whether therapy is in group or individual form, the needs or limitations of the participant(s), and the preferences of the facilitator.

Individual Music Therapy

Music therapy on an individual basis can be carried out in as simple a format as playing individually selected music in an older person's room or home for 30 minutes or 1 hour daily. The individual should be observed before, during, and after the presentation of music, at least at the beginning of therapy, and any changes in behavior should be noted (Gerdner & Swanson, 1993). If the older individual lives independently, the observation may be recorded by a family member or by the individual, if he or she is capable of doing so. If the older person or nursing staff report a recurring low point in the day, when negative thoughts and feelings seem to predominate, the therapy session should be rescheduled to that time (Hanser, 1990).

Common problems such as insomnia can be addressed directly through music therapy. Music that the insomniac older individual finds relaxing can be played at bedtime to assist him or her in falling asleep. The music player must have a quiet, automatic shut-off mechanism so as not to jar the client awake. At the other extreme, lively foot-tapping music may be used at times when an older person feels the least energetic, often in the morning hours (Hanser, 1990).

Music Therapy Program Plan

Client _____ Date _____

Activity planned or being considered _____

_____

Format ____ Individual ____ Group ____ Estimated no. of participants

Expected level of participation in the activity_____

_____

Goals

____ Improve interpersonal relationships   ____ Increase self-confidence
____ Increase opportunity to socialize   ____ Improve coordination
____ Elevate mood   ____ Sensory stimulation
____ Increase concentration and attention   ____ Reminiscence
____ Increase sense of well-being   ____ Relaxation
____ Improve memory functioning   ____ Exercise (small muscles)
____ Promote sense of belonging to a group ____ Exercise (large muscles)
____ Increase pleasurable activities   ____ Decrease apathy

Frequency of activity ____ Daily   ____ Twice a week   ____ Weekly

                      ____ Every other week   ____ Monthly

                      ____ Other (specify) _____

_____

Number of weeks music activity will be provided _____

Location of activity _____

A Life Worth Living: Practical Strategies for Reducing Depression in Older Adults, by Pearl Mosher-Ashley and Phyllis Barrett. ©1997 Health Professions Press, Inc., Baltimore.

Music Therapy Assessment Interview

Client _____ Date _____

Respondent _____
        (___ Family ___ Friend ___ Caregiver)

Activity planned or being considered _____

Musical preferences
    a = To listen to   b = To participate in

    ___ Sing-alongs   ___ Big band   ___ Classical   ___ Folk

    ___ Player piano   ___ Jazz   ___ Opera   ___ Blues

    ___ Religious   ___ Country/western   ___ Other

What types of music don't you like? _____

_____

Which of the following kinds of ethnic music do you enjoy?
    ___ Irish Celtic ___ Cajun ___ Polkas

    ___ Spirituals ___ Latin/Salsa ___ Other (please specify)

_____

Which of the following would you like included in a music program?

Song _____

Composer _____

Singer _____

Musical style _____

Do you play a musical instrument? ___ Yes ___ No

Are you willing to learn a simple instrument? ___ Yes ___ No

    ___ Tambourine   ___ Ukulele

    ___ Maracas   ___ Guitar

    ___ Kazoo   ___ Autoharp

A Life Worth Living: Practical Strategies for Reducing Depression in Older Adults, by Pearl Mosher-Ashley and Phyllis Barrett. ©1997 Health Professions Press, Inc., Baltimore.

Another type of music therapy that may be helpful to older individuals living independently is one that requires the music therapist to prescribe various homework exercises to be completed along with playing certain music selections. Selections used early in the course of therapy should be familiar pieces chosen by the client. Observations made by the therapist during the course of treatment can shed light on the potential effectiveness of other pieces, including classical works, which have helped other clients. In this way, an individualized program is developed (Hanser, 1990). The homework assignments may include gentle exercise while listening to soothing music, working out tight muscles in a pleasing way; progressive muscle relaxation, in which parts of the body are relaxed slowly and individually to slow, soothing music; and the replacement of dysfunctional thoughts and worries with familiar, pleasant visual imagery while listening to a favorite piece of music (Hanser, 1990). Clients are usually asked to find a comfortable and relaxed position at a time when interruptions are least likely to occur in order to practice at least one of these techniques daily. The practitioner overseeing the music therapy visits the home weekly to monitor and discuss progress (Hanser, 1990). In order to evaluate the overall effectiveness of this type of program, a pretest should be used to establish baseline observations about depression, mood, and stress levels. At least four standardized tests are available for this purpose: the Geriatric Depression Scale (GDS), created by Yesavage et al. in 1983; the Brief Symptom Inventory (BSI), created by Derogatis and Spencer in 1982; the Self-Esteem Inventory (SEI), created by Rosenberg in 1979; and the Beck Depression Inventory (BDI), created by Beck et al. in 1961 and revised in 1996 (see Chapter 1); the Life Satisfaction in the Elderly Scale (Chapter 2) is also recommended. A posttest can then be administered to document changes in the status of depression, mood, and stress, or other targeted problems. Clients should be encouraged to continue to use the techniques introduced during the course of the formal therapy after it ends, making changes in the music used in order to avoid boredom.

Group Music Therapy

Group music therapy sessions usually are 1 hour in length, but can last upward of 2 hours. One reason for this suggested length is the limited physical stamina of frail older individuals. The sessions should be scheduled at a time when other activities will not prevent participation (Short, 1992). Each session should include a period for greeting other group members and settling into the therapeutic process. Individuals may form a circle, making the session slightly more intimate. A discussion before the music begins is sometimes recommended: At the first meeting, this period allows for an explanation of the therapeutic process and a verbal outline of the session. At subsequent meetings, group members should be asked how they are feeling, and their input regarding past or future sessions should be welcomed (Short, 1992).

Music should be selected based on its therapeutic value in relation to the goal or theme chosen for the particular session, keeping in mind the participants' input and musical preferences. For example, if relaxation is the goal and classical music is a preference for some members of the group, Bach's "Air on a G String" or Vaughan Williams' "Fantasia on Greensleeves" may work effectively (Rosling & Kitchen, 1992). If stimulation is the goal, songbooks compiled by decade or song sheets reproduced in large-print format can be passed around to provide everyone with lyrics for a rousing sing-along (Moore, 1986). If musical instruments are to be used, Moore (1986) recommends investing in a few good-quality instruments rather than relying on inexpensive rhythm instruments because their sound quality is generally poor. (Kazoos are effective, however, if participants are instructed to hum into them because the sound mimics vocalization.) Good-quality instruments that are perhaps the easiest to incorporate into a music therapy session are the autoharp, ukulele, and guitar because many songs require that only two or three chords be played on these instruments. A pitch pipe also can be useful in establishing a key, preferably one low enough to accommodate most mature voices (Clair, 1996; Moore, 1986).

Some experts in music therapy recommend instituting an induction period prior to presenting the music. Participants are asked to make themselves as comfortable as possible, and topics from the premusic discussion or suggestions from group members are selected for a short period of relaxation and imagery. Progressive relaxation techniques may be used, provided that necessary modifications are made for people with physical disabilities, as noted previously (Short, 1992). Moore (1986) suggests breathing exercises adapted from yoga. Once the participants are relaxed and receptive, each should be greeted by name in a welcoming song, as recommended by Clair and Bernstein (1990). Following this introduction, the music selection can be played or the group can be led in song. During this period, the group facilitator should monitor any nonverbal cues given by the participants. After allowing sufficient time for individuals to return to full consciousness, if the technique being used involves imagery, a postmusic discussion may follow (Short, 1992). All individuals should be invited to comment on any aspect of the music presentation, the images they experienced, their feelings, or memories that surfaced (Rosling & Kitchen, 1992).

Music therapy can also be coordinated with other types of therapeutic activities. Drawing or painting while listening to certain music selections is one possibility. Individuals can then share their artwork with the group in the postmusic discussion, along with feelings and memories experienced (Rosling & Kitchen, 1992). Exercise or dance movements can accompany music therapy, but the physical limitations of some of the older adult participants must be taken into account (Hanser, 1990).

Maintaining attendance records, along with records of behavior and emotional states before and after each session is recommended (Rosling & Kitchen, 1992). (A sample form designed for this purpose is included on p. 238.) Because it is almost impossible to lead the session and observe behavioral and emotional states simultaneously, sessions can be videotaped so that at a later time the therapist can note such things as communicating, including verbal response; one participant watching another participant or the therapist; singing; interacting with an instrument; or remaining seated without the use of restraints (Clair & Bernstein, 1990).

Music Therapy Record Form

Activity _____

Date of session _____ Location _____

Behavioral observation key   b = Before activity, a = After activity, d = During activity, NA = Not applicable.

Participant name	Smiled	Laughed	Talked with others	Silent	Observed facilitator	Observed participants	Interacted with instrument	Sang	Other

A Life Worth Living: Practical Strategies for Reducing Depression in Older Adults, by Pearl Mosher-Ashley and Phyllis Barrett. ©1997 Health Professions Press, Inc., Baltimore.

Another option is to use objective outside observers, perhaps undergraduate interns from a local college, who can review the videos and make detailed observations. They may even be able to record the duration of desired behaviors in seconds or minutes (Clair & Bernstein, 1990).

More research is needed in order to continue to improve the structuring of appropriate and successful music therapy experiences (Clair & Bernstein, 1990). Research involving a control group might be the most helpful in determining whether the overwhelmingly positive informal responses of older adults to the therapy has most to do with the therapist, the techniques, or the music itself (Hanser, 1990).

VARIATIONS ON USING MUSIC THERAPY WITH OLDER ADULTS

Numerous possibilities exist for bringing music into the lives of older people, whether they live independently or in a group setting. Some of these possibilities are live performance; musical games; player piano; karaoke; bell choir; and music, drawing, and imagery activities.

Live Performance

Live music can be presented in two modes, although the variations on this theme are obviously infinite: passive listening and participation. Passive listening involves bringing live music to an audience in order to entertain and perhaps educate. Commentary from the audience should be encouraged, but the most important goal is the enjoyment derived from watching and listening to a live performance. In selecting the kind of music to be performed, the educational, cultural, and ethnic backgrounds of group members should be considered. Before the performance the activity director or music therapist should also share information about the composer of the music, the artist(s) performing it, the work and its place in musical history, and related topics. This introduction is followed by the performance itself, with an informal session of response, comment, and general discussion afterward (Kartman, 1990).

The other approach is more active, with musicians brought into a long-term care facility, senior center, or other gathering place with the express intent of engaging older adults in song and making music. A western Massachusetts duo, "The Sunshine Boys" (Tom Griffin, age 71, and his partner, Roger Wapner, 54), perform four to six shows a week at area nursing facilities. They report that performing for older adults is their way of paying back the people who "made this country great" (Thamel, 1995, p. B8). Wapner, a cancer and stroke survivor, plays banjo and Griffin sings. Their repertoire includes popular tunes from the 1920s to the 1940s, and the audience is encouraged to sing along. Griffin has even been known to pass the microphone around to accommodate participants in wheelchairs. A woman in one audience appreciated a rendition of "My Wild Irish Rose," a song that brought back warm memories of her late husband; another woman reported that she sang along with all the songs, and a staff person noted that even people with Alzheimer's disease sang and danced during the performance (Thamel, 1995).

A simple sing-along conducted by a staff member or therapist without the presence of guest performers is also possible. Moore (1986) recommends the kind of songs "The Sunshine Boys" perform. She suggests starting with songs traditionally sung in groups, then moving on to popular songs, show tunes, and humorous songs. Making "environmental sounds" such as clapping and rapping tabletops add to the fun. Swaying and nodding "to and fro" to the music, as opposed to side to side (which may cause some participants to feel that they are out of sync with the music or doing something wrong), can be encouraged as well. After building up to more stimulating songs, Moore suggests gradually backing off and ending the session on a calm note. She emphasizes that the facilitator does not need to be an exceptional singer or musician; in fact, too polished a performance sometimes inhibits group members' participation (Moore, 1986, p. 432). Clair and Bernstein (1990) propose a similar session, incorporating the use of professional-quality tambourines, hand-held drums, maracas, and claves (i.e., a pair of cylindrical hardwood sticks that are used as a percussion instrument).

Musical Games

Messenger (1995) suggests the use of a musical quiz as a means of encouraging socialization, building self-esteem, and providing opportunities for pleasant recollections. Music of the big bands and music associated with famous radio programs, movies, bands, or singers are possible categories for the quiz. Other ideas include bodies of water mentioned in song, musical geography (cities, states, rivers, and countries mentioned in song), and boys' and girls' names in songs, particularly if someone in the group shares one of the names (Kartman, 1990). The format can mimic a popular television quiz show, with a master of ceremonies encouraging participants to pick a category, receive a musical clue (perhaps played on the piano), and identify the tune. It is also possible to ask the group to sing a few lines of the tune after it has been identified.

Moore (1986) has devised a musical bingo game. The materials needed are 10 songbooks in large-print format, 10 sturdy 9" × 15" cards, 35 songs appropriate for the players, and 35 small pieces of paper. The name of each song to be used should be written on a small piece of paper. Then the cards should be turned into bingo cards by making 25 squares on each (5 rows across and 5 rows down). Each vertical column should be headed with the letters in the word MUSIC. The squares in each vertical row should be filled with song names chosen from five separate lists of seven songs each, ensuring that no two cards have the same combination of songs. The middle square can be designated a free space.

To play musical bingo, the cards should be distributed. Song titles should be called out by the song leader/group facilitator by choosing from the small pieces of paper (perhaps placed in a bowl or a hat) until someone has m-u-s-i-c (b-i-n-g-o). The whole group can then sing the songs in the winner's line (Moore, 1986).

Player Piano

The heyday of the player piano was the years before and after World War I. It provided accompaniment to the jazz age of the 1920s and was often the "voice" of silent movies. For some older people, it may have been the focal point of music at home as well. In 1923 alone, over 200,000 player pianos were purchased. For these reasons, Olson (1984) decided that the player piano was perfect for use in music therapy with older people. To implement this idea it is not necessary to have a player piano on the premises. In the 3-week study that Olson conducted, a 1922 Kimball player piano was used to play 20 piano rolls, which were tape recorded and presented to a group of older adults. The treatment consisted of five sessions, with four songs played per session, each of about 2–4 minutes' duration. The songs were selected by a consultant from the Michigan State University Department of Music and were similar in style and arranged according to tempo variations. University students, some of whom were majoring in music therapy, served as observers and recorders in order to assess the success of the therapy. They looked for clients' attempts to keep the rhythm, movement of extremities, body movement, and smiles, and found more of all of these signs of enjoyment and involvement during the music than they did before or after it was played. When participants were asked if they knew the songs, if they liked or disliked them, and how the songs made them feel, verbal responses were 98% positive (Olson, 1984). This technique seems to address several common goals of music therapy: increased physical activity, an enhanced sense of well-being, and pleasant reminiscence.

Karaoke

Laser karaoke is an audiovisual device that encourages a person to sing along with recorded music. A monitor displays a colorful video as well as the words to the song being played. The nurses at Toronto's Queen Elizabeth Hospital got the idea for introducing karaoke to their patients from noticing its popularity at area nightspots (Mavely & Mitchell, 1994). Although there is an initial expenditure in obtaining the equipment, this therapy is easy to implement. When the machine was installed on the chronic care unit at Queen Elizabeth's, the nurses first invited volunteers to test it. Then they held an informational session for residents and their families, and all were invited to participate or just to listen. Soon, attendance at regular sessions swelled; even people who avoided singing in other activities wanted to sing along with the karaoke machine. In fact, the activity was instantly and continuously popular, even with residents whose physical limitations made it impossible for them to participate fully. When asked about their karaoke experience, residents responded with comments such as "Music is life, a renewal of life," "Music is feeling," "Singing is fun and wonderful," and "I do not think I could live without music" (Mavely & Mitchell, 1994, p. 23). Family members were equally enthusiastic. One resident who had not spoken for months broke into tears and began to sing softly with the recording on the karaoke machine; at a subsequent session, his wife joined him in singing along. Soon, he began to speak again. The music connected people with feelings and relationships from bygone times, uplifted the spirits of many, and allowed for a kind of transcendence, a way of forgetting for a time some of the less pleasant realities of aging and life in a hospital (Mavely & Mitchell, 1994).

Bell Choir

One of several therapies explored by Christie (1992) was the formation of a bell choir. The group in her study consisted of 12 relatively high-functioning women between the ages of 61 and 88. The members of the group had expressed interest in bell ringing and in music in general. They lived with various disabilities: impaired hearing or sight, cognitive losses, and problems with ambulation. The goals of the therapy were to increase their ability to attend to their surroundings and to improve their musical performance. Progress in establishing eye contact with the facilitator and in hitting the right notes on cue was recorded at each of six biweekly sessions. Improvement was achieved in both areas, and the performers even rated themselves musically. This therapy is relatively easy to implement, requiring only the set of bells and a room appropriate for practice sessions. Bell choir is best suited for individuals with some musical background; obviously, basic familiarity with the notes of the scale is helpful. The choir may also provide an opportunity for older adults to perform for their peers, enhancing the self-esteem of the performers and contributing to the establishment of a pleasant atmosphere in a residential setting. This activity can be offered to independent-living older adults at a senior center as well.

Music, Drawing, and Imagery

Noting that even in a humane setting, individuality is suppressed by residential living, Rosling and Kitchen (1992) initiated a 14-week music therapy program in a long-term care facility using relaxation, recorded music, art materials, writing, and discussion to explore the feelings and memories of the participants. The primary goal of the therapy was to combat depression by nurturing each participant's inner world. An area in a resident lounge was partitioned for privacy, large tables were moved together to create a work space, and large sheets of drawing paper were taped to the tables before the start of each session. Relaxing music having the natural rhythms of the heart and breathing was chosen. Some of the music selections used were Satie's "Gymnopedies," Bach's "Air on a G String," Pachelbel's "Canon in D," and Vaughan Williams' "Fantasia on Greensleeves." A facilitator began by leading the group through a short, simple guided imagery or gentle physical exercise set to the music, encouraging participants to concentrate on their breathing. Then a facilitator would demonstrate use of the drawing materials—large block crayons for ease of grasp or felt-tip pens. More music—ethnic, pop, or New Age music—was then played, and the group was instructed to choose a favorite color. Later they would be instructed to draw in time to the rhythm of the music; to choose a new color appropriate to the mood of the music; to draw something that symbolized what they were feeling; to look across the table and draw the face of a neighbor; and, finally, to close their eyes and move their hand to the music. During the drawing exercise, facilitators circulated among the group, encouraging and assisting members. After 25–30 minutes, the participants were asked to title their work. Then the group was led in a discussion of this experience, their memories, and more. Silences were respected. Members gave various responses to this course of therapy: Some participants found the drawing portion too difficult, but enjoyed other aspects of the sessions. Some experienced pleasant memories, others painful ones. For some group members, the drawing vented frustrations or was a better way for them to communicate than speaking.

Although this type of therapy would not be difficult to provide in a practical sense (the materials are inexpensive and readily available), any therapy that encourages this level of introspection, and, specifically, the use of imagery, must be conducted by a professional music therapist who is equipped to handle potentially strong and often painful reactions.

USE OF MUSIC THERAPY FOR PEOPLE WITH ALZHEIMER'S DISEASE

Smith (1990) contends that music therapy provides people with Alzheimer's disease with a sense of accomplishment, a source of energy and stimulation, and a way to find words with which to communicate, in addition to triggering memories. Music therapy can also provide relaxation and comfort for both people with Alzheimer's disease and their caregivers. Many people with the disease can sing or play a simple instrument, such as an autoharp or omnichord, when there seems to be little else of which they are still capable. Singing or playing an instrument can give the individual a sense of competence and accomplishment. The rhythm of the music can also encourage movement and exercise, both of which can mitigate the restlessness that people with Alzheimer's disease experience at certain times of the day. It is difficult not to move to "The Beer Barrel Polka" or Benny Goodman's "Sing, Sing, Sing," notes Smith. A caregiver or nursing staff member using music with a person with Alzheimer's disease can sit or stand in front of the person, giving verbal and visual instructions for exercises to be performed to music of an appropriate rhythm and tempo. It is important to work through the instructions slowly and to ask the person to repeat the movements until they are done correctly (or nearly so). Some other strategies include playing balloon volleyball, tossing a ball, walking, dancing, or swaying to the music.

As Alzheimer's disease progresses, the cortex of the brain shrinks, affecting both recall and verbalization. Consequently, it is difficult for people with Alzheimer's disease to initiate a conversation. However, automatic language skills (e.g., "Hello, how are you?" "Fine, thanks") may be retained. Encouraging a person with Alzheimer's disease to complete the lyrics to well-known songs is a way of triggering his or her automatic language ability, giving him a positive experience, perhaps even a chance to talk (Smith, 1990). If an individual cannot easily complete the lyric, it will be clear immediately and the therapy should be discontinued.

The restlessness that is symptomatic of Alzheimer's disease can be treated with the introduction of soothing music (Smith, 1990). Some audiotapes specifically designed for relaxation are available (see the resource list at the end of this chapter); religious music may also be appropriate in some cases. However, it is important for a caregiver to be prepared for the possibility that someone who has this disorder may react quite unexpectedly to any given piece of music; the caregiver's own response to the music may not be shared.

It is also possible to use music therapy with a group of people with Alzheimer's disease or a mixed group of individuals with both cognitive and physical impairments. Christie (1992) recommends that the group facilitator seat the participants close together, maintain a calm demeanor, and introduce familiar songs for group sing-alongs. Sessions can be held weekly or biweekly and should last no longer than 30 minutes.

MUSIC THERAPY FOR HIGH-FUNCTIONING OLDER ADULTS

In a pilot program at the Montefiore Home for the Aged in Cleveland Heights, Ohio, Shapiro (1969) found that the ambitious activities he planned broke down barriers between ethnic groups, led to physical stimulation, and resulted in animated conversation over the dinner table following the sessions. Shapiro began by choosing a comfortable room, furnished with colorful furniture that was placed in rows facing a piano and a blackboard. He also made occasional use of a record player. Several different activities were introduced. Among these was an activity in which two different rhythm patterns were explained and assigned to two groups. The patterns were also written on the blackboard. After some practice, the two groups "played off" their parts against the piano using tambourines, maracas, drums, and other rhythm instruments.

Another activity introduced the group to conducting. A $\frac{3}{4}$ meter was discussed and outlined on the blackboard. The group practiced the pattern, first by moving just their index fingers in time, then by moving the whole hand (to the wrist), then the forearm, and then the entire arm. They sang and conducted simultaneously as a group. Finally, a volunteer was asked to come forward and conduct the group. The participants responded to this activity with great enthusiasm. This movement exercise is especially appropriate as rehabilitation for people with arthritis, rheumatism, and post–CVA symptoms.

In an effort to increase attention span and to improve memory and the ability to associate, Shapiro devised an activity involving training the ear. Four notes were played on the piano. Then the group was instructed to listen for a change in one note and determine whether the new note was higher or lower. Eventually, participants were asked to identify and describe two changes in a series of six notes.

Shapiro (1969) also asked participants to graph the mood of musical selections on paper, creating an image similar to that created by a polygraph machine; this activity allows older adults to vent their hostility, aggression, and depression. Introducing certain songs for group sing-alongs, such as "Don't Fence Me In," also affords participants an opportunity to safely express some of their own feelings of confinement or frustration through someone else's words.

Music therapy has numerous applications for older people. As Moore (1986) points out, the beat and rhythm of song reach the most primal areas of the brain, energizing the whole nervous system and creating physiological changes. Wolfe

(1978) used music therapy successfully with people with chronic pain. Although music therapy can be simply a source of fun and entertainment for many older people (Kartman, 1990), it can also arouse extremely withdrawn people, who have been beyond the reach of verbal communication (Moore, 1986). Rima Starr specializes in singing for and with people who are terminally ill. (Starr is on the staff of the Jacob Perlow Hospice of Beth Israel Medical Center, New York City.) Among her clients was an 87-year-old woman with advanced Alzheimer's disease, whom she visited weekly. Typically, on her arrival Starr would find the woman in bed, moaning. Before long, however, the two would be singing songs, such as "Has Anybody Seen My Gal?," "Baby Face," "By the Light of the Silvery Moon," "Daisy," and "(I'll Be Loving You) Always," together. The woman knew most of the words and also kept time using maracas. On one occasion, when they came to the line, "We trip the light fantastic," in the song "The Sidewalks of New York," the client's face lit up. "Anyone could see that she really liked that line and whatever she associated with it," Starr reported (Kaufman, 1995, p. B8).

It is apparent that music can be appreciated by even the most severely disabled or ill older person. Hanser (1990) notes that older adults often rediscover the familiar but forgotten calming influence of music when it is reintroduced to them through music therapy. Some older people are even moved to learn to play an instrument. Music can also be a stimulus for positive life review. And, as Kartman (1990) noted, just having a good time can affect emotional equilibrium, affect psychosomatic illness, and offset some of the losses of aging.

REFERENCES

Bell, J.C. (1987). Music and the elderly. *Educational Gerontology, 13*, 147–155.

Bennett, S.L., & Maas, F. (1988). The effect of music-based life review on the life satisfaction and ego integrity of elderly people. *British Journal of Occupational Therapy, 51*, 433–436.

Biley, B. (1992). Use of music in therapeutic care. *British Journal of Nursing, 1*, 178–180.

Blumenthal, S.J., & Kupfer, D.J. (Eds.). (1990). *Suicide over the life cycle: Risk factors, assessment, and treatment of suicidal patients.* Washington, DC: American Psychiatric Press.

Bright, R. (1987). The use of music therapy and activities with demented patients who are deemed "difficult to manage." *Clinical Gerontologist, 6*, 131–144.

Choi, B.-C. (1995, September 1). Music therapy in South Korea. *Korean Music Therapy Newsletter*, pp. 1–2. (Available via the Internet at http://falcon.cc.ukans.edu/memt/Korea.html.)

Christie, M.E. (1992). Music therapy applications in a skilled and intermediate care nursing home facility: A clinical study. *Activities, Adaptation & Aging, 16*(4), 69–86.

Clair, A.A. (1996). *Therapeutic uses of music with older adults.* Baltimore: Health Professions Press.

Clair, A.A., & Bernstein, B. (1990). A preliminary study of music therapy programming for severely regressed persons with Alzheimer's-type dementia. *Journal of Applied Gerontology, 9*, 299–311.

Clair, A.A., & Bernstein, B. (1994). The effect of no music, stimulative background music and sedative background music on agitated behaviors in persons with severe dementia. *Activities, Adaptation & Aging, 19*(1), 61–70.

Gerdner, L.A., & Swanson, E.A. (1993). Effects of individualized music on confused and agitated elderly patients. *Archives of Psychiatric Nursing, 7*, 284–291.

Hanser, S.B. (1990). A music therapy strategy for depressed older adults in the community. *Journal of Applied Gerontology, 9*, 283–297.

Kartman, L.L. (1990). Fun and entertainment: One aspect of making meaningful music for the elderly. *Activities, Adaptation & Aging, 14*(4), 39–44.

Kaufman, M.T. (1995, July 22). Songs soothe those in twilight of life. *Springfield Union-News*, pp. B8–B9.

Lynch, L. (1987). Music therapy: Its historical relationships and value in programs for the long-term care setting. *Activities, Adaptation & Aging, 10*(1–2), 5–15.

Mavely, R., & Mitchell, G.J. (1994). Consider karaoke. *Canadian Nurse, 90*(1), 22–24.

McCloskey, L.J. (1985). Music and the frail elderly. *Activities, Adaptation & Aging, 7*(2), 73–75.

Meddaugh, D.I. (1987). Exercise-to-music for the abusive patient. *Clinical Gerontologist, 6*, 147–154.

Messenger, B. (1995). *The power of music: A complete music activities program for older adults* (pp. 72–81). Baltimore: Health Professions Press.

Moore, E.C. (1986). A music therapist's perspective. In I. Burnside (Ed.), *Working with the elderly: Group process and techniques* (2nd ed., pp. 426–440). Boston: Jones & Bartlett.

Noble, C.J. (1996, April 10). Young musician has a mission. *Springfield Union-News*, pp. C4–C5.

Olson, B.K. (1984). Player piano music as therapy for the elderly. *Journal of Music Therapy, 21*, 35–45.

Palmer, M.D. (1977). Music therapy in a comprehensive program of treatment and rehabilitation for the geriatric resident. *Journal of Music Therapy, 14*, 190–197.

Rosling, L.K., & Kitchen, J. (1992). Music and drawing with institutionalized elderly. *Activities, Adaptation & Aging, 17*(2), 27–38.

Shapiro, A. (1969). A pilot program in music therapy with residents of a home for the aged. *Gerontologist, 9*, 128–133.

Short, A.E. (1992). Music and imagery with physically disabled elderly residents: A GIM adaptation. *Music Therapy, 11*(1), 65–98.

Smith, S. (1990). The unique power of music therapy benefits Alzheimer's patients. *Activities, Adaptation & Aging, 14*(4), 59–64.

Thamel, P. (1995, July 6). Performers spread sunshine with music and memories. *Springfield Union-News*, p. B8.

Weiss, R. (1994). The right therapist and the right music. In *Music therapy: Doctors explore the healing potential of rhythm and song*. Silver Spring, MD: National Association for Music Therapy.

Wolfe, D.E. (1978). Pain rehabilitation and music therapy. *Journal of Music Therapy, 15*, 162–178.

Yon, R.K. (1984). Expanding human potential through music. In B. Warren (Ed.), *Using the creative arts in therapy* (pp. 106–130). Cambridge, MA: Brookline Books.

Appendix
Music Therapy Resources

Music Therapy Associations

American Association for Music Therapy, Inc.
Post Office Box 80012
Valley Forge, Pennsylvania 19484
Phone (610) 265-4006
Fax (610) 265-1011
Both the American Association and the National Association circulate job opportunity notices to members; listings are free to employers

Institute of Music Therapy
Hochschule für Music und Theater
Hamburg, Germany
e-mail wcmt96rrz.uni-hamburg.de
Web site http://www.uni-hamburg.de/musicmed
A source of information, in English and in German, and sponsor of an annual world conference, in conjunction with the World Health Organization

National Association for Musical Therapy, Inc.
8455 Colesville Road, Suite 930
Silver Spring, Maryland 20910
Phone (301) 589-3300
Fax (301) 589-5175
e-mail infonamt.com
Web site http://www.namt.com
A source of information on all aspects of music therapy

Music Sources

Creative Concepts Publishing Corp.
2290 Eastman Avenue #110
Ventura, California 93003
Phone (800) 222-9745 (U.S., Canada only)
Phone (805) 339-2999
Fax (805) 339-2994
Web site http://www.creativeconcepts.com
A source of sheet music for piano and guitar; catalogs can be ordered or browsed

Playtime Music Company
17214 Front Beach Road
Panama City, Florida 32413
Phone (904) 230-8283
Fax (904) 230-1877
e-mail playtimebeaches.net
A source for player piano music, the catalog includes such categories as Roaring 20s, sounds of the 30s, marches and patriotic songs, polkas, and sacred music

West Music
Phone (800) 397-WEST
Web site   http://www.westmusic.com
Offers a catalog of music specifically selected for use by music therapists; orders may be placed by phone or via the Internet

Other Resources

Best Practice in Music Therapy Utilizing Group Percussion Strategies for Promoting Volunteerism in the Well Older Adult (Book)
Volunteering with a Beat (Brochure)
Volunteerism with a Beat: Development of a Well Older Adult Volunteer Group Percussion Program (Video)
Rhythm for Life
Barbara Crowe, R.M.T.-BC, Executive Director
A Project of The Tides Foundation
2051 South Dobson #17-383
Mesa, Arizona 85202
Phone (619) 594-2814 or (602) 965-7413
The book provides a complete outline of this 10-week training program, as well as suggestions, how-to advice, and marketing strategies; the brochure is designed to promote interest in music in older adults, and the video is for use at an introductory therapy session

The Joy of Music in Maturity: Innovative Programs for Seniors (1993), by Joan Shaw, R.M.T.-BC, 488 pages, $39.95
MMB Music, Inc.
Contemporary Arts Building
3526 Washington Avenue
St. Louis, Missouri 63103-1019
Phone (800) 543-3771
Fax (314) 531-8384
e-mail   mmbmusic.com
Web site   http://mmbmusic.com
A complete resource for anyone who wants to implement a music therapy program for older people; the book is organized around the idea of a "theme for the month," includes musical games, menus, and song sheets, and has a large-print format

Where Do I Go From Here?, music by Ken Medema, dialogue with Janice Winchester Nadeau, Ph.D., $24.95 per set
Personal Therapy Resources
Post Office Box 120321
St. Paul, Minnesota 55112
Fax (612) 780-3133
Three 1-hour audiotapes blending music and conversation to help people cope with grief and loss; intended to supplement the services of a therapist, member of the clergy, or a funeral director
e-mail   bwalto19skypoint.com
Web site   http://scream.iw.net/ptr/where.html

A thing of beauty is a joy for ever:
Its loveliness increases; it will never
Pass into nothingness . . .
John Keats, "Endymion"

Drawing on Experience

Art Therapy

When he was 85 years old, Michelangelo was concentrating on a series of drawings of Christ being carried to the tomb (The Armand Hammer Collection, 1987); in the 20th century, Pablo Picasso, Marc Chagall, and Andrew Wyeth were still painting in their 80s. The primitivist Grandma Moses is the artist most often associated with extraordinary creativity in old age. Unlike Moses, who took up painting late in life, most creative older adults show a predilection for creative outlets in early childhood and maintain long-term and consistent involvement in their chosen art form (Dohr & Forbess, 1986). Obviously, creativity is not reserved for young people. It can be a mode of self-expression and self-revelation throughout the life span.

Older adults who seek out art programs or engage in creative activities at home perceive an increase or a stabilization, rather than a decline, in their creativity with age. Among creative people, peak periods of artistic engagement seem to occur before the late 30s and early 40s, when art takes a back seat to family and work obligations, and after 60, when time becomes available again. The motivation for creative endeavor later in life seems to be both intrinsic, fueled by the creative interests of the individual, and extrinsic, spurred by the presence of an interesting and engaging program or by the support of family and friends (Dohr & Forbess, 1986).

Art therapy, the employment of the visual arts in the service of education, psychotherapy, and rehabilitation, has existed since just after World War II (Morrin, 1988). This therapy has proven to be an effective means of helping individuals explore their feelings and conflicts and communicate them to others. According to Virshup (1986), the creation of art is in many ways a road to the unconscious whose product exists and can be reviewed as often as desired. It allows people to reexamine experiences and emotions and is a vehicle through which earlier, hurtful misconceptions, relived emotionally, can be refashioned, often making life experiences more understandable and less painful (Saul, 1988).

Phillips (1982) identifies three types of art therapy: *art psychotherapy*, in which art is used as a means of or aid to psychotherapy; *functional art therapy*, in which art is used as part of a rehabilitation process; and *psychoeducational art therapy*, in which educational goals are combined with psychological awareness and sensitivity. Rugh (1985) differentiates art therapy in general from art education, while acknowledging that where art therapy stops and art education begins is a hotly debated topic: One focuses on mental and emotional issues first and on technique second; the other reverses the emphasis. The introduction of art to older adults lies at the crossroads between the two fields, says Rugh.

Art therapy can provide an opportunity for older adults to socialize and interact with others (Mango, 1992; Sterritt & Pokorny, 1994). Because it involves some physical activity, art therapy can also help rehabilitate individuals who require muscle retraining or strengthening and can contribute to improvements in coordination and range of motion (Morrin, 1988). In addition, art therapy can lead to improvement in reality orientation and in cognitive ability in people with organic mental disorders, can help aphasic patients to communicate, and can make dying meaningful (Weiss, 1984). Because art minimizes verbal demands on the individual, it can provide an alternate outlet for negative feelings in an environment where it is safe to release them. In fact, many procedures in art therapy are designed to assist in making favorable changes to personality, based on a widely held belief that the forces involved in creativity are related to those underlying personality development in general (Morrin, 1988; Saul, 1988).

The use of art therapy has been widely successful in society's institutions (e.g., schools, rehabilitation clinics, nursing facilities), especially with individuals who resist traditional therapies (Colli, 1994; Sterritt & Pokorny, 1994; Virshup, 1986). Older individuals may be especially appropriate candidates for art therapy as many are apprehensive about other types of therapy. Older people are often traumatized by the aging process, suffering from depression, hopelessness, and a sense of loss of control over their lives. Even the small gain of control over the art materials can boost self-esteem (Sterritt & Pokorny, 1994; Virshup, 1986), and exposure to art and participation in art activities can lead to a brighter, more exciting, and more forward outlook for frail older adults (Saul, 1988).

Older adults who have an opportunity to participate in an art therapy program report benefits such as intellectual stimulation, a sense of emotional well-being, improved physical health, and an enjoyable recreational experience (Dohr & Forbess, 1986). Older people like to work with art materials, despite their own initial perception that they lack talent and experience and despite the fact that many of them have taken a long hiatus from this kind of activity (Harrison, 1980). Some older adults especially enjoy the social aspects of the activity, whereas others appreciate an opportunity to create something that they can give as a gift to a relative or friend (Dohr & Forbess, 1986).

Art therapy can be offered to individuals or to groups and is feasible and beneficial in many different environments (e.g., independent living, congregate housing, long-term care facilities). In a residential setting the art therapist is frequently part of a team, working with psychiatrists, psychologists, social workers, psychiatric nurses, and physical therapists (Morrin, 1988). An art therapy program can be added to existing programs within a facility through the therapeutic recreation or activities department, which can provide great benefit at very little cost (Barker & Brunk, 1991). If the goals of a program are more recreational and social than therapeutic, it is possible for a general activity director or other staff person to introduce art into the recreational offerings of a facility. Requisites for either the art therapist or the health care professional are a respect for the older adults involved and a level of comfort in dealing with older people.

Although all older people experience similar ills, losses, and needs to adapt, they are not a homogeneous group, any more than individuals in other stages of life are all alike. (In fact, as people age, they become less and less alike.) Treatment should be individuated. However, the introduction of one or more of the visual arts is an appropriate tool in improving the quality of life of most older people, whether they are frail, bedridden, disabled, or in generally good health (Saul, 1988; Weiss, 1984).

USE OF ART THERAPY WITH OLDER ADULTS LIVING INDEPENDENTLY

Mr. Sayles lost his wife to cancer about a year ago. He still manages to attend the programs at the senior center in the local Congregational church once or twice a week, but he seems withdrawn and at loose ends. In fact, he is agonizing over whether to give up the home he and his wife shared for 34 years. It is really too much for him to keep up by himself, particularly because he always relied on his wife to attend to the basic housekeeping duties. Dusting, vacuuming, laundering curtains, and the like are new and foreign activities for him. Still, most of his memories of his wife are associated with this familiar place, and he cannot quite picture himself living somewhere else.

One day, on his way to the room where the men often play cards, Mr. Sayles passed through a common area at the center, which was abuzz with activity. Several of the regular women attendees were working on a patchwork quilt. Scraps of material littered the card tables usually reserved for tag sale fund-raisers, and the women were busy with scissors, thread, and a sewing machine. Mr. Sayles thought of his wife, who often did needlework as they watched television together. To be sociable, he asked what the women were making. They explained that they were making a communal quilt comprising individual squares that represented their homes and other familiar buildings in the community surrounding the church. They said they planned to hang the finished product on the wall of the common area. He complimented them on their work. Almost jokingly, they invited Mr. Sayles to contribute a square to the project.

Mr. Sayles was intrigued. He is not at all comfortable with what he calls "women's work," but found the already-completed squares attractive and full of meaning: One square depicted the local public library, another a corner drug store, which is now a vacant storefront but was once a cornerstone of the community. In addition, many of the women were working on renditions of their own homes. The women encouraged Mr. Sayles by offering to help with the actual sewing. Slowly, he sat down and found himself choosing from the scraps of fabric and reminding his helpers that his home is a Cape Cod–style house with two dormers and a central doorway.

When the quilt was finally hung in its place of honor, Mr. Sayles seemed proud that his home had been included in it. He also seems more like his old, outgoing self, laughing when the other men at the center ribbed him good-naturedly about having been part of the "quilting bee." Perhaps seeing his home memorialized in this way will make it a little easier for him to consider moving on.

For older adults living independently, an art therapy program can be offered through a local senior, community, or adult day center. In addition, local hospitals or long-term care facilities may invite community members to participate in their weekly or biweekly art therapy sessions (Barker & Brunk, 1991). Any location that provides a semiprivate area with tables and chairs is appropriate. It is important that transportation of some sort be provided for participating individuals and that the facility director be receptive to the particular type of program being offered.

One painting group that met in a small community mental health center in Charlottesville, Virginia, set a goal of reaching older people before they became incapacitated or troubled. In this program personal growth and creativity were valued more than the products of the clients' efforts. The work of art was seen as a personal statement (Harrison, 1980). The 12-week program initially introduced green tempera paint and various shapes and sizes of bristle and hair brushes. At the first session participants were encouraged to move the brushes freely, accustoming themselves to the tools of the trade. In the next two sessions participants worked on mixing paints to achieve a variety of colors. Then, each individual was asked to create a simple landscape. Finally, after seeing slides of work by Grandma Moses and Ralph Fasanella (two artists who began painting late in life) and discussing memories, photographs, and scrapbooks, each participant chose something unique as the subject for a painting—an old home, a hometown, family, friends, or a favorite possession (Harrison, 1980).

Encouraging older people to work through both good and painful memories via the medium of artistic expression allows a safe way to express feelings within the confines of a structured exercise (Morrin, 1988). Allowing them to choose their own subjects provides them with an opportunity to make decisions at a time in life when too many things seem to them to be out of their control. Displaying the work provides the participants with an opportunity to share their creativity with family, friends, and the community. It can also draw positive media coverage, reinforcing positive attitudes about older adults and aging. The participants themselves can experience increased self-esteem and an improved ability to solve problems and think creatively, skills learned through the artistic process that are transferable to their daily lives (Harrison, 1980).

USE OF ART THERAPY WITH OLDER ADULTS LIVING IN CONGREGATE HOUSING OR LONG-TERM CARE FACILITIES

When Sadie was young, she dreamed of being an artist. Her favorite medium was watercolor, and she spent many an afternoon in the public park across the street from her home trying to capture the special quality of the light on the trees at that time of day and in different seasons. But that was during the Great Depression, and Sadie was practical enough to realize that a career in art was no more than a pipe dream. So she studied bookkeeping at the local high school of commerce, went to work for an insurance company, and ended up marrying her boss. When her first son was born, she left work and busied herself at home for several years, returning to work at the insurance company part time once her youngest boy started school. She hardly gave painting a thought during those busy days.

Sadie is now a resident of the Jewish retirement community in the town where one of her sons lives. The other residents are friendly, but Sadie misses the old neighborhood, her friends, and her husband, who died 5 years ago. The days seem long, and Sadie finds herself bored for perhaps the first time in her long life. When one of the staff members mentions that an art therapist will be presenting a program at the nursing facility in the coming months and asks for resident input, Sadie thinks of those long-ago afternoons in the park with her easel, paint box, brushes, and water jar. She asks if it might be possible for the art therapist to include watercolor painting in the program and is delighted to hear that it is included. Despite a little arthritis in her hands and eyesight that isn't what it once was, she looks forward to the first lesson with obvious enthusiasm.

For individuals living in congregate housing or in long-term care facilities, an art therapy program often can be implemented on the premises. The program can be integrated into existing activities or recreational therapy programs. The support of the facility's director, an adequate and well-lit space, and fairly minimal supplies are all that are required in order for the therapist to offer a program. Within the art therapy group, individuals should be given the opportunity to interact spontaneously with the therapist and with other members of the group in what Morrin (1988) calls a "therapeutic alliance" (p. 245). Although some frail residents in long-term care may tend to withdraw from others in an attempt to preserve some individuality, most are actually eager for human contact and the chance to express themselves, which an art therapy group can provide. Several overtures may need to be made to these reluctant residents, but eventually many will respond. An experience with the arts can lift the spirits of frail older adults without demanding a great deal in return (Saul, 1988).

One successful program was initiated by Alta Bee Wolcott (1978), who at age 79 started an art therapy group in a nursing facility where she had briefly been a resident herself. An artist who espoused the philosophy that art is about feeling and sensing rather than intellectualizing, Wolcott decided that idle and bored residents of nursing facilities would benefit from a carefully structured introduction to art. Wolcott emphasized the aesthetic, not the practical, in her sessions, believing that skill is secondary to a sense of design (e.g., of color, form, line), a means rather than an end in the experience of creating art.

Wolcott chose to start with a group of the most disabled residents in the facility, including some individuals who were extremely hostile and averse to involvement in the program. She made it clear from the start that participants need not try to please her, that they were free to do things their own way. In an assignment to draw "sausage figures," Wolcott pointed out that at the very time the group was meeting, Pablo Picasso, famous for his "sausage figures," was himself ill and no doubt in a wheelchair, as were most of the group members. The connection proved inspirational: The group loved Picasso's drawings and came to believe that what they were creating was in fact real art. Wolcott found that although these individuals were well acquainted with their own inner images and stored-up life experiences, they were unsure at first about how to put them on paper. Her nurturing, nonjudgmental approach helped them to find their individual ways of creating. The first year proved so successful that group members requested the chance to continue, and some members of a second group, which focused on painting, were given their own art supplies so that they could paint outside of class time (Wolcott, 1978).

One may assume that art therapy would be inappropriate for people who are severely physically or mentally disabled—even Wolcott (1978) asked that her initial group members be able to see and hear and have one good hand—but, in fact, this therapy has proven successful even with people in the advanced stages of Alzheimer's disease. Hypothesizing that the stages of Alzheimer's disease may parallel the stages of cognitive development in children, Vance, Camp, Kabacoff, and Greenwalt (1996) looked to the work of Maria Montessori, the children's educator, for inspiration. They treated clients with respect and introduced art projects that required the skills of an appropriate developmental stage. For example, when the therapists discovered that some individuals were not participating because they could not hold the scissors, they patiently taught straight-line cutting and then curved-line cutting, in the manner in which Montessori introduced such skills to young children (Vance et al., 1996).

One out of every five older adults will be hospitalized at some point, whether briefly, for an extended period, or permanently (Rugh, 1985). Many of them will spend their final years in long-term care facilities or in congregate housing, which will provide nursing care when needed. In a long-term care facility most caregiving efforts are directed toward maintaining physical health, sometimes in a setting that lacks opportunities for emotional and mental fulfillment. Art therapists, art educators, and others in the humanities try to develop programs that can speak to the mental, emotional, and social needs of older adults (Rugh, 1985). These innovative ideas are exciting alternatives to the sad, stereotypical image of older people seated for hours before television screens that they do not even watch (Vance et al., 1996).

PRECAUTIONS TO TAKE AND ACCOMMODATIONS TO MAKE IN IMPLEMENTING ART THERAPY WITH OLDER ADULTS

Art therapy can be beneficial for many older individuals. The creative process alone can be therapeutic. However, Weber (1981) cautions that therapists may sometimes push older people to "do something" simply for the sake of activity. The challenge is to offer an art therapy program that genuinely stimulates creativity and self-expression, while being sensitive enough to know when someone is content to "be" rather than to "do" (Weber, 1981).

Some dangers are also inherent in interpreting the art of older people. First, there is a great deal of dissension over appropriate modes of interpretation in both the literary and visual arts. Proponents of hermeneutics, formalism, structuralism, phenomenology, depth psychologies, feminist critical theory, Marxist critical theory, and deconstruction are likely to have radically different perspectives on a drawing or painting (Franklin & Politsky, 1992). Second, particularly with older people, it may not always be constructive to bring unconscious material too close to the surface by putting into words obviously painful themes. Some years ago, one of the authors' clients produced a pastel drawing depicting the members of her art therapy group. One of the participants had been depicted in dark shades that obscured her features. Privately, the client confided that, after some consideration, she decided that her feelings about this woman had influenced her drawing. The client asked the author if she thought the woman was likely to guess how she felt about her by viewing the drawing. Although she found the woman annoying, she noted that the woman's only son had recently passed away and she did not want to add to her pain. This case illustrates Morrin's (1988) contention that often it is wiser to convey interest and empathy without specifically commenting on the latent content of an individual's picture.

If interpretation is to be an integral part of the therapeutic process, it is important to recognize that some individuals may uncover extremely upsetting issues while participating in art therapy. Although it may be helpful to discuss these issues within the group, the group facilitator must be careful not to cause the individual to feel vulnerable. Older people benefit from a sequence of cumulative psychotherapy sessions. Issues raised during sessions should not be left for individuals to ruminate on. Intervention leading to a measure of closure before the end of a session should be offered (Wolk, 1993).

Because older people are often preoccupied with issues of health, impending death, and the loss of loved ones, these topics probably will be discussed in the course of art therapy sessions. This kind of sharing is a positive outcome of the program being offered, but the therapist or activity facilitator must be equipped to control emotionally charged situations effectively (Morrin, 1988). In addition, group dynamics will not always be idyllic. Many older people have physical, cognitive, and emotional afflictions, and, like people of any age, some are malcontents and obstructionists. Members of the group may also have pent-up rage as a result of accumulated negative life experience. It is important for the therapist or group facilitator to provide the opportunity for a safe emotional outlet (Morrin, 1988).

Any critique of artwork created by an older person should foster self-esteem and self-confidence, not undermine a fragile ego by harshly judging the work on technical terms (Rugh, 1985; Wolk, 1993). Respect for all levels of artistic expression must be demonstrated in order to avoid discouraging older people who may already think of themselves as being without talent and merit (Rugh, 1985).

Accommodations can be made in some tools and materials to help individuals with disabilities participate in art therapy sessions. For example, activities can be placed on carts, and shelves can be placed on wheels to bring materials to people with mobility problems. Adjustable table heights are helpful in accommodating wheelchairs (Vance et al., 1996). Rubber pencil grips, available at educational supply houses, make pens and pencils easier to hold for people with arthritis or weakness in the muscles of their hands (Edelson, 1991). Paintbrushes may be easier to grip with the addition of materials such as wooden dowels and strapping tape. Brushes can be attached to the foot or the head, or held in the mouth. Paint jars can be prevented from spilling by anchoring them in a weighted kitchen spice rack (Harlan, 1991). Some therapists have noted that older people seem to prefer lighter colors, particularly pastels; this preference can be taken into account in choosing supplies (Morrin, 1988; Tate & Allen, 1985).

Harlan (1991) suggests that crayons, finger paints, and other media traditionally associated with children be avoided, particularly with older people with mental retardation, because part of the therapeutic goal is to foster age awareness and to engender dignity of the individual. This suggestion may also hold true for older adults with cognitive impairment, particularly those in the early stages, when they have insight into the changes that are taking place within them. Harlan also argues that crafts are not a good choice because craft work emphasizes adherence to specific techniques and to a step-by-step approach rather than the therapeutic goal of freedom of expression associated with the creation of art. For example, the art of pottery allows for more interaction with materials and more freedom in designing and finishing a product than does the craft of ceramics.

Caution should be exercised when using any potentially harmful materials. Strong-smelling paints and sharp scissors should be avoided or used with extreme care. A pleasant and safe environment adapted to the specific needs of older people should be created by the facilitator.

If works of art or photographs of them are to be recorded or displayed, it is important to have some type of permission form signed by either the participants or their families. It is also crucial that nursing staff and caregivers understand the importance that the art may hold for the older adult artist; the casual discarding of drawings, paintings, and other creations can cause emotional devastation.

IMPLEMENTATION OF AN ART THERAPY PROGRAM

Implementing a successful art therapy program is somewhat labor intensive for the facilitator, but pays large dividends to those willing to invest their efforts. The steps included here have been tested and proven effective by numerous art therapists.

Initial Steps

The first step in implementing any type of art therapy program is establishing a site for the sessions. A private room with large tables (or one large table) and chairs to accommodate all participants, even those in wheelchairs, is essential. It is important to be able to situate participants so that few have their backs to one another (Barker & Brunk, 1991). Easy access to a water tap and a washbasin is helpful, as is space for storing supplies and projects (Morrin, 1988). Adequate lighting and access to rest rooms are also necessary.

Most art supplies are reasonably inexpensive. The materials needed depend on the medium that is being used. Paper and pencil are sufficient in some cases. Other materials include paint, charcoal, clay, string, ink, paper cups, paper plates, paper cutouts, glitter, paper towel and toilet tissue tubes, and dried pasta. Depending on the particular session, a supply of glue, paintbrushes, and scissors should be on hand. Morrin (1988) recommends using 12" × 16" sheets of paper because larger sizes can be intimidating. Additional supplies can be purchased or gathered for specific projects as needed. If music is to serve as a mood-setter or inspiration for participants, some sort of player and selected music should be available.

A program that requires more sophisticated equipment and more specialized space (e.g., a kiln for firing pottery and space to accommodate it, a darkroom and equipment for developing photographs) may require a substantial investment. Rather than seek funding for art therapy programs from clinically oriented foundations, Malchiodi (1987) suggests approaching local and state arts councils. Some states run arts lotteries and some cities have private foundations (e.g., the Community Foundation in Springfield, Massachusetts) that fund arts- and education-oriented projects.

The second step is that approval be obtained from the director of the appropriate facility for the type of art therapy program being implemented. Often, a demonstration is helpful in familiarizing the administration and staff with this nontraditional form of therapy. One possibility is to ask that the administrators and staff members actually participate in a simulated art therapy session. An alternative is to offer a one-time activity for some of the residents that can be observed by administrators or staff members.

After approval has been received, the therapist or program facilitator should become familiar with the group participants. Information about specific abilities, disabilities, and interests can be obtained through interviews with prospective participants prior to the start of an art program or before or after the first session. An alternative is to require that participants fill out survey cards either before the program begins or during the first session. In the case of participants with cognitive impairments, a relative might be interviewed in order to ascertain the participant's likely interests. Any special accommodations for individuals with disabilities can be made prior to or during the first session.

Volunteers may be needed to attend sessions because some older individuals may need one-to-one assistance (Barker & Brunk, 1991). Also, some older adults may be hesitant to participate and the prospect of working one-to-one with the volunteers may encourage them to become part of the group (Rugh, 1985). The exhibit on page 259 is a form that can be used by facilitators in planning an art therapy activity.

Activities

Art activities should be sufficiently challenging to involve the participants without overwhelming their abilities or causing anxiety (Sterritt & Pokorny, 1994). The activities should also be planned with the primary goal or goals—whether rehabilitative, therapeutic, educational, recreational, or social—in mind. Many art therapy programs stress the social aspects of sharing ideas with other participants or showing one's art, but some of the participants may be more interested in programs that stress aesthetics and provide the opportunity for individual expression and interpretation (Dohr & Forbess, 1986). Others may be interested in developing and enjoying art skills at their own pace for personal satisfaction as well as for an outlet for emotions. It should be remembered that everyone, regardless of IQ or innate talent, has imagination and the capacity for creativity (Morrin, 1988). Another specific goal of an art therapy program may be life review, with activities designed to help the individual review major life events and come to terms with the past and the self (Bergland, 1982). It is important for the facilitator to carefully consider the needs and desires of the participants when planning activities for the sessions.

Structure of Group Sessions

Group sessions can be held weekly or biweekly. The optimal length of a session is between 60 and 90 minutes (Morrin, 1988). A group of 6-8 or perhaps as many

Art Therapy Program Plan

Art activity planned_____

No. of sessions needed to complete activity _____

Estimated no. of participants _____

Prospective participants

_____   _____

_____   _____

_____   _____

_____   _____

_____   _____

Objectives

____ Improve interpersonal relationships   ____ Increase self-confidence

____ Increase opportunity to socialize   ____ Improve coordination

____ Elevate mood   ____ Sensory stimulation

____ Increase concentration and attention   ____ Foster reminiscence

____ Increase sense of well-being   ____ Foster relaxation

____ Improve memory functioning   ____ Promote sense of belonging to group

____ Exercise (hand and finger muscles)   ____ Exercise (large muscles)

____ Foster creativity   ____ Foster self-exploration

Frequency of activity

____ Daily   ____ Twice a week   ____ Weekly   ____ Every other week

Materials needed (cost)

_____

_____

_____

Funding source _____

Cost to each participant _____

How activity is to be evaluated _____

_____

A Life Worth Living: Practical Strategies for Reducing Depression in Older Adults, by Pearl Mosher-Ashley and Phyllis Barrett. ©1997 Health Professions Press, Inc., Baltimore.

as 15 participants is ideal (Morrin, 1988; Weiss, 1984). Each session should begin with the greeting of each member individually, and the atmosphere of the group should be one of warmth and encouragement. Participation should be voluntary (Morrin, 1988).

Early sessions should feature simple assignments that require no particular ability; more intricate projects can be assigned later in the program (Morrin, 1988). Weiss (1984) and Hubalek (1997) suggest playing lively music in the background and establishing a theme to be explored in each session. One possible sequence of activities moves from scribble drawing (a loosening-up activity) to the drawing of a timeline of each individual's life, marking major points and generating group discussion of commonalities. Participants can also be asked to draw pictures of their families or of idealized families, to draw a picture of a place they would like to be, and of themselves engaged in a favorite activity or with a favorite companion. Group murals, self-portraits, and journal writing and drawing are other advanced project possibilities (Weiss, 1984). Another interesting project evokes reminiscence through the use of slides, films, books, objects, and conversation. An attempt is made to capture the essence of each person's reaction to the stimulus in a work of art. Finished and unfinished work is hung and discussed; then unfinished work is taken down and completed at another session (Rugh, 1985). Although it is often recommended that the art experience be completed in a single session, Rugh cites the effectiveness of ongoing projects and continuity for older people. Having something to look forward to is especially important to them. Throughout the program, emphasis should be placed more on the process than on the product, and feedback should be frequent and uniformly positive (Morrin, 1988). In art there is no right or wrong, no good or bad—simply opportunities for unique personal expression (Rugh, 1985).

Each session should end with a discussion. Individuals can display their artwork and describe certain aspects of it, as well as talk about feelings that may have surfaced while creating it. It is important to allow the participants to talk as much as possible about their own work. The group facilitator should withhold comment at first, allowing the artists to arrive at their own meaning (Franklin & Politsky, 1992). Feedback from the group should also be encouraged (Sterritt & Pokorny, 1994).

It is in viewing and discussing the artwork that the group serves its most important purpose for both the members and the therapist. The group provides a chance for interaction among older people whose life experience has narrowed. The symbolic content of the work can also signal common emotional experiences among group members. If the group responds without censorship, the artist will gain self-confidence and enjoy a release of tension while maintaining self-control. Sharing one's artwork with other people in the group can be extremely gratifying (Morrin, 1988).

Structure of Individual Sessions

Although most older people enjoy the social aspects of group sessions, some do not. It is possible to design an art therapy program for an individual that has components similar to those of a group program. Individuals who feel uncomfortable sharing artwork and emotions in the intimate environment of the group may nevertheless enjoy the opportunity to display their work publicly; to have it highlighted in a publication; or to become involved in a letter, telephone, or video exchange or mentor network (Dohr & Forbess, 1986).

Program Evaluation

Some sort of evaluation of the program is necessary. If specific psychotherapeutic goals for individuals in the program have been set, the art therapist may elect to make use of pre- and posttests, such as a depression scale (see Chapter 1) or Salamon and Conte's Life Satisfaction in the Elderly Scale (1984; see Chapter 2), to measure success or failure in meeting those goals. An informal evaluation can be conducted through observations and interviews during the sessions. Observation data may include willingness or desire to participate, focus of attention, expressions (verbal and nonverbal) of pleasure, and interaction with the group. Interview data may include comments about activities and how they made the person feel, and the desire to do the activity again (Sterritt & Pokorny, 1994). Page 263 is a sample record form. Harlan (1991) suggests interviews with staff, observations about attendance and functioning of individuals within a group over time, the gathering of feedback from participants, and an examination of the art produced (see p. 264 for a sample evaluation form).

VARIATIONS ON ART THERAPY

Many ingenious projects have been developed by art therapists and health care professionals for older people in general and for older people with disabilities.

General Art Activities for Older Adults

Self-Portrait

The objectives of self-portrait are to create an awareness of self, to focus on the sense of touch, and to build self-esteem. Participants are reminded of their facial features, reaffirming in a sensory way their individuality, which for many individuals may have been undermined by living in a long-term care setting. Achieving a handsome product is less important than capturing an impression of the self (McMurray, 1990). The materials needed are vine charcoal, newsprint or 12" × 18" charcoal paper, and paper towels.

Participants are encouraged to create a charcoal self-portrait after feeling their features with their eyes closed. They may need to take breaks in the process of reviewing their features in order to rest their arms. They may need to remove their glasses in order to adequately explore their facial features. Participants should ask themselves the following questions:

Is my hair wiry, fluffy, straight, or curly?
Is my forehead rounded, flat, wide, narrow, high?
Are my eyebrows thick, thin, continuous, or shaped like crescents?

Are my eyes deep set, drooped at the corners, or do they end abruptly?
Do I have laugh lines?
Is my nose longer or shorter than my eyebrow?
Are there bumps or a hook to my nose?
Is there a triangle between the tip of my nose and my nostril?
Are there wrinkle lines from my nose to my mouth?
Are my cheeks rounded?
Are my cheekbones prominent?
Are my lips ample or thin?
What is the relationship in size between my upper and lower lip?
Is my chin pointy or round?
Are my ears large or small?
Are the muscles of my neck long or short?
Are my shoulders fat or bony?

Once the participants' review is complete, they should open their eyes and use the charcoal, which smudges easily to create shadows and tones, to draw their self-portraits.

Participants are unlikely to draw a complete self-portrait, but they do usually manage to put down on paper some recognizable aspects of their individual appearance. They may laugh at the finished product, but individuality is reinforced by the obvious differences between each person's drawing. This project also may be undertaken in clay to achieve a three-dimensional portrait (McMurray, 1990). It should be noted that freely drawing self-portraits is an inappropriate activity for older adults with a dementing illness unless the therapist is prepared to cope with the anxieties associated with the loss of cognitive abilities.

Masks & Face Plates

Barker and Brunk (1991) originally designed the making of masks and face plates for individuals with traumatic brain injury, but it can be implemented with older individuals or groups. The materials needed are paper plates, paper bags, and construction paper cutouts (precut facial features as well as other three-dimensional decorations can be purchased or clipped from magazines).

Participants are asked to make a mask from a paper bag using the features and other cutouts supplied to express their own self-image. Higher-functioning participants might be asked to make a face plate: Images are created on each side of a paper plate; one side expresses how the artist perceives him- or herself and the other side expresses how the artist feels others perceive him or her.

Folk Art Mural

Background

One way to minimize feelings of isolation as well as boredom in older people is to design a group project. Weber (1981) suggests creating a cloth mural depicting the participants' community. Decisions about precisely what should be included

Art Therapy Record Form

Activity _____   Date of session _____   Location _____

Behavioral observation key   b = Before activity, a = After activity, d = During activity, NA = Not applicable.

Participant name	Smiled	Laughed	Talked with others	Silent	Positive comments about self	Negative comments about self	Expressed pride in item made	Worked on task	Other

A Life Worth Living: Practical Strategies for Reducing Depression in Older Adults, by Pearl Mosher-Ashley and Phyllis Barrett. © 1997 Health Professions Press, Inc., Baltimore.

Art Therapy Evaluation Form

Art activity _____ Date _____

Location of sessions _____

No. of sessions taken to complete activity _____

Average no. of participants _____

Participants	No. of sessions attended	Pre-treatment score	Post-treatment score
_____	_____	_____	_____
_____	_____	_____	_____
_____	_____	_____	_____
_____	_____	_____	_____
_____	_____	_____	_____
_____	_____	_____	_____
_____	_____	_____	_____

Measure used _____

General reports from participants _____

_____

_____

_____

Reports from staff _____

_____

_____

_____

Were results formally exhibited? ___ Yes ___ No

Location of exhibit _____

A Life Worth Living: Practical Strategies for Reducing Depression in Older Adults, by Pearl Mosher-Ashley and Phyllis Barrett. ©1997 Health Professions Press, Inc., Baltimore.

should be left to the participants in order to give them an opportunity to exercise decision-making skills and personal control over the activity. Because the group members are reflecting on their environment and their experiences, the project may contribute to self-esteem and an enhanced sense of identity.

The folk art mural project can be carried out in a room specifically designated for the arts in a long-term care facility or in a communal meeting area in a senior center or adult day center. Because many people can participate, a core group that works in a public area encourages others to get involved by contributing ideas and feedback, such as in the earlier vignette concerning "Mr. Sayles." The materials needed are burlap (for the backing), cloth remnants (for cutting and applying to the burlap), scissors, needles, and thread.

The cloth remnants are cut into geometrical shapes approximating parts of buildings (e.g., windows, chimneys, doors) and then appliquéd onto the burlap backing. The stitching need not be extremely fine because the finished product will be ornamental rather than durable. Some of the items likely to be represented are individuals' homes (including perhaps a replica of a high-rise congregate housing complex), churches, and familiar grocery and drug stores. Trees, flowers, seasonal wreaths on the doors of houses, even clotheslines complete with laundry are other possible additions. And, of course, people and pets can be represented in the mural.

It is unlikely that buildings and people will be rendered in appropriate proportions, given both the group nature of the endeavor and some of the infirmities of the participants. However, it is interesting to note that a characteristic of folk art is that realistic proportions are often ignored in favor of convenient sizes for including the details that are important to the creators (Weber, 1981).

The finished product may be an appropriate decorative addition to the room in which it was created or to another area in which people can admire the group's creation.

Artist as a Role Model

Phillips (1982) used the art of one older woman as a means of encouraging individuals in a long-term care facility to reminisce and review their lives. The goals of the program were psychoeducational: Both art application and psychological themes were explored.

Elizabeth Layton (known as "Grandma Layton"), the role model in Phillips' project, took her first art class when she was 68 years old. Subsequently, her art was exhibited throughout the world. Her subjects are universal. One work depicts two older people running toward each other with open arms through a field of daisies; another depicts a Peter Pan-like figure tied to his mother's apron strings. The technique Layton used was a modified version of contour or "blind" drawing. Except for an occasional glance in order to reposition the pencil, the artist looks at the object being drawn, not at the paper, while drawing. Layton's experience with art helped her to overcome a 40-year history of clinical depression.

Phillips's art therapy program presented Grandma Layton's work to the participants through the medium of slides. Fourteen works were photographed and slides were made, each accompanied by a quote from the artist. The works and the quotes inspired life review and reminiscence during group presentation and discussion (Phillips, 1982). This kind of project costs relatively little and could be administered by existing staff in a facility. Although an art therapist would have valuable contributions to make in such a program, introducing art in this way does not require specific skills because it allows the art to speak for itself (Phillips, 1982). Participants can be introduced to the contour or "blind" drawing technique that Layton employed. The project can be adapted by creating slides of the work of any artist—famous or unknown—and used to introduce various drawing, painting, photographic, or other art techniques. It could also be introduced on either an individual or a group basis.

Miscellaneous Activities

Mango (1992) suggests that people draw the way that they feel, a picture of their illness, or something funny that happened to them. Sterritt and Pokorny (1994) use precut paper in a variety of shapes and sizes to allow people to freely create an original design. Barker and Brunk (1991) encourage seasonal activities such as making masks for Halloween, Valentines in February, and Pilgrim and turkey ornaments for Thanksgiving. Any of these activities can be implemented with an individual or in a group.

Art projects can be undertaken by partners or teams. Older people can be asked to work together to draw or paint a mural inspired by a theme or to create totems onto which wide strips of paper bearing participants' symbols for themselves are affixed (Barker & Brunk, 1991). A team can even construct three-dimensional model vehicles or buildings from household items such as toilet paper or paper towel tubes, plastic lids, caps, and containers, all spray painted individually and then glued together (Barker & Brunk, 1991).

Art Therapy for Older Adults with Depression

Landgarten (1983) notes that the medium of art provides both artist and therapist an opportunity to understand the feelings and desires of the depressed person. Exercising creativity can also be a kind of proof of existence for those who feel they are invisible or useless and can lead to a sense of mastery and of the ability to tackle problems. Positive reinforcement can come from the sense of accomplishment and recognition of the artist's work by others. The art materials provided by the therapist may even be seen as a valuable gift and an expression of positive attention.

Simple materials are used: pictures from magazines, felt markers, oil pastels, colored plasticene, and colored paper. The participants should be instructed to describe pictorially some of their concerns and goals. The art therapist should also assign some positive topics to be explored through use of the materials (e.g., the depiction of each individual's abilities or hobbies) because, left to their own devices, depressed individuals are more likely to dwell on their problems and to depict them in their art. The therapist may even offer to collaborate on the work of art, providing symbolic as well as actual support. Clients should also be encouraged to create art between the formal sessions, or the effects of the therapy on their depression are likely to be temporary. The therapist should be alert to any suggestion in the artwork of suicidal thoughts so that psychotherapeutic intervention can be offered.

Once a piece is completed, the artist should be encouraged to title it or write something about its meaning on the artwork. The individual has then made both a graphic and a written statement. The discussion period following the creation of the work allows for verbal sharing. The artwork can be a starting point from which the person can begin to explore feelings with others (Landgarten, 1983), which could lead to referral in severe cases and to participation in other forms of treatment for individuals who continue to exhibit symptoms.

Art Therapy for Older Adults with Alzheimer's Disease

It appears that older adults with a progressive dementia can experience both a slowing of decline and even some gains when engaged in novel and stimulating activities. These findings have been attributed to a decrease in excess disability fostered by low self-esteem, feelings of worthlessness, and increased dependence on others. According to Vance and Greenwalt (1996), two kinds of cognitive skills can be called on in making the accommodations needed to allow people with Alzheimer's disease to participate in traditional art projects: First are the procedural skills (e.g., riding a bicycle, brushing one's teeth), which have been shown to be more resistant to the ravages of the disease than are other kinds of memory-based skills. Second are what Vance and Greenwalt (1996) call the Piagetian skills (named for the French child psychology theorist, Jean Piaget), the cognitive skills that are acquired by children in a precise, orderly pattern and that seem to be lost by people with Alzheimer's disease in reverse order of their acquisition. Specifically, the art therapist can capitalize on what Piaget referred to as the preoperational stage of development (i.e., Piaget's second stage, his term for 2–7 year olds, characterized by the inability to distinguish between one's own perspective and another's or to logically grasp such things as the reversibility of mental representations) and the sensory–motor stage of development (i.e., Piaget's first stage, his term for children from birth to age 2, during which the infant constructs an understanding of the world by coordinating sensory input, such as seeing or hearing, with physical actions).

In introducing people with Alzheimer's disease to an art therapy program, the facilitator should design activities that are neither too difficult nor too easy, thereby encouraging the participants to use their existing cognitive abilities. Tasks should be compatible with the level of cognitive ability of the participants, and sensory stimulation should be emphasized through the use of color and multimedia modalities. Vance and Greenwalt (1996) suggest projects geared to the specific functional level of the participants.

The objectives of the rock painting activity are tactile stimulation of the materials, a chance to capitalize on a procedural skill (the use of the paintbrush), and the satisfaction of seeing a change in the color and appearance of the rock. The materials needed are crystalline rocks (can be found in stream beds and lakes), paintbrushes, a bowl of water, and a place mat or dish towel.

Participants are instructed to place the rock on the mat or dish towel next to the water bowl and brush. Then the facilitator demonstrates dipping the brush into the water and spreading the water onto the rock. The participants are then encouraged to use their own equipment to follow suit. The result is that the dull rocks now sparkle.

The materials needed for creating color gradations are color tiles (paint samples or pieces of construction paper), glue (optional), scissors (optional), and tape (optional). The activity facilitator places a series of color tiles in front of the participant, arranging shades of a given color sequentially in order of diminishing hue. Once this is done and then discussed, the samples are mixed up and the participant is instructed to rearrange them again in the original order. A variation is to arrange the colors of the spectrum as in a rainbow, disarrange them, and then rearranged in the order in which they appear in the rainbow. The arrangements can be temporary or can be glued or taped into place to create a piece of art.

This task is fairly difficult for participants with Alzheimer's disease, so it is important that there be a fairly sharp contrast between the shades of color being used. In addition, because older adults have difficulty distinguishing between darker colors, bright colors may be a better choice.

The materials needed for sorting by color are color tiles (paint samples or pieces of construction paper, including various shades of the same colors, and, optionally, cards bearing the names of colors). The facilitator mixes up the color tiles and places them in a pile. The participant is instructed to create piles of like colors, grouping the various shades of each color together. Participants who are higher functioning may be asked to label each pile with the card bearing the appropriate color name. More contrast in color is needed by lower-functioning individuals. The activity reinforces discrimination and decision-making skills.

The objective of the creating lid designs activity is the provision of a sense of order and control and affirmation of the procedural skill of opening bottles and jars learned early in life. The materials needed are colored lids and colored bottles. The participant with Alzheimer's disease is given a variety of lids to choose from and instructed by the facilitator to pick up the lids and screw them onto the bottles that match in color and size. It is best for the facilitator to introduce the materials one at a time. As the individual becomes more proficient, more choices for combinations can be presented.

The objective of the creating a Mardi Gras tree activity is the creation of a Christmas tree decorated with Mardi Gras ornaments, which reinforces a sense of time and season (appropriate for use in reality orientation). Because tree trimming at holiday time foments a conditional emotional response that in general has positive associations, this response is affected by Alzheimer's disease very little. The materials needed are Christmas tree (any size) and tree stand, Mardi Gras beads (preferably green, gold, and purple because these colors are easier for older adults to distinguish), strand of electric lights (preferably in matching colors), and other types of traditional Mardi Gras decorations.

Each participant should be given some beads and instructed to place them on the tree. The facilitator should demonstrate and encourage enthusiastic, free engagement with the materials. Decorations can be adapted to celebrate any holiday. The tree should be placed in an easily accessible area so that the participants and others can enjoy it.

Art Therapy for Older Adults with Mental Retardation

Harlan (1991) notes that older people with mental retardation face the same losses and physical changes as do others in their age group, but are even more poorly equipped to deal with these challenges given their cognitive, emotional, and experiential limitations. Art programs can help address these issues by providing age-appropriate creative activities for people who often lack meaningful pursuits. A good program addresses the developmental issues of aging and fosters self-esteem and autonomous functioning.

According to Harlan (1991), the format of an art therapy program for older adults with mental retardation should be open-ended, leaving participants free to choose their materials and subject matter. They should be allowed to explore the concerns of the moment, given an opportunity for independent decision making, and accommodated in ways that address their varying abilities and interests. Given the freedom inherent in this approach, the facilitator must provide a consistent support structure: Meeting days, times, place, and membership in the group should be consistent. The choice of materials should be adequate but not overwhelming.

Materials should be sturdy, attractive, well-maintained, and not too difficult for people with arthritis or limited grip strength to use. Accommodation for reduced vision or other physical impairments may also be necessary. Oil pastels, tempera paint, and drawing pencils are essential materials, and felt-tip markers, chalk pastels, colored pencils, watercolors, and collage materials are other good items to have on hand. Clay is another good medium, particularly if a kiln can be accommodated on the premises.

The guidance of an art therapist is also recommended for working with older people with mental retardation. The role of the activity facilitator or therapist is twofold: to establish the appropriate environment—ensuring privacy and a spacious work area, with adequate lighting and freedom from distractions—and to motivate the participants by intervening to solve problems and offering positive feedback on the specific abilities of individuals. Many participants either are afraid of or feel apathetic about participating because art involves challenge and risk. Those who are reluctant to participate should not be pressed to do so. They may eventually pick up materials after watching others.

It is important that the facilitator establish a sense of safety and security and ensure some early successes, while offering consistent, nonjudgmental acceptance and reassurance. It may be necessary, for instance, to overcome earlier experiences that have suggested to the participants that all art is representational. Rugh (1985) suggests showing older adult artists works of modern art to alter their sense of what is acceptable. In providing feedback a generalization such as "That's lovely" is not helpful; it is better to emphasize the unique qualities of an individual's work: "I noticed you decided to use colored pencil instead of pastel. Which one seems to work best for you?" (Harlan, 1991, p. 73).

People with mental retardation are often accustomed to trying to please others. They need to be encouraged to state their own preferences and make their own decisions during the art therapy sessions. For example, they can decide where they would like to sit, what size paper they prefer to draw on, how long to work on a project, and so forth. They must also feel that both positive and negative artistic expressions are valid. These individuals are more aware of death, including their own, than many people realize. Artwork may allow them to begin to express ideas, fears, and wishes about their own health or the deaths of friends and family members, which may trigger reminiscences. The art therapist must be prepared to handle difficult emotional situations (Harlan, 1991).

Day Activities for Older Adults with Mental Retardation

In contrast to people who argue for the supremacy of aesthetics over practicality in art therapy applications and for offering experiences with art as opposed to crafts (Harlan, 1991; Morrin, 1988), Edelson (1991) argues that salable art and fine handicrafts can provide older adults with mental retardation with avocational opportunities, stimulation, and enhanced social acceptance late in their lives. Edelson notes that many of these individuals have either no access to day programs or access only to a minimal number of activity options. They need to develop motor skills and self-care skills in order to prevent regression, and art-based activities are very appropriate to these ends. In addition, arts and crafts are considered socially acceptable pursuits for older people, including those with mental retardation. The goals of Edelson's type of program are obviously somewhat different from those of many of the programs previously examined: Instruction in the production of the artwork or craft takes precedence over free self-expression, and more emphasis is placed on the product itself than in other programs. Edelson believes that the experience should be vocational as well as recreational. The emphasis is on art as work, rather than as therapy or hobby. However, gains in self-esteem and a sense of accomplishment, social opportunities, and greater acceptance by the larger community have something in common with the results of therapeutic-oriented approaches.

The Gateway Approach, the program described by Edelson, is a prevocational training program conducted by a large nonprofit human services corporation in Boston and funded by the Massachusetts Department of Mental Retardation. The setting for the program is a loft space with natural northern lighting. Participants in the program are trained in fine arts (e.g., watercolor); ceramics; paper graphics, including card and wrapping paper design; weaving; fabric printing; and silk screening. Professionalism, salability, and production goals are stressed in higher-functioning participants, who attend 5 days a week, 6 hours each day. An attempt is made to capitalize on past experience and the abilities of the participants. For example, a deinstitutionalized 72-year-old man, who had some weaving experience, has developed a level of expertise that led to the exhibition of his work at local juried craft fairs; an older man with moderate mental retardation who drew as a hobby had his work exhibited in New York City art galleries and reviewed by the *Boston Globe*. Clients with visual impairments are given bright colors with which to work; weaving and ceramics have been found to be skills that can be developed by people who are legally blind. Emphasis is placed on what each individual does well, and new tasks are introduced one at a time. One-to-one instruction is often necessary. Some may need to start with craft kits (e.g., latticework) and graduate to creating original designs. Participants may also need to be exposed to works of art in order to fully appreciate the importance of what they are doing.

Finding that they can indeed do certain high-level tasks helps many older adults with mental retardation to overcome the "learned helplessness" that is often the legacy of institutionalization. By accentuating skills and abilities through sales and exhibits, the program also does much to destigmatize older people with mental retardation, helping them to be respected, contributing members of their communities (Edelson, 1991).

. . .

The arts are a part of our humanity, and the ability to appreciate and create art does not diminish with age. In fact, there is some evidence to suggest that people simply create differently during different stages of their lives (Saul, 1988). Individuals in their 60s and beyond may feel free to express themselves originally and openly, in ways they might not have felt able to in years past. Nurses and other health care professionals must become knowledgeable about the potential that creativity and art have for healing and growth (Sterritt & Pokorny, 1994). Many older people who may be embarrassed to seek counseling respond positively to the opportunity to participate in an art therapy program (Weiss, 1984). Art therapy can also result in improved functioning of people with Alzheimer's disease and in the reduction of the medications they need (Sterritt & Pokorny, 1994). In general the arts can offer older adults a sense of hope, an orientation toward the future for those who otherwise may be preoccupied with lost yesterdays and the seemingly useless present (Saul, 1988).

Participating in art activities allows older people to identify positively with the feelings and experiences of others while expressing their inner selves. Sharing or exhibiting their art provides them with a chance to showcase their abilities and demonstrate their self-worth. To be an artist is to be a valuable, contributing, vital part of society, regardless of one's age.

REFERENCES

The Armand Hammer Collection. (1987). Los Angeles: The Armand Hammer Foundation.

Barker, V., & Brunk, B. (1991). The role of a creative arts group in the treatment of clients with traumatic brain injury. *Music Therapy Perspectives, 9,* 26–31.

Bergland, C. (1982). The life review process in geriatric art therapy: A pilot study. *Arts in Psychotherapy, 9,* 121–130.

Colli, L.M. (1994). Aims in therapy and directives in society: Observations on individuation and adaptation. *Arts in Psychotherapy, 21,* 107–112.

Dohr, J.H., & Forbess, L.A. (1986). Creativity, arts, and profiles of aging: A reexamination. *Educational Gerontology, 12,* 123–138.

Edelson, R.T. (1991). Art and crafts—not "arts and crafts"—alternative vocational day activities for adults who are older and mentally retarded. *Activities, Adaptation & Aging, 15,* 81–97.

Franklin, M., & Politsky, R. (1992). The problem of interpretation: Implications and strategies for the field of art therapy. *Arts in Psychotherapy, 19,* 163–175.

Harlan, J.E. (1991). The use of art therapy for older adults with developmental disabilities. *Activities, Adaptation & Aging, 15,* 67–79.

Harrison, C.L. (1980). Creative arts for older people in the community. *American Journal of Art Therapy, 19,* 99–101.

Hubalek, S.K. (1997). *I can't draw a straight line: Bringing art into the lives of older adults.* Baltimore: Health Professions Press.

Landgarten, H. (1983). Art psychotherapy for depressed elders. *Clinical Gerontologist, 2*(1), 45–53.

Malchiodi, C. (1987). Strategies for obtaining art therapy funding from arts-related sources. *American Journal of Art Therapy, 25,* 91–94.

Mango, C. (1992). Emma: Art therapy illustrating personal and universal images of loss. *OMEGA, 25,* 259–269.

McMurray, J. (1990). Self-portraits. *Activities, Adaptation & Aging, 14,* 51–53.

Morrin, J. (1988). Art therapy groups in a geriatric institutional setting. In B. Maclennan et al. (Eds.), *Group psychotherapies for the elderly* (pp. 245–256). Madison, CT: International Universities Press.

Phillips, J. (1982). The art of Grandma Layton: An art therapy tool with the elderly. *Activities, Adaptation & Aging, 2,* 3–10.

Rugh, M.M. (1985). Art therapy with the institutionalized older adult. *Activities, Adaptation & Aging, 6,* 105–120.

Salamon, M.J., & Conte, V.A. (1984). *The Salamon-Conte Life Satisfaction in the Elderly Scale.* Odessa, FL: Psychological Assessment Resources.

Saul, S. (1988). The arts as psychotherapeutic modalities with groups of older people. In B. Maclennan et al. (Eds.), *Group psychotherapies for the elderly* (pp. 211–221). Madison, CT: International Universities Press.

Sterritt, P., & Pokorny, M. (1994). Art activities for patients with Alzheimer's and related disorders. *Geriatric Nursing, 15,* 155–159.

Tate, F.B., & Allen, H. (1985). Color preferences and the aged individual: Implications for art therapy. *Arts in Psychotherapy, 12,* 165–169.

Vance, D.E., & Greenwalt, L. (1996, March). Practicing Various Types of Art at an Alzheimer's Adult Day Care Center. Paper presented as part of an idea exchange at the 42nd Annual Meeting of the American Society on Aging, Anaheim, CA.

Vance, D.E., Camp, C., Kabacoff, M., & Greenwalt, L. (1996, Winter). Montessori methods: Innovative interventions for adults with Alzheimer's disease. *Montessori Life,* pp. 10–12.

Virshup, E. (1986). Group art therapy in a methadone clinic lobby. *Journal of Substance Abuse Treatment, 2,* 153–158.

Weber, B.L. (1981). Folk art as therapy. *American Journal of Art Therapy, 20,* 47–52.

Weiss, J.C. (1984). *Expressive therapy with elders and the disabled.* New York: Haworth Press.

Wolcott, A.B. (1978). Art therapy: An experimental group. In I. Burnside (Ed.), *Working with the elderly.* Boston: Jones & Bartlett.

Wolk, R.L. (1993). The role of interpretation in psychotherapy with the aged. In E. Hammer (Ed.), *Use of interpretation in treatment: Technique and art* (pp. 332–338). Northvale, NJ: Aronson.

Appendix
Resources for Art Therapy

Art Therapy Associations

American Association for Art Therapy (AAAT)
Ed Steyger, Executive Director
1202 Allanson Road
Mundelein, Illinois 60060
Phone (708) 949-6064
Fax (708) 566-4580
Purpose of the association is to progressively develop the therapeutic use of art, to advance research, to improve standards of practice, and to provide vehicles for the exchange of information and experience

South Texas Art Therapy Association (an affiliate of the AAAT)
Web site http://www.hal-pc.orgwheeler
An organization offering professional development opportunities and timely information to local practitioners, as well as a taste of the field to anyone with access to its home page

Arts Projects Sources

The Full Circle Center
Madeline M. Rugh, Ph.D., A.T.R., Director
910 Nebraska
Norman, Oklahoma 73069
Phone (405) 329-6435
The Center has developed a series of seminars, workshops, training courses, and slide/text packages on art and older adults; price list supplied on request

Making Your Own Mark:
A Drawing and Writing Guide for Senior Citizens
by Francine Ringold, Ph.D., and Madeline Rugh, M.A., A.T.R.
$14.95 plus $2.00 S & H
Available from Council Oak Books
1428 South St. Louis
Tulsa, Oklahoma 74120
Phone (800) 247-8850 or (918) 587-6454

A self-directed study and practice guide for adults interested in sharing experiences and discovering creative ability; illustrated with photographs and samples from older adult artists and writers

Nasco Catalogs
Web site http://www.nascofa.com/Catalogs
Nasco offers educational and specialty catalogs in numerous disciplines, including arts and crafts and activity therapy (supplies for nursing facility programs)

Other Resources

Alyce Marholin, M.A., and Stacie Zibel R.N., B.S.N., founders of Age of Discovery: The Artist in Later Life, A Long-Term Care Creative Arts Program
Alyce Marholin
30 Timberwood Road
West Hartford, Connecticut 06117

Stacie Zibel
15 Trumbull Lane
West Hartford, Connecticut 06117
Phone (203) 232-6685
Marholin and Zibel have developed an arts program for older adults in a residential setting that could be adapted for use by others

"When you walked into my life that afternoon I hadn't been able to work or make anything for nearly a year . . . and I was beginning to think I wouldn't ever again, that I had reached the end. . . . You revived my life."

Helen Martins, to her friend, Elsa, in Athol Fugard's *The Road to Mecca*

Lean on Me

Support Groups

Support groups can help older people work through difficult feelings and problems, obtain objective feedback in a caring environment, and explore alternative strategies to cope with personal issues. In addition, support groups offer older adults an opportunity to form intimate relationships in a relatively short period of time. With supervision and training, health care and social services professionals can incorporate group work into the delivery of their services.

Research has shown that a support system is vital to the health of every individual. People who maintain a support system of friends and relatives have a lower incidence of death and illness (Minkler, 1985; Syme & Berkman, 1990). In general, these people are sick less often, recover more rapidly when they are sick, and engage in more healthy and health-related behaviors than people who lack social supports (Berkman, 1985; Wortman & Coneway, 1985). Face-to-face contact with older people permits those in the support network to observe changes in health or general well-being (O'Bryant, 1985) and to make recommendations to see a physician if the changes are negative. A support network also has positive effects on appetite and nutrient intake (McIntosh, Shifflett, & Picou, 1989). Older people who are socially isolated tend to eat alone, which can lead to less regularly scheduled meals, overreliance on convenience foods, and a reduction in the amount and type of food eaten.

Social support has also been found to play a critical role in the maintenance of well-being in older adults (Biegel, 1984). For most older people social support derives from spouses, their adult children, friends, and neighbors. Confidants and companions tend to contribute more to a person's overall happiness than do a person's social contacts. Chappell and Badger (1989) found that measures of straight counts of individuals (e.g., daily or weekly contact), marital status, living arrangements, or having adult children were not related to subjective well-being. However, the quality of the relationship with people in the network was related to subjective well-being—it had a significant impact on it. Lee and Ishii-Kuntz (1987) report that friends play a greater role than do family members in reducing loneliness and increasing morale in older adults. The authors attribute this finding to the positive regard gained by choosing and being chosen as a friend. In addition, older adults tend to help their friends, thereby fostering independence from their adult children and reducing concern that they are a burden to their children (Roberto & Scott, 1986).

As compared with younger people, older people tend to maintain smaller networks of people with whom they discuss important matters, which in turn means that they have fewer social roles and fewer social contacts (Morgan, 1988). Most older adults maintain a circle of long-standing relationships (Kahn & Antonucci, 1980; Morgan, 1988). For older men their confidants are often their wives, who are frequently perceived to be their closest friends, and, in some cases, their adult children (Reisman, 1988). Older women tend to cultivate deep friendships with other women with whom they can talk (Keith, Hill, Goudy, & Powers, 1984). Men experience decreased numbers of contacts with friends and assign less importance to friendships over time, whereas women's contacts and their commitment to friends do not seem to change (Field & Minkler, 1988). Men tend to be dependent on their wives to coordinate and schedule social relationships (Depner & Ingersoll, 1982). These gender-specific differences may explain Lee and Ishii-Kuntz's (1987) finding that interaction with neighbors reduces loneliness and increases morale for men, but not for women. On the one hand, most women expect intimacy in relationships that they find rewarding. On the other hand, men's friendships are based on shared activities, and they may not expect more from relationships. However, when intimacy is available to men in a relationship such as marriage or with children, it is valued.

Factors that influence close nonfamilial relationships include income and education (Morgan, 1988). Income allows continued contact with long-standing members of the network: Sufficient disposable income must be available to go out with friends for a shared activity (e.g., lunch or dinner, movies) or even cover the transportation costs of a visit. Education may play a role in the initial acquisition of friends and continued range of contacts. Older adults with an advanced education tend to maintain professional contacts after retirement. Also, highly educated individuals may have acquired more friends in the past because friendships at younger ages tend to be influenced by information seeking (Carstensen, 1993, 1995).

Most older adults have satisfying relationships well into later life. Only 16%–20% of those studied report not having confidants (Chappell & Badger, 1989; Peters & Kaiser, 1985). These people risk loneliness, a common source of distress in older adults (Mosher-Ashley, 1994a) and a state that has a major, negative effect on morale (Lee & Ishii-Kuntz, 1987). Chappell and Badger (1989) caution, however, that health care and social services personnel should use qualitative measures to assess the type of relationships older adults experience: Living alone or reduced social contacts should not be automatic indicators of loneliness, and marriage should not exclude an older adult from the risk for loneliness.

Several researchers (Kahn & Antonucci, 1980; Morgan, 1988) propose that the types of long-term relationships that contribute to well-being in later life are not easily replaced through mere substitution. This may be attributable, in part, to the length of time needed to develop the level of intimacy required for a person to disclose feelings and personal problems. Support groups can help assuage this feeling of loss because they are designed to foster intimacy among their members and provide a forum in which to share problems.

The therapeutic benefits of support groups for older people are many. Improvements in interpersonal and social functioning; opportunities to gain new friendships, adjust to new lifestyles, or both; and the enhancement of a sense of belonging and well-being all have been associated with participation in support groups (Abraham, Niles, Thiel, Siarkowski, & Cowling, 1991; Clark & Vorst, 1994; Stone & Koonin, 1986). Most support groups are formed on the basis of a theme. Examples are being an older man living in a community setting or residential facility composed predominantly of older women; widows or widowers coping with the loss of a spouse; retirees coping with the loss of work identity; and survivors grieving the recent death of a sibling, friend, or pet. Often, deeply concealed feelings of fear, loneliness, or anxiety associated with depression can be identified and expressed after receiving support from other group members who share similar emotions (Capuzzi, Gross, & Friel, 1990; Caserta & Lund, 1993). Various methods of coping can also be explored (Tross & Blum, 1988).

Support groups can also be formed for the sole purpose of friendship (Bentov, Smith, Siegal, & Doress-Worters, 1994). This type of group work can be characterized as social therapy (Tross & Blum, 1988) and is used to counteract the effect that the loss of friends through death, illness, relocation, or being out of touch with them for long periods because of passivity or depression has on older adults. These groups offer older adults an opportunity to socialize and even exercise social skills that may have deteriorated from disuse or that may have been affected by major stressors such as bereavement, relocation, and extended family disruption (e.g., children who live a considerable distance away and who are consumed by their own activities, conflicts that have resulted in alienation between family members).

Some differences exist between groups comprising older members and those comprising younger participants. These differences are culturally based and do not represent age-related physiological changes (Lakin, 1988). On average, older adults are less educated and consequently less familiar with psychological ideas and terminology than are younger adults. Older adults are also more reluctant to admit a need for psychological assistance. Although some psychotherapists report that older people have more difficulty disclosing personal information, it should not be assumed that all older adults will display this tendency. In carefully conducted observations of different age groups, Lakin (1988) found that older adults talked with relative ease and little hesitation about profound experiences such as loneliness, fear of abandonment, problems of widowhood, and feelings of rejection and vulnerability in the face of apparent indifference in the environment. A comparative group of younger adults exhibited more tension and punctuated their description of experiences with anxious pauses.

Implementation of a support group is feasible in a range of environments and can be modified to fit the needs of many older people (Abraham et al., 1991). For those residing independently, in congregate housing, or in long-term care facilities, support groups can be an accessible option, with severe cognitive, communicative, or physiological disabilities being the only barriers (Abraham et al., 1991; Clark & Vorst, 1994).

Several different types of groups have been developed for use with older adults. Many of these groups share common features with support groups. The type of group selected for implementation depends on the type of problem exhibited and its severity. This chapter focuses on support groups, although much of the information presented can apply to all of the groups listed in the following:

Psychotherapy groups—Usually led by a therapist formally trained in providing mental health services; group members are encouraged to identify and express feelings and find support from other members who share similar feelings, with the goal of continued personal and psychological development

Support groups—Led by a professional, paraprofessional, or peer; designed to facilitate the sharing of feelings, empathic responses among members, and the discovery of coping strategies

Self-help groups—Similar to support groups, but are often initiated by peers who share a common problem; although one individual tends to take over responsibility for coordinating the group, all members have equal status

Mutual-help groups—Similar to self-help groups in that they tend to focus on problems and members have equal status; however, these groups are more goal oriented, with the expectation of devising mutually beneficial solutions for all members

Topic-specific groups—Focus is on a topic or activity to foster contentment, self-realization, or increased knowledge; topics can include assertiveness training, physical concerns, or retirement planning; activities can include music, art, literature, or writing

Social therapy groups—Designed to provide socialization either to promote relationships or improve social skills

It should be noted that group interventions for older adults historically have been implemented by practitioners from many disciplines (Tross & Blum, 1988). Health care and social services professionals have been conducting support groups for older people in a variety of settings. Their involvement in the delivery of services places them in an advantageous position to start and conduct groups in community centers, retirement communities, and residential or day treatment centers. In addition, these professionals are not usually associated with mental health services, lessening the resistance some older adults may feel with regard to attending a support group.

USE OF SUPPORT GROUPS WITH OLDER ADULTS LIVING INDEPENDENTLY

Nate Timmons, a 73-year-old retired executive, is by nature an organizer, one who likes to get things done through people. In college he was class president, the chairman of various school clubs, a cheerleader, and the director of social affairs. On the surface he appears to be an outgoing, carefree person, but internally he is shy and eager to please. Because of his organizational and promotional abilities, he served successfully as president of an employer–employee relations association, rescuing it from imminent demise and making it one of the best in the United States, with a significant increase in membership and income. Nate tends to be a worrier and suffered from insecurity in his younger years, when he often did not know where his next dollar was coming from. A spiritual man, he finds comfort in his religious faith. Having experienced a heart attack, several operations, and arthritic knees and back, he strives to stay physically fit by swimming laps two or three times a week. Nate remains active by serving on several community organization boards and sporadically taking courses at a local university. He has received awards for outstanding leadership for his contributions to his profession and to the community. In addition, he maintains a solid family life with his wife and two children.

Despite his accomplishments, Nate is plagued by thoughts that he has not done enough. Also, he feels the loss of influence he once enjoyed among his peers and in the community. Nate always felt a need to be liked, to be accepted, and to stand out as a leader. In retirement, his opportunities to shine have been fewer. Although he has remained active in several organizations, he found himself in need of a forum to air his disappointments, his phobic thoughts, his attitudes about death, and his constructive ideas for the betterment of the community. With this need in mind, he formed what turned into a self-help therapy group. The other members were two retired business executives with whom he had lunched regularly. Nate schedules meeting times and is looked to by the other participants to keep the sessions alive. Ordinarily, the topics of discussion are world events, local activities, humor, and the well-being of mutual friends. A buzzword such as "sons," "business," "health," "feelings," or "family" will usually touch off a discussion of inner concerns that plead for expression. The group's success in helping the three men air their feelings and create a mutually supportive interchange can be seen in the name they have given the group—"The Terrorpeutic Club"—and in the regularity with which they meet. Group meetings are given preference over other events in the lives of the participants.

Older people living independently can benefit from support groups established in settings such as senior centers, adult day programs, churches, community centers, and libraries (Capuzzi, Gross, & Friel, 1990; Caserta & Lund, 1993). It is necessary to find a group that will be suitable for and beneficial to the older individual. Support groups may state general objectives that deal with confronting the many issues related to aging, or they may be established specifically to deal with a problem facing all members. It is important for older adults to feel comfortable and welcome within the group, and differences in race, religion, intellectual capacity, or cultural background, if present, are usually overcome rapidly. Similar previous emotional experiences and problems, rather than similar backgrounds, become the basis for the alignment of a group (McWhorter, 1980).

A means of transportation is essential in order for independent-living older adults to attend support groups regularly. If the individual or his or her family is unable to make this accommodation, public transportation or a senior van service may be an option. If several older adults will be relying on a senior van for transportation, it is advisable to contact the agency to coordinate timing of the group session and van availability.

USE OF SUPPORT GROUPS WITH OLDER ADULTS LIVING IN CONGREGATE HOUSING OR LONG-TERM CARE FACILITIES

Ginger is an 86-year-old woman who has resided in a nursing facility for 4 years. At first, her son and daughter-in-law visited frequently, about once a week. After a few months, the number of visits began to taper off to twice a month, then monthly; eventually, the couple visited only on major holidays. Ginger had married and divorced early in life. Her son was an only child. She had no siblings, was not close to her cousins, and had not made friends within the facility. Although Ginger appeared to have adjusted to life in the nursing facility, staff members were concerned about her tendency to spend a great deal of time alone.

The facility social worker was forming a self-help group designed for residents with intact cognitive abilities who had few visitors and were loners in the facility. She elected to include Ginger in the group. The number of participants was limited to eight because the goal was to facilitate the formation of friendships. Each individual invited to join the group had been carefully screened to ensure that participants were compatible with each other.

The group met twice a week in a small staff lounge. Coffee and cookies were served during a 15-minute social period preceding the formal group session, which lasted 45 minutes. During the formal session, the social worker asked each group member to take turns in sharing personal information. A chronological approach was taken with members, beginning with childhood events and progressing to the present. Members were free to decide how many sessions were to be devoted to a given chronological period. The decision to remain with a certain period or move on to another was made at the end of a session. In this way, the discussion of enjoyable periods could be extended and, if an individual member had not contributed to the discussion, he or she could do so at the next meeting.

Ginger attended each meeting and shared information about herself with the group. When the group began to discuss late adolescence and early adulthood, Ginger described her troubled marriage. She was 18 when she married and 4 months' pregnant. Her husband, who was only 19 at the time, was not ready to settle down and spent much of his free time with his friends at local bars. After 2 years of arguments and recriminations, they separated. Her husband returned to live with his parents. Ginger elected to stay on in their apartment because her mother had passed away several years earlier and her father lived in a rooming house. Ginger arranged for a friend to watch her son while she worked part-time. Her husband paid the rent and visited their son infrequently. This arrangement continued for several years until Ginger's father-in-law passed away unexpectedly. At that time she learned that her in-laws had been paying her rent. Ginger's husband had moved away and was living with a woman who was pregnant. He asked Ginger for a divorce so that he could remarry, offering to help her out with the rent in the future. She agreed and received checks to cover the rent until the divorce decree came through. After the divorce, the checks stopped, and Ginger did not hear from her ex-husband, who had moved, leaving no forwarding address. Attempts to locate him through relatives proved fruitless. In addition, she was made to feel that she had entrapped her ex-husband and had "sponged off" his parents for years.

The years following the divorce were hard for Ginger; she and her son lived in virtual poverty on her meager pay as a waitress in a diner. She described her intense feelings of guilt over not being able to provide a better childhood for her son. Her need to work full-time and much overtime left her little time and energy for the boy. Her guilt was so pervasive that when the boy objected to her seeing a man who was interested in her, Ginger quietly acquiesced. Ginger also described how her son had to shoulder the responsibility for his education. Fortunately, he was an excellent student, and his social world centered on school-based activities. He earned a scholarship and assistantship that enabled him to attend college and graduate school.

Ginger attributed her son's few visits to the lack of role models for family affinity and devotion, although she confessed that at times she felt his actions were the result of her fatigue and preoccupation with the need to work while he was growing up. Following Ginger's story several members of the group praised her efforts to rear her son without the customary supports. The topic shifted to a discussion of family visits and how important they were to the participants. Another woman in the group, Louise, described her pain at not being visited regularly by her daughter, who lived only 30 minutes away. These revelations formed the basis of a friendship between Louise and Ginger.

The group continued to meet for 2 months. During that time, some members formed friendships and some did not. Louise and Ginger's relationship continued, and they spent part of each day together. They met at some of the structured activities, particularly the "Koffee Klatch" group on Monday mornings. They also watched an early evening television program together. Their friendship lasted for 2 years, until Louise's death. Ginger frequently mentioned how important the group had been in helping her to get some issues "off her chest" and in meeting her best friend, Louise.

Support groups are quite feasible for older adults living in congregate housing or in long-term care facilities (Abraham et al., 1991). A group can be established and sessions can be held at the facility in a conference room or recreation room. The room must be large enough to accommodate a circle of group participants, some of whom may be in wheelchairs (Clark & Vorst, 1994; Puppolo, 1980).

Residents' interests and needs should be assessed prior to implementing such a group (McWhorter, 1980). Staff members may help in identifying residents who may benefit most from participation in a support group. However, it is important that older people be invited to attend, not be required to do so (Capuzzi, Gross, & Friel, 1990; Stone & Koonin, 1986). Also, because regular attendance is necessary to establish and maintain group identity, it is important to consult the staff when drawing up the support group schedule in order to avoid holding sessions at times when other activities have been planned (Abraham et al., 1991; Puppolo, 1980).

Therapists working in long-term care must actively verbalize concerns that members find difficult to express and to integrate comments made (Leszcz, Feigenbaum, Sadavoy, & Robinson, 1985; Sadavoy & Leszcz, 1987). In part, verbalization is necessary because of the limited psychological sophistication of the group members and the passivity found in many residents.

PRECAUTIONS TO TAKE AND ACCOMMODATIONS TO MAKE IN IMPLEMENTING SUPPORT GROUPS

The implementation of a support group, whether it be in a community setting or within a residential facility, requires certain considerations. For instance, privacy is essential, and choosing a location that is convenient and nonthreatening, such as a community center or a library, may be conducive to discussions of feelings. Providing a comfortable physical environment with access to bathroom facilities is also advised (Capuzzi, Gross, & Friel, 1990). Even giving the group a generic name—for example, "Men's Group," "Widows'/Widowers' Group"— may ease the minds of those who are fearful of mental health services and their connotations (Bratter, 1986; Caserta & Lund, 1993).

Group Size and Attendance

Group size may vary; however, small groups of 10 or 12 are recommended. Because a member is likely to be absent from each session, selecting a group size slightly larger than desired is wise (Puppolo, 1980). Some groups may be conducted with variable attendance, with some members participating in every session and others attending only monthly (Matorin & Zoubok, 1988). This type of format is appropriate for socialization groups but may not be suitable for small support groups designed to encourage members to share feelings and personal information. Some groups (see, e.g., Matorin & Zoubok, 1988) are launched with all members participating in every session and, once group cohesion has taken place, move to a variable format to meet the needs of individual members.

Regular attendance is important. Because memory deficits are common in many older adults, certain techniques must be employed to ensure each member's presence at group sessions. One solution is to send a note to forgetful group members specifying the date and time of the next group meeting (Puppolo, 1980). In residential care facilities, group facilitator–nursing staff collaboration may be necessary. The staff may post the names of the group members along with dates and times of group meetings on a bulletin board and assist in reminding them and preparing them for group sessions (Abraham et al., 1991).

Schedules

Schedules must be planned carefully. Taking the schedules of group participants and the facility (if applicable) into consideration is essential (Abraham et al., 1991; Puppolo, 1980). Scheduling support group sessions during times when group members are more alert is also recommended (Capuzzi, Gross, & Friel, 1990; Matorin & Zoubok, 1988). For example, early morning sessions can be taxing and stressful for some participants. Transportation may be difficult to arrange or obtain early in the morning. Rush-hour traffic can present a problem to older drivers. Also, many older adults, especially those with physical impairments, require more time to complete their activities of daily living (ADLs). Evening sessions are also problematic. Many older people do not like to be out after dark and those in residential care settings are usually placed in bed early (Burnside, 1986). Mid-morning is a particularly good time to work with depressed older adults because they are more likely to be alert and are less subject to fatigue (Clark & Vorst, 1994).

Many experts recommend that support group sessions for older people be limited in length. Often, shorter and more frequent sessions are better suited for people with physical or psychological limitations (Lakin, 1988). For residents of nursing facilities a session should last no longer than 1 hour (Abraham et al., 1991). Cognitively intact older adults, even those with physical disabilities, can tolerate longer sessions of up to 2 hours (Kemp, Corgiat, & Gill, 1991–1992). Support groups may meet biweekly, weekly, bimonthly, or monthly.

Effective Group Facilitators

The success of a support group is dependent on the facilitator possessing certain qualities. Patience; acceptance; empathy; creativity; abundant energy; and genuine concern for and knowledge of the socioeconomic pressures, health problems, and diseases that can compound the stressors of aging are essential qualities in a successful group facilitator (Abraham et al., 1991; Matorin & Zoubok, 1988; McWhorter, 1980). A group facilitator should also possess good communication and organization skills (Burnside, 1986).

Often, there is a marked age difference between the facilitator and members of a group. Although this difference may not present a problem, it is possible that older adults may be skeptical of the competence and ability of a younger individual to understand their feelings, their situation, or both. It may benefit the group if the facilitator chosen is closer in age to that of the members of the group. However, good training in geropsychology may help younger people better understand the problems faced by older people (Lakin, 1988). It is also important that facilitators resolve their own intergenerational issues before undertaking group work with older adults (Benitez-Bloch, 1988). In particular, facilitators need to come to terms with their own feelings about death, disability, and loss and should be comfortable with the expression of feelings about these issues (Capuzzi, Gross,

& Friel, 1990). Frequently, there will be deterioration in the physical condition of members if the group continues over a considerable period of time (Burnside, 1986). The death of a member may also occur. These events can have a traumatic effect on the group facilitator and on group members. The physical condition, deterioration in health, and even death of group members have been known to lead to depression in group facilitators (Burnside, 1986).

Issues of gender have been known to play a role in groups in which cofacilitators have been of equal status and mixed gender. Older adults who were raised during a time in which women rarely became professionals have been found by Lothstein (1988) to treat male cofacilitators with greater respect than they do female cofacilitators. However, gender issues concerning a single female facilitator or female cofacilitators have not been raised in the literature, nor have they been experienced by the authors.

Accommodation of Participants

People who have hearing, visual, or other physical disabilities can benefit from support groups, provided they are not extremely debilitated (Abraham et al., 1991; Clark & Vorst, 1994). Screening individuals for these types of deficits is necessary to ensure that any problems can be compensated for in a group setting (Clark & Vorst, 1994). Certain accommodations, such as choosing a room large enough for wheelchair access, using a microphone and amplifier for people with hearing impairments, and providing a pencil and paper for people with aphasia or other speech limitations, are necessary and can be made rather easily (Abraham et al., 1991; Clark & Vorst, 1994; Puppolo, 1980; Stone & Koonin, 1986).

Although a support group can be beneficial for older people with aphasia or other speech limitations, it is important to limit the number of nonverbal members of a group in order to maintain active interaction (Puppolo, 1980). By the same token, it is just as important to encourage the participation of a nonverbal group member. It is easy to unintentionally ignore such individuals. A conscious effort must be made by the facilitator to attend to aphasic or other silent group members at every session (Puppolo, 1980).

Support groups are not suitable for all older people. Support groups should not be used in place of individual therapy or psychotherapy groups for troubled older adults in need of such services. Prospective participants should be assessed for severity of the symptoms displayed and referred for appropriate mental health services. Older individuals who are unwilling to be referred for traditional psychotherapy may be considered for a support group, but only after every effort has been made to encourage them to undergo psychotherapy. Also, certain individuals' personalities, prejudices, or physical limitations prevent them from receiving any benefit from support groups (Abraham et al., 1991). An alternative therapy should be sought for these people (Lakin, 1988). Other older adults may possess personality traits that make it difficult for groups to assimilate them. For example, Matorin and Zoubok (1988) reported a case in which a clearly lonely and isolated woman coped with dependency needs and despair because of her increasing loss of vision with sharp, sarcastic, and vituperative behavior. In some cases such older people can reduce group cohesion and the benefits received by other members. A skillful group facilitator can minimize the problems posed by difficult members and create opportunities for members to learn from negative interchanges. However, in peer-facilitated and self-help groups, it may be better to let difficult members, who tend to drop out anyway, leave.

IMPLEMENTATION OF A SUPPORT GROUP

Preliminary Steps

The implementation of a support group program in a community setting, in congregate housing, or in long-term care facilities requires following several preliminary steps, all of which have been discussed in greater detail in preceding sections.

Choosing a Competent Group Cofacilitator

Choosing an older person as cofacilitator can be advantageous (Fisher, 1988). The peer facilitator can assist members both within and outside of the group. Within the group, the peer can support and clarify statements; outside of the group, the peer can be responsible for reminding members when meetings are to take place and contacting members who missed a session to express concern and to encourage them to attend future sessions. Burnside (1986) has successfully used long-term care residents as cofacilitators. The cofacilitator position in Burnside's groups was rotated weekly, and several members volunteered for the opportunity to serve. When properly trained, paraprofessionals have also been found to be effective group facilitators (Gallagher, 1981; Zimberg, 1969). The group facilitator's attention to structuring and scheduling group sessions is critical. A facilitator who is late, cancels, or reschedules meetings frequently sends a message to the participants that the group is less important than his or her other responsibilities.

Finding an Appropriate Room in Which to Hold the Sessions

It is important that the space selected for the group sessions meet the needs of the members and not be changed if possible during the length of the group intervention. As previously noted, the room should be located close to bathroom facilities and not be subject to distractions. Privacy is necessary in order for members to disclose personal information. Also, shuffling the group from area to area can increase confusion and inhibit group cohesion and the group process.

Recruiting Suitable Candidates to Become Group Members

A contract should be established between each member and the group facilitator. This contract can be verbal or written. The advantage of a written contract is that it can be referred to by the participants or family members if an aspect is forgotten. Written contracts should be used when prospective members are forgetful or disoriented. According to Burnside (1986), the contract should include time at which the sessions will be held; place where the sessions will be held; duration of the individual session; expected length of the series of sessions; list of other members; purpose of the group, with a clear description of objectives and goals; and name of the facilitator and a phone number at which he or she can be reached should the prospective member have any questions. Abraham et al. (1991) caution that the contract may need to be somewhat informal given the reluctance of some older people to sign forms.

The selection of members should be considered carefully. The facilitator should keep in mind that the therapeutic aspects of the group are not mediated by the therapist but by the members who provide acceptance, support, and hope through interpersonal feedback, testing (i.e., challenging inappropriate perceptions in other members, practicing new ways of responding), and learning (Yalom, 1985). The criteria in selecting participants should include the ability to express oneself adequately, to listen to feedback, and to participate in a conversation without disrupting it (Clark & Vorst, 1994).

A variety of people is needed to complete the group, but the variety should not be wide. For example, two hearing-impaired or three silent, withdrawn, depressed older adults can increase the work of the group facilitator. A well-balanced group requires both talkative and quiet people (Burnside, 1986). Interestingly, differing educational level has not been found to be a variable that negatively affects group cohesion (Burnside, 1986). Older adults of differing cognitive levels should not be combined (Burnside, 1986; Weiss, 1994). Older adults who are severely withdrawn can be admitted to a group if they can respond to simple questions and, even minimally, to requests for feedback.

Older adults who ask specifically to join a group should be included if possible (Burnside, 1986). Such a request reflects a proactive step toward resolving their problems and taking responsibility for their own lives, two popular goals of group intervention.

The interview with the prospective group member should be used as an opportunity to assess the individual's abilities, to explain the function of a support group, and to establish the expectations of the members (Clark & Vorst, 1994).

Establishing Group Size

The size of the group should be kept within a manageable range but not be too large (more than 12) or too small (less than 4). A facilitator may be tempted to add extra members without considering the impact that this addition may have on the group. Open groups, into which new members are freely added and from which members periodically terminate, can be larger than closed groups, in which the membership is stable and the sessions are time limited. Socialization groups can also absorb a larger number of members, as can groups with cofacilitators. Groups involving frail older adults should begin with 12 members because if the average 30% dropout rate (common with frail older adults because of illness) holds true, the group size will still be substantial with 8 members (Weiss, 1994).

Scheduling

A schedule should be formulated after careful consultation with group members, staff, family, or all three. Family members may resent the group if it interferes with their own schedules (Burnside, 1986). Residential care staff can also sabotage a group if they perceive it as interfering with their responsibilities to the resident. The group must last long enough to enable members to develop group cohesion and for the therapeutic process to take place. Short-term groups usually involve approximately 14 weeks, and long-term groups often last 6 months to 1 year (Weiss, 1994). A schedule of ongoing contacts between the group facilitator and staff members should be arranged because the facilitator should be aware of events taking place within the community center or residential facility that may have an impact on members.

Considering Costs

The costs of conducting the group should be considered carefully (Burnside, 1986). These costs include group facilitator's (or facilitators') time, refreshments, transportation, and staff time to assist in assembling participants for the group. The amount of time spent by the group facilitator goes well beyond the time spent in the group sessions. Much time is expended in the selection of participants, which includes interviewing each candidate. Also, progress notes on each participant must be recorded following each session. Contacting absent members may also be time consuming. Although it may be tempting to forgo refreshments as a cost- and time-saving measure, serving coffee and tea helps to relax the participants and provides a stimulus to socialization. The amount of time staff need to prepare a resident to attend a group session should not be underestimated. The facilitator will need to spend time explaining the importance of the group and expressing appreciation to each staff person involved on an ongoing basis. Failing to meet these costs may result in a less-than-successful experience for group participants.

Accommodating Medical Limitations

Any medical problems experienced by the group members should be taken into consideration when implementing a support group. Prospective members should be asked if they have medical problems that may affect their ability to sit for a continuous hour in a group meeting. However, participants should be reassured that accommodations can be made to meet their medical needs. For example, men with prostate problems may need to sit near an exit so that they can excuse themselves to use the bathroom (Burnside, 1986).

Goals and Topics for Discussion

Some groups are established with a topic area or problem that will be the focus of all group sessions. (Group facilitators who wish to conduct a problem-focused group may find the sources listed in the appendix at the end of the chapter useful.) The fundamental aspects of supportive therapy focus on strengths and setting realistic goals (Yalom & Terrazas, 1968). Once the preliminary steps are complete, it is important to define the goals and objectives of the support group carefully (Abraham et al., 1991). Through consultation with nursing staff, family, and group members and review of each member's chart (if available), group facilitators will gain a sense of what the support group should and can accomplish (Matorin & Zoubok, 1988).

In the first session of a general, nonspecific topic group the facilitator may wish to survey members as to what topics or themes they would like to discuss. Offering a list from which they may select topics can expedite the process (Stone & Koonin, 1986). Some examples of general goals and topics for discussion that apply to most older adult support groups follow:

Goals
Express common concerns
Share ways to cope with common experiences
Decrease social isolation
Express feelings more freely
Increase personal interaction and group cohesiveness
Create a supportive environment and provide opportunities for socialization

Possible topics/themes
Problem-solving skills (e.g., asserting oneself, resolving problems with family)
Emotional difficulties of aging
Bereavement/depression
Adjustment to a different lifestyle
Loss of the ability to drive and be mobile
Fear of becoming nonfunctional and being placed in a nursing facility

In general, it is best to begin with "safe" topics (e.g., having participants provide a short autobiography, describe their immediate family, share their interests and hobbies) until group members become more familiar with and trusting of each other. More personally relevant topics (dependent on the theme of the group; e.g., in a bereavement group the participants can be surveyed to determine who has experienced a common emotional response, such as anger and guilt following the death of a loved one) may then ensue (Abraham et al., 1991). In the first few sessions, the general goals for group members are to become comfortable with speaking in the group, to learn and use the names of other members, and to be able to respond at least minimally to questions (Clark & Vorst, 1994).

Format of Sessions

The format of support group sessions can and should be flexible in order to meet the needs of the group members. The first session should provide a model for the sessions to follow. Participants should be seated in a circular arrangement. If refreshments are served as part of the meeting, it may be wise to seat members around a table. Cofacilitators should be seated diagonally across from each other, with an equal number of members on each side. This arrangement permits them to establish eye contact with as many members as possible and to assist two members with deep emotional needs on each side (Burnside, 1986). The group facilitator should introduce him- or herself and suggest that group members introduce themselves to each other (Abraham et al., 1991). The goals of the group and the location, frequency, and duration of the sessions should be made clear. The importance of attendance should be stressed as well as the need for confidentiality (Abraham et al., 1991; Puppolo, 1980; Stone & Koonin, 1986). The group facilitator can include in the original contract a statement that group members are to honor confidences (Burnside, 1978). In addition, this subject should be raised and discussed at some length in one of the early sessions. If the facilitator is placed in the position of needing to share information raised in the group with others (e.g., family, health care professionals) outside of the group, permission of the group member(s) must be obtained.

Anxiety is a common response among participants in the initial meetings. Anxiety can be observed in chain smoking, talking rapidly, monopolizing the discussion, and exhibiting nervous mannerisms in the extremities (e.g., tremors, fidgeting, excessive or repetitive movement). Some members may exhibit anxiety by staring out the window or at the floor and avoiding eye contact with others, especially the group facilitator (Burnside, 1986). Certain warm-up techniques can be initiated by the facilitator in order to ease the tension some people feel about being in a group of strangers. One technique is to serve refreshments at each session. Arranging for group members to alternate bringing a refreshment or snack, often one that is homemade, can help to foster an atmosphere of personal warmth and familiarity (Matorin & Zoubok, 1988). Other techniques for warming up the group include using ambient (background) music or even singing and dancing (Lakin, 1988; Stone & Koonin, 1986). Facilitators who are concerned that refreshments may distract participants from dealing with serious issues during the session should consider scheduling a 10–15 minute social interaction period before the formal session begins. The session could be held in a separate room adjacent to the area where the social is held.

Early in the sessions, participants should be informed that the group discussions may cause anxiety (Weiss, 1994). As participants grow in understanding the issues they raise, they may feel depressed or anxious and may feel compelled to leave the group. They should be encouraged not to give up on the group but to air these feelings, which will undergo change over the progression of the sessions and the therapeutic process. The group facilitator should keep in mind that his or her function is to highlight strengths individual members exhibit, which are then supported and reinforced by other group members.

It is important for the group facilitator to be mindful of the following things during group discussions:

Sharing and comparing are helpful; these should involve not only common concerns but also common pleasures and satisfactions.

Support, empathy, and encouragement are essential; these are best achieved through active listening (see Chapter 8).

Energy is vital; physical and mental energy must be maintained in older adult support groups and often can be contagious.

Patience is necessary; allow group members to set the pace while also supplying necessary encouragement and stimulation for progress.

Flexibility is necessary to meet the wide range of needs presented by older adults.

Member participation (to the best of his or her ability) in each session is encouraged; asking certain questions or requesting a topic for group discussion may facilitate this goal.

Mentioning absent members or asking group members to name them ("Who isn't here today?") is a way to help group members to become more concerned about each other, and may stress the importance of attendance.

Avoidance of the use of psychological concepts, terminology, and descriptions of behavior is advised.

Lakin (1988) recommends that group interventions with older adults emphasize an atmosphere of acceptance, encouragement, support, and nonconfrontation. Yalom (1985) has pointed out that members are likely to terminate membership in a group when the punishments or disadvantages of group membership outweigh the rewards or anticipated rewards. These disadvantages can include feelings of anxiety, frustration, discouragement, and rejection arising from the group experience. Burnside (1986), who has had considerable experience in conducting groups and training facilitators, cautions that groups with a confrontational style are not appropriate for older people. Ego enhancement and mutual support should be encouraged. Clark and Vorst (1994) also recommend that a nonthreatening and undemanding atmosphere be maintained.

Special effort should be made to help an older adult with impaired hearing participate in the group process. This may mean asking the individual to sit near the therapist or a peer facilitator and encouraging members to speak more audibly. However, as mentioned previously, several people with hearing impairments should not be included in the same group.

Members should be encouraged to send a card, to telephone, and even to visit a member who is not able to attend the group because of a prolonged illness or hospitalization. Matorin and Zoubok (1988) described the emotional gains one hospitalized member of their group experienced by receiving a visit from her group. At the very least, the group facilitator or cofacilitator should contact absent members to ask why they did not attend the meeting, to express concern for them, and to encourage them to attend future sessions. Absenteeism is one of the most frequently encountered problems experienced by novice group facilitators (Burnside, 1986).

Some therapists have found that incorporating caregivers and family into groups for older adults can be beneficial (Dunlop, Skorney, & Hamilton, 1982; Fisher, 1988; Matorin & Zoubok, 1988). This approach can help these people as well as the members. The group facilitator has an opportunity to model for both parties appropriate patterns of communication and conflict resolution. Although family involvement can be beneficial, it should not be undertaken by new facilitators. Coordinating group dynamics involving both the client and a family member, particularly when there is a conflict or issue between the individuals, requires skill and experience.

Group Process

Group intervention follows a stage progression (Corey, 1985). The first stage centers on *orientation* and *exploration,* during which members feel socially isolated from each other and direct most of their attention toward the facilitator. Group facilitators need to use tact and diplomacy to minimize jealousy among group members or to handle issues of overdependency on or overattachment to them on the part of some members (Burnside, 1986). Group facilitators must be willing to relinquish their authority and move toward group autonomy or overdependency will likely take place (Abraham et al., 1991). They may need to be directive, prompting discussion and self-disclosure (Capuzzi, Gross, & Friel, 1990). However, this need is more evident when the participants have little formal education (Lakin, 1988): Better-educated participants require less facilitator guidance. Groups based in long-term care facilities require more initial direction from the group facilitator (Abraham et al., 1991).

In the second stage, the *transition* stage, group members experience increased anxiety, defensiveness, and conflict as they begin to move toward group cohesion. During this stage, the facilitator must be sensitive to the needs of members and be supportive. The third stage, the *working* stage, involves the actual exchange of feelings and thoughts between members. During this stage, informal facilitators emerge and group cohesion takes place. According to Abraham et al. (1991), this phase may not occur until the 10th or 11th week, supporting Weiss's (1994) recommendation that short-term groups should last at least 14 weeks. And, Knight (1989) and Mosher-Ashley (1994b) have found that old-old (age 80 and older) clients tend to require more therapy sessions.

The focus of the fourth stage, the *consolidation* stage, is on applying what has been learned in the group and putting it to use in everyday life (Corey, 1985). Frequently, role-playing is employed to accomplish this goal. Requiring group members to practice different ways of responding to the significant people in their lives enables them to obtain valuable feedback from others and to consider new alternatives to old behaviors. This final stage also involves *termination.* Some anxiety may be observed in group members as the end of the therapeutic process nears. Some active members will display anxiety by growing silent during the termination phase (Abraham et al., 1991). Others may fall asleep. Abraham et al. (1991) feel that at least five sessions should be devoted to termination. Group members should be encouraged to formally say goodbye to the facilitator and other members. This can be accomplished by having each member express what he or she enjoyed most about the group experience. Facilitators should never promise to come back for a visit if they cannot absolutely do so (Burnside, 1986)—it is easier for everyone to say goodbye than to look forward to an event that does not take place. The act of termination is more complicated in open groups because only one or two members terminate and the majority of the members continue in therapy. In such cases the facilitator should ask each member to say goodbye formally and to share how the member terminating will affect him or her (Clark & Vorst, 1994). The person terminating should also share his or her feelings about leaving the group.

Evaluation

It is necessary to monitor the progress of a support group because some participants may demonstrate subtle gains over time that may not be noticed unless detailed records are kept. Factors that should be assessed include the amount of participation and attendance within each group meeting for each individual group member, or both; the content of discussions; and the characteristics and behavior of the group before, during, and after participation in the support group. Summarizing the discussion at the end of each session may be helpful (Caserta & Lund, 1993; Matorin & Zoubok, 1988). Any other information that the group facilitator finds pertinent or interesting should be recorded on a group record form (see exhibit on p. 293). In addition, any unusual group member behaviors, events, or accidents should be reported to nursing staff, family members, or both (Abraham et al., 1991).

Pre- and postassessments should be conducted on each participant to determine the therapeutic gains made or lack thereof. Depending on the goals of the group, a life satisfaction scale (e.g., Life Satisfaction in the Elderly Scale, developed by Salamon & Conte, 1990; see also Chapter 2) or a depression scale (e.g., Geriatric Depression Scale, developed by Brink et al., 1982; see also Chapter 1) should be employed. Progress within the group should be formally monitored using a form similar to that shown on page 293. Progress forms should be completed immediately following the group session because details may be forgotten. Forgetting is particularly likely to occur with less active group members. Although noteworthy impressions may be remembered, details concerning the involvement of each individual may be lost. Follow-up measures may also include a self-report completed by the participants regarding their mood, perception, and insight into self and others, along with activity level and level of social interaction (Weiss, 1994). Some feedback on the group facilitator is also recommended. Regrettably, a form designed to assess facilitator effectiveness does not exist. Questions concerning the facilitator's therapeutic style, personality, understanding, and competence with a particular group should be incorporated into the self-report as an additional scale that can be submitted separately to ensure anonymity (Weiss, 1994).

Challenge of Working with Difficult Group Members

Members monopolizing the group discussion is the most common problem experienced by novice group facilitators (Burnside, 1986). One strategy to contain a member who tends to monopolize the group is to seat the individual near the group facilitator, who can place a restraining hand gently onto the member's arm or hand. Another approach is for the facilitator to interrupt the person periodically, stating that he or she would like to hear what others have to say. The monopolizer could be thanked for initiating the discussion and given the responsibility of encouraging others to share and discuss the issues raised. Lakin (1988)

Group Record Form

Group _____ Date of Session _____ Location _____

Participants	Eye contact	Verbal comments	Nonverbal comments	Support to others	Insightful comments	Disruptive behavior	Notes

Issues raised:

Absent members	Contact date	Reason for absence	Attending next session?	Notes

A Life Worth Living: Practical Strategies for Reducing Depression in Older Adults, by Pearl Mosher-Ashley and Phyllis Barrett. © 1997 Health Professions Press, Inc., Baltimore.

postulated that older people are self-protective and avoid strong, overt reactions to other members. Consequently, critical feedback to some older participants may be more difficult to mobilize. This is problematic when trying to curb long-winded members who tend to monopolize sessions. The group facilitator should not rely on the members to support critical comments to an individual monopolizing a session. This approach may actually discourage participation in the very individuals the facilitator is trying to encourage.

It is the responsibility of group facilitators to provide for the safety of the members (Burnside, 1986). People who are likely to become verbally or physically abusive should not be included in a group. Such individuals may be known to the other members and inhibit group cohesion. An outburst in the group may also prevent members from freely expressing their thoughts and feelings in future meetings. Boundaries may need to be established for people with strong religious or political convictions who feel compelled to convert other members (Burnside, 1986). Setting boundaries can be accomplished by establishing a ground rule that religion and politics cannot be discussed in the group sessions. Older adults who exhibit symptoms of a cognitive disturbance or bipolar disorder should not be included in the group unless their condition has remained stable for a considerable period of time. Burnside (1986) cautions against including hypochondriacal people as well.

Levine and Poston (1980) describe a group intervention for older female psychiatric outpatients with severe character disturbances who were chronic complainers. After encountering some resistance to an analytical group intervention, the therapists terminated the formal group and introduced an alternative informal "coffee bar" approach featuring refreshments; social contact; a forum in which to vent concerns; and brief, individual attention from the therapists. The coffee bar atmosphere led to group cohesion, and the cohesiveness spontaneously generated formal group discussions.

If several difficult members cannot be managed in a group, it may be more effective to combine them into a small subgroup of their own, in which they can receive more individual attention and can cope with group members who are as assertive and emotionally needy.

Groups for Residents of Long-Term Care Facilities

Novice group facilitators tend to underestimate the potential of group members in long-term care facilities (Burnside, 1986). Often, in long-term care settings short-term therapy is conducted for only 6 or 8 weeks because of the frail condition of the residents and limitations in staff time (Weiss, 1994). As mentioned earlier, Weiss (1994) recommends a group be conducted for at least 12–14 weeks, the common duration for short-term therapy. It is critical that staff members be supportive of the residents' involvement in group work. (Abraham et al., 1991; Burnside, 1986). Also, residents are encouraged to freely express their feelings, thoughts, and needs in the group. Staff support is needed if this behavior is to generalize to everyday experience. Most residents of long-term care facilities are expected to be dependent and cooperative. Without active encouragement from the staff, the gains made in the group will probably diminish (Weiss, 1994). Weiss (1994) recommends that staff members participate in their own weekly group therapy program for 1 month as a means of increasing their awareness and empathy toward the residents' situation and to encourage residents' participation in therapy.

Older adults with distinctly different levels of cognitive functioning should not be combined in a group (Burnside, 1986; Weiss, 1994). People who are cognitively alert and verbal will dominate the group and feel that they cannot relate to individuals whose cognitive functioning is impaired. In fact, being placed in the same group may result in lowered self-esteem because people who are cognitively alert will assume that they are perceived to be similar to people who have diminished cognitive skills. Also, losing one's cognitive skills is a major fear for many older adults (Cavanaugh, 1993). Increased intimacy and proximity with people who are cognitively impaired will most likely increase anxiety. People who are less cognitively alert will be reluctant to join in the conversation when placed in a group with people who are cognitively alert. Also, their losses will appear to be greater in comparison to their more able peers.

Prior to each session, the facilitator of a group based in a long-term care facility should meet with each group member for 5–10 minutes (Abraham et al., 1991). Weiss (1994) observed two different types of needs expressed by group members in long-term care settings. The first involved problem-solving needs that were focused around ADLs. The second involved emotional growth needs, such as coping with grief, that are related to the changes experienced as a result of the aging process. Ideally, a group should focus on one of these need areas. Mixing people of different cognitive levels and needs can slow and even inhibit the development of a group focus, group cohesion, and trust, thereby limiting the therapeutic gains to be achieved.

Some residents of long-term care facilities may have difficulty with the open communication and intimacy of a group. Some of these individuals may have limited experience in confiding in people other than family members. Also, the loss of privacy and limited personal space in residential care settings may create more rigid psychosocial boundaries (Weiss, 1994). They may fear revealing themselves, thereby losing the respect of other residents, or becoming too vulnerable.

Group members should attend sessions wearing street clothing (i.e., no bathrobes, nightgowns, pajamas) and prosthetic devices. Failure to do so communicates that to them, the session is not an important function. Also, not wearing a hearing aid or dentures can affect the participants' ability to communicate (Burnside, 1986).

Weiss (1994) recommends that group work be an ongoing activity in long-term care settings. New residents should be encouraged to join a group for 3 months in order to facilitate their adjustment to the new setting. Theme-focused groups could be offered to all residents. Participants who do not resolve their issues by the conclusion of a series of theme-focused group sessions can elect to join another group. If an experienced health care or social services professional is not available to provide group treatment, long-term care facilities may wish to contract with local counselor training programs to become practicum sites for advanced students. Another approach is to contact the local community mental health center about the possibility of asking a therapist to conduct a series of weekly short-term groups. Third-party reimbursements may be obtained from Medicaid or Medicare.

Christenson (1984) designed an interesting variation on a support group for older residents of a nursing facility. The therapist-directed self-help group was designed for residents who were diagnosed as having symptoms of depression or who were at risk for developing such symptoms. Groups averaging five to six members learned to set short-term goals and work toward regaining control over certain areas of functioning. The goals included increasing decision-making ability, increasing abilities in ADLs, increasing flexibility and strengthening areas on the body, pursuing recreational activities, and improving or developing social skills. Group sessions focused on reviewing individual progress toward goals and on completing an activity involving learning social skills such as assertiveness training, planning leisure time, identifying and expressing feelings, and setting goals. Group members were encouraged to interact and provide feedback to each other.

Groups for Older Adults with Cognitive Impairment

The use of support groups has been explored with older people who are undergoing cognitive losses as a result of a dementing illness. Yale (1991) has pointed out that the erosion of cognitive functioning is bewildering and frightening. According to Yale, support groups can reduce the participants' sense of isolation, facilitate the grieving process over the losses being experienced, and enable participants to exchange information and resources concerning coping with the changes taking place.

Relatively little attention has been directed toward providing support groups to older adults with cognitive impairment. In one of the few studies to explore the use of support groups with these older adults Snyder, Quayhagen, Shepherd, and Bower (1995) propose that participants eligible for such a group score 20 or above on the Mini-Mental State Examination (Folstein, Folstein, & McHugh, 1975) or score 100 or above on the Dementia Rating Scale (Mattis, 1988). (Chapter 3 contains more detailed information on the Mini-Mental and the Dementia Rating Scale.) Thompson et al. (1990) recommend that potential participants score at least at the mild dementia phase on the Clinical Dementia Rating Scale (Hughes, Berg, Danzinger, Coben, & Martin, 1982) or a 3 on the Global Deterioration Scale (Reisberg, Ferris, DeLeon, & Crook, 1982) (see Chapter 3). Snyder et al. (1995) employed a format in which patients and caregivers met both together and separately in sessions to discuss personal issues within the context of a structured sequence of topics. In this way the independent needs of both groups were met while providing opportunities to enhance communication and sharing between the two parties. The meetings were structured in an 8-week block, with weekly sessions of $1\frac{1}{2}$ hours' duration. Each session was devoted to a specific topic. An introductory session was followed by sessions on how to cope with memory problems, ADL issues, self-esteem, social and family relationships, legal and financial concerns, and health maintenance. A final session was held to review and handle future issues.

Yale (1995) has written an excellent book on how to develop and carry out a support group for individuals who are in the early stages of Alzheimer's disease and related dementias. She also advocates an 8-week-long, time-limited format, although she indicates that longer sequences of up to 15 weeks have been conducted by others. The meetings last for 90 minutes and average 6–8 participants, depending on the comfort level of the group facilitator. Like Snyder et al. (1995), Yale emphasizes sharing feelings and developing coping strategies within the context of a topical format. Four useful forms have been developed by Yale (1995) to 1) interview and screen prospective participants, 2) record observations of participants during a session, 3) record observations of the group as a whole during a session, and 4) evaluate the impact of the group on participants and caregivers following the conclusion of the group.

When working with people with cognitive impairment, the size of the group should be limited to six. Burnside (1986) recommends that a concerted effort be made to communicate with confused clients. Quite frequently, these clients respond with a nod when asked if they understand what has been said. The nodding may simply reflect their desire for the facilitator to go away. During group sessions, the facilitator should frequently repeat the purpose of the meeting because group members may be anxious, have difficulty remembering, or both.

Groups for Minority Older Adults

Evidence suggests that people from minority groups do not require different therapeutic approaches (Tross & Blum, 1988). Group facilitators, however, must be familiar with and appreciate the cultures, values, customs, and ways of interacting represented by minority participants. When a group is made up of several members of a specific ethnic group and the facilitator does not share the cultural heritage, the facilitator should ask a peer facilitator or cofacilitator to represent the minority group. Efforts should be made to include at least two people from the same ethnic group in a support group (Burnside, 1978). This inclusion will facilitate the group process because people belonging to the ethnic group will be more likely to voice their concerns if they feel they are not alone. They will also be less likely to feel alienated. The decreased sense of alienation may prevent such an individual from terminating from the group.

The Association for the Blind in Melbourne, Australia, has established several ethnic support groups using teleconferencing technology (Gibbons, 1984a). Groups have been developed for French-, Greek-, and Slavic-speaking people, and are run entirely in the native language. The focus of the groups has been on the particular needs of people with visual impairment within the ethnic group. This type of program could be extended easily to other frail, homebound older adults who find comfort in socializing with other members of their ethnic group.

Intergenerational Groups

Group interventions involving people of various ages offer certain advantages. The benefits include better understanding of the developmental phases of the life cycle, an opportunity to act out family roles, an opportunity for older adults to provide support and advice to younger people, and an opportunity for older members to review their values and experiences (Burnside, 1986). However, novice group facilitators should not attempt to undertake an intergenerational group until they have some experience with a more homogeneous group. Burnside (1986) reports that working with group members of the same age will decrease some of the variables with which a novice group facilitator must cope.

Mutual-Help Groups

Mutual-help groups focus on a specific shared issue such as a troubled relationship with an adult child, arthritis, allergies, or urinary incontinence (Bentov et al., 1994). They differ from traditional self-help groups in that the mutual-help group works toward finding solutions to the problems raised by the group members. For example, Samuels and Samuels (1975) describe a group of older adult women who joined together for the purpose of enabling members to continue living in their own homes. The group organized a pool of younger volunteers and paid workers who helped with housekeeping, repairs, transportation, companionship, and a variety of other personal services.

Mutual-help groups may or may not have a facilitator. The facilitator keeps track of the time during each session, so that each person has a chance to speak, and keeps the discussion focused on the theme. Each member is regarded as an expert on his or her problem and able to recognize what is needed. Each member of the group should be encouraged to discuss his or her needs. Members with professional expertise should participate as equals (Bentov et al., 1994).

Telephone Support Groups

Although face-to-face group involvement has advantages, many older adults, most notably those who are visually impaired, physically impaired, or both, have difficulty negotiating attendance at weekly meetings. For these individuals, the telephone can provide a useful means of facilitating group involvement. Telephone support groups can be directed by a therapist or facilitated by a peer. Standard group techniques are carried out in a teleconferencing format.

Participants must become familiar with the technology before they can begin to experience the therapeutic benefits of a teleconferencing group. Many beginners feel uncomfortable about when they should contribute to the ongoing discussion. Some fear that everyone will speak at once and are therefore reluctant to speak at all. One solution to this problem, advocated by Gibbons (1984b), is to assign each person a position around an imaginary clock face. Participants can then take turns speaking in a clockwise direction. As the participants relax and begin to recognize the different tones of voice and word orders of individual members, the discussions become more free-flowing. Some members may experience difficulty concentrating on what is being said and who is saying it. This difficulty tends to be verbalized as a hearing problem. Encouragement from the facilitator, patience, and experience with teleconferencing will increase concentration.

Therapist-Conducted Groups

Professionals interested in conducting telephone-based support groups must locate a sponsor or obtain a grant because the cost can be high. The options available consist of an access fee and a per-minute per-participant rate. This option would require participants to call a toll-free telephone number at the designated time. To schedule an operator-coordinated call, a fee per participant would be added to the per minute rate charge. Some older people could share in the expense of the teleconferencing sessions by paying a fee for participating in the program, but they should not be expected to assume the bulk of the cost.

Evans and Jaureguy (1981) describe a teleconferencing program in which a social worker trained in cognitive-behavioral strategies treated three clients with visual impairment for psychosocial problems over the telephone for 8 consecutive weeks. The highly structured group counseling sessions resulted in lowered self-ratings of depression and loneliness. Involvement in outside social activities and domestic chores increased as well.

Gibbons (1984b) conducted her telephone-based support groups for an average of 8 weeks. Following the termination of a group, she contacted each member for reassessment and offered them the opportunity to participate in further group work, if necessary. Many of the participants developed friendships as a result of their group experience. They exchanged telephone numbers and engaged in regular one-to-one telephone contact.

Peer-Facilitated Groups

In 1979 the Association for the Blind in Victoria, Australia, established a telephone support program called Telelink. In the program peer helpers provide assistance to people with visual impairment, most of whom are older (Albertson, 1982; Gibbons, 1984a, b). Six to eight clients are connected in their own homes with a peer group facilitator and with each other for a 1-hour session. The groups usually meet for 8 weeks, then take a 4-week break. During the break, some clients join special interest groups that discuss topics such as history, football, and music. Thomas and Urbano (1993) assessed the effectiveness of Telelink groups and compared the telephone sessions to Yalom's work on group dynamics in terms of their therapeutic effect. The group data indicated that the main benefits of Telelink were the provision of support, sharing of information, discussion of current affairs, and expression of humor. Using cofacilitators was found to be necessary in balancing the flow of conversation and ensuring all members were involved without one dominating the session.

The Telelink program was particularly effective in helping people belonging to various minority groups. These individuals used the telephone support group to discuss adjustment issues and past experiences. This finding suggests that teleconferencing would be an effective strategy to provide support to frail older adults who are experiencing a common problem (e.g., bereavement, loneliness, family conflicts).

Computer Alternatives

Given the cost involved in carrying out a support group over the telephone, a more practical alternative may be to employ the procedural aspects of Telelink programs using the Internet. Although many older people find learning to use a computer daunting, some have begun to explore the benefits of this technology. SeniorNet, established on the Internet in 1986, has provided information and a source of friendship and support to 15,000 older adults (Dickerson, 1995). Older adults are able to "log on" and visit a "chat room" in the organization's station on the provider, America Online.

Equipment is being designed with the sole function of accessing the Internet (Elmer-Dewitt, 1996). With the cost projected at $300–$500, this equipment will be considerably less expensive than current computer systems, making access to the Internet available to a wider audience. WebTV is a service that allows individuals to access the Internet through their television set with the use of a set-top box and keyboard that closely resemble a home video game (contact Magnavox, Philips Consumer Electronics Corp., 800-531-0039, for more information).

As in other instances, the technology that many fear leads to dehumanization may, in fact, provide an invaluable source of contact for those who might otherwise be isolated by distance, disability, or other factors. Still, there is no substitute for the face-to-face contact that can tell a health care provider or a friend much more than words can communicate about an older person's physical and emotional states, and that can also lead to improvement in an older person's overall sense of well-being.

REFERENCES

Abraham, I., Niles, S., Thiel, B., Siarkowski, K., & Cowling, W.R. (1991). Therapeutic work with depressed elderly. *Nursing Clinics of North America, 26,* 635–650.

Albertson, L. (1982). Telelink rescues housebound. *Australian Society, 1,* 9–10.

Benitez-Bloch, R. (1988). Including the active elderly in group psychotherapy. In B. Maclennan, S. Saul, & M.B. Weiner (Eds.), *Group psychotherapies for the elderly* (pp. 33–41). Madison, CT: International Universities Press.

Bentov, M., Smith, D., Siegal, D.L., & Doress-Worters, P.B. (1994). Aging and well-being. In P.B. Doress-Worters & D.L. Siegal (Eds.), *The new ourselves, growing older* (pp. 3–21). New York: Touchstone.

Berkman, L.F. (1985). The relationship of social networks and social support to morbidity and mortality. In S. Cohen & L. Syme (Eds.), *Social support and health* (pp. 241–262). Orlando, FL: Academic Press.

Biegel, D. (1984). *Building support networks for the elderly: Theory and applications.* Beverly Hills, CA: Sage Publications.

Bratter, B. (1986). Peer counseling for older adults. *Generations, 10*(3), 49–50.

Brink, T.L., Yesavage, J.A., Lum, O., Heersema, P., Adey, M., & Rose, T.L. (1982). Screening tests for geriatric depression. *Clinical Gerontologist, 1,* 37–43.

Burnside, I. (1978). *Working with the elderly: Group process and techniques.* Monterey, CA: Wadsworth Health Sciences.

Burnside, I. (1986). *Working with the elderly: Group process and techniques* (2nd ed.). Monterey, CA: Wadsworth Health Sciences.

Capuzzi, D., Gross, D., & Friel, S. (1990). Recent trends in group work with elders. *Generations, 14*(1), 43–48.

Carstensen, L.L. (1993). Motivation for social contact across the life span: A theory of socioeconomic selectivity. In J.E. Jacobs (Ed.) *Nebraska symposium on motivation, Vol. 40, Developmental perspectives on motivation* (pp. 209–254). Lincoln: University of Nebraska Press.

Carstensen, L.L. (1995). Evidence for a life-span theory of socioemotional selectivity. *Current Directions in Psychological Science, 4,* 151–156.

Caserta, M., & Lund, D. (1993). Intrapersonal resources and the effectiveness of self-help groups for bereaved older adults. *Gerontologist, 33,* 619–629.

Cavanaugh, C. (1993). *Adult development and aging* (2nd ed.). Pacific Grove, CA: Brooks/Cole.

Chappell, N.L., & Badger, M. (1989). Social isolation and well-being. *Journal of Gerontology, 44,* S169–S176.

Christenson, I. (1984). Self-help groups for depressed elderly in the nursing home. *PT & OT in Geriatrics, 3*(4), 39–47.

Clark, W., & Vorst, V. (1994). Group therapy with chronically depressed geriatric patients. *Journal of Psychosocial Nursing, 32*(5), 9–13.

Corey, G. (1985). *Theory and practice of group counseling* (2nd ed.). Monterey, CA: Brooks/Cole.

Depner, C., & Ingersoll, B. (1982). Employment status and social support: The experience of mature women. In M. Szinovacz (Ed.), *Women's retirement: Policy implications of recent research* (pp. 61–76). Beverly Hills, CA: Sage Publications.

Dickerson, J.F. (1995, Special Issue, Spring). Never too old. *Time, 145*(12), p. 41.

Dunlop, J., Skorney, B., & Hamilton, J. (1982). Group treatment for elderly alcoholics and their families. *Group Work with Groups, 5,* 87–92.

Elmer-Dewitt, P. (1996, January 22). Why JAVA is hot. *Time,* pp. 58–60.

Evans, R.L., & Jaureguy, B.M. (1981). Group therapy by phone: A cognitive behavioral program for visually impaired elderly. *Social Work in Health Care, 72,* 79–90.

Field, D., & Minkler, M. (1988). Continuity and change in social support between young-old and old-old or very-old age. *Journal of Gerontology, 43,* P100–P106.

Fisher, D.B. (1988). Activity group psychotherapy for the inner-city elderly. In B. Maclennan, S. Saul, & M.B. Weiner (Eds.), *Group psychotherapies for the elderly* (pp. 121–130). Madison, CT: International Universities Press.

Folstein, M.F., Folstein, S.E., & McHugh, P.R. (1975). Mini-Mental State: A practical method for grading the cognitive state of patients for the clinician. *Journal of Psychiatric Research, 12,* 189–198.

Gallagher, D. (1981). Behavioral group therapy with elderly depressives: An experimental study. In D. Upper & S. Ross (Eds.), *Behavioral group therapy* (pp. 187–224). Champaign, IL: Research Press.

Gibbons, J. (1984a). Telelink: Teleconferencing and social welfare services. *Programmed Learning & Educational Technology, 21,* 329–332.

Gibbons, J. (1984b). Live wires. *Social Work Today, 15*(24), 14–15.

Hughes, C.P., Berg, L., Danzinger, W.L., Coben, L.A., & Martin, R.L. (1982). A new scale for the rating of dementia. *British Journal of Psychiatry, 140,* 566–572.

Kahn, R.L., & Antonucci, T.C. (1980). Convoys over the life course: Attachment, roles, and social support. In P.B. Baltes & O.G. Brim (Eds.), *Life-span development and behavior*. New York: Academic Press.

Keith, P.M., Hill, K., Goudy, W.J., & Powers, E.A. (1984). Confidants and well-being: A note on male friendships in old age. *Gerontologist, 24*, 318–320.

Kemp, B.J., Corgiat, M., & Gill, C. (1991–1992). Effects of brief cognitive-behavioral group psychotherapy on older persons with and without disabling illness. *Behavior, Health, and Aging, 2*, 21–28.

Knight, B. (1989). *Outreach with the elderly: Community education, assessment, and therapy*. New York: New York University Press.

Lakin, M. (1988). Group therapies with the elderly: Issues and prospects. In B. Maclennan, S. Saul, & M.B. Weiner (Eds.), *Group psychotherapies for the elderly* (pp. 43–55). Madison, CT: International Universities Press.

Lee, G.R., & Ishii-Kuntz, M. (1987). Social isolation, loneliness, and emotional well-being among the elderly. *Research on Aging, 9*, 459–482.

Leszcz, M., Feigenbaum, F., Sadavoy, J., & Robinson, A. (1985). A men's group: Psychotherapy of elderly men. *International Journal of Group Psychotherapy, 35*, 177–196.

Levine, B.F., & Poston, M. (1980). A modified group treatment for elderly narcissistic patients. *International Journal of Group Psychotherapy, 30*, 153–167.

Lothstein, L.M. (1988). Psychodynamic group therapy with the active elderly: A preliminary investigation. In B. Maclennan, S. Saul, & M.B. Weiner (Eds.), *Group psychotherapies for the elderly* (pp. 67–87). Madison, CT: International Universities Press.

Matorin, S., & Zoubok, B. (1988). Group psychotherapy with geriatric outpatients: A model for treatment and training. In B. Maclennan, S. Saul, & M.B. Weiner (Eds.), *Group psychotherapies for the elderly* (pp. 107–119). Madison, CT: International Universities Press.

Mattis, S. (1988). *Dementia rating scale: Professional manual*. Odessa, FL: Psychological Assessment Resources.

McIntosh, W.A., Shifflett, P.A., & Picou, J.S. (1989). Social support, stressful events, strain, dietary intake, and the elderly. *Medical Care, 27*, 140–153.

McWhorter, J.M. (1980). Group therapy for high utilizers of clinic facilities. In I.M. Burnside (Ed.), *Psychosocial nursing care of the aged* (pp. 114–125). New York: McGraw-Hill.

Minkler, M. (1985). Social support and health of the elderly. In S. Cohen & S.L. Syme (Eds.), *Social support and health* (pp. 199–216). New York: Academic Press.

Morgan, L.L. (1988). Age differences in social network participation. *Journal of Gerontology, 43*, S129–S137.

Mosher-Ashley, P.M. (1994a). Diagnoses assigned and issues brought up in therapy by older adults receiving outpatient treatment. *Clinical Gerontologist, 15*, 37–65.

Mosher-Ashley, P.M. (1994b). Termination from therapy and persistence patterns of elderly clients in a community mental health center. *Gerontologist, 34*, 180–189.

O'Bryant, L.L. (1985). Neighbor's support of older widows who live alone in their own homes. *Gerontologist, 25*, 305–310.

Peters, G.R., & Kaiser, M.A. (1985). The role of friends and neighbors in providing social support. In W.J. Sauer & R.T. Coward (Eds.), *Social support networks and the care of the elderly*. New York: Springer Publishing.

Puppolo, D.H. (1980). Co-leadership with a group of stroke patients. In I.M. Burnside (Ed.), *Psychosocial nursing care of the aged* (pp. 253–270). New York: McGraw-Hill.

Reisberg, B., Ferris, S.H., DeLeon, M.J., & Crook, T. (1982). The global deterioration scale for assessment of primary degenerative dementia. *American Journal of Psychiatry, 139*, 1136–1139.

Reisman, J.M. (1988). An indirect measure of the value of friendship for aging men. *Journal of Gerontology, 43,* P109–P110.

Roberto, K.A., & Scott, J.P. (1986). Equity considerations in the friendships of older adults. *Journal of Gerontology, 41,* 241–247.

Sadavoy, J., & Leszcz, M. (1987). *Treating the elderly with psychotherapy: The scope for change in later life.* Madison, CT: International Universities Press.

Salamon, M.J., & Conte, V.A. (1990). *The Life Satisfaction in the Elderly Scale.* Woodmere, NY: Adult Development Center, Inc.

Samuels, M., & Samuels, N. (1975). *Seeing with the mind's eye.* New York: Random House.

Snyder, L., Quayhagen, M.P., Shepherd, S., & Bower, D. (1995). Supportive seminar groups: An intervention for early stage dementia patients. *Gerontologist, 35,* 691–695.

Stone, I., & Koonin, M. (1986). A support group in a retirement home. *Aging, 352,* 18–20.

Syme, L.S., & Berkman, L. (1990). Social class, susceptibility, and sickness. In P. Conrad & R. Kern (Eds.), *The sociology of health and illness: Critical perspectives* (pp. 28–33). New York: St. Martin's Press.

Thomas, T., & Urbano, J. (1993). A telephone group support program for the visually-impaired elderly. *Clinical Gerontologist, 13*(2), 61–71.

Thompson, L.W., Wagner, B., Zeiss, A., & Gallagher, D. (1990). Cognitive/behavioral therapy with early stage Alzheimer's patients: An exploratory view of the utility of this approach. In E. Light & B.D. Lebowitz (Eds.), *Alzheimer's disease treatment and family stress: Directions for research* (pp. 383–397). Rockville, MD: National Institute of Mental Health.

Tross, S., & Blum, J. (1988). A review of group therapy with the older adult: Practice and research. In B. Maclennan, S. Saul, & M.B. Weiner (Eds.), *Group psychotherapies for the elderly* (pp. 3–29). Madison, CT: International Universities Press.

Weiss, J.C. (1994). Group therapy with older adults in long-term care settings: Research and clinical cautions and recommendations. *Journal for Specialists in Group Work, 19,* 22–29.

Wortman, C.B., & Coneway, D.R. (1985). Reactions to victims of life crisis: Support attempts that fail. In I.G. Sarason & B.R. Sarason (Eds.), *Social support: Theory, research, and applications* (pp. 463–489). Dordrect, Germany: Martinus Nijhoff.

Yale, R. (1991). Support groups for newly diagnosed Alzheimer's clients. *Clinical Gerontologist, 12,* 86–89.

Yale, R. (1995). *Developing support groups for individuals with early-stage Alzheimer's disease: Planning, implementation and evaluation.* Baltimore: Health Professions Press.

Yalom, I.D. (1985). *The theory and practice of group psychotherapy* (3rd ed.). New York: Basic Books.

Yalom, I.D., & Terrazas, F. (1968). Group therapy for psychotic elderly patients. *American Journal of Nursing, 68,* 1690–1694.

Zimberg, S. (1969). Outpatient geriatric psychiatric in an urban ghetto with non-professional workers. *American Journal of Psychiatry, 125,* 1697–1702.

Appendix
Resources for Groups Dealing with Specific Problems

Caserta, M., & Lund, D. (1993). (widows and widowers).

Dunlop, J., Skorney, B., & Hamilton, J. (1982). Group treatment for elderly alcoholics and their families. *Group Work with Groups, 5,* 87–92. (alcoholism in older adults)

McWhorter, J.M. (1988). Group therapy for high utilizers of clinic facilities. In I.M. Burnside (Ed.), *Psychosocial nursing care of the aged* (pp. 114–125). New York: McGraw-Hill. (frequent utilizers of medical facilities)

Puppolo, D.H. (1980). Co-leadership with a group of stroke patients. In I.M. Burnside (Ed.), *Psychosocial nursing care of the aged* (pp. 253–270). New York: McGraw-Hill. (stroke victims)

Snyder, L., Quayhagen, M.P., Shepherd, S., & Bower, D. (1995). Supportive seminar groups: An intervention for early stage dementia patients. *Gerontologist, 35,* 691–695. (people with cognitive impairment)

Yale, R. (1995). *Developing support groups for individuals with early-stage Alzheimer's disease: Planning, implementation and evaluation.* Baltimore: Health Professions Press. (people with cognitive impairment)

"Ah, my poor friend, men have sunk very low . . .
They've let their bodies become mute and they
only speak with their mouths."

Nikos Kazantzakis, *Zorba The Greek*

Let's Get Physical

Exercise

The benefits of regular exercise to a person's health and well-being are widely recognized. We can all point to older adults whose energy and vitality we hope to emulate in our own later years. One of the authors' aunt and uncle, at ages 80 and 81, respectively, are active participants in many of the activities offered by their neighborhood senior center. They play volleyball at least once a week at the center, bowl in a senior league each Thursday morning, and square dance almost every Friday night. Like other active older adults, they exemplify the fact that exercise is an antidote to the deterioration of health that is usually associated with aging (Shephard, 1994).

Most older adults, however, rarely participate in exercise programs. The reasons for this vary. The emphasis on exercise and fitness in their generation usually ended after elementary or secondary school, or perhaps with military training (Edmunds, 1991); the phenomenon of health clubs and exercise equipment for home use is largely associated with the baby boom generation that followed. Socioeconomic status early in life seems to influence attitudes toward exercise in later life, and cost can be a factor, especially for people living on a fixed income (Shephard, 1994). In addition, many professionals who care for older adults, as well as the adults themselves, believe that exercise is too dangerous and the risks for injury too high (Dawe & Curran-Smith, 1994; Weiss, 1988). Others reason that it is too late to bother with exercise, that it does no good for individuals past "a certain age" (Jamieson, 1982).

Contrary to these fears and beliefs, programs consisting of range-of-motion (ROM) exercises, strength training, and carefully monitored cardiovascular exercises can produce phenomenal results for older adults. Exercise improves muscular strength and range of motion and helps to maintain bone mass, prolonging the capacity to perform the independent activities of daily living (ADLs) (Dawe & Curran-Smith, 1994; Flatten, Wilhite, & Reyes-Watson, 1988; Hooker, 1990). Although there is some risk when stress is imposed on an older person's body, the physiological benefits of regular exercise have been found to far outweigh the costs of a sedentary lifestyle (Waldo, Ide, & Thomas, 1995). A longitudinal study that included the responses of 6,780 participants found a strong correlation between better health and being more active than one's peers, including walking 1 or more miles at least once a week (Wolinsky, Stump, & Clark, 1995). Another 10-year longitudinal study found that of inactivity, obesity, and smoking, inactivity had the most significant negative impact on the health of older people (Forbes, 1992).

In addition to the physical benefits of exercise, studies have shown that regular exercise may also have psychological benefits: Body and mind are not easily separated. Often, there is a reciprocal effect between the mental and physical consequences of an illness. When older people do not feel well physically, there is an inclination for them to become less mobile and therefore to be exposed to fewer stimuli. The result is often a generalized feeling of malaise. Consequently, people's dependency needs tend to increase. In addition, instead of reaching out for help and connection to the outside world, older people may become introspective and experience a sense of isolation and loneliness as well as poor self-esteem (Forbes, 1992). Several studies have suggested that exercise may help to improve self-esteem, cognitive performance, and body image (Dawe & Curran-Smith, 1994; Kirkcaldy & Shephard, 1990).

Some studies have revealed positive mood effects, such as relief from mild depression, resulting from exercise (Brown, 1992; Fillingham & Blumenthal, 1993; Gitlin et al., 1992). Studies examining exercise and mood effects conflict, however. Most older adults report "feeling better" after participation in an exercise program (Gitlin et al., 1992). Whether this feeling is the result of an actual reduction in depression or the opportunity to participate in a meaningful, goal-oriented program with peers is not known (Gitlin et al., 1992). An exercise program can provide an opportunity for social interaction, which is often lacking in many older adults' lives. This opportunity alone can bring meaning and enjoyment to some older adults.

Exercise programs for healthy older people and older people with chronic conditions such as arthritis, diabetes, or cardiovascular disease come in many varieties and are feasible in numerous settings. Older adults living independently and those living in congregate housing or in long-term care settings can all benefit from some type of exercise program (Flatten, Wilhite, & Reyes-Watson, 1988). Although part of the benefit of an exercise program may stem from actual participation in a group, it is also possible to provide an exercise program on an individual basis.

Activities such as aerobic dance, yoga, or tai chi chuan (also known simply as tai chi) require little equipment and can be led by an informally trained staff person or volunteer at a senior center or in the day room of a congregate living or nursing facility. Activities such as strength training can be offered using a minimal amount of equipment (e.g., a pair of 2-lb dumbbells, resistance bands), a well-trained facilitator, and perhaps a slightly more specific kind of space. ROM exercises, which can be performed in a seated position and even in bed, can be implemented by a nurse or other staff member in a medical setting. Walking is excellent exercise both for older adults living in a long-term care facility and those living independently. Whatever exercise program is chosen should be appropriate for the individual, and his or her physician should be consulted before any exercise progam is initiated.

USE OF EXERCISE THERAPY WITH OLDER ADULTS LIVING INDEPENDENTLY

Mr. and Mrs. Reed, a couple in their 70s, are the instructors of a tai chi class for older adults at a small town council on aging. "I'm no expert," laughs Mrs. Reed, relating that she and her husband learned what they know about the Chinese art from classes they took at the local community college. The Reeds were so taken with the exercise program, which stresses slow movement and deep breathing as various extremities and even internal organs are targeted for attention, that they wanted to share it with others. For several years now they have offered a 1-hour Wednesday afternoon class to older adults.

The group meets in a small gymnasium that has a hardwood floor and a small stage at one end, where the Reeds, both slim and agile, with perfect posture and much grace, alternately model the "form" for the group. Their students range in age from the 60s to the 80s, including one gentleman who remembers watching his own grandmother perform the traditional exercises when he was a child in his native Shanghai. Each session includes about 15 minutes of warm-up movements, followed by 15–30 minutes of a traditional sequence of movements (i.e., "form") set to calm, quiet music, which almost masks the sound of children playing in an adjacent room. Then the group generally breaks into smaller groups, some resting and chatting, some practicing particular elements of the exercise with one of the Reeds, before reconvening for one last synchronized repetition of the day's program.

"I feel great when I come here, and I feel great when I leave," says one woman who has been a regular participant for 2 years. She suffers from minor heart problems and has some difficulty with her legs, occasionally taking a break in the middle of an exercise session. Tai chi has had such a positive impact on her physical health and overall sense of well-being that she now practices it each morning on her own, often concentrating on specific elements associated with improvement in the function of the heart. Recently, she started taking lessons in country line dancing ("The instructor says I can substitute something for the jumps") and plans to cool down after this strenuous exercise by volunteering to be a "grandmother rocker" for the babies in the day care area. Other group members comment, "I feel better about myself," because of the tai chi class, and that the class provides "great exercise and a feeling of tranquility and well-being." "There would be a big hole in my life without these sessions," says one woman. As a result of tai chi, says another, "I am on the road to being more in contact with my *real* self." (Sneed & Mosher-Ashley, 1997)

An exercise program can be designed in several ways for older adults living independently. A group program is ideal for most people. A community center, adult day center, senior center, church, or local school is an appropriate setting for gathering as long as the location is accessible to the participants through public or other modes of transportation. One illness prevention-oriented health education program initiated in several large senior centers in New York served 7,000 older adults who demonstrated nutritional improvement, weight loss, and improvement in exercise level (Cox & Monk, 1989). After 10 months of weekly exercise classes, participants in tai chi classes at a senior center in Massachusetts reported improvements in balance, leg strength, posture, concentration, and the ability to relax (Hitchner, 1995).

Local long-term care facilities and hospitals may offer some type of program that invites older adults from the community to join them on a weekly or biweekly basis. For example, a supervised exercise program at the Veterans Administration Hospital in Durham, North Carolina, included older participants with chronic illnesses such as arthritis, hypertension, and heart disease, as well as healthy older people, and produced improvement in participants in all areas assessed. The participants in the program were primarily military veterans between the ages of 65 and 75 who used an outpatient clinic at the hospital. In the program they exercised 3 times a week for 90 minutes at 70% of each participant's maximum capacity. The exercises included stationary cycling, stretching, weight training, and walking. Pre- and postassessments were conducted, with the participants' "before" status serving as the control. A registered nurse explained the program goals and exercise activities and obtained patient histories to assess for coronary risk. Balance, range of motion, and joint pain were also evaluated, and stress tests were performed. Problems requiring treatment were attended to before the program began, and no one was excluded for health reasons. The outcomes assessed were cardiovascular fitness, flexibility, and strength. Although preexisting chronic disease did seem to correlate with the likelihood of participants dropping out of the program before the 4-month assessment, those who persevered through the 6th month committed to the program. The study showed that it is possible to carry out a regular exercise program for older people, even those who are chronically ill, that results in improved cardiovascular fitness.

Further research is needed to determine the best type and frequency of exercise programs for older adults, and more consideration needs to be given to making accommodations for older people with conditions such as arthritis. In addition, researchers are interested in whether the beneficial effects of an exercise program can be long term for older people, as they are for middle-age people. Preliminary findings suggest that older adults may be more willing and able to adopt more active lifestyles than might be expected, given their desire to maintain their health and independence (Morey et al., 1989).

An alternative to attending a group exercise program is to bring an individually designed program directly into the older adult's home once or twice a week (Fastiggi & Mosher-Ashley, 1997). This arrangement may be ideal for people who are unable to leave their homes or who do not have access to transportation. A visiting nurse or a relative or friend could assist a bedridden older person in ROM exercises that can be performed while seated or could help an ambulatory older adult to maximize mobility through assisted walking in the adult's home. Although this type of program does not have the benefits of a large social gathering, the individual attention to the older person's needs is a plus.

USE OF EXERCISE THERAPY WITH OLDER ADULTS LIVING IN CONGREGATE HOUSING OR LONG-TERM CARE FACILITIES

At 86, Mrs. Mason has survived her husband by some 20 years, as well as two bouts with cancer. Among other disabilities, she has painful arthritis in her hands and back, which makes most sitting positions uncomfortable and necessitated her giving up her tradition of writing Christmas notes to scattered friends and family. Failing eyesight has already made her dependent on others for transportation, and a hiatal hernia and the loss of her sense of smell has taken most of the joy out of eating. Mrs. Mason had been receiving loving care from her younger sister, but as the disabilities mounted, her sister realized she needed help. She enlisted the assistance of a visiting nurse, but eventually even the nurse could not provide the level of care Mrs. Mason required. Reluctantly, her sister placed her in a nursing facility.

The coaxing and cajoling, first of the visiting nurse and later of the nursing facility staff, aimed at getting Mrs. Mason to walk and exercise were met with uncharacteristic resistance (she had always been timid and low in self-confidence). Family members who visited her at the facility noted that other residents found the notion that exercise was important to be foolish and either resisted completely or went along with the staff's suggestions or with an organized program in a mechanical or halfhearted way.

Traditionally, the activity level of older residents of nursing facilities is low; in fact, only about 50% of the residents in the facilities involved in one study indicated a willingness to participate in an exercise program being offered. However, those who are willing are quite enthusiastic about overcoming the limits imposed by facility life and their own infirmities (McMurdo & Rennie, 1994). Older adults need to be encouraged in a positive fashion to participate in and commit to an exercise program.

For older adults living either in a long-term care facility or in congregate housing, the ideal exercise program is one that is conducted on the premises. A recreation room or community area is an appropriate area for an exercise program as long as there is ample space. It is important to coordinate the day and time of the sessions so that they do not conflict with other activities. Exercise to musical accompaniment is a popular activity with few requirements for sophisticated equipment. A variation to accommodate people who are not physically fit is seated exercise to music, which can be conducted in a group format, much like an aerobics class. One program involved volunteers at randomly selected nursing facilities in twice-weekly, 45-minute seated exercise sessions. Among other gains made, this group of frail older adults showed improvement in quadriceps strength, suggesting that it is possible to train the muscles of even old–old (age 80 and older) people (McMurdo & Rennie, 1994).

Another option for older adults living in a long-term care facility is to bring an individually designed program to them in their rooms several times a week. This type of program is ideal for older adults who are bedridden or those who for other reasons cannot participate in a group. One study found some improvement in the short-term memory of older adults with cognitive impairment who were encouraged to perform slow, rhythmic motions while seated and to take short walks. Researchers found that a single session of these low–intensity exercises improved their short-term memory for at least 30 minutes following the session (Dawe & Moore-Orr, 1995). Such exercises could easily be directed by nurses, nursing assistants, or recreational personnel and incorporated into the daily routine of older adults, but staffing shortages in facilities may create obstacles. For example, whereas one study indicated that a walking program for residents of nursing facilities both benefited frail older residents and provided nurses with valuable information about their actual ability to walk, at least one director of nursing cited insufficient staff to ensure the safety of the residents as a deterrent to implementing a walking program (Spier & Meis, 1994). This is a potentially tragic problem, given that the researchers in this study found the strongest indicator of early death among the residents to be "the presence of a mild impairment of mobility" (p. 277). Typically, physical therapy is undertaken early in the recovery process and then discontinued, but frail older people regain mobility at different rates. Spier and Meis found evidence of continued progress in ambulation long after physical therapy had been terminated. Because this type of individual program requires one-to-one attention, training family members or friends to help the older adult with the exercises may be a solution. This strategy has the added benefit of giving the family member or friend a productive task to do and may lessen the pain associated with interacting with a loved one with cognitive impairment.

Precautions to Take and Accommodations to Make in Implementing an Exercise Program for Older Adults

Exercise fitness programs for older adults are becoming popular throughout the United States. These programs can be found at or in hospital wellness centers, neighborhood senior centers, adult residence complexes, churches, and other community organization centers. Unfortunately, few of these programs employ a program director specifically trained in the physiology and exercise needs of older adults. Although there are many benefits to be gained by older adults through appropriate exercise, there are also very real health risks when an exercise program is not designed with the needs of older people in mind (Forbes, 1992).

Exercise falls into two general categories: dynamic and static. *Dynamic exercise* involves the rhythmic contraction and relaxation of large muscle groups over extended periods of time. The goal of dynamic exercise is to improve cardiorespiratory fitness. This exercise is sometimes called aerobic, isotonic, or endurance exercise, and includes such activities as aerobic floor exercise or dance. In contrast, *static exercise* involves the continuous contraction of a muscle group to the point of fatiguing it. Sometimes called anaerobic, isometric, or resistive exercise, it includes such activities as weightlifting, pushups, and pullups. Some static exercise is inappropriate for older adults, especially those with chronic illnesses, because it increases the work of the heart and can lead to acute elevation of the blood pressure (Edmunds, 1991). However, studies in the mid-1990s have indicated that some older adults can safely undertake strength training programs and benefit from them. Strength training can help prevent the loss of oxygen capacity and muscle and bone mass that occurs with aging, as well as prevent weight gain (Smith, 1996). Participation in a strength training program has also been shown to improve dietary intake for older adult women (Tucker, Harris, & Martin, 1996) and may reduce the incidence of both vertebral and nonvertebral fractures in women with osteoporosis (Sambrook & Krucoff, 1996).

Most important for facilitators to remember when beginning an exercise program in any situation is to obtain approval from each participant's physician prior to the beginning of the program. One way of doing this is to submit the proposed exercise program to the physician, explaining each exercise to be included, the frequency and length of sessions, and any other pertinent information (Weiss, 1988). The physician will review the proposal and add extra exercises or delete any exercises that are inappropriate for his or her patient. In addition, the physician will advise the patient of any special precautions that must be taken. For example, exercise can affect insulin dosage requirements and can have an impact on blood pressure levels. A person's aerobic capacity is also affected by the existence of cardiovascular disease and by the use of beta-blockers. Participants who use tranquilizers or diuretics may experience dizziness and, potentially, falls. People with musculoskeletal disease require additional protection against damage to joints and bones (Forbes, 1992). Most physicians will be delighted that their patients are beginning an exercise program. However, some circumstances may warrant the recommendation that there be no exercise at all, and this decision must be respected for reasons of safety and liability (Weiss, 1988).

Once a program is undertaken, it is important that the facilitator help the participants be aware of their own bodies. They should monitor their breathing and be able to talk comfortably during exercise. The instructor should observe participants closely and ensure that each exercise is being performed correctly. Older adults' joints, tendons, and ligaments move less freely and are less elastic than those of younger adults. Their bones are more brittle and can break easily, and often, their muscles are not as strong as they once were.

The facilitator should also ensure that the participants are not overdoing their workout by watching them for body and facial signals (e.g., tentative movements, grimaces). Excessive exercise can have adverse physical and psychological consequences (Kirkcaldy & Shephard, 1990). Facilitators should know how and be able to teach participants how to spot signs of overexertion or exhaustion and when to slow down or stop exercising. The signs of overexertion or exhaustion are being out of breath, experiencing chest or stomach pains, experiencing cramps, experiencing unusual or unfamiliar pain *of any kind*—"going for the burn" is dangerous, and sweating excessively (Flatten, Wilhite, & Reyes-Watson, 1988). Special precautions should be taken during summer or humid weather: exercise should be less vigorous and participants should be encouraged to drink extra water (i.e., more than the amount they usually drink) both before and after exercising (Allen & Steinkohl, 1987). If any of the danger signs occur, the exercise session should be stopped. If a participant feels lightheaded, dizzy, or nauseous, feels pain in the left arm, or feels digestive heartburn, the session should be stopped immediately and the person should lie down, preferably on a couch, bed, or exercise mat. The person's doctor should be called and no attempt should be made to give water or medicine, unless nitroglycerin is prescribed and available. Notes should be made, if possible, as to when the problem began and the symptoms and changes experienced. The exercise program should be reevaluated at a later time (Flatten, Wilhite, & Reyes-Watson, 1988).

Falls may occur during an exercise therapy session. To prevent falls, older adults should exercise while being supported by or sitting in a chair (Jamieson, 1982; Weiss, 1988). Participants should always be helped into a safe position before beginning exercise. If a fall does occur, it is best not to try to help the participant to get up. The person should be reassured, calmed, and encouraged to lie still for awhile. After the person is calm, inquiries should be made as to whether any pain is felt. If the person does not feel pain, he or she should be helped to gently move one limb at a time. If the person continues to not feel pain, it is safe to help the person to stand. If pain exists in any joint or bone, the person should be covered with a blanket and his or her physician should be called (Flatten, Wilhite, & Reyes-Watson, 1988).

Although there are risks for anyone who exercises, serious risks such as heart attack or broken bones are actually quite rare. If appropriate precautions are taken, even older people with chronic illnesses can enjoy the benefits of exercise (Edmunds, 1991). For example, although exercises can be beneficial for people with arthritis, no part of the body that is painful should be exercised (Weiss, 1988).

Session length should also be limited to approximately 60 minutes because most older adults have limited energy level and attention span.

Exercise programs are feasible for older adults in that they usually do not require many or expensive materials. Obviously, a program involving the use of sophisticated weightlifting equipment would need to be carried out in a well-outfitted gymnasium. Some strength training exercises may require the use of weights or props. Although these pieces of equipment are not mandatory, they may help to increase muscle strength over time. It is not necessary to purchase expensive weights, however. Cans of food, sand-filled plastic bottles with handles, and socks filled with beans can all be used as weights. In addition, bicycle inner tubes from flat tires or elastic surgical tubing from medical supply stores can be used as resistance bands for strength training (Flatten, Wilhite, & Reyes-Watson, 1988; Jamieson, 1982).

Yoga, tai chi, aerobic exercise, and dance require little more than a space large enough to accommodate the participants and their movements. The ideal room is one having a carpeted or wood floor, which is less resistant to falls and provides more of a cushion for joints. Armless straight-back chairs can be used for support and safety during exercising. The room should be well-lit and air conditioned or heated. The room should contain a clock with a second hand so that participants can check their target heart rate periodically (Weiss, 1988).

Participants should be dressed in comfortable clothes that allow a full range of motion. At least one study indicates that like younger people, older people tend to experience "physique anxiety," a self-consciousness about the body's appearance, and that many older people avoid exercise because of this anxiety (McAuley, Bane, Rudolph, & Lox, 1995). The recommendation that participants wear loose, sweatsuit-like clothing may circumvent this problem. Proper shoes, with no hard soles or heels, should be worn. Tennis shoes are acceptable (Flatten, Wilhite, & Reyes-Watson, 1988; Weiss, 1988).

Music can be a pleasant accompaniment to the exercise sessions. However, its inclusion is dependent on the instructor/facilitator. If music is desired the selections should correspond to the tempo of the exercises and to the preferences of the participants. A range of music styles makes the class more interesting (Weiss, 1988). A portable cassette or compact disc player is probably the most economical and convenient source of musical accompaniment.

According to Forbes (1992), the primary criteria in selecting an exercise activity should be the safety of its use by the participants, the level of interest the activity holds for the participants, and the improvement of cardiorespiratory endurance; improvement in muscular strength and endurance are less important goals. Once an appraisal of the health of each participant has been made and once it is understood that the most appropriate kind of exercise for older participants is regular, moderate exercise, the program can be implemented.

IMPLEMENTATION OF EXERCISE THERAPY

When implementing an exercise program for older adults, the first step is to designate a facilitator/instructor for the program. The best models seem to involve volunteers and workers within existing networks of service to older people. An exercise program can be integrated into a therapeutic recreation or occupational therapy program within a facility. It is suggested that facilitators/instructors attend a training program in order to orient themselves to the special characteristics of older adults as well as the necessary procedures for safe and effective exercise for these individuals. Many local YMCA programs offer this type of training.

Choosing a site is the second step. As mentioned earlier in the chapter, the room should be spacious, properly cooled or heated, have carpeted or hardwood floors, and have a clock with a second hand. Necessary props such as chairs, broomsticks, resistance bands, and weights should be obtained or made, and music, if desired, should be chosen and prepared for the sessions. After proper approval has been received from all participants' physicians, an appropriate exercise program can be designed (see p. 315 for a sample program planning form). Many free pamphlets, books, and videotapes are available describing specific exercises for older adults and outlining special considerations for people with chronic health problems (see appendix at the end of the chapter). Some type of arrangement of ROM exercises, muscle strengthening exercises, cardiovascular exercises, or all three should be designed in order to suit the participants of the program. ROM exercises move each of the body's joints through the full range of isotonic motion. Joints are moved to the point of minimal resistance without causing pain. These exercises can be performed lying down, sitting, or standing and are appropriate for almost every older adult. ROM exercises can be done independently by the client or with assistance from the instructor/facilitator (Dawe & Curran-Smith, 1994).

Muscle strengthening exercises increase muscle strength and help to give stability to vulnerable joints. They help to improve the participants' ability to bear weight, lift objects, and sustain movement (Weiss, 1988). This type of exercise can be done with or without weights. Before performing an exercise with weights, a participant should be able to perform the exercise properly and confidently without the weights. Cardiovascular exercises help participants to increase endurance. Walking, swimming, bicycling, and dancing are examples of cardiovascular exercises. Participants in exercise programs that include this type of endurance exercise should be examined by a cardiovascular specialist before beginning the program, and they should start and progress slowly (Flatten, Wilhite, & Reyes-Watson, 1988). This type of exercise may not be suitable or necessary for all older adults, however.

Each session should begin with a 5-minute warm–up period of gently swinging the arms, stretching the limbs, rotating the hips, and other related stretches and exercises to warm up the muscles. At the end of each session, a cool-down period is necessary, consisting of stretches and gentle movement exercises that allow the body to slowly cool down. In addition, a target heart rate should be taken at least twice during each session (once at maximum endurance).

Exercises most commonly included in exercise programs for older adults include slow, easy movements using the full range of motion. Typically, a person sits in a chair or stands and moves fingers, forearms, arms, feet, or calves in a flexing then straightening manner. Many exercises include slow, circling actions

Exercise Program Planning Form

Client _____ Date _____

Instructor/Clinician _____

Examined by physician? ____ Yes ____ No

Current Functional Status

___ Able to walk 1 mile   ___ Able to walk around the mall or block

___ Able to walk down the hall   ___ Able to walk unaided

___ Walks with aid (___ cane ___ walker)   ___ Needs assistance in walking

___ Climbs stairs unaided   ___ Climbs with aid (___ cane ___ walker)

___ Needs assistance in climbing   ___ Uses wheelchair

___ Able to navigate chair alone   ___ Able to transfer to chair unaided

___ Able to assist in transfer to chair

Short-Term Goal

_____

Long-Term Goal

_____

Exercise Regimen

Type   ___ Range of motion   ___ Strengthening   ___ Cardiovascular

Length of sessions   ___ 30 minutes   ___ 45 minutes   ___ 60 minutes

Specific exercises to be carried out

1.

2.

3.

4.

5.

A Life Worth Living: Practical Strategies for Reducing Depression in Older Adults, by Pearl Mosher-Ashley and Phyllis Barrett. © 1997 Health Professions Press, Inc., Baltimore.

at a particular joint, such as circling each finger or circling arms in a slow, swimming-type action (Flatten, Wilhite, & Reyes-Watson, 1988). It is important for the instructor/facilitator to be aware of individual differences in ability and learning methods. In general, older people learn best by doing. Reinforcement and feedback are very important. When the older person performs the exercise correctly, these actions need to be encouraged. Instructions for correction of movement may also need to be given.

The instructor should be in a position where he or she can be seen and heard clearly, and he or she should know the exercise routine thoroughly. Instructions should be clear and brief, and presented one step at a time. A demonstration is necessary, and the participants should be given an opportunity to ask questions. Older adults should be allowed time to practice the exercise, with the instructor/facilitator guiding the effort, making corrections as necessary. The session should not be focused on competition. Participants should be allowed to work at their own pace and asked to do only the number of repetitions that they can accomplish comfortably—with older adults there is no such thing as "no pain, no gain" (Flatten, Wilhite, & Reyes-Watson, 1988).

ASSESSMENT AND EVALUATION

An evaluation of any exercise program is a necessity. Ideally, assessment should include the recording of the history, objectives, and organization of the program, and information about staffing needs, time frame, accompanying counseling activities, and so forth. Predisposing, enabling, and reinforcing factors that may affect outcomes, including health-risk profiles of the participants, should be acknowledged. A questionnaire administered onsite can be used to gather pertinent information, including health status, health-risk behaviors (e.g., smoking, high fat intake), health care practices, level of interest in programs, level of participation, and level of satisfaction, both before and after the program. A control group is also needed in order to accurately assess any findings (Cox & Monk, 1989). However, given the limitations in time, expertise, and resources of senior centers, nursing facilities, and other likely providers of exercise programs for older adults, ideal assessments are highly unrealistic. Inexpensive, quick, unobtrusive evaluations of programs and individual sessions make more sense and will serve the purpose. Any good fitness program needs to be evaluated regularly in order that informed decisions can be made for improving, expanding, and even deleting aspects of the existing program. The Functional Fitness Assessment (FFA) for Adults Over 60 Years may be a more helpful prepackaged test than tests designed for younger adults (Alessio & Leviton, 1990).

A helpful assessment is one that tests for muscle strength, muscle endurance, cardiovascular endurance, flexibility, and body composition, and can be administered with limited time spent on task and with limited resources (Alessio & Leviton, 1990). Muscle strength and endurance can be tested using an arm curl test, which is safer than pushups or pullups for older adults, and the one-legged stand, timed. Cardiovascular endurance can be judged fairly accurately based on the time required to walk 1 mile. To test for flexibility, the participant can sit on a bed or on the floor and extend the legs so that the heels of the feet are set on the 25-inch mark of a yardstick, with the yardstick placed between the participant's legs and the "0" facing toward the participant. With the hands placed one on top of the other, the participant should slowly reach forward along the yardstick as far as possible and hold this position for 2 seconds. An appropriate range for an older person is between 10 and 30 inches. Finally, to test for body composition, the simple ratio of body weight to body height can be taken with equipment no more sophisticated than a bathroom scale and a yardstick, and standard weight charts can be used for evaluation (Alessio & Leviton, 1990). Page 318 is a simple form to use in evaluating various activities and fitness goals. This form can be easily adapted to reflect the more specific components or goals (or both) of any particular exercise program.

VARIATIONS ON EXERCISE THERAPY FOR OLDER ADULTS

Several variations on exercise therapy are beneficial for older adults, including tai chi, yoga, dance/movement therapy, swimming, strength training, and guided imagery.

Tai Chi

Tai chi is a type of moving meditation that originated in China. It is different from other forms of exercise in that it takes a holistic approach to fitness. The aim of tai chi is to harmonize the actions of the body with those of the mind. A number of clinicians have reported that tai chi can have therapeutic benefits for people of all ages (Jin, 1992). Tai chi is excellent exercise for older adults because its movements are slow paced and not strenuous. It is a series of calculated movements. Tai chi does not tax the body; instead, it tends to create strength and energy. Participants have reported achieving a new sense of balance, improvement of posture, and an increase in the ability to relax (Hitchner, 1995).

A typical tai chi program includes a 5- to 10-minute warm-up period, followed by the synchronized performance of a "form," or routine. The instructor/facilitator stands facing the group, perhaps in an elevated position, so that all movements can be observed and mirrored easily. A "soft" tai chi form includes various movements with names such as "ward off," "deflect," and "repulse the monkey," derived from the martial arts tradition of tai chi. Following the performance of the form, participants typically relax briefly or request individual or small-group instruction from the instructor/facilitator in order to perfect individual elements in the form. Then the form is repeated.

Tai chi allows every part of the body—muscles, joints, bones—a chance to exercise. It may also improve the natural functions of organs, increasing vigor and strengthening them against disease. If practiced regularly tai chi can lead to both mental and physical well-being and may even lengthen one's life (Jin, 1992).

Exercise Assessment Form

Client _____ Date _____

Instructor/Clinician _____

Date of last assessment _____

How long has client been participating in exercise program? _____

Short-term goal _____

_____

Long-term goal _____

_____

Formal assessment (specify test employed) _____

_____

Results _____

_____

Informal assessment (specify criteria employed) _____

_____

Results _____

_____

Changes to be made to program _____

_____

A Life Worth Living: Practical Strategies for Reducing Depression in Older Adults, by Pearl Mosher-Ashley and Phyllis Barrett. © 1997 Health Professions Press, Inc., Baltimore.

Older adults with chronic health conditions should consult their physician before beginning tai chi. Experienced tai chi instructors should be sensitive to the individual health needs of their students (Jin, 1992). Loose clothing should be worn to permit easy movement. Shoes should be comfortable and lightweight.

The length of practice and the particular movements that should be taught will vary according to the individual's age, physical condition, and ability. Tai chi sessions may be held indoors in recreation rooms of community or senior centers (Sneed & Mosher-Ashley, 1997); however, outdoors is the traditional and preferred environment. Traditionally, tai chi is practiced in the early morning hours, although any time of day is acceptable (Hitchner, 1995; Jin, 1992). Sessions for older adults should not last longer than 1 hour. No single exercise should be done for more than a few minutes or beyond the point of exhaustion.

Yoga

Like tai chi, yoga is a meditative exercise with Asian roots. The earliest evidence of yoga was found during archaeological excavations in the Indus Valley of India in the 1920s, which uncovered, among other objects, a seal depicting a man seated in the lotus position. This artifact has been dated to the 3rd century B.C. (Worthington, 1982). In fact, yoga is the oldest system of personal development for body, mind and spirit, and is practiced around the world (Bhat, 1996).

Yoga can be practiced by people of any age, in almost any physical condition. Athletes can use yoga to restore energy and improve stamina; working adults may turn to it to reduce stress. Proponents believe that yoga improves the memory and concentration of both children and older adults and that it is a tonic for insomnia, emotional imbalance, and headaches (Bhat, 1996). Yoga may be especially appropriate for older adults in that it consists of gentle movements, stretches, and flexes. Yoga requires no equipment and no special accommodations and can be practiced standing or sitting in a chair or on the floor.

In addition to the physical benefits derived from the practice of yoga there is evidence that it is a more effective therapy for various psychosomatic and psychiatric disorders than are talk therapies (Goyeche, 1979, cited by Allen & Steinkohl, 1987). In one study psychiatric patients who met twice a week for 90-minute sessions reported that they felt "more relaxed, less tense, more energetic, and more limber" and that the exercises gave them "a sense of mastery" (Allen & Steinkohl, 1987, p. 65). Participants surprised themselves when they continued practicing yoga beyond the initial 6-month pilot program. Researchers reported good attendance and enthusiasm throughout the course of the program, noting that it provided both social and exercise experience (Allen & Steinkohl, 1987).

Typical exercises include a posture that encourages a rich supply of blood to flow to the brain, helping to relieve headache, sinus congestion, and back pain, and simultaneously massaging the abdominal area, relieving cramps, improving digestion, and strengthening the sciatic nerves. Another posture is a powerful backward bending movement that strengthens the spine, preventing slipped discs and other back ailments and encouraging proper breathing. Other postures are helpful for people who stand or sit for prolonged periods. Neck movements, shoulder socket rotations, and eye exercises help to relax the upper back, neck, and eye muscles. One of these movements is practiced lying down and involves the practice of slow, smooth breathing, which is believed to have generalized healing properties (Bhat, 1996). (Further information on these exercises can be found in the Appendix.)

Dance/Movement Therapy

A combination of structured and unstructured movements, dance/movement therapy emerged from modern dance in the 1940s as an alternative to "talk therapy." It helps people to express their feelings without words, and can therefore be used with small children who lack the language skills to express themselves adequately; with adults who have lost touch with their feelings; and with older adults who are so lonely, depressed, or confused that they are unable to express themselves. Increasingly, dance/movement therapy is being used in nursing facilities, psychiatric hospitals, and schools for children with disabilities (Brody, 1995).

Various techniques can be used with older adults. For example, some therapists move with their clients in supporting and mirroring roles; others act as empathic observers. The dance is usually performed in a group and involves touch between participants. Physical contact alone often helps to relieve feelings of loneliness and isolation and provides a source of sensory stimulation (Brody, 1995). Some movement can also induce relaxation and even improve muscle tone, flexibility, and range of motion—all appropriate goals of any exercise for older people.

Two therapists who have worked with older adults in Connecticut nursing facilities and senior centers, Dr. Susan L. Sandel and Amy Hollander, have found that dance/movement therapy helps older people deal with "feelings of loss, [it] counters social withdrawal, encourages creativity, and fosters self-esteem" (Brody, 1995, p. C2). Another therapist, Dr. Fran J. Levy, recounts the story of a 56-year-old man who had become withdrawn after suddenly losing his sight. At first a hesitant participant, he reported a greater comfort level in navigating both indoors and outside after six dance/movement therapy sessions. After 25 sessions, he was able to vent some of his resentment and frustration about his blindness and to get on with his life (Brody, 1995).

Water Exercise

Water exercise, also called aqua-aerobics, aqua exercise, aquatic dance exercise, water workouts, or hydroaerobics, is an activity performed most often in the shallow part of a swimming pool. It provides participants with an enjoyable physical conditioning program and is designed to improve overall fitness by providing a workout for the heart and lungs and toning and strengthening muscles. Water exercise is frequently accompanied by music, and a program can be designed for either swimmers or nonswimmers. This exercise is appropriate for any age group, healthy people, people who are overweight, individuals who are recovering from injury, or those who have various health problems (Clark, 1994). Water exercise is ideal for older adults, especially those with health problems, because swimming is a low-impact exercise. For people who have experienced difficulty exercising on land, the buoyancy of water provides the opportunity for a stimulating workout while participants enjoy a sense of weightlessness.

Instructors need not be exceptional swimmers themselves; in fact, instruction seems to be most effective when the instructor remains on deck, in full view of the participants. A lifeguard should also be on duty so that the facilitator can concentrate on the instruction. Instructors must possess a caring attitude, common sense, good judgment, sensitivity, open-mindedness about the abilities of older adult participants, and a sense of humor. Certification in aquatic exercise, which is available from many colleges, is a great advantage.

The other requirement for this type of exercise program is a swimming pool with easy access to parking and entry, a water temperature in the 84°–86° range, decks with nonslide surfaces, and access for people with disabilities (e.g., chair lifts in addition to the customary ladder). The facility should be clean and well maintained, with good lighting and high-quality safety equipment (Clark, 1994).

A typical water exercise program should include a warm-up period followed by tailor-made exercises for participants of varying abilities. Some individuals may need to use kickboards or the pool wall for support during exercises, whereas others may not. Exercises that work major muscle groups and improve fine motor skills should be included in an exercise program. Other elements of the program may consist of water walking, partner exercises, and opportunities for socializing. Any kind of music can be incorporated into the exercise program. The instructor must be aware of any medications that participants are taking because these may affect heart rate and should be taken into account in determining the appropriate intensity of exercise for individuals (Clark, 1994). The goals of a water exercise program should be fun and safety coupled with a reasonable physical challenge. A good program fulfills both physiological and social needs and can lead to increased self-esteem and an opportunity for self-actualization (Clark, 1994).

Strength Training

With age, muscle mass declines and the composition of muscle changes, resulting in declining muscular strength and endurance. A strength training program for older adults is an exercise regimen designed to slow and even reverse the decline. Muscular strength is important for older adults because it is essential to the completion of normal ADLs and to their general independence. A strength training program involves many components that ensure both success and safety for the participants. Important elements include pretesting, the setting of individualized goals, designing the training regime, and establishing methods for evaluation (Topp, Mikesky, & Bawel, 1994).

According to the American College of Sports Medicine (ACSM), potential participants should be categorized through a pretest into people who are apparently healthy, those at higher risk for injury or cardiovascular disease, and those with diagnosed disease, with individuals in the latter two groups requiring a physician's consent before proceeding with a program involving moderate or vigorous exercise. (Most strength training for older adults is geared to a moderate level of exertion.) However, even apparently healthy men over age 40 and women over age 50 should have a physical examination and take a diagnostic exercise test before engaging in strength training (Topp, Mikesky, & Bawel, 1994).

Individualized goals should be established based on the person's objectives, the initial level of muscular strength, the person's other time commitments, and the availability of and access to exercise facilities. The program design follows the same basic principles as those for a younger person, emphasizing proper exercise form and technique, the maintenance of a training record, and the employment of different types and modes of strength training. In general, the program should stress the muscles beyond what they encounter in regular daily activity, the stress imposed should be increased gradually, and the training should be persistent and geared to the needs of the individual. Because many older adults have limited financial resources, limited transportation, and limited access to sophisticated exercise equipment, it is important to find inexpensive, convenient ways to ensure the consistency required of a strength training regimen. One inexpensive mode of training involves the use of elastic surgical tubing. Tubing costs $.50 a foot, can be carried anywhere, and can be used in many ways. For example, "loops can be tied in the ends of the tubing and the hands placed through the loops to decrease the need for isometric grip strength, which has advantages for those with arthritis or hypertension" (Topp, Mikesky, & Bawel, 1994, p. 270).

Goals can be set for strength and endurance or other measurable criteria, and there are normed tests for determining the achievement of the goals. However, older adults may have developed criteria of their own involving valued functions such as being able to walk up stairs, get up from a chair, lift things, or perform other ordinary ADLs (Topp, Mikesky, & Bawel, 1994).

The Appendix lists some of the many resources available for use in establishing dance, general fitness, rehabilitation, water exercise, tai chi, and yoga programs appropriate for older adults.

Enhancement of Rote Exercise

Almost any exercise program can be set to music, although there is little statistical proof that the efficacy of the exercise is enhanced by music. Attempts have been made to enhance the appeal of rote exercise—the kind of exercise required of people with arthritis, for instance—by accompanying the exercises with music such as jazz (Bernard, 1992). Another approach to solving the motivation problem inherent in rote exercise is that of using guided imagery to add purpose to the seemingly purposeless repetition. Guided imagery is the psychological process that allows one to evoke the physical characteristics of objects or events that are not actually seen (Riccio, Nelson, & Bush, 1990). In other words, it is possible to form a mental picture of a flower when no flower is physically present. A study of 27 women between the ages of 62 and 96, selected from a nursing facility, a residential retirement facility, and a foster care home introduced the imaginary activity of apple picking (Riccio, Nelson, & Bush, 1990). The researchers felt that most people would have positive feelings about the "activity" and that it would motivate them to do the necessary exercise. A control group performed the same rote exercises without using guided imagery. The results were as the researchers predicted: The people who employed imagery along with the exercise enjoyed greater success. The subjects' responses after the exercise were generally consistent with the statistical findings. They said such things as "My apple tree is plentiful," "I will have to go to another tree when I finish here," and "I used to pick apples" when they were involved in the reaching-up exercise, and "I will be rich pretty soon" during the reaching-down exercise. In contrast, the control group replied with comments such as "This is silly" or "I'm not tired, but I want to stop."

It is simple to implement a guided imagery-enhanced exercise program. No props are required, though exercise equipment of various types may be employed. The most effective image topics that can be suggested to the exercisers are those that bring back vivid, well-remembered, even well-loved activities and events.

Adherence to an exercise program is difficult for everyone, not just for older adults. However, given that studies on the aging of the human body indicate that up to 50% of the body's decline can be attributed to simple inactivity (O'Brien & Conger, 1991), it is important to find the means to motivate older adults to remain active or become active. They may need to be reminded that even routine ADLs such as personal hygiene and vacuuming are actually light exercise, and that gardening, hobby painting, and walking are moderate exercise (Forbes, 1992). Also, they may need to be introduced to the exercise resources of the local community and reassured about the safety of undertaking appropriate exercise regimens.

. . .

What factors motivate older adults to be active? O'Brien & Conger (1991) studied the life philosophy of adults who chose to participate in a Senior Games competition in Alberta, Canada, exploring the beliefs, strategies, and future life orientation of the participants. Some participants were married, some were widowed; some reported arthritis, heart conditions, the loss of a lung, diabetes, or cancer. The general findings of the study suggested that these older adults were "fun-loving, competitive, and action oriented" and "optimistic about the future" (p. 85). Furthermore, many of the respondents "aggressively embraced physical activity, social activity through volunteer work, and personal hobbies as a way of staying healthy, and many of them expressed achievement goals related to sport, physical fitness, work, and major home projects" (pp. 85–86).

Perhaps relatively few older adults will fit the mold of 72-year-old Warren Miller, a sports photographer and enthusiast, who planned a trip to Maui to windsurf and another to the Rocky Mountains to ski (Martinez, 1995). Still, numerous studies, including one by Topp and Stevenson (1994), indicate that even moderate levels of commitment to regular exercise lead to cognitive, physical, and psychological rewards for older adults. Those who, unlike Warren Miller, have not developed a philosophy that embraces lifelong activity may, therefore, benefit from a nudge into a more active and healthy lifestyle.

REFERENCES

Alessio, H., & Leviton, D. (1990). Field tests that evaluate adult physical fitness: A new emphasis on ease of administration, low cost and safety. *Activities, Adaptation & Aging, 14*(4), 45–56.

Allen, K.S., & Steinkohl, R.P. (1987). Yoga in a geriatric mental clinic. *Activities, Adaptation & Aging, 9*(4), 61–68.

Bernard, A. (1992). The use of music as purposeful activity: A preliminary investigation. *Physical Therapy & Occupational Therapy in Geriatrics, 10*(3), 35–45.

Bhat, V. (1996, March 20). Benefits of yoga to modern life. *INDOlink: Health & Fitness: YOGA.* (Available at http://www.genius.net/indolink/Health/yoga.html)

Brody, J. (1995, October 20). Dance shoes replace therapist's couch. *Springfield (Massachusetts) Union-News,* pp. C1, C2.

Brown, D. (1992). Physical activity, ageing, and psychological well-being: An overview of the research. *Canadian Journal of Sport Sciences, 17,* 185–193.

Clark, G. (1994). Water exercise for senior adults—prescription for fun and fitness. *Journal of Physical Education, Recreation & Dance, 65*(6), 18–21.

Cox, C., & Monk, A. (1989). Measuring the effectiveness of a health education program for older adults. *Educational Gerontology, 15,* 9–23.

Dawe, D., & Curran-Smith, J. (1994). Going through the motions. *Canadian Nurse, 90*(1), 31–33.

Dawe, D., & Moore-Orr, R. (1995). Low-intensity, range-of-motion exercise: Invaluable nursing care for elderly patients. *Journal of Advanced Nursing, 21,* 675–681.

Edmunds, M.W. (1991, December). Strategies for promoting physical fitness. *Nursing Clinics of North America, 26,* 855–866.

Fastiggi, L., & Mosher-Ashley, P.M. (1997, March). *An outreach fitness program for frail, homebound elders.* Paper distributed in a program exchange at the 44th annual meeting of the American Society on Aging, Nashville, TN.

Fillingham, R.B., & Blumenthal, J.A. (1993). Psychological effects of exercise among the elderly. In P. Seraganian (Ed.), *Exercise psychology: The influence of physical exercise on psychological processes* (pp. 237–253). New York: John Wiley & Sons.

Flatten, K., Wilhite, B., & Reyes-Watson, E. (1988). *Exercise activities for the elderly.* New York: Springer Publishing.

Forbes, E.J. (1992). Exercise: Wellness maintenance for the elderly client. *Holistic Nursing Practice, 6*(2), 14–22.

Gitlin, L., Lawton, M.P., Windsor-Landsberg, L.A., Kleban, M., Sands, L., & Posner, J. (1992). In search of psychological benefits: Exercise in healthy older adults. *Journal of Aging and Health, 4,* 174–188.

Hitchner, G. (1995, February 3). Benefit for body, mind: Seniors in South Hadley revel in t'ai chi classes. *Springfield (Massachusetts) Union-News,* pp. 17–18.

Hooker, S. (1990). *Caring for elderly people* (3rd ed.). New York: Tavistock/Routledge.

Jamieson, R.H. (1982). *Exercises for the elderly.* Verplanck, NY: Emerson.

Jin, P. (1992). Efficacy of Tai Chi, brisk walking, meditation, and reading in reducing mental and emotional stress. *Journal of Psychosomatic Research, 36*(3), 361–370.

Kirkcaldy, B., & Shephard, R. (1990). Therapeutic implications of exercise. *International Journal of Sport Psychology, 21,* 165–184.

Martinez, A. (1995, November/December). King of the hill. *Modern Maturity,* p. 24.

McAuley, E., Bane, S.M., Rudolph, D.L., & Lox, C.L. (1995). Physique anxiety and exercise in middle-aged adults. *Journal of Gerontology, 50B*(5), P229–P235.

McMurdo, M.E.T., & Rennie, L.M. (1994, May). Improvements in quadriceps strength with regular seated exercise in the institutionalized elderly. *Archives of Physical Medicine and Rehabilitation, 75,* 600–603.

Morey, M.C., Cowper, P.A., Feussner, J.R., DiPasquale, R.C., Crowley, G.M., Kitzman, D.W., & Sullivan, R.J. (1989). Evaluation of a supervised exercise program in a geriatric population. *Journal of the American Geriatrics Society, 37,* 348–354.

O'Brien, S.J., & Conger, P.R. (1991). No time to look back: Approaching the finish line of life's course. *International Journal of Aging and Human Development, 33*(1), 75–87.

Riccio, C.M., Nelson, D.L., & Bush, M.A. (1990, August). Adding purpose to the repetitive exercise of elderly women through imagery. *American Journal of Occupational Therapy, 44,* 714–719.

Sambrook, P.N., & Krucoff, C. (1996, May/June). New treatments for osteoporosis. *Saturday Evening Post, 268*(3), 74 77.

Shephard, R.J. (1994). Determinants of exercise in people aged 65 years and older. In R. Dishman (Ed.), *Advances in exercise adherence* (pp. 343 360). Athens. University of Georgia Department of Human Kinetics.

Smith, T. (1996, February). Older people need strength training too. *Consumers' Research Magazine, 79*(2), 19–22.

Sneed, S.M., & Mosher-Ashley, P.M. (1997, March) *A peer-facilitated approach to activity using tai chi in a community senior citizens center.* Paper distributed in a program exchange at the 44th annual meeting of the American Society on Aging, Nashville, TN.

Spier, B.E., & Meis, M. (1994). Maintenance ambulation: Its significance and the role of nursing. *Geriatric Nursing, 15,* 277–281.

Topp, R., Mikesky, A., & Bawel, K. (1994, September/October). Developing a strength training program for older adults: Planning, programming, and potential outcomes. *Rehabilitation Nursing, 19,* 266–273.

Topp, R., & Stevenson, J.S. (1994). The effects of attendance and effort on outcomes among older adults in a long-term exercise program. *Research in Nursing & Health, 17,* 15–24.

Tucker, L.A., Harris, K., & Martin, J.R. (1996, April). Participation in a strength training program leads to improved dietary intake in adult women. *Journal of the American Dietetic Association, 96*(4), 388–390.

Waldo, M.J., Ide, B.A., & Thomas, D.P. (1995, February). Postcardiac-event elderly: Effect of exercise on cardiopulmonary function. *Journal of Gerontological Nursing, 2*(2), 12–19.

Weiss, J.C. (1988). *The "feeling great!" wellness program for older adults.* New York: Haworth Press.

Wolinsky, F.D., Stump, T.E., & Clark, D.O. (1995). Antecedents and consequences of physical activity and exercise among older adults. *Gerontologist, 35,* 451–462.

Worthington, V. (1982). *A history of yoga.* London: Routledge & Kegan Paul Ltd.

Appendix
Resources for Specific Exercise Programs

Dance

Jodi Stolove's Chair Dancing
Stock No. 14-44776-7
Starcrest of California
19465 Brennan Avenue
Perris, California 92599
Phone (909) 657-2793
A no-impact exercise program giving cardiovascular benefits; available on video-
and audiocassette; ideal for arthritis sufferers and for those desiring to become
active after years of inactivity

Line Dancing for Seniors
Stock No. 21-33784-5
Starcrest of California
19465 Brennan Avenue
Perris, California 92599
Phone (909) 657-2793
Instructional and entertaining video introduces older adults to five different dances
with progressive degrees of difficulty; moderate aerobic exercise

*More Than Movement for Fit to Frail Older Adults: Creative Activities for the Body,
Mind, and Spirit*
Pauline Postiloff Fisher
Baltimore: Health Professions Press, 1995
A practical resource that uses dance, art, poetry, sensory training, and intergen-
erational games to encourage movement among older adults of varying abilities

General Fitness

Angela Lansbury's Positive Moves: My Personal Plan for Fitness and Well-Being
New York: Delacorte Press, 1990
A fitness book by the popular star of the television show *Murder, She Wrote*,
designed for older adults

Camp Rediscovery
Dr. Dan Leviton
Department of Health Education
University of Maryland
College Park, Maryland 20740
A health and well-being program designed for adults over age 55; week-long
overnight camp sessions feature meal preparation, physical activities, and the shar-
ing of current health information

Do It Debbie's Way: Debbie Reynolds' Exercise Video
Coast to Coast Video

An 85-minute exercise video featuring the musical comedy stage and film star, geared toward older adults and available in many libraries

Fitness After Fifty: Elaine LaLanne's Complete Fitness Program
Lexington, MA: The Stephen Greene Press, 1986
A fitness book for older adults by the wife of famed fitness expert Jack LaLanne, available in many libraries

Healthy Aging
Box 307
Coventry, Connecticut 06238
Covering general fitness issues of older adults; a video, discussion kit, and a guide are available as a package or separately; the video profiles nursing facility residents "pumping iron" from their wheelchairs, a woman controlling her diabetes with the help of exercise on a treadmill, and so forth; for use by health care professionals

Living Fit (A Guide to Fitness At Any Age)
from *Shape Magazine*
Phone (800) 340-8957
Magazine designed for women age 35 and over; inspiring and motivating articles enrich commitment to a fit lifestyle; latest information on nutrition, exercise, health, beauty, and personal growth

Rehabilitation

Cardiac Comeback
Levels 1,2,3
Dr. Alan Xenakis Cardiac Rehab Series
Wood/Knapp Video
Los Angeles, California, 1990
Available in many libraries, these 50- to 60-minute videos were developed by a cardiologist to lead heart patients through the stages of recovery after a heart attack

Strength Training

Harvard/Tufts Strength Building Program
Maria A. Fiatrone, M.D.
Fit for Your Life Research Studies
1200 Centre Street
Boston, Massachusetts 02131
Program originally developed by researchers at Harvard Medical School and Tufts University for resident volunteers at Boston's Hebrew Rehabilitation Center for the Aged; its three steps target the muscles of the upper and lower body and the trunk, helping a person to maintain and strengthen muscle mass and increase flexibility

Weight Training: Steps to Success
T. Baechle & B. Groves
Champaign, IL: Leisure Press, 1992
A step-by-step introduction to weight training for all ages

Water Exercise

The Power of Water
Ursula Pahlow
Champaign, IL: Sagamore Publishing, 1991
Available in libraries, this book examines the therapeutic possibilites of swimming and other water exercise

Aquacises
M.S. Giles
Bedford, MA: Mills & Sanderson, 1988
Available in libraries, this book outlines various water exercises appropriate for older adults

Tai Chi Chuan

The Art of Tai Chi: A Practical Guide
Paul Crompton
Rockport, MA: Element Press, 1993
A book that introduces this Asian exercise to participants of any age; available in many libraries

Tai Chi for Seniors
Publishers Choice Video
Post Office Box 4171
Department IS41-PB
Huntington Station, New York 11746
A video introduction to the exercise tradition practiced daily by millions of Chinese older adults

Yoga

Easy Does It Yoga for Older People
A. Christensen & D. Rankin
New York: Harper & Row, 1975
An illustrated book that introduces yoga specifically to older adults; available in many libraries

Yoga for Seniors
Publishers Choice Video
Department IS41-PB
Huntington Station, New York 11746
Simple postures and slow stretching are demonstrated by 69-year-old Patricia Laster and her class of older adults; 55 minutes

All the world's a stage,
And all the men and women merely players;
They have their exits and their entrances,
And one man in his time plays many parts . . .

William Shakespeare, As You Like It

Everybody Is a Star

D rama is not just what happens when professional performers take the stage. It is the communication of imagination through action, and it affects interactions with others, whether on stage or in daily life. Everyone has many roles to play, and the roles change according to one's relationships and situation. Often, these changes are the result of circumstances beyond one's control (Warren, 1984). Perhaps no time in life presents more challenges in this regard than old age. Some roles—spouse, caregiving parent, worker—may have ended. New roles—widow, patient, parent dependent on adult children—may be uncomfortable, even distressing.

Until the 1950s psychological interventions were considered inappropriate for older people, and since the mid-1980s there has been a reluctance to tackle negative emotions and attempt to solve problems (Johnson, 1985). The number of mental health professionals trained to serve older adults is insufficient (Davis, 1985). The lack of mental health services is particularly apparent in nursing facilities (Carman & Nordin, 1984). Drama therapies are among the interventions that continue to be underutilized.

It may be assumed that a group such as frail older adults would be incapable of taking part in dramatic activities, but that view is unfounded. It is within the power of the human imagination to overcome mental and physical limitations as well as emotional barriers (Warren, 1984). The drama therapies cannot reverse the aging process. However, they can help older people discover an enhanced vitality and creativity, help them maintain their imagination and mental faculties, and help them face the end of life with dignity and a sense of reconciliation (Langley, 1987). The drama therapies can help older people develop self-respect and respect for one another as they struggle with the problems inherent in the last years of life. They provide older people with access to their past experiences, help them to come to terms with losses and perceived failures, and draw on the experience and wisdom of a lifetime to help them confront the challenges of old age. Perhaps best of all, participation in the dramatic arts is one way in which older people can fulfill their important, traditional roles of storytellers and transmitters of culture and resume a position of dignity and value in society (Mazor, 1982).

Although some cultures revere older adults as sources of wisdom and continuity, all too often Western culture pronounces older people socially dead long before their physical demise. A distinction has not always been made between the normal aging process and disability attributable to stress and physical and mental illness. It has taken many years to acknowledge that older people need more than nursing care, that they must be helped to maintain their bodily and mental faculties and to reconcile the problems and conflicts of later life. The introduction of the creative arts to older people is still in its infancy, but awareness is growing that the arts are not just for the young (Langley, 1987).

Psychodrama, a group therapy approach in which the client is encouraged to dramatize a past, present, or anticipated life experience or role in order to achieve understanding or catharsis (Corey, 1985), was created and developed by Jacob Moreno (Bielanska, Cechnicki, & Budzyna-Dawidowski, 1991). Moreno drew on psychoanalytical theory, gestalt therapy, developmental psychology, existential philosophy, and Jungian analysis in developing a conceptual framework for this drama therapy. He believed that acting out a past, current, or potential role or event allowed an individual to circumvent habitual responses and find a channel for feelings and new behaviors (Corey, 1985). He argued that a balance needed to be struck between spontaneity and institutionalization, between too loose a social fabric and too dehumanized a society (Davies, 1987). Although Moreno initially worked with people with mental illness, delinquent youths, and people who were socially disadvantaged (Davies, 1987), psychodrama is not primarily concerned with responding to pathology (Altman, 1983). Rather, it is a mechanism for promoting growth and development in any group of people. Based in developmental theory and the belief that all of life involves stages of development (Johnson, 1982), it is particularly applicable to the situations and challenges presented by older people. The standard techniques of psychodrama lead to lively group interaction, the exploration of interpersonal problems, and experimentation with new ways of approaching other people and of reducing isolation (Corey, 1985).

Psychodrama is based on *creative drama,* an improvisational, nonexhibitional form of drama in which participants work without a script and usually without props, and are led to imagine, enact, and reflect on human experience (Thurman & Piggins, 1982). In creative drama, which was developed to train people for the theater, actors are given a conflict situation and asked to create a dramatic sequence around it, including the improvisation of a resolution to the conflict (Davis, 1987). In psychodrama, emphasis is placed on the experience rather than on the performance (Huddleston, 1989).

The structure of psychodrama has three phases: A session begins with a warm-up period, during which issues are brought up and someone is chosen to be that day's protagonist (i.e., lead performer). Many of the techniques in psychodrama center around this individual, who is working on a specific issue or issues. The protagonist, however, is usually not the only person benefiting from the session. Often, other group members are able to relate to the protagonist's issues and, by participating in the session, can resolve issues of their own (Schloss, 1988).

The warm-up period is followed by the action itself, the dramatization of an issue of importance to the protagonist and to the rest of the group (Altman, 1983). *Encountering* is the term assigned to the point at which individuals immediately and meaningfully confront themselves or significant others on stage. Because the action is spontaneous rather than rehearsed, there is always an element of surprise in this moment. The encountering leads to *tele,* the two-way flow of feelings between people in the group. Whether the result is positive or negative, it is *tele* that binds the group (Corey, 1985).

Finally, a sharing period in the psychodrama allows for reactions and discussion. The session may lead to catharsis, which in this context implies not just a release of emotion but also an opportunity for new perceptions and cognitions (Altman, 1983). The emotions avoided as too painful within existing relationships or role expectations often can be released within the safe framework of the drama (Davies, 1987).

Unlike Freudian psychoanalysis, psychodrama can lead to sudden, quickly achieved breakthroughs. Reliving and reexperiencing a scene from the past can elicit details about the situation that can result in a new understanding and permit a corrective emotional experience. The individual can evaluate past actions in terms of present circumstances (Mazor, 1982). It is also possible to test assumptions and fantasies against the group's response and to glean suggestions for action or understanding from peers. Group members act as therapeutic agents for each other (Altman, 1983). By taking various roles, participants can also try on others' situations and learn to view life from diverse perspectives (Corey, 1985). Moreno believed that in order to know ourselves we must see ourselves through others' eyes (Davies, 1987).

The most important goal of the therapy is the achievement of spontaneity and the enhancement of creativity (Altman, 1983). It is spontaneity, contend Moreno's disciples, that allows for mental health, social competence, and interpersonal involvement (Corey, 1985). Children are naturally spontaneous; as people age they become less so and need to relearn the value of spontaneity. Of course, clients still must work through emotional issues in order to achieve lasting resolutions (Corey, 1985).

Since Moreno's pioneering efforts, several variations on his theory and technique have evolved. For example, *dramatherapy* developed in the United Kingdom in the 1960s and 1970s, largely through the efforts of Sue Jennings, whose background was in anthropology and group analysis (Davies, 1987). The emphasis in dramatherapy is on reliving events, and it is grounded in developmental theory. Although some approaches stress restoring balance or putting things right, the concentration here is on overcoming barriers to development (Johnson, 1982). Jennings began by using games and exercises to increase body awareness and nonverbal communication, often using masks, puppets, mime, and role-plays. Dramatherapy has gradually moved in the direction of psychotherapy (Davies, 1987), emphasizing enrichment of life, goal-specific learning (e.g., social skills, rehabilitation, assertiveness training), and the resolution of neurotic conflicts (Langley, 1987). Dramatherapy allows older people to play again, although they must not be made to feel childish. For older adults with diminishing faculties, dramatherapy also reinforces simple social skills such as the exchange of greetings or the way to initiate a conversation or handle a social situation in a shop or restaurant. Finally, it allows individuals to grapple with major life changes, trauma, loss, and impending death (Langley, 1987).

Sociodrama, a synthesis of group psychotherapy and theatrical presentation, places emphasis on empowerment in the political and social arenas. One important program, developed at the Bellevue Mental Hospital in Jamaica, New York, in 1978, addressed the checkered history of treatment of people with mental illness; the issues surrounding deinstitutionalization; and the relationships among patients, staff, and the larger community (Hickling, 1989).

Geriadrama is the term coined by Claire Michaels to describe her work with drama in nursing facilities and senior centers. A variation on psychodrama, geriadrama's purpose is helping older people to recover lost aspects of their personalities, particularly creativity and spontaneity. Geriadrama also provides relief from the anguish of physical and mental deterioration; older people can be energized by their experience of the arts, rather than immobilized by medication. With an acceptance that the future is limited, geriadrama stresses the present; takes physical and mental disabilities into account; and incorporates pantomime, kinesics, improvisation, body movement, transformation games, verbal games, nonverbal games, physical games, poetry, music, the enactment of scenes from plays, and the consideration of news topics (Michaels, 1981).

All of the drama-based psychotherapies stress the establishment of the therapeutic alliance, the reexperience of suppressed feelings and fantasies, and the gradual achievement of a more harmonious and realistic equilibrium in current relationships (Davies, 1987). The various therapies complement rather than conflict with each other (Langley, 1987), and they all have the potential to provide older people with a forum for exploring difficult issues and the fears of old age (Thurman & Piggins, 1982). Professionals who plan to emphasize drama therapies in their work should consider obtaining training. Information on training is available from the organizations listed in the Appendix.

Older adults must address numerous changes in their lives, whether related to the aging process, new family roles, new technologies, or loss of job or spouse. Some older people experience diminished self-esteem and self-confidence as a result of these changes (Davis, 1987). Depression, anger, feelings of isolation, and boredom are problems that occur in a significant number of older people. However, many of those who are suffering fail to use existing mental health services for a variety of reasons (Nordin, 1987). The drama therapies may be beneficial for individuals who fear the stigma of therapy because they provide an emotional outlet and an opportunity to socialize in a setting that is less threatening than that of traditional psychotherapy (Davis, 1987).

The flexibility of the drama therapies also makes them suitable for working with older people. Various games, activities, and improvisational scenes provide opportunities to explore problems, gain self-esteem, expand creativity, and alleviate feelings of isolation and depression (Davis, 1987; Huddleston, 1989; Schloss, 1988). Verbal and nonverbal exercises can help individuals express ideas and opinions, gaining an awareness of themselves and the people around them (Huddleston, 1989). Participants learn that others share their concerns, and they benefit from the human contact in the group. Drama also anchors memories in the present and provides linkage between what was and what is. Finally, it is a refreshing new activity, something to anticipate with pleasure (Thurman & Piggins, 1982). Older individuals who live independently, in congregate housing, or in long-term care facilities may all find enjoyment and therapeutic benefit in the drama therapies.

USE OF DRAMA THERAPIES WITH OLDER ADULTS LIVING INDEPENDENTLY

They call themselves the "Broadway Players." They visit local elementary schools and nursing facilities, performing scenes from popular Broadway musicals, in full costume and using the few props that the senior center van can accommodate. Everyone in the group is more than 60 years old, with women outnumbering men by about 4:1. That ratio accounts for the fact that many of the male roles are taken on by women, who have a lot of fun donning cowboy hats and boots for a segment of *Oklahoma* or a pinstripe suit and spats to portray a fast-talking character in *Guys and Dolls*.

Despite their "aches and pains," the group members look forward to the rehearsals and the physical workout of being on stage—not to mention the chance to ham it up a bit. Some mention the affection among group members as an important part of the experience; others comment that performing "keeps them young." The reception they enjoy from both old and young audiences is also a source of inspiration.

Given their ages, it is not surprising that some members occasionally miss rehearsal or even disappear for a time. One 90-year-old participant missed a whole winter because of illness, but was back in the spring to take part in the upcoming roadshow, undaunted by the fact that her wheelchair would have to figure in the chorus line.

The drama therapies are available to older individuals living independently if they have access to a senior center, adult day center, or other community organization wishing to offer a program and being able to attract enough interested individuals to form a group (Stern, 1988). All that is needed is a room large enough to accommodate the participating members and a facilitator, an individual who will lead the sessions. Depending on the goals of the activities offered, the facilitator should be an individual trained in group therapy work and in one or more of the drama therapies. Another possibility is to have a health care professional and a volunteer with some theater experience cofacilitate the group. Schedules must be set up so that public transportation can be utilized, and the director and/or staff of the facility should be consulted in order to gain their cooperation (Johnson, 1986; Stern, 1988).

One creative drama program implemented in a senior center located in a church building near Pennsylvania State University involved teaching a variety of relaxation and concentration exercises, theater games, and dramatic skills. It allowed participants to integrate thoughts, words, actions, and emotions through improvisational plays that reviewed participants' lives. The purpose of the program was to enhance a sense of well-being, not to remediate pathological conditions. Group members created dramatic situations together, and the audience participated in the productions. Frequently, actors disclosed things about themselves spontaneously in the course of the improvisation. Roadblocks to creativity often seemed to fall away in the dramatic context. Although the research conducted to discern levels of hostility, anxiety, hope, and the capacity for human relationships before and after the program proved inconclusive in some areas, individual sessions obviously had a significant impact on the participants (Davis, 1985).

Because much of the benefit of the drama therapies stems from the group setting, which enhances socialization skills and allows for interactions with others, older individuals who are homebound or otherwise unable to participate in group activity are not able to gain those benefits. Therefore, an alternative therapy must be found.

USE OF DRAMA THERAPIES WITH OLDER ADULTS LIVING IN CONGREGATE HOUSING OR LONG-TERM CARE FACILITIES

When the new activity director at the nursing facility realized that many of the residents seemed to know very little about each other, she decided to develop a getting-to-know-you activity with a dramatic twist. For the pilot project, she invited several high-functioning residents to a mid-morning get together, telling them only that she had an idea for getting people better acquainted with each other and that she needed help in trying it out.

When the eight volunteers arrived, the activity director introduced the dramatic form called pantomime. She asked if any of them remembered seeing Marcel Marceau, the master of the form, on television variety shows. Some of them had seen him, though they said that they would not have remembered his name. The activity director also asked if anyone had ever played charades, a game that uses some of the techniques of pantomime. None had, but most of them were familiar with the game. When the activity director suggested that it might be fun to share some information about themselves (e.g., their former line of work; favorite hobbies, sports, and activities; least favorite activities), the participants agreed.

In the first session they decided to pantomime clues to their favorite activities when they were young adults. The activity director suggested that everyone take a few minutes to visualize a process involved in the activity. For example, to pantomime fishing, a participant might want to carry an imaginary rod and pail to a chair, sit down, bait the hook, cast the line, and so forth. Because of time restraints, only two participants were able to mime their activities during that first session: One man successfully communicated a love for baking pies; another kept the group guessing as he silently waxed an invisible car. Those who were not able to participate during the first session seemed disappointed and said that they looked forward to their chance to perform at the next session.

One of the emphases of several of the drama therapies is the reevaluation of one's roles in life in light of the changes connected with aging. Older people who continue to live independently can define themselves as shoppers, country club members, volunteers, even grandparents, but older people living in long-term care facilities often are forced into extremely limited roles. It was once assumed that withdrawal and disengagement were natural components of aging, but there is an increasing awareness that older people can be actively involved in life. Although physical and cognitive impairments may make role reengagement difficult or impossible for some individuals, the principle of spontaneity employed by the drama therapies can reverse the process of role reduction and some of the behavior patterns that typically result from the restrictions of living in a long-term care setting (Altman, 1983).

The drama therapies are particularly well suited to individuals living in congregate housing or long-term care facilities. This is because the residents, some of whom may be quite frail, need not be transported to an unfamiliar and perhaps threatening environment. In addition, relationships among people who, for better or worse, must live together, stand a good chance of being enhanced through drama therapy. Staff members can also be called on to participate or assist in the therapy, encouraging better relations among all constituencies in the facility (Carman & Nordin, 1984).

Recreation rooms or lounge areas are appropriate sites for holding drama group sessions, as long as they provide some privacy and are unlikely to be interrupted. An individual skilled in theater and a professional with experience in the group process are needed to facilitate the group, and a sufficient amount of interest must be expressed by the older adults. The director or staff (or both) of the facility should be consulted and agreeable to the idea (Stern, 1988). Gaining support from staff members and coordinating a schedule with that of other residential activities is critical to the success of the program (Johnson, 1986; Stern, 1988).

A program initiated by social workers at Hebrew Home of Greater Washington in Rockville, Maryland, succeeded in creating fun and joy for residents, family members, and staff. A tradition was inaugurated of producing a humorous play on the annual family-sponsored Staff Appreciation Day. The premise of one plot was that the entire nursing staff could not make it to work one day and family members had to fill in for them. The family members turned out to be "all thumbs," taking blood pressure around ankles, confusing medications, and the like. Another skit focused on the common problem of lost items in nursing facilities, dealing with this often-trying situation in a comical way. Through the humor of the storyline, staff members came to know how much their efforts and professionalism were appreciated.

Humor allowed people to express feelings that they had found difficult to put into words, boosting staff self-esteem and creating a positive effect on the atmosphere of the facility. Another by-product was the esprit de corps established among family members as they gathered props, shared rides, and collaborated in writing funny song lyrics set to familiar melodies. Before long, families were asking for news of other families' loved ones, and a support system began to grow. The production and its preparation allowed family members to take a lighthearted break from the difficult realities of their situations, lifting their spirits and those of the residents and staff (Weisberg & Haberman, 1992).

PRECAUTIONS TO TAKE AND ACCOMMODATIONS TO MAKE IN IMPLEMENTING DRAMA THERAPIES WITH OLDER ADULTS

The external environment in a drama therapy session comprises the physical location, the spatial arrangement of participants, the dramatic activities themselves, and the roles of the therapist and group members. At the outset, these components must be structured, stable, and understandable; later, most people will be able to cope with less structure (Johnson, 1982). A regular time and place for group sessions should be established. Adequate space for a circle of chairs and wheelchairs is necessary. Interruptions can be very disruptive, and this must be taken into consideration when choosing a room in which to hold the sessions (Johnson, 1986; Michaels, 1981; Stern, 1988). Sessions may be held weekly or biweekly for 1- or 2-hour periods, depending on the needs of the group members.

Group size, according to Michaels (1981), should not exceed 15 participants. Langley (1987) warns that diagnosis, chronological age, and mental and physical disability status may not be the best criteria for grouping older people. A more useful gauge is high versus low dependency. For people who are able to dress and feed themselves and who retain some social skills, even if they are in the early stages of cognitive loss, virtually any kind of drama therapy is appropriate. However, those who are highly dependent or have short attention spans or severe limitations because of physical disability must be accommodated in smaller groups of perhaps three to four individuals. Activities must be less complex, and, if possible, an assistant should be made available to the facilitator (Langley, 1987).

Few materials are mandatory for a drama therapy program because of the improvisational nature of most of the techniques. Costumes and props may be introduced to stimulate characterizations. In addition, posters, paintings, and photographs may be used to describe themes of the day (Huddleston, 1989; Michaels, 1981). A tape recorder can be used for keeping a record of each session and playing music. Although props, scripts, and other enhancements may lend structure to the dramatic undertaking, they also increase the level of complexity and are usually not necessary (Johnson, 1982).

The nature of the drama therapies requires group members to speak frequently and sometimes use body movements. When working with older adults, the facilitator must keep in mind their possible physical and verbal limitations, and should relate requests for movements and speech to their capabilities (Michaels, 1981). It is important for the facilitator to be knowledgeable about both physical and psychological disorders that affect older people in particular and to draw on the expertise of other professionals in the facility in which drama therapy is being offered (Langley, 1987).

In addition, the more cognitively or developmentally impaired the group members, the more important it is to start with simple activities and slowly advance to more complex ones. Problems will always occur during transitions between activities with different levels of complexity, but each session should be built carefully on what has gone before in order to minimize adjustment difficulties for the participants. Close observation of the individuals in the group will usually reveal which level of structure, media, complexity, affect, and interpersonal demand each person finds most comfortable. Attention to these issues can help the facilitator understand the participants better and predict their likely behavior in a variety of situations (Johnson, 1982).

Facilitators should recognize their own limitations in deciding on either the composition of the group or on the complexity of the activities undertaken. The facilitator's role should remain directive, allowing the group members to choose the content of the interactions (Kane, 1992). Participants do need to know that they will not be coerced to work on issues that they prefer not to explore and reassured that this will be a safe environment. Less significant events should be explored first, leaving more traumatic events for later in the course of the program. The facilitator should be vigilant, ensuring that no participant is vulnerable to attack from other members of the group. The purpose of the group is to be supportive, not confrontational. It is extremely helpful for the facilitator to have personally experienced the role of protagonist in a psychodrama session in order to appreciate the needs of individuals for protection and support in this particular therapy (Corey, 1985).

Sometimes the facilitator may feel that group discussions are superficial, but it is important to respect the developmental stage of the participants and not to force an individual or the group to grapple with matters that are, at the moment at least, too threatening (Johnson, 1982). In addition, it should be recognized that all problems will not be solved and that deep psychological areas should be left to facilitators who are properly trained in psychotherapy (Michaels, 1981). This is not to say that emotional issues should not be addressed. It is necessary, however, to allow sufficient time to work through and bring closure to the deeply emotional components of a session (Kane, 1992).

Finally, facilitators must be aware of their own attitudes and feelings about aging and about the societal assumptions and prejudices about older people. Working with older adults may cause facilitators to experience strong emotions about their own mortality or about unresolved conflicts with their own parents or relatives. It is important for facilitators to monitor their feelings in order to prevent them from clouding their perceptions of what is happening in the dramatic session (Langley, 1987).

IMPLEMENTATION OF THE DRAMA THERAPIES

Initial Steps

Because many people tend to think of themselves as without talent and experience in the arts, the announcement of a new drama program at a nursing facility or senior center may intimidate some potential participants. A better tactic might be to invite residents or attendees to an auction, a mock trial, a treasure hunt, or a reenactment of a classic television show such as *This Is Your Life*. It may even be possible to piggyback the drama program on an existing activity (e.g., creative movement could be included at exercise time, a dramatic game could be introduced during the intermission of a bingo game). After people have had a good time participating in a nonthreatening drama-related activity, they can be invited to join a drama club. Another possibility is to invite an existing drama group—local high school or college students, older adults, or a community theater troupe—to make a presentation at the facility and perhaps return to do a workshop for those interested in becoming involved. Of course, the direct approach—a simple invitation to participate in a drama group—can also be used, especially if staff put in a good word for the new program. Further interest can be inspired by sending written invitations, distributing or posting fliers, or publishing an announcement in a newsletter. People can also be invited by telephone or in person (Thurman & Piggins, 1982).

The materials needed to implement a drama program are minimal. Posters, rhythm instruments, taped music, costumes, and other props may be gathered to set the mood for productions or help to develop a character (Michaels, 1981), but none of these things is required. The room used should be large enough to accommodate a circle of chairs and wheelchairs and also allow for a separate section to be designated the "stage" (Corey, 1985). Moreno's ideal stage was 12–15 feet in diameter and elevated 1–2 feet above floor level, with two surrounding stepped lower areas, a "Juliet" gallery, seating for the audience, and lighting equipment. Although such specific accouterments are far from necessary, Moreno's point was that therapeutic theater, like a church, should be a special setting in which transformation can occur (Davies, 1987). At minimum, the room used should be removed from the traffic of a busy facility and free of interruptions from telephones and public address systems (Michaels, 1981). It should be well ventilated and warm enough or cool enough for the season (Thurman & Piggins, 1982).

Sessions are best scheduled in mid-morning or later in the afternoon, after rest time, in order for people to feel fresh (Michaels, 1981). An appropriate session length is between 1 and 2 hours. It is difficult to get down to business in less than 1 hour; however, most participants will tire or lose their concentration if the session is much longer than 1 hour (Thurman & Piggins, 1982).

Formation of the Group

The ideal size for a group is approximately 8–10 individuals, 12–15 if the facilitator has an assistant, and only 3–4 if participants are highly dependent (Thurman & Piggins, 1982). Some natural groups may exist at an adult day center or senior center; otherwise, a group can be recruited with this specific activity and purpose in mind (Langley, 1987). The interests and abilities of the group must be taken into account before planning the sessions. In a nursing facility setting, for example, many participants are likely to have physical and cognitive impairments, to be in wheelchairs, among other disabilities. Therefore, there are some obvious limitations to the activities that can be undertaken. In contrast, more can be attempted with older people who can ambulate freely and with independent-living older adults who frequent a senior center (Michaels, 1981). Once the group has formed, it is important to establish ground rules: Michaels (1981) recommends that all agree that there will be no private conversations during sessions and no airing of personal hostilities. Although attendance cannot be mandatory with a volunteer and sometimes frail clientele, participants must commit to arriving on time and being prepared to participate when they do attend if the group is to become cohesive and be successful.

Facilitator's Role

Like a good teacher, a drama group facilitator should be well-organized and interested, and possess a warm personality. Some of the problems he or she will face are those that confront any teacher (e.g., invariably, the group will comprise both reluctant and dominating participants). Other problems are specific to older adults: vision and hearing deficits, problems with ambulation, and sporadic attendance because of illness (Thurman & Piggins, 1982). The facilitator is a therapist, a producer, a catalyst, an observer/analyzer, all at the same time (Corey, 1985). The facilitator's duties include planning sessions, providing a tolerant and safe atmosphere, warming up the group, supporting and directing the actors, encouraging spontaneity, facilitating interaction, and summarizing the group's feedback. The position calls for creativity, courage, and charisma (Corey, 1985). A sense of humor and finely honed listening skills are also crucial (Thurman & Piggins, 1982). A successful facilitator helps older participants address extremely difficult questions such as "Where has it all gone?" "What do I do now?" "Who cares?" (Michaels, 1981, p. 177). By guiding the exploration and reexperience of personal histories and memories, the facilitator can help group members find meaning in their lives and an enhanced sense of self-worth.

Goals and Guidelines

It is important to establish goals when implementing a drama-based therapy. Modifications may be necessary to fit the needs of specific groups and situations; Stern (1988) recommends the following goals for older adult drama groups: maintain an atmosphere in which common concerns can be discussed freely; listen to one another; proceed in one's own way (there is no "right" way in improvisation); develop flexibility and promote risk taking; encourage the sharing of experiences through speaking, listening, acting, and reacting; debunk myths about older adults; be honest; be open to new experiences; be open to how one is perceived by others; be imaginative; generate supportive behaviors; and have fun! In certain situations it may be sufficient to summarize the goals as simply getting to know the other group members and sharing feelings with the group (Johnson, 1985). Whatever the goals, they should be presented to the group at the first meeting and agreed to by consensus (Stern, 1988). On page 341 is a form that can be used in developing a plan and specific goals for a drama therapy activity.

Early Sessions

The facilitator may need to take an especially active role in early sessions, asking questions to establish common ground and introducing warm-up activities to break the ice. Sadly, even older people who live together in a long-term care facility may not know each other very well (Thurman & Piggins, 1982). Questions about former homes, travel destinations, birthdays, ethnicity, former jobs, and holiday traditions can stimulate people to talk about themselves and their lives (Altman, 1983). Early on it is important to provide time for talk, to elicit information to be used as a basis for later activities, and to encourage the bonding of the group (Thurman & Piggins, 1982).

At the very first session the facilitator needs to set the tone by being sure to use participants' names, make personal comments, and greet group members with a handshake or another form of physical contact. Participants should be seated in a circle so that they can see one another and in order to reinforce the idea that all participants have equal status in the group (Thurman & Piggins, 1982). At first, activities in which everyone participates at the same time and no one feels singled out may prove to be the most comfortable. The improvisational nature of planned activities should also be stressed at this time, so that participants do not develop fears that they may be asked to memorize a script.

Drama Therapy Program Plan

Drama activity planned _____

Group facilitators_____

No. of sessions needed to complete activity _____

Estimated no. of participants _____

Prospective participants

_____   _____

_____   _____

_____   _____

_____   _____

_____

Objectives

___ Improve interpersonal relationships   ___ Increase self-confidence

___ Increase opportunity to socialize   ___ Improve social skills

___ Elevate mood   ___ Improve sensory stimulation

___ Increase concentration/attention   ___ Promote reminiscence

___ Increase sense of well-being   ___ Promote relaxation

___ Improve memory functioning   ___ Promote sense of belonging

___ Address losses   ___ Address environmental restrictions

___ Foster self-exploration   ___ Foster creativity

___ Increase assertiveness   ___ Foster enjoyment

Frequency of activity ___ 2X/week ___ Weekly ___ 2X/month ___ Monthly

Materials needed _____

_____

How activity is to be evaluated _____

_____

A Life Worth Living: Practical Strategies for Reducing Depression in Older Adults, by Pearl Mosher-Ashley and Phyllis Barrett. © 1997 Health Professions Press, Inc., Baltimore.

At this stage, as later, a unifying theme is more effective than a series of unrelated activities. Sessions seem more meaningful when a particular issue is explored. The activities built around the theme should be varied in order to provide for change of tempo, rest periods, and retention of interest (Thurman & Piggins, 1982). Early sessions can be based on such nonthreatening topics as how each individual got his or her name. Group members can adopt the roles of family members and act out the decision-making process (Altman, 1983). The importance of humor in the introductory sessions cannot be underestimated. Group members need to have fun, to gain confidence in themselves and trust in the other group members, and to feel free to be spontaneous before they can be asked to share their hopes and fears (Warren, 1984).

Structure of Sessions

As mentioned earlier, traditional psychodrama consists of three elements: a warm-up period, the action or dramatization, and an opportunity for group discussion and feedback. The purpose of the warm-up is to break down awkward barriers of silence and to help group members overcome inhibitions and reservations about performing and working with each other (Michaels, 1981; Schloss, 1988). When a session begins, a period of time should be allowed for greeting one another and settling in. Name tags may be useful in helping everyone, including the group facilitator, to remember first names (Michaels, 1981). During the warm-up period, the facilitator should greet participants personally, explain or reiterate the nature and purpose of the therapy, and invite questions. Each participant is then briefly interviewed and asked specifically about a particular topic, perhaps a relationship. Then the group brainstorms for a focus for the day's session (Corey, 1985). If this is a first session the group can participate in an introductory name game during the warm-up period, possibly sharing childhood nicknames or other personal information (Michaels, 1981). The warm-up period in later sessions should include a review of previous sessions (Michaels, 1981).

It is important for group members to relax. Many techniques can be used to work toward this objective. Sometimes listening to music and being encouraged to accompany it with flowing body movements can alleviate tension (Huddleston, 1989). Also, games can be utilized for this purpose. Group members can be asked where they might be or what they might be doing if they could be anywhere, doing anything. The facilitator could point to an empty chair and ask each group member to imagine someone—famous, fictitious, or from their own lives—sitting in the chair and to begin a dialogue with that person. Group members can also be asked to choose a time in their childhood and describe to the group what life was like then (Michaels, 1981). Another possibility is to ask each member of the group what feeling is most prominent at the moment and to elicit discussion on that theme (Nordin, 1987).

The warm-up activity or technique helps to engage the emotions of the group. It is an important part of psychodrama because it is from this element that the rest of the session develops (Michaels, 1981). A chance remark, a bit of information, or an individual's heightened emotions may develop into a productive session. It is important for the group facilitator to watch for these contributions and lead the group toward them when they surface (Michaels, 1981; Schloss, 1988).

In preparation for the second phase of the activity, the action, a protagonist is selected by the facilitator and other group members to provide the focus for the day's dramatic exploration. Themes may come from books, television, personal interests of members of the group, or the experience of the group facilitator. For example, the theme may be a vacation trip. Group members can be asked to brainstorm images, bring in posters and souvenirs, and try to recall their own trip experiences. Then the "vacation" can be broken into parts, all of which can be dramatized: booking the reservations, attending a concert or visiting a museum, ordering food in a restaurant, dealing with language differences, and so forth. Dramatizing familiar events in literature is another possibility (Thurman & Piggins, 1982).

Another approach is to perform an improvisation by supplying the who, what, when, where, and why for a character in a given situation. For example, family members decide that it is time for their grandfather to move in with them, but he refuses to leave his own home. In setting the drama in motion, it should be explained that people improvise all the time in real life. Limited props (e.g., man's hat, cane) add a nice touch to this activity, but are not required (Thurman & Piggins, 1982). Eventually, practitioners will evolve their own repertoire of applications, and they should look to the older people themselves for creative ideas (Langley, 1987).

Once the theme has been agreed on, protagonists should be prompted to explore it dramatically. Although they may begin with a verbal recounting of imaginary events or events in their own life, they should be encouraged to move toward acting out the event rather than describing it. Pretending that significant other people are present can further intensify the reality of the dramatic situation. Auxiliary egos, who may resemble significant people in protagonists' lives, can be chosen from the group and instructed by protagonists in how to play their roles. They can also take the parts of inanimate objects, pets, and the like. Although the audience is not directly involved in the action, they can identify with the protagonists, empathize with their situations, and gain insights about their own lives (Corey, 1985).

In the final stage, the discussion period that follows the action, the audience provides feedback. As ideas and emotional responses are shared, the facilitator should always supply support for anyone who needs it, particularly when emotionally charged issues are proposed (Corey, 1985). Michaels (1981) argues that drama therapy activities for older people should focus primarily on the positive, providing respite from preoccupation with ill health and losses (Michaels, 1981). In order to ensure that the experience is positive, it is important for the facilitator to model spontaneity, risk taking, self-disclosure, humor, creativity, empathy, and acceptance at all times, so that the members of the group are likely to be similarly supportive (Corey, 1985).

Evaluation

It is important to maintain records of the group's progress (p. 345 is a form that can be used for recording observations). Tape recording sessions and picture taking may be helpful in reviewing what has taken place. Written permission should be obtained beforehand for any photographs taken (Michaels, 1981). Michaels (1981) warns that it may take as many as five or more sessions for group members to become excited and involved. Consequently, it is probably best to delay making any observations about group cohesiveness and productivity until the fifth session or later. It is helpful to assess the extent to which participants remember what went on at previous sessions, the number of times participants make comments indicating that the workshops help them to forget their troubles and have a good time, the number of displays of pleasure and affection during sessions (e.g., smiles, hugs, kisses, handshakes), and the incidence of members offering thanks for the availability of the activity (Michaels, 1981). It is important that the facilitator not become discouraged and allow time for the participants to become familiar with each other and the process.

VARIATIONS ON DRAMA THERAPIES WITH OLDER ADULTS

Numerous drama activities have been developed for use with older adults or adapted for use from other venues. Many reflect the slightly different emphases of the specific drama-based therapy or school in which they originated. For convenience, the examples that follow are categorized by their theoretical place of origin, whether in psychodrama, dramatherapy, sociodrama, geriadrama, or creative drama in general. Whereas some activities require a highly trained practitioner in a given area, many can be used or adapted for use by caring health professionals with experience in group work, especially if assisted by theater aficionados with an empathy for and a good rapport with older people.

Psychodrama Activities

Psychodrama can be used in numerous activities, such as those described in the following paragraphs (Corcy, 1985).

In self-presentation protagonists play themselves as they typically function in a situation or relationship. If, for example, the goal is to improve the dynamics of a relationship with a family member, protagonists should demonstrate how they usually approach the person in a situation that involves a conflict. The protagonists may also state the problem and say something about the other individual.

In presentation of the other, rather than portray themselves, protagonists take on the role of the significant other person—family member, friend, or mate. In a completely subjective manner, protagonists act as they perceive the other person to act, allowing the facilitator and the rest of the group to understand how protagonists view the other person.

In role reversal protagonists are encouraged to switch roles with another person on stage. Protagonists take the role of the significant other, and the second

Drama Therapy Group Record Form

Drama activity _____ Date of session _____ Location _____

Use the behavioral observation key to score each participant's behavior during the session.

Behavioral observation key   b = Before activity,   a = After activity,   d = During activity,   NA = Not applicable.

Participant	Smiled	Laughed	Talked with others	Silent	Positive comments about self	Negative comments about self	Participated actively	Emotionally upset	Other

Follow-up on clients who were emotionally upset during session

Participant	Issue addressed during session	Seen individually after session	Other

A Life Worth Living: Practical Strategies for Reducing Depression in Older Adults, by Pearl Mosher-Ashley and Phyllis Barrett. © 1997 Health Professions Press, Inc., Baltimore.

actor takes the real-life role of the protagonist. This technique allows protagonists to understand better how the other person feels about them and why that person might react and behave in certain ways within the relationship.

Soliloquy, a monologue addressed directly to the audience, allows protagonists to express uncensored feelings and thoughts. Rather than constitute a separate activity, the soliloquy is best used as part of another application (e.g., during the course of a role reversal).

In the double technique an actor functioning as an auxiliary ego stands behind protagonists, acting with and even speaking for them on occasion. The double is often able to discern and express thoughts that protagonists are not comfortable articulating. If this technique is used in the context of an interaction between protagonists and an actor portraying a significant person in their life, the comments of the double may serve to escalate the interaction and to move protagonists closer to catharsis and self-revelation. A variation allows for multiple doubles, with different actors taking sides to make protagonists' ambivalence manifest.

After protagonists have left the stage, an auxiliary ego assumes their role, mirroring their posture, gestures, and words. By observing their own behavior as another mimics it, protagonists can begin to see themselves as others see them. The mirror technique can guide protagonists to a more objective picture of themselves.

Frequently used as part of the warm-up phase but adaptable for use as part of the primary action of a session, the Magic Shop encourages protagonists to imaginatively trade certain existing qualities for qualities they would prefer in their place. The exercise helps protagonists with values clarification, making them focus on what personal attributes might contribute to more rewarding interpersonal relationships.

Through the future projection technique, individuals are helped to deal with anticipated events that provoke anxiety and fear. Rather than simply talk about an upcoming meeting, interview, reunion, move, or life change, protagonists act out the future scene, preparing themselves psychologically to meet its challenges and receiving feedback from the group on ways to ensure a positive outcome.

Whereas psychoanalysis encourages the verbalization of dreams, psychodrama encourages the acting out of dreams. Protagonists may begin by pretending to recline in bed and then leaving the bed while reconstructing what was dreamed. Other group members can be assigned parts to act out. Protagonists should be given the freedom to change parts of the dream, thus gaining insight into personality patterns that may have contributed to the dream's original and altered forms.

Dramatherapy Activities

Costumes and Props

As a way of encouraging reminiscence of happy times and fulfilling roles in life, drama group participants can be asked to bring in articles from a bygone era to pass around, demonstrate, and discuss. The group facilitator might also be able to procure a particular kind of item (e.g., costume hats) for group members to try on or to work with. A mirror should be available so that all can admire themselves. Another variation is to invite members of a local theater group to put on a fashion show of period costumes for the group. A related activity uses audio-visual aids (e.g., photographs, slides) to conjure up stories of the past. Group members may be encouraged to improvise a short scene typical of a bygone era while standing alongside a projected picture of a familiar locale (Langley, 1987). A variation suggested by Thurman and Piggins (1982) involves the introduction of a quilt and the encouragement to speculate on its history, its maker, its owner(s), and the like. Warren (1984) uses a dilapidated briefcase or bag and asks group members to speculate on its history and owner or owners.

A more personal approach to reminiscence is suggested by Mazor (1982). Using music (e.g., Grieg's *Peer Gynt Suite*) to evoke visual and sensory images of nature, the facilitator asks participants to verbalize any image that comes to mind. Frequently, a scene from childhood or youth will occur to a group member and leading questions asked by the facilitator can help flesh out the scene and lead to its simple dramatization. Mazor uses the example of a man who recalled boyhood strawberry-picking excursions. When asked such questions as "What equipment do you need?" or "What should we do with the berries?," group members shared memories of appropriate berry-picking gear and the woodstoves and primitive ice boxes important in transforming berries into jam, pie, and other delicacies.

Reminiscence Theater

A community theater group concerned with older adults can be invited to perform at a long-term care facility or senior center. Using a format based on the British music hall or American vaudeville traditions, the performers can select appropriate songs and events from the past and include them as part of an informal show. The audience can be invited to sing along and participate in a postperformance discussion. To make the activity interactive, the theater group members could interview the older people prior to the performance, tailoring their questions to the specific memories and song preferences of the audience. Another variation would allow for even more spontaneity, with performers prepared to allow the audience to interject memories and requests during the actual performance. In this way they can guide the actors in an improvisational performance that is responsive to the audience's interests (Langley, 1987).

Group Reminiscence Theater

In group reminiscence theater group members are encouraged to reminisce about events in their own lives and to dramatize them (Langley, 1987). Michaels (1981) suggests posing questions such as "Where were you on the day that _____?," filling in the blank with the day a war ended, a scandal broke, or an assassination occurred as a prompt. More personal recollections, such as a childhood trauma or a rite of passage, are also appropriate for this activity. Although some older adults will be reluctant to participate, thinking perhaps that their own memories are unworthy of dramatization, staging more generic skits based on shared or similar memories may encourage participation (Langley, 1987).

Theater

Keeping disabilities and limitations in mind, it is possible to mount an actual theatrical production with a group of older people. It may be best to start with a one-act play or with familiar scenes excerpted from longer works. Anxiety can be lessened for the group participants who plan to appear on stage by de-emphasizing the need to memorize lines; scripts can be read or dialogue can be improvised around the storyline. Other group members can enjoy the camaraderie of the behind-the-scenes aspects of production: prop gathering, scene building, costume making, making up the actors, music arranging, lighting, and the like (Langley, 1987).

Michaels (1981) has generated lively discussion among older adults through the use of two famous pieces of literature in particular. In a nursing facility setting a group read from the scene between mother and son in Tennessee Williams's *The Glass Menagerie* and offered alternatives for the mother's behavior that might have fostered a better relationship. Another activity focused on the Langston Hughes poem "Mother to Son," and drew comments from every member of the group. Huddleston (1989) also cites the value of generating a group discussion about an issue raised by the performance of a literary work.

A Sociodrama Activity: Reenacting History

In a long-term care facility it is possible to map out a series of performances over a number of years dealing with the history of the facility or perhaps of facilities similar to it. Hickling (1989) took on as a project the dramatization of the history of a mental health facility, from inception to deinstitutionalization. The history or nature of other facilities—nursing facilities, senior centers, congregate housing complexes—may also be explored. The purpose of sociodrama is to give voice to a usually silent group. Older individuals may find it therapeutic to be able to speak out about the situation in which they find themselves, and the community may be better informed if invited to attend a performance of this type. Even the potential for change in the facility itself exists.

A Geriadrama Activity: Pantomime

As a warm-up activity, participants can be asked to mime how they are feeling at the moment, likes or dislikes, past career or leisure activities, and what they did earlier in life (e.g., before coming to live in a nursing facility). The activity encourages the use of the body while recognizing limitations attributable to infirmity. Alternatively, the facilitator may volunteer to mime with the help of instructions from an individual who is physically disabled (Michaels, 1981). This activity can also introduce individuals to other members of the group.

Creative Drama Activities

Older adults can be exposed to other creative drama activities, such as Living Pictures, Proverbs, Safety on the Streets, the Magic Box, storytelling/character creation, and To Be Continued (group storytelling).

In Living Pictures (a variation on the childhood game, Statues), pictures of groups of people in different poses and suggested relationships are introduced to small groups. The group is invited to speculate on the individuals, relationships, and situations pictured, based on body language, clothing, and other observations. Then group members are asked to create a living picture: Taking on the roles of the individuals in the still picture, the group sets things in motion briefly before being instructed to freeze. The scene can be pantomimed or spontaneous dialogue can be incorporated. Pictures used may suggest topics such as the arrival of a new baby, a wedding, an auto accident, or winning the lottery. The group can be encouraged to introduce a problem into the scenario (e.g., the groom has misplaced the ring at his wedding) and to improvise a scene (Thurman & Piggins, 1982). This activity can be made more relevant to a group of older adults by choosing pictures that suggest that the pictured group is dealing with a hospitalization, an individual's move to a congregate living complex, and so forth.

In the Proverbs activity a group is asked to improvise a scene embodying the truth of a well-known expression. Expressions such as "Every cloud has a silver lining," "Actions speak louder than words," or "Two heads are better than one" may be appropriate for a group of older people, particularly if participants are encouraged to apply the adage to important situations from the past or to current issues in their lives. The facilitator can start by encouraging the participants to think of proverbs they remember from childhood, discuss the meaning of one of them for further exploration, and then create a situation through which to demonstrate the wisdom of the saying. This activity might also lend itself to a discussion of changing mores or values during the participants' lifetimes, abiding, timeless truths, or both (Thurman & Piggins, 1982).

Safety on the Streets is a particularly appropriate activity for older adults living independently. The facilitator can begin by introducing a newspaper clipping about a recent mugging, telephone scam, or other safety issue that is relevant to older people. Then the facilitator takes the role of interviewer in a man-on-the-street format, asking group members questions about their perception of crime (e.g., Is it getting worse?), of news coverage (e.g., Is crime exaggerated in the media?), the causes of crime, self-help possibilities, and so forth. Improvisations can be set up later based on the viable ideas that arise during the question/answer activity. Ideas can also be shared with local law enforcement agencies, community watch groups, and the media (Thurman & Piggins, 1982).

Based on a technique used by Stanislavski in the training of actors for the theater, the Magic Box begins with a decorated box and the question "What do you suppose is in the box?" The group is encouraged to free-associate, with the facilitator being more or less directive, perhaps helping the group narrow its theme (e.g., food, treasure). Another approach is for the facilitator to direct the group through a series of questions about the probable texture, size, weight, or design of the imagined object. Conjectures can be incorporated into a scene to be acted out. Related activities include a "magic newspaper," which encourages group members to pass around a real newspaper and imaginatively make something else out of it (e.g., telescope, hat, airplane), and "magic clay," in which participants are encouraged to mime the manipulation of imaginary clay. All of the exercises encourage creativity, imagination, spontaneity, and even body movement (Warren, 1984).

In storytelling/character creation participants are encouraged to move from recounting family stories to actually playing the parts of various family members. This activity, which is guided by a supportive facilitator and derives feedback from a group of peers, may provide an individual with the role flexibility, communication skills, and confidence to transfer the performance to the more important potential audience of adult children and grandchildren (Warren, 1984).

To Be Continued allows the group to create their own script or story, one that has significance for them. The group sits in a circle, and the facilitator offers a starting point for the story, mentioning time, place, protagonist—whatever comes to mind. Each member of the group then contributes a word, phrase, or sentence to the evolving story. Contributions can come from individuals according to the seating order or a Nerf ball can be tossed from one participant to a randomly chosen participant in order to liven up the proceedings. This part of the activity can be audio- or videotaped and written down later, if desired. Either during the evolution of the story or after the fact, the group can act it out (Warren, 1984).

References

Altman, K.P. (1983). Psychodrama with the institutionalized elderly: A method for role re-engagement. *Journal of Group Psychotherapy, Psychodrama & Sociometry, 36*(3), 87–96.

Bielanska, A., Cechnicki, A., & Budzyna-Dawidowski, P. (1991). Drama therapy as a means of rehabilitation for schizophrenic patients: Our impressions. *American Journal of Psychotherapy, 45*, 566–575.

Carman, M.B., & Nordin, S.R. (1984). Psychodrama: A therapeutic modality for the elderly in nursing homes. *Clinical Gerontologist, 3*(1), 15–24.

Corey, G. (1985). *Theory and practice of group counseling* (2nd ed.). Pacific Grove, CA: Brooks/Cole.

Davies, M.H. (1987). Dramatherapy and psychodrama. In S. Jennings (Ed.), *Dramatherapy: Theory and practice for teachers and clinicians* (pp. 104–123). Cambridge, MA: Brookline Books.

Davis, B. (1985). The impact of creative drama training on psychological states of older adults: An exploratory study. *Gerontologist, 25*, 315–321.

Davis, B. (1987). Some roots and relatives of creative drama as an enrichment activity for older adults. *Educational Gerontology, 13*, 297–306.

Hickling, F.W. (1989). Sociodrama in the rehabilitation of chronic mentally ill patients. *Hospital and Community Psychiatry, 40*, 402–406.

Huddleston, R. (1989). Drama with elderly people. *British Journal of Occupational Therapy, 52*, 298–300.

Johnson, D.R. (1982). Developmental approaches in drama therapy. *Arts in Psychotherapy, 9*, 183–189.

Johnson, D.R. (1985). Expressive group psychotherapy with the elderly: A drama therapy approach. *International Journal of Group Psychotherapy, 35*(1), 109–127.

Johnson, D.R. (1986). The developmental method in drama therapy: Group treatment with the elderly. *Arts in Psychotherapy, 13*, 17–33.

Kane, R. (1992). The potential abuses, limitations, and negative effects of classical psycho-dramatic techniques in group counseling. *Journal of Group Psychotherapy, Psychodrama & Sociometry, 44*, 181–189.

Langley, D. (1987). Dramatherapy with elderly people. In S. Jennings (Ed.), *Dramatherapy: Theory and practice for teachers and clinicians* (pp. 233–256). Cambridge, MA: Brookline Books.

Mazor, R. (1982). Drama therapy for the elderly in a day care center. *Hospital and Community Psychiatry, 33*, 577–579.

Michaels, C. (1981). Geriadrama. In G. Schattner & R. Courtney (Eds.), *Drama in therapy* (pp. 175–192). New York: Drama Book Specialists.

Nordin, S. (1987). Psychodrama with the elderly. *Journal of Group Psychotherapy, Psychodrama & Sociometry, 39*, 51–61.

Schloss, G. (1988). Growing old and growing: Psychodrama with the elderly. In B. Mac-lennan, S. Saul, & M.B. Weiner (Eds.), *Group psychotherapies for the elderly* (pp. 89–104). Madison, CT: International Universities Press.

Stern, R. (1988). Drama gerontology: Group therapy through counseling and drama tech-niques. In B. Maclennan, S. Saul, & M.B. Weiner (Eds.), *Group psychotherapies for the elderly* (pp. 251–265). Madison, CT: International Universities Press.

Thurman, A.H., & Piggins, C.A. (1982). *Drama activities with older adults: A handbook for leaders*. New York: Haworth Press.

Warren, B. (1984). Drama: Using the imagination as a stepping-stone for personal growth. In B. Warren (Ed.), *Using the creative arts in therapy*. Cambridge, MA: Brookline Books.

Weisberg, J., & Haberman, M.R. (1992). Drama, humor, and music to reduce family anxiety in a nursing home. *Geriatric Nursing, 13*(1), 22–24.

Appendix
Resources for Drama Therapies

Organizations

American Board of Examiners in
   Psychodrama, Sociometry and Group Psychotherapy
Box 844
Cooper Station
New York, New York 10276
Founded in 1975, the Board establishes professional standards and certifies qual-ified professionals; a booklet is available listing trainers and practitioners

American Society of Group Psychotherapy & Psychodrama (ASGPP)
6728 Old McLean Village
McLean, Virginia 22101
Phone (703) 556-9222
Fax (703) 556-8729

Professional organization for therapists specializing in working with groups, offering professional development opportunities

National Coalition of Arts Therapies Associations (NCATA)
2000 Century Plaza
Suite 108
Columbia, Maryland 21044
Phone (410) 997-4040
Fax (410) 997-4048
An alliance of professional associations dedicated to the advancement of the arts as therapeutic modalities

National Association for Drama Therapy (NADT)
6 Woods Road
Sherman, Connecticut 06405
Phone (203) 350-1620
Fax (203) 355-3838
A membership organization for working drama therapists and those interested in the field of drama therapy; the Association oversees undergraduate and graduate training programs and certifies Registered Drama Therapists (R.D.T.), a credential needed to work in mental health facilities in many states

Bring me the sunset in a cup,
Reckon the morning's flagons up
And say how many Dew,
Tell me how far the morning leaps—
Tell me what time the weaver sleeps
Who spun the breadths of blue!

Emily Dickinson, Poem #128

Is It Working?

Monitoring Client Progress and Evaluating the Program

For the facilitator, monitoring clients' progress and evaluating the effectiveness of the therapeutic intervention program is as important as selecting and designing the initial treatment plan. These aspects should be considered prior to implementing treatment. Otherwise, some measures that could be effective will not have been administered. Record keeping is frequently the least enjoyable aspect of planning and implementing intervention programs. This is particularly true for professionals who have selected their field of specialization because of the opportunity it provides for helping and working with clients. However, accurate and adequate record keeping is an essential component of providing treatment. Using structured forms and requiring clients to record their own behavior can reduce the amount of time spent in paperwork, reserving more time for the other aspects of successful intervention.

INITIAL ASSESSMENT

The initial assessment is usually conducted in the first two interviews with the client. The first session should focus on establishing rapport with the client and obtaining a narrative report about his or her situation. If the client appears to be comfortable discussing the situation, a depression or life satisfaction scale may be administered at this time. If more time is needed to establish rapport, the scale can be given in the second session. During the second session a specific target problem should be selected for change. It is best to select only one problem. If the client presents several issues—feelings of depression, loneliness, conflict with family members, desire for greater independence in functioning—the issue with highest priority should be selected. The other issues can be set aside for future intervention or the point can be made that changes must be undertaken one step (i.e., one problem) at a time. In selecting the problem targeted for change, one should choose an issue within the scope of one's experience and expertise. For example, resolving conflicts with family members requires skills not addressed in this book. If these conflicts are addressed by someone without the appropriate training and supervision, a situation could be made worse. However, if the client identifies an area within the caregiver's field of specialization (e.g., greater independence in functioning), intervention is ethically appropriate.

Once a problem has been targeted for change, short-term and long-term goals should be established. The short-term goal should be an outcome that can feasibly be met by the third or fourth session. The long-term goal is what can be realistically expected at the conclusion of treatment. Every effort should be made to encourage the client to provide these goals. Goals can be reframed more realistically if the initial expectations do not appear to be achievable. Next, the client should explore the different treatment modalities and be encouraged to select one that appeals to him or her. If a group is being established for one of the treatment approaches, the client could be invited to join or wait for an alternative, preferable treatment, if possible.

Preferably, the records concerning the individual's depressed state and steps taken to remediate it should be addressed in a separate section of each client's case record. The purpose is twofold: First, the person who is designing and implementing the plan can quickly review and make modifications in the plan based upon the client's progress. Second, the accumulation of information concerning the treatment offers a cohesive package for administrative review (Pinsker & Sporn, 1980). A complete record can also serve as the basis for reports and case presentations (e.g., Betz, 1980). A sample form to be used for the initial assessment and planning of treatment can be found on page 356.

DEVELOPMENT OF A TREATMENT PLAN

In working with older adults one must keep in mind that many of them have little familiarity with psychological concepts and treatment (Knight, 1986). Clients need to be educated about the therapeutic process as it unfolds. This can be accomplished by simply explaining the steps being taken, the concepts involved (e.g., short-term and long-term goals), and the rationale for actions.

The treatment should be time-limited. A fixed number of sessions conducted over a specific period of time should be established and agreed on by the therapist and the client. Another time-limited period of treatment can be negotiated at the conclusion of the first course if it seems necessary. Starting and ending dates for treatment should be identified at the beginning of treatment. During each session progress toward the goal should be reviewed and monitored. Modifications should be made if gains are not achieved in a reasonable number of sessions. The gains to be made depend on the treatment modality employed and the severity of the depression experienced by the client. For example, in cognitive-behavioral therapy, improvement should not be expected until well into treatment (e.g., in the change phase). Also, clients who experience severe depression require extensive intervention or a special type of treatment before they begin to show improvement.

Clients should be differentiated as to whether the depressive symptoms are caused by the client's outlook on life and lack of coping skills or by some other event, such as loss of a spouse, physical illness, lack of social network, insufficient pleasurable activities, or boredom. In the latter situation the client frequently has drifted into a pattern of living that is not rewarding and offers much time to ruminate about losses. Often, there is some overlap in these two differentiation categories, and effort is required to determine what is fueling the client's depressive affect. If the underlying cause of the client's inability to influence change is a belief that efforts are hopeless and change is not possible, a cognitive-behavioral approach should be used. If the feelings of depression are attributable to loneliness or feelings of worthlessness, or if they are secondary to some other situation, one of the ten other interventions described in Chapters 4 through 13 is recommended.

Traditionally, clients have not participated in the process of planning mental health interventions (McLean & Miles, 1974). However, their involvement in identifying the problem and elucidating treatment goals enhances communication, increases their motivation to participate in treatment efforts, and increases the

Initial Assessment Form

Client _____ Address_____

	Date completed	Pretreatment measure used	Score
1.	_____	_____	_____
2.	_____	_____	_____

Problem from the client's perspective

_____

_____

_____

Reports concerning the problem from others' perspectives

_____

_____

_____

Goals

Short-term _____

_____

Long-term _____

_____

Treatment Plan

Treatment modality to be used _____

    Individual _____ Group _____

Proposed intervention plan _____

Expected duration _____

Frequency of contact ___ 2X/week ___ Weekly

               ___ 2X/month ___ Monthly

Who will implement plan _____

Others involved _____

chances that the treatment gains can be generalized beyond the duration of the intervention.

To ensure that clients have participated in the planning of their treatment, Menenberg (1995) recommends that they sign a written outline of the plan. Although an excellent suggestion, Abraham, Niles, Thiel, Siarkowski, and Cowling (1991) point out that many older adults are reluctant to sign forms. Clients may feel some hesitancy if a signature is required as proof of having planned an intervention.

PROGRAM EVALUATION

Evaluating the effectiveness of a program can be conducted on two levels: its impact on the individual and its usefulness in treating a larger number of people who share a common problem. The latter is usually used to convince administrators or prospective funding sources to expand the program to treat a larger number of people and, consequently, requires a carefully designed plan.

Anecdotal Reports

Many treatment programs developed by well-meaning professionals in all of the disciplines have relied on "anecdotal" support. Anecdotal support consists of reports by staff, family, and the client as to the effectiveness of the procedures used. The reports are regarded as anecdotal because they are not based on any formal assessments. They do not involve any record forms, specific scales, or even a review of other documentation kept concerning the client. The anecdotal report represents an intuition about or an overall sense of what has happened. As such, the report can be influenced easily by "social desirability," the willingness of the person who is being asked to report on the effectiveness to describe what the other wishes to hear. The client and family or staff also may be affected by the amount of time and effort expended on the problem. Simply having something done about a problem situation may result in a placebo effect, whereby the client improves as a result of the belief that the treatment is working. Given these potential sources of error, anecdotal reports are not considered to be reliable.

The anecdotal report may reflect the perception that things are better and the problem is resolved. However, if the factors maintaining the lowered sense of well-being have not been corrected, the perceived improvement likely will be temporary. Also, if an intervention is time consuming or costly to implement, it would be advantageous to know whether it indeed works before implementing it on a larger scale.

Administrative personnel who are involved in quality assurance are not impressed by anecdotal reports. However, the ability to support claims of effectiveness with objective data will sway them. Collecting objective data involves some planning and the use of comparative measures.

Pre- and Postmeasure Assessment

Pre- and postmeasure assessments compare the client's behavior before and after treatment. Depending on the client, either a depression or life satisfaction scale can be administered. It may make sense to use one of each in order to understand which aspect reflects the most change.

It is important to select an assessment scale that measures accurately the change sought and that is sufficiently sensitive to detect the type of changes expected from the intervention. It is wise to select several measures. For example, one of the authors' clients used a series of structured relaxation exercises with a cued recall to help reduce feelings of tension during stressful periods of the day. Before beginning an audiotaped relaxation exercise, he would tap himself on the shoulder. Later, when he found himself in a stressful situation (e.g., driving in traffic), he used a tap on the shoulder to elicit a relaxation response. At the beginning of treatment, he completed a self-report measure to determine the amount of anxiety he was experiencing and the degree to which it interfered with his life. The self-report measure was readministered at the end of treatment 3 months later. Very little change was reflected in the measure. However, the client reported feeling better. In discussing the reasons behind his feelings, he described how he had consumed a bottle of 100 antacid tablets every week prior to treatment. At the conclusion of treatment, he had not consumed a full bottle of tablets in the previous month. Additional measures that can be used to assess effectiveness include a weekly record of people interacted with, activities attended, tasks accomplished, or any other responses that are indicative of improvement. The weekly record can be maintained for 3 weeks prior to treatment and 3 weeks after the end of treatment.

Follow-up assessments should be conducted to ensure that the effects of treatment continue beyond the duration of treatment. Knowing that the effects are long-lasting will provide impetus to the therapist to implement the intervention with other clients and help to demonstrate its effectiveness to administrators. If the effects wear off, this is an indication that there may be other factors influencing the client's initial improvement or that some changes need to be made in the treatment to ensure maintenance of the gains achieved. Ideally, follow-up assessments should be conducted at 2- and 6-month intervals. These assessments should include a readministration of the scales used for the pre- and postmeasure assessments. In addition, a narrative report in which clients are asked to provide a subjective assessment of their well-being is helpful. The follow-up may be conducted over the telephone. Telephone follow-ups are employed commonly by mental health professionals and have also been used by medical professionals (e.g., Closson, Mattingly, Finne, & Larson, 1994). A sample record form for the follow-up assessment is provided on page 359.

Incorporation of Clients as Controls

The use of a control group is an effective approach to assess how well an intervention plan has worked with several people who share a common problem. A control group is made up of two or more people who are as similar (e.g., gender, closeness in age, physical condition, cognitive functioning, health) as possible to the individuals receiving the treatment being assessed. The number of people in the control group should equal the number of clients receiving treatment. Even

Follow-Up Assessment

Client _____

Address _____

Date of follow-up _____

Follow-up conducted ____ in person _____ over the phone

Treatment modality _____

Date treatment ended _____

1.   Have you had any difficulty with sadness or feeling down? (If no, go to Question 4.)

2.   Are the feelings as bad as when we started _____?
                                                                (specify treatment)

3.   Have you been doing anything special to cope with these feelings? (Ask for specific examples.)

4.   Have things improved in any way? (Ask for specific examples.)

5.   Describe an average day for you.

6.   Do you get out to see ____ friends ____ family ____ others?

     Who specifically? _____

7.   Have you received many visitors?

8.   Do you ____ make ____ or receive phone calls from friends, family or others?

9.   Readminister scale used as the premeasure and the postmeasure.

     Scale _____

     Score _____

A Life Worth Living: Practical Strategies for Reducing Depression in Older Adults, by Pearl Mosher-Ashley and Phyllis Barrett. ©1997 Health Professions Press, Inc., Baltimore.

when only one client is receiving an intervention, another client should be selected to serve as a control. The best approach is to begin with pairs of matched clients and then to select one to serve as the control by using a random procedure such as the flip of a coin. (It is important to bear in mind that a strong feeling that one client should receive the treatment while another is put on hold for a future time could inadvertently bias the results. Feelings about the client who is to receive the treatment and about the type of interaction that takes place could produce the bulk of the effect that one is inclined to attribute to the intervention.) The controls are given pre- and postmeasure assessments, but they are not exposed to the intervention plan. Because the controls do not receive treatment, their scores on the pre- and postmeasure assessments are not expected to show improvement. Individuals selected to serve as controls should be clients who can benefit from the intervention plan. In fact, they may be clients for whom intervention is planned in the future. In this way data collected about their functioning can be compared to responses collected before and after future intervention, thereby increasing the documentation concerning the program's effectiveness.

When a control group is used to compare the effectiveness of the treatment on a group of clients, both the premeasure and the postmeasure should be administered. It may be tempting to administer only a postmeasure assessment. However, without the premeasure it will not be clear whether the two groups differ in their level of depression or life satisfaction. For example, the treatment group may have comprised more severely depressed clients than did the control group. On the postmeasure, the treatment and control groups could have scores that do not differ significantly. However, a comparison of the pre- and postmeasures could reveal considerable difference for one group but not the other.

Single-Client Designs

When only a few clients are to receive treatment and no others are available to serve as controls, it is possible to design the intervention to permit each client to act as his or her own control. This strategy can be implemented in several different ways, the most common being a reversal of treatment and a multiple baseline design (Christensen, 1994).

Reversal of Treatment

In reversal of treatment response measures are recorded in numerical form (e.g., number of times the client visited friends or engaged in activities outside his or her home) on a daily or weekly basis. The measures can consist of any indicator of the client's well-being, including the number of pleasurable activities engaged in, number of tasks completed, amount of unstructured time spent brooding, number of contacts with others in which a conversation took place, and so forth. The same measure selected should be recorded for all phases of the program. A reversal of treatment design typically comprises four phases (Barlow, 1992). The first phase consists of the period prior to treatment. The response measure is recorded for 2 or more weeks to determine the level of functioning before efforts are made to improve it. During the second phase, the introduction of treatment, the response measure should demonstrate an improvement over the pretreatment period. To ensure that it is the treatment at work and not some other factor, the therapist should institute the third phase, in which the treatment is discontinued for a period of time. Without treatment, the response level should worsen. Treatment is reinstituted in the fourth stage, and the response level should improve once again. For demonstration purposes, the response measure is usually displayed in graphic form. A sample graph of a treatment plan employing a reversal of treatment design is supplied on page 362.

A reversal of treatment design is a useful method to demonstrate the effectiveness of an intervention in a single client. However, the discontinuation of treatment simply to demonstrate its effectiveness may not feel ethically appropriate. Exposure to treatment may also influence the client in such a way that its discontinuation may not result in the expected decline. Experience with treatment may lead the client to the realization that some events are indeed within his or her control. In such cases an alternative design is available.

Multiple Baseline Across Clients

A multiple baseline design can take three forms: across clients, across behavior, and across settings. For the type of interventions described in this book, the multiple baseline across clients is the most suitable. At least three but preferably four clients should receive treatment. The clients should not come in contact with each other prior to or during treatment. Each client undergoes the same intervention but at different points in time. The same response measure (e.g., task completion, contact with friends, activities outside the home) is recorded by all three clients for a period of 2 to several weeks. The treatment is then begun with the first client, but not with the second and third clients. The response measure continues to be recorded by all three clients. After the first client has experienced the treatment for approximately 4 weeks and is showing improvement based on the response measure, the same treatment is initiated with the second client but not with the third. Both the first and second clients receive treatment, and all three clients record the response measure. After the second client has been receiving treatment for a period of several weeks and improvement has been demonstrated, the treatment is begun with the third client. At this juncture, all three clients receive treatment and continue to record their responses. If improvement in the response measure takes place uniformly when treatment is initiated with each client, the effectiveness of the treatment will be demonstrated. Because more than one client has shown improvement, it can be argued that the treatment, not some other artifact of the process involved, is responsible for the improvement. As with the reversal of treatment design, the response measure is usually presented graphically in order to demonstrate the program's effectiveness. A sample multiple baseline across clients graph is shown on page 363 (readers should note that space constraints prevent the presentation of daily data, but the data should be recorded and graphically presented every day).

Reversal of Treatment Design

A Life Worth Living: Practical Strategies for Reducing Depression in Older Adults, by Pearl Mosher-Ashley and Phyllis Barrett. ©1997 Health Professions Press, Inc., Baltimore.

Multiple Baseline Across Clients Design

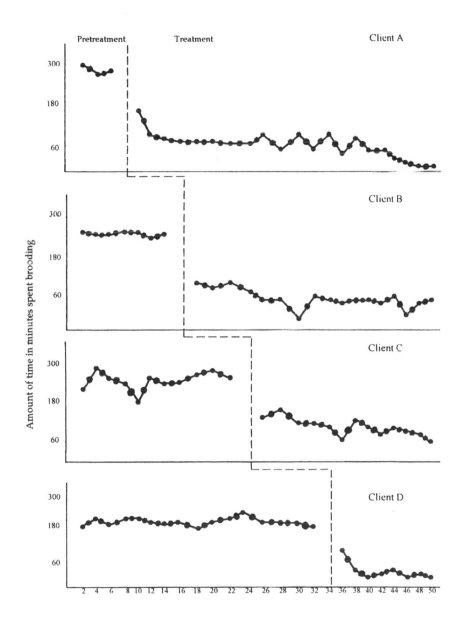

A Life Worth Living: Practical Strategies for Reducing Depression in Older Adults, by Pearl Mosher-Ashley and Phyllis Barrett. ©1997 Health Professions Press, Inc., Baltimore.

CLIENT PROGRESS MONITORING

Typically, health care and social services professionals employ a systematic approach in maintaining records about their interventions. They should do so when undertaking an intervention concerned with an affective problem. The particular system employed is not important as long as it provides a detailed and accurate account of what transpired during treatment and its outcomes. Efforts should be made to avoid the use of a record-keeping system that is overly complicated. Many professionals have found that elaborate recording is time consuming and reduces the amount of contact with clients (Addy-Keller & McElwaney, 1993; Brider, 1992). Records must be maintained, but a simple yet comprehensive approach is best.

Case Records

Since the beginning of the 1970s the trend in mental health interventions has been toward a problem-focused approach to record keeping. Initially, records were maintained in a format called the narrative chart. The narrative chart was an ongoing record with little structure on which the therapist and various staff in residential settings added assessment data, observations, and treatment ideas as they occurred. This form of charting was perceived to be disorganized, unreadable, and lacking in clarity (Dayringer, 1978). Recording information on narrative charts was also perceived by staff in residential settings as a chore unrelated to providing care (Williams, Jacobs, Debski, & Revere, 1974). One of the first departures from the narrative chart format was the problem-oriented record developed by Lawrence Weed.

Problem-Oriented Record

The problem-oriented record (POR) was initially designed to shift the focus from diagnostic labels and their symptoms to the client's specific functional problems (Harvey, Atkinson, Gale, & Lantinga, 1974; Katz & Woolley, 1975). The POR is a method of documenting all information concerning a given client, usually in a psychiatric hospital or a mental health center. It consists of five major components (Gilandas, 1972):

Database—These data include identification, chief complaint, present illness, medical history, social history, family and marital history, and psychological assessment.

Problem list—The problem list represents all of the problems exhibited by the client, based on the data collected. The problems are numbered and labeled descriptively.

Treatment plan—A plan for dealing with each of the problems identified is developed and is cross-indexed by a number for each problem.

Progress notes—The client's progress is noted at regular intervals and recorded and cross-indexed by the problem number. Both subjective and objective information are provided, along with material related to the treatment plan.

Discharge summary—Discharge summary refers to the termination of treatment. Conclusions concerning outcome, prognosis of future recurrence, and recommendations for maintenance of gains or future help are described.

The POR has several advantages over the narrative chart. The information contained in the case record is written in a structured form, permitting therapists and others to follow the client's progress in treatment and to identify effective and ineffective aspects of the treatment (Gilandas, 1972; Harvey et al., 1974). The format of the database and progress notes also enables individuals from all disciplines to review the information and add to it (Katz & Woolley, 1975; Williams et al., 1974).

Alternative Approaches

The POR has been criticized for the limitations it places on the recording of progress notes. According to McLean and Miles (1974), there are only two options in recording the notes: either noting the date when the problem has been resolved or making no comment because the problem has not been resolved. Also, although the POR focuses on problems and their treatment, the sequential nature of the records (with several problems being addressed on the same page every day) makes it difficult to perceive interventions for a single problem as a whole (Pinsker & Sporn, 1980). In response to the latter problem Berni and Ready (1974) recommended that the material be organized into chapters, each addressing a discrete problem. A variation on this theme was proposed by Pinsker and Sporn (1980), who advocated that a new page, divided into areas designated by discipline (e.g., nursing, activities, social work, mental health) be employed each day.

Although the focus is still on the client's functional problems and their treatment, the elaborate system of the POR is no longer in general use. The basic components, however, have been retained; for example, the detailed database is universally used, as are progress notes and the discharge summary. The treatment plan is usually developed in response to an adaptive problem and recorded as such. It should be noted, however, that the treatment of pathological conditions tends to be directed to the syndrome and is not limited to symptomatic problems (e.g., Zawacky, Levit, Khan, & Bhattacharyya, 1992). Treatment must clearly specify outcomes and be designed to reach these goals. The progress notes tend to involve a detailed summary of what transpired during each treatment session. Some information concerning the client's progress toward the goal of treatment is also included.

The POR approach is also used in health care disciplines other than mental health. This approach has been used in documenting nursing care (Buckley-Womack & Gidney, 1987), postanesthesia care (Reed, 1991), nursing education (Schuster & Colvin, 1986), and pastoral counseling (Dayringer, 1978). In many cases the systems developed to address the problems dealt with in these fields may be adapted for use with programs to reduce depression or increase life satisfaction.

Progress Notes

The most common approach used by mental health professionals to record the steps taken in treatment and monitor the client's progress is progress notes. Typically, at the conclusion of a session the therapist records a brief narrative account of what transpired. Individual progress notes are prepared for each client and are placed in that individual's file. The date, time, and location of the session (if it is a place other than the therapist's office) must be included. A general summary of what transpired in the session, highlighting the most prominent issues addressed, is also included, as is a brief description of the aspect of the treatment provided and the client's reaction. The progress notes should also include an evaluation of the client's progress, based on criteria established in the treatment plan (Lechowicz & Carmack, 1974). Some therapists ask the client to complete a brief depression scale prior to each session, whereas others write a brief report of the client's verbal description of how he or she fared on the specific criteria during the period since the last session. Objective information (i.e., direct observation of the client's progress) should be differentiated from subjective information (i.e., client-based reports). Progress notes tend to be about one third to a full page long, handwritten. If further detail needs to be added to any of the items listed, the reverse side of the page can be used. (See page 367 for a sample form for recording progress notes.)

The method employed in recording progress notes can vary according to setting. In some settings, particularly psychiatric inpatient clinics, each discipline records notes on different sections of the chart. In other residential settings all or some disciplines write sequentially on the same page (Pinsker & Sporn, 1980).

Pinsker and Sporn's approach (1980) to record keeping, in which a new page, divided into different areas by discipline, is used each day, is particularly useful in residential care settings. Devoting a section to the client's depression or lack of life satisfaction would enable nursing staff to record observations and the implementation of any aspects of the treatment for which they are responsible.

Given the large amount of charting nursing personnel must complete, it is best to consider a brief, checklist-type format if nurses or direct care staff are to record their observations of the client's emotional state or the implementation of treatment. Permission to include a new data gathering section on the chart must be obtained and the recording system approved before it is introduced. Lucatorto, Petras, Drew, and Zbuckvich (1991) recommend a simple 24-hour record containing a column of specific observations or tasks completed and three check-off columns beside it representing the three different shifts (i.e., 7 A.M.–3 P.M. 3–11 P.M., 11 P.M.–7 A.M.). The direct care staff or nurses assigned to the older adult or to monitor treatment record their initials in the respective shift column. Similar recording systems have been advocated by other medical professionals (e.g., Addy-Keller & McElwaney, 1993; Buckley-Womack & Gidney, 1987). Checklists and flow sheets with specific behaviors and responses listed are most frequently recommended. A checklist of depressive symptoms applicable to a wide range of clients can be prepared, duplicated, and used for all clients. It is important to include specific responses, otherwise, vague and even trivial statements such as "doing OK" will be recorded (Buckley-Womack & Gidney, 1987). In assessing treatment effects emphasis should be placed on outcome measures. It is also wise to require the staff member responsible for the client on a specific shift to include a signature or initials designating the respondent. Noncompliance in extra charting

Client Progress Notes

Client _____

Address _____

Session no. _____   Location _____

Date _____   Time _____ A.M. / P.M.

Status since last session _____

_____

_____

_____

_____

Treatment implemented _____

_____

Progress made toward goal _____

_____

_____

_____

_____

_____

_____

_____

_____

_____

A Life Worth Living: Practical Strategies for Reducing Depression in Older Adults, by Pearl Mosher-Ashley and Phyllis Barrett. ©1997 Health Professions Press, Inc., Baltimore.

of this type is a frequent problem. Knowing who the respondent is will enable the staff member to receive the proper appreciation. Staff who do not record may be approached discreetly and their help requested. (See p. 369 for a sample form to be used for staff records.)

Client Involvement

Requiring clients to assume partial responsibility for recording their feelings, thoughts, and behavior results in comprehensive records and reduces the amount of recording by the therapist. It is common to ask clients to complete assessment forms independent of the therapist. Even other disciplines (e.g., nursing) are asking clients to complete self-assessment devices prior to receiving treatment (Hirshfield-Bartek, Hassey Dow, & Creaton, 1990). Several clinicians have recommended involving clients in recording progress notes. Badding (1989) recommends that clients be asked at the end of the session to summarize what was covered and what was most important to them. The clinician then writes this information into the record along with his or her impressions. This practice was found to contribute to greater retention of treatment plans, improved concentration on the work, and a feeling that therapy was an easier process, presumably because there was less anxiety about what was written in the notes and more clarity about the procedures involved. In addition, asking clients to assist in recording progress notes helped practitioners to complete that portion of the file in a timely manner. In this era of accountability and client rights, involving clients in recording progress notes reduces the risk that misunderstandings will take place. Albeck and Goldman (1991) report that some clients can participate effectively in codocumentation in the progress notes. Using their approach clients dictate their view of the issues covered in treatment during the last several minutes of a session. The therapists then dictate their comments in the presence of the clients. The notes are transcribed from the tape into a written record, which is then reviewed by both parties at the beginning of the next session.

When considering client involvement in case recording, therapists should introduce the documentation procedure in a simple, nonthreatening manner (Badding, 1989). If the client appears interested, as reflected by requests for more information, the client can be asked to participate. If the client appears reticent about being involved, it is best not to pursue the matter. Many clients who are depressed or anxious may feel threatened by the added responsibility. They can be invited to participate in the recording of progress notes later in their intervention. Another option, recommended by Solomon (1987), is to write the notes in the presence of the client and read them to him or her for input on the accuracy of the therapist's impression. In this manner the records maintained are demystified, accuracy is ensured, and the client becomes an active participant without feeling that a greater degree of cognitive functioning is required.

Computerized Records

Many therapists have begun to use computer-based records to save time and organize the material more effectively. Zemcov, Barclay, Brush, and Blass (1984)

Staff Record Form

Client _____ Date _____

Behavioral observations	7 A.M.–3 P.M.	3–11 P.M.	11 P.M.–7 A.M.
Affect			
Smiled			
Laughed			
Appeared sad			
Wept			
Interactions			
Initiated conversation with staff			
Initiated conversation with residents			
Responded to comments by staff			
Responded to comments by residents			
Activity level			
Attended scheduled activities			
Engaged in individual activity			
Sat for periods doing nothing			
Watched TV for much of the time			
Purposeful activity			
Helped another resident			
Helped staff			
Engaged in other helpful activity			
Involvement with family and friends			
Made telephone calls			
Received visitors			
Other			

A Life Worth Living: Practical Strategies for Reducing Depression in Older Adults, by Pearl Mosher-Ashley and Phyllis Barrett. ©1997 Health Professions Press, Inc., Baltimore.

provide highly detailed computer-compatible forms for the evaluation and follow up of outpatients with a dementing illness. These forms include medical, neurologic, psychiatric, psychometric, and clinical laboratory examinations. Included in the exams are a number of standardized scales (e.g., the Hamilton Rating Scale for Depression [see Chapter 1] and the Blessed, Tomlinson & Roth Information-Memory-Concentration Test [Blessed, Tomlinson, & Roth, 1968]) as well as computerized formats for progress notes and follow-up assessments. The data collected can be easily retrieved at a future date and can be analyzed as part of a larger data set for investigative purposes.

Word processing software is making the process of record keeping much easier. Zawacky et al. (1992) prepared a standardized format for each psychiatric syndrome with accompanying goals and treatment methods that are stored as a word processing macro (i.e., a single computer instruction that stands for a sequence of operations). The relevant macro is "called up" by a therapist who is working on a case in which the client displays symptoms indicative of the particular syndrome. Modifications can be made to individualize treatment, but considerable time is saved by not including all of the customary material. This format is particularly adaptable to the treatment modalities described in this book. A general treatment plan can be prepared for one or more of the interventions commonly used. When the treatment is to be initiated with a new client, the prepackaged plan can be called up and modifications quickly made to meet the special needs of the individual.

Mead, Cain, and Steele (1985) reported on a computer-oriented database management system designed to be used in marriage and family therapies. Forms similar to those created by Zemcov et al. (1984) were developed for the client database treatment plan. These forms consist of a problems, goals, and interventions list and progress notes. The sample forms provided in this chapter can be easily typed into a word processing program and used or modified.

Termination of Treatment

At the conclusion of treatment it is customary to complete a form describing the outcome of treatment and reasons for termination (see p. 371 for a sample form). In most cases termination occurs at an agreed-on point and by the mutual agreement of therapist and client. On occasion, the therapist or client elects to discontinue treatment. For example, the client may no longer wish to attend therapy sessions. It is always important to keep in mind the client's right to terminate a therapeutic intervention. In some cases the therapist may feel frustrated by a client's noncompliance and decide that the treatment is not appropriate. The client or therapist may become ill and not be able to continue. Also, given the age and medical conditions of this group of clients, it is not unusual for some of them to die unexpectedly during treatment. On rare occasions a family member may wish to discontinue the treatment or the client may move, making continuing treatment unrealistic.

Keeping a record of how the treatment ended helps to provide closure on an intervention. It can also help as a quick reference should the client have dif-

Termination of Treatment

Client _____

Address _____

Target problem _____

Treatment modality _____

Date of last session _____

Was treatment completed?   ___ Yes ___ No

Person initiating termination   ___ Therapist ___ Client

                                        ___ Mutual agreement ___ Other

Reason for termination _____

_____

_____

Outcome of treatment ___ Improved ___ No change ___ Worse

Criteria employed _____

_____

_____

Explanation of outcome _____

_____

_____

Recommendations for maintenance of gains _____

_____

_____

Prognosis

Likelihood of recurrence ___ Low ___ Likely ___ Very likely

Recommendation if client needs further help in handling problem

_____

_____

_____

_____

_____

A Life Worth Living: Practical Strategies for Reducing Depression in Older Adults, by Pearl Mosher-Ashley and Phyllis Barrett. ©1997 Health Professions Press, Inc., Baltimore.

ficulty with depression or decreased life satisfaction in the future. Reviewing the information concerning termination can jog the therapist's memory as to strategies the client was to employ to maintain gains obtained in treatment. Concerns over potential recurrence also may have been noted under prognosis for future reference.

REFERENCES

Abraham, I., Niles, S., Thiel, B., Siarkowski, K., & Cowling, W.R. (1991). Therapeutic work with depressed elderly. *Nursing Clinics of North America, 26,* 635–650.

Addy-Keller, J., & McElwaney, K. (1993). A new documentation tool. *Nursing Management, 24*(11), 46–50.

Albeck, J.H., & Goldman, C. (1991). Patient-therapist codocumentation: Implications of jointly authored progress notes for psychotherapy practice, research, training, supervision, and risk management. *American Journal of Psychotherapy, 45,* 317–333.

Badding, N.C. (1989). Client involvement in case recording. *Social Casework, 70,* 539–548.

Barlow, D.H. (1992). *Single case experimental designs.* Needham Heights, MA: Allyn & Bacon.

Berni, R., & Ready, H. (1974). *Problem-oriented medical record implementation: Allied health peer review.* St. Louis: Mosby.

Betz, B.J. (1980). Curtain on schizophrenia: A twenty-five-year clinical follow-up. *American Journal of Psychotherapy, 34,* 252–260.

Blessed, G., Tomlinson, B.E., & Roth, M. (1968). The association between quantitative measures of dementia and of senile change in the cerebral gray matter of elderly subjects. *British Journal of Psychiatry, 114,* 797–811.

Brider, P. (1992, September). The move to patient focused care. *American Journal of Nursing,* pp. 27–33.

Buckley-Womack, C., & Gidney, B. (1987). A new dimension in documentation: The PIE method. *Journal of Neuroscience Nursing, 19,* 256–260.

Christensen, L.B. (1994). *Experimental methodology.* Boston: Allyn & Bacon.

Closson, B.L., Mattingly, L.J., Finne, K.M., & Larson, J.A. (1994). Telephone follow-up program evaluation: Application of Orem's self-care model. *Rehabilitation Nursing, 19,* 287–292.

Dayringer, R. (1978). The problem-oriented record in pastoral counseling. *Journal of Religion and Health, 17,* 39–47.

Gilandas, A.J. (1972). The problem-oriented record in a psychiatric hospital. *Hospital and Community Psychiatry, 23,* 336–339.

Harvey, R.T., Atkinson, C.A., Gale, J.M., & Lantinga, L.J. (1974). Toward a more efficient use of the problem-oriented record in psychiatry. *Hospital and Community Psychiatry, 25,* 42–43.

Hirshfield-Bartek, J., Hassey Dow, K., & Creaton, E. (1990). Decreasing documentation time using a patient self-assessment tool. *Oncology Nursing Forum, 17,* 251–255.

Katz, R.C., & Woolley, F.R. (1975). Improving patients records through problem orientation. *Behavior Therapy, 6,* 119–124.

Knight, B. (1986). *Psychotherapy with older adults.* Beverly Hills, CA: Sage Publications.

Lechowicz, J.S., & Carmack, N.D. (1974). Systematic approach to client care in a rehabilitation facility: Adaptation of a medical model. *Vocational Evaluation and Work Adjustment Bulletin, 7,* 14–19.

Lucatorto, M., Petras, D.M., Drew, L.A., & Zbuckvich, I. (1991). Documentation: A focus for cost savings. *Journal of Nursing Administration, 21*(3), 32–36.

McLean, P.D., & Miles, J.E. (1974). Evaluation and the problem-oriented record in psychiatry. *Archives of General Psychiatry, 31*, 622–625.

Mead, D.E., Cain, M.W., & Steele, K. (1985). A computer data based management system for a family therapy clinic. *Computers and Family Therapy, 1*(1–2), 49–88.

Menenberg, S.R. (1995). Standards of care in documentation of psychiatric nursing care. *Clinical Nurse Specialist, 9*, 140–142, 148.

Pinsker, H., & Sporn, A. (1980, April). A new approach to psychiatric progress notes. *Medical Record News, 51*, 39–41.

Reed, R.D. (1991). A standards of care plan in the postanesthesia care unit. *Journal of Post Anesthesia Nursing, 6*, 255–264.

Schuster, S.E., & Colvin, M.K. (1986). Clinical progress notes: A challenge for the nurse educator. *Journal of Nursing Education, 25*, 33–36.

Solomon, J.G. (1987, September 7). Should a psychiatrist share his notes with patients? *Medical Economics*, p. 103.

Williams, D.H., Jacobs, S., Debski, A., & Revere, M. (1974). Introducing the problem-oriented record on a psychiatric inpatient unit. *Hospital and Community Psychiatry, 25*, 25–28.

Zawacky, C.A., Levit, V.G., Khan, M.M., & Bhattacharyya, A. (1992). Psychiatric paperwork enhancement through quasi automated office systems development. *Computer Applications in Mental Health, 8*, 63–85.

Zemcov, A., Barclay, L.L., Brush, D., & Blass, J.P. (1984). Computerized data base for evaluation and follow-up of demented outpatients. *Journal of the American Geriatrics Society, 32*, 801–842.

Index

About the Authors

Pearl M. Mosher-Ashley, Ph.D., is Professor of Psychology at Worcester State College. She admits that her first job, as a nursing assistant in a long-term care facility, prepared her for a long and rewarding career in the field of aging. Although the facility was deplorable (pre-OBRA regulations), she found the residents delightful and a source of wisdom, warmth, and optimism, even under their primitive living conditions.

While in graduate school, she was drawn to what has since become the field of geropsychology through her work with Dr. Patricia Wisocki, a psychologist specializing in work with older adults. While completing her doctorate in counseling psychology, she was part of a team developed to work solely with older adults in a community mental health center. For several years following she worked as a clinician in a residential and day treatment program for older people with profound mental illness. In this capacity she had an opportunity to gain first-hand experience in designing and implementing the treatment strategies described in this book.

Dr. Mosher-Ashley is a licensed psychologist in Massachusetts, and at Worcester State teaches two to three sections of the psychology of aging each semester to students in occupational therapy, nursing, communication disorders, gerontology, and psychology. She is an active researcher and has published numerous articles in professional journals.

Phyllis W. Barrett, Ph.D., is Professor of English at Holyoke Community College, where she was named to the 1997–1998 Elaine Marieb Chair for Teaching Excellence. In addition to teaching courses in developmental writing, freshman composition, advanced writing, the literary genres, American literature, and the modern novel, Dr. Barrett frequently co-teaches with her colleague, Dr. Mark Lange, in psychology/literature learning communities. She is preparing an interdisciplinary honors colloquium on the topic "Millennium" to be offered in 1999 and 2000. Dr. Barrett is also the secretary of the Massachusetts Community College Council, the union that represents the faculty and professional staff at all 15 public community colleges in the Commonwealth.